CW00497325

Ezra Pound and the Career of Modern Criticism

Studies in American Literature and Culture: Literary Criticism in Perspective

Brian Yothers, Series Editor
(*El Paso, Texas*)

About *Literary Criticism in Perspective*

Books in the series *Literary Criticism in Perspective* trace literary scholarship and criticism on major and neglected writers alike, or on a single major work, a group of writers, a literary school or movement. In so doing the authors—authorities on the topic in question who are also well-versed in the principles and history of literary criticism—address a readership consisting of scholars, students of literature at the graduate and undergraduate level, and the general reader. One of the primary purposes of the series is to illuminate the nature of literary criticism itself, to gauge the influence of social and historic currents on aesthetic judgments once thought objective and normative.

Ezra Pound and the Career of Modern Criticism

Professional Attention

Michael Coyle
and
Roxana Preda

Rochester, New York

First published 2018
by Camden House

Camden House is an imprint of Boydell & Brewer Inc.
668 Mt. Hope Avenue, Rochester, NY 14620, USA
www.camden-house.com
and of Boydell & Brewer Limited
PO Box 9, Woodbridge, Suffolk IP12 3DF, UK
www.boydellandbrewer.com

ISBN-13: 978-1-57113-192-8
ISBN-10: 1-57113-192-2

Library of Congress Cataloging-in-Publication Data

Names: Coyle, Michael, 1957– author. | Preda, Roxana, 1959– author.
Title: Ezra Pound and the career of modern criticism : professional attention / Michael Coyle and Roxana Preda.
Description: Rochester, New York : Camden House, 2018. | Series: Studies in American literature and culture: Literary criticism in perspective | Includes bibliographical references and index.
Identifiers: LCCN 2018019945| ISBN 9781571131928 (hardcover : alk. paper) | ISBN 1571131922 (hardcover : alk. paper)
Subjects: LCSH: Pound, Ezra, 1885–1972—Criticism and interpretation. | Criticism—United States—History—20th century.
Classification: LCC PS3531.O82 Z62368 218 | DDC 811/.52—dc23 LC record available at https://lccn.loc.gov/2018019945

Gone now forever that heroic age
When roaring Ezra stormed our country stage!
His stride was long, his shout was long and high,
Flame rolled in all directions from each eye;
And if his fist spun round and clapped his ear,
It mattered little, since the bent was clear.
He made our grandsires slubber in their seats,
Time-serving editors hunt safe retreats;
And when the lion turned away and slept,
His enervated victims softly wept;
Each fool was breathless not to make a sound,
Sweating with terror lest he awaken Pound.

—Yvor Winters, "The Critiad"

Contents

Preface

The historical relevance of literature is not based on an organization of literary works which is established post factum, but on the reader's past experience of the "literary data."

—Hans Robert Jauss, "Literary History as a Challenge to Literary Theory"

The reception history of Ezra Pound arguably entails the history of academic criticism itself. To make that argument is not necessarily to reaffirm Hugh Kenner's vision of "the Pound era," but rather to recognize that, after the Second World War, Pound's work became the decisive battleground upon which the new critics initially established their dominance, and over which subsequently swept successive forms of feminist and poststructuralist theory.[1] Pound's work was and remains a challenge to all critical models. At once inviting and resisting exegesis, *The Cantos* in particular has been for three quarters of a century the ultimate proving ground. By the second decade of the twenty-first century, questions of canonicity came to seem less urgent, but Pound's work continues to attract new approaches, even if these no longer accelerate more general professional anxieties and concerns. In other words, without ever having achieved unchallenged canonical status, Pound's work has long been central to questions of what disciplinarity in English might mean.

Professional attention, in the context of Anglo-American departments of English, is shaped and regulated by the dynamic rules of disciplinarity. These rules have changed over time, are changing still, and doubtless should change with the evolving role of academic writing and authority in the culture at large. But at any particular moment rules and conventions—both explicit codes and regulations like double-blind referees—as well as implicit conventions about fairness or avoiding merely *ad hominem* attacks—govern critical behavior. Academic communities are formed with inner dissensions and agreements—the strength lies in numbers and in the endless revision of accepted and shared knowledge. Moreover, such expectations govern not just what is said, and how, but also where such work is suitably published. This much is evident in the straightforward instructions of the series in which this volume participates, "Literary Criticism in Perspective," to its authors:

> "Literary criticism" as used here means scholarly literary analyses written by academics, professional reviewers or writers and published

> in scholarly books or periodicals and, where applicable, in widely disseminated, serious periodicals such as the *Times Literary Supplement, Die Zeit, The New York Review of Books*, the *New York Times Book Review* and so on.

Part of the reason for instructions like this is to disentangle intellectual exchange from the discursive torrents of the marketplace. But one of the interesting things about following Pound's reception is that it unfolds contemporaneously with the development of academic literary criticism. Nevertheless, because Pound's poetry always aimed for readers' reach rather than their grasp, it wasn't until the Bollingen controversy that popular periodicals and papers gave Pound much notice. Between 1910–1930, his work was most often reviewed in the "little magazines" that targeted the intellectual and often marginal audiences that followed letters and the arts. With Pound living in Rapallo and largely removed from American attention, the 1930s represented a period of transition and the 1940s were generally preoccupied with the war. By the time the Bollingen controversy was settled, Pound criticism had moved almost entirely into the newish world of academic publications.

In her introduction to *New Approaches to Ezra Pound* (1969), Eva Hesse wrote that "scholarly studies of Ezra Pound began with Lawrence Richardson's essay 'Ezra Pound's Homage to Propertius' in the *Yale Review* in 1947, Hugh Kenner's two essays in *Hudson Review* in 1949 and 1950, and an essay by Hugh Gordon Porteus in Peter Russell's symposium of the same year" (Hesse 51). Six years later, Donald Davie proffered that "anything [published on Pound] before the truly pioneering study, Hugh Kenner's *The Poetry of Ezra Pound* (1951), is of mostly historical interest" (Davie 1975, 124). These comments offer us an interesting point of departure, for more time separates us from Hesse and Davie than separated them from Kenner. The title of Davie's book, *Ezra Pound*, signifies a legitimated object for serious literary study. "Ezra Pound" has become a known quantity for many of the kinds of literary study now conducted in Anglo-American institutions of higher learning. Beyond any doubt, as we shall see, Kenner's book established the conditions for such study. Kenner's book, quite simply, put Pound on the map and established the terms in which subsequent study would be conducted, or at least to which it must respond. Kenner *was* the pioneer.

But as American history records, or at least has recorded recently, few pioneers encounter previously uninhabited Edens. In staking and holding his claim, Kenner had both to displace earlier societies and also to defeat rival claims from other academic colonizers. Beyond this point, however, the pioneer analogy reverses itself. Because the kind of criticism Kenner pioneered did not relegate other critical discourses to reservations—it expelled them *from* the reservation. Other models, having become insufficiently formalist and so unprofessional, were left to do their work outside of academe. With Kenner's work, "Pound criticism" first developed as such. It was Kenner who transferred the study of Pound from middle- and high-brow popular monthlies and quarterlies into academic organs, superseded the review with the scholarly study, and transformed the poet and polemicist into an academic subject. This book will examine some of the consequences of that process, but without Kenner's precedent it would have no place in the series "literary criticism in perspective."

Nevertheless, Davie's comment should not be taken to suggest that no previous discussion of Pound's work managed insight or understanding. Pound's reception was first shaped by poets, especially the two who were nearest to him: Eliot and Yeats. They provided the axes of reference (and also the limitations) for the new critics' discussion of Pound's work and for the tenor of his general reception until 1950. But after Kenner's *The Poetry of Ezra Pound* those discussions altered in kind, and assumed purposes alien to earlier discussions. Consequently, previous discussions were unlikely to meet the expectations of readers anticipating academic discourse; they have come in this way to be "of mostly historical interest."

This book is about that history, and part of its purpose is to affirm that the success of Kenner and so many others in making Pound academic has exacted a high price—unavoidable perhaps, especially after the Bollingen controversy, but dear, nonetheless. Assessing that price is an important part of putting "literary criticism in perspective," and our necessary focus on "literary criticism" as it has come to be construed after the New Criticism successfully institutionalized it should not lead us to forget that there are different *kinds* of criticism as surely as there are different schools of literary criticism. What's more, as we explore in Chapter One, Pound himself preferred other kinds of critical discourse to those sanctioned by and given a regular place in the academy.

This book offers a reception history of Ezra Pound, but rather than providing a blow by blow chronology, it regards the Bollingen controversy as a crucial moment that largely changed the terms of Pound's reception in both America and in Britain—and continues to affect Pound's reception by asking a question that has not been satisfactorily answered, even today: in what way and to what extent is Pound's poetry vitiated by his politics? The subsequent evolution of professional attention has thrown out of court the Fellows' contention that politics should be excluded as a criterion for evaluation and that Pound's poetry is to be considered only as literature, with no effect or relevance on the world as we know it. Consequently, borrowing from Dominick LaCapra's *The Trial of Madame Bovary*, we will treat the controversy surrounding Pound's Bollingen Prize as a "reading" of the work. In several important respects, the controversy quickly became meta-critical. The initial outcries against the award argued that the American public had been betrayed by intellectuals; but arguing about Pound's particular merit soon contributed to widespread reassessment of the relation of poetry and politics. More recent contests among, say, New Historicism, deconstruction, feminist, minority, eco-criticism and Marxist ideology-critiques demonstrate that that reassessment continues. This reception history considers the changing terms of Pound criticism—it is difficult in such a book as this to avoid so reifying a phrase—in terms of changing meta-critical—theoretical—language. The Bollingen controversy, the ongoing case of the case that won't go away, will serve to organize our account of previous and subsequent developments.

♦ ♦ ♦

Pound himself always demonstrated a keen interest in what late-twentieth-century critics came to call "reception history," or *Rezeptionsästhetik.* For Pound, the operative term was "impact," and his aim was to discern changes in cultural sensibility, rather than changes in the ways that critics and readers endeavor to make sense of particular texts.[2] Pound knew that, at different times, particular writers have been understood in different ways; but for Pound these differences had always sought controversy, often fomented it, and many antagonists took the opportunity of Pound's indictment (July 26, 1943) to condemn what Pound seemed to have become. Carl Sandburg, for one, did not even wait for the indictment, responding to news of the broadcasts by declaring simply (April 18, 1943) that "once among American major poets Pound rated. Now he's out" (259). The tone and content of Sandburg's verdict anticipated much of what followed.

The singularities of Pound's reception have prompted us in some cases to move from a strictly chronological organization. We offer, for instance, a chapter on the many *Lives* of Ezra Pound. Perhaps because Pound himself always resisted attempts to separate the poet from the poem, the art from politics and all manner of "extra"-literary concerns, he has inspired a still growing number of biographical studies. And the allusive texture of much of his work has also exegetical work of fairly distinct order: the *Ezra Pound Newsletter* that John Hamilton Edwards and William Vasse compiled, as well as their subsequent *Annotated Index of Ezra Pound*, followed by the decades-long work of *Paideuma* and *Sagetrieb*, in America, and *Agenda* in Britain, and of course the two-volume *Companion to The Cantos of Ezra Pound* compiled by Carroll F. Terrell's team centered at the University of Maine, Orono. Collectively considered, Pound criticism embodies the best and the worst of professional literary studies: sometimes brilliant, often hagiographical, occasionally tendentious and thesis-driven, but at its best, despite the defensiveness that set in with the Bollingen battles and has reappeared often since, mindful of the sociocultural obligations of critical discourse.

Ours is not a triumphalist history, wherein the misunderstood-in-his-own-day poet finally gets the audience he deserves; such triumph over skeptics might, once upon a time have seemed inevitable, as when in 1960 Richard Landini imagined that "the bulk of negative criticism of [*The Cantos*] was written before 1940" and that "recent criticism has been on the whole favorably disposed toward Pound." He allowed the "obvious exception [of] the irresponsible commentary which critics, particularly of the *Saturday Review*, brought to bear on the award of the Bollingen Prize," but expected that that kind of thing had played itself out (49). Landini's expectation is in retrospect understandable: within the ecology of American academe at that time the ideology critiques of the late century might have seemed unimaginable. Reception history is not, however, about readers and critics generally changing their minds over a question—it's about the questions themselves changing. It's not that later readers "saw the light" that earlier readers missed so much as that, for historically specific reasons, readers and critics came to ask different questions and sought to meet challenging work in different ways.

This reception history illuminates the role of Pound studies in shaping the very forms of modern literary study. Some critics, especially European ones, have long sensed as much. Over half a century ago, G. S. Fraser submitted that sometimes violent disagreements over Pound's poetry existed "long before Pound had involved himself, self-hurtingly, in politics" (87). N. Christoph de Nagy went further still, noting how Pound's "skepticism turned into irritation and anger when he saw, after 1920, the unparalleled growth of criticism in England and America—with a function diametrically opposed to that circumscribed by him" (Nagy 1966, 11). Even today, there is no consensus about the status or even nature of Pound's work, but almost from the beginning, and certainly from the essays of the first wave of the postwar era, critics understood that Pound's work represented a radical challenge to their own enterprise. Critical orthodoxy is harder to identify today than it was for the generation of Pound's first academic criticism, but it remains difficult to imagine an academic critical model that could be anything but antagonistic to Pound's ambitions and purposes. Finally, the potential of Pound's work to continue challenging academic writing in radical ways remains a sign of its enduring value to criticism in all its forms.

Notes

[1] Karen Leick (2002) has argued that much of the fury surrounding Pound's award resulted from, first, the cynical manipulations of the editors of the *Saturday Review of Literature* and, second, from a kind of rearguard seizing of the Pound question as a means of getting at Eliot.

[2] Michael Coyle (1995) has questioned this idea (35–78).

Acknowledgments

THIS BOOK HAS HAD a long gestation, begun at an earlier moment in Michael Coyle's life and at an earlier moment in the career of Pound criticism. It sat unattended—though never forgotten—for ten years. That ten-year period saw the formation of the Modernist Studies Association and the rejuvenation of the Ezra Pound Society. It also saw the rapid development of computer technologies, so that this book was begun on a PC using one software program and completed on a Mac using another that couldn't communicate with the first. These changes all impacted the course of the narrative we tell here, often creating new opportunities along with the new problems to be solved.

By the early twenty-first century, Pound criticism has developed into a rich tradition, too much of an industry for new readers to take in quickly. This book is offered as a way in, less a summary than a mapping of still-active fault lines. Once-heated arguments don't so much disappear as mutate and become new bases for further critical constructions. Contemporary critical positions on Pound, on his writings, on the relations between them are informed by history precisely because the poet and his work have excited so much controversy, from the time of his earliest publications.

Very special thanks must go to our editor, Jim Walker, who contacted Michael some years after he had shelved this book and invited him to return to it. That gesture in itself was extraordinary. But so, too, was his continuous good will and encouragement. This project received another chance at life due to the collaboration with Roxana Preda, the co-author of this volume. While Michael felt more at ease with the older research and the emergence of Pound studies as a well-defined field of scholarship, Roxana focused on the more recent developments in the discipline. This is reflected in the structure of the present book. Michael is responsible for the introduction and the first four chapters, Roxana for bringing the story into the present and writing the conclusion.

Michael's research assistant, Rahil Uppal, volunteered extra hours to track down missing citations and create chapter bibliographies. The Interlibrary Loan office at Colgate University was indefatigable in its efforts on our behalf, unfailingly delivering book reviews from small journals and articles from hard-to-find periodicals. This project was helped hugely by Volker Bischoff's *Ezra Pound Criticism 1905–1985: A Chronological Listing of Publications in English* (Marburg: Schriften der

Universitätsbibliothek Marburg, 1991); his work, particularly in his listing of reviews after their subject, suggested many turns and numerous questions. We wish to thank Colgate University Dean of the Faculty, Tracey Hucks, and Richard Braaten, Chair of the Colgate University Research Council, for their support. And, finally, both for her long patience with the disappearing act that this project required, as well as for her absolutely invaluable work on the index of this book so chocked full of proper names, Michael wishes to thank Kara Rusch.

Roxana in her turn wishes to thank Archie Henderson, bibliographer extraordinaire of Pound studies. Without his selfless bibliographic work for the Ezra Pound Society and his continuous friendly support, her chapters might not have seen the light of day. She is also grateful to David Moody, who took the time to discuss the art of biography with her, both in the pages of *Make It New*, and in the informal conversation of an unforgettable summer evening in Edinburgh.

1: From Wabash to Washington, 1907–1947

A poet is justified not by the expression of himself, but by the public he finds or creates; a public made by others ready to his hand if he is a mere popular poet, but a new public, a new form of life, if he is a man of genius.

—William Butler Yeats, *Essays and Introductions*

Amateurs, Experts, and Professionals

POUND'S "A FEW DON'TS," one of the pre-war manifestos with which he fomented poetic revolution, opens with a warning to poets and writers to "pay no attention to the criticism of men who have never themselves written a notable work" (200). The force of this advice might, a century and more later, be mistaken for a caution about academic criticism. It wasn't. In 1913 academic culture in general was still inchoate and English—which continued to focus more on philological than on hermeneutic, or even stylistic questions—as a particular discipline was just beginning to move from its Arnoldian mission.[1] In the first quarter of the twentieth century, English criticism was still essentially a gentleman's affair and had yet to define itself in professional terms. If Pound's mature poetry challenged that establishment, his early criticism actively militated against it.

Each of the installments of Pound's first important critical essay, "I Gather the Limbs of Osiris" (serialized in the *New Age* from November 30, 1911, through February 22, 1912) ran under the standing rubric, "Mr. Pound will continue expositions and translations in illustration of 'The New Method in Scholarship.'"[2] A. Walton Litz and Lawrence Rainey have identified this serial essay as an important moment in the development of Pound's distinction between the professional and the expert: "Taking up the question of who should assess poetry, amateurs or professionals, Pound writes: 'I should not discriminate between the "amateur" and the "professional," or rather I should discriminate quite often in favour of the amateur, but I should also discriminate between the amateur and the expert.'" For Litz and Rainey, this discrimination is important, not least because it was struggling against a mainstream that was already gathering force—and this struggle portended trouble for Pound in future:

> Pound's usage of "expert" in this passage does not reinforce a rhetoric of professionalism; instead, it undermines it. Whereas 'the specialist' and the 'professional' are those whose position derives from impersonal systems of training and practice, 'the expert' is one whose authority derives from unusual ability or mastery which is the result of experience, something in addition to mere training and practice. (66)

The poet-critics who shaped the first half-century of Pound's reception might have aspired to be "experts," but they were not in the modern sense "professionals," even though many of them depended on the income from reviews. Very few of the contemporaneous reviews of Pound's work were by academics, and what few academic responses there were we remember today, if at all, as subjects of ridicule—most infamously the review of *Propertius* by University of Chicago Professor of Classics William G. Hale, titled "Pegasus Impounded," in which Hale judged that "if Mr. Pound were a professor of Latin, there would be nothing left for him but suicide" (55).

"Criticism" was then, in the first three decades of the twentieth century, almost by definition *not* academic, still the purview of experts rather than academic professionals; as Eliot wrote of Pound at mid-century in his introduction to *Literary Essays of Ezra Pound*, literary criticism was to be identified by "its concentration upon the craft of letters, and of poetry especially" (xiii). The emphasis was on craft, possibly as a reflection of sensibility, and the practitioners of this criticism were themselves most often poets—or at least aspiring poets. Pound's first "don't" ("Use no superfluous word, no adjective, which does not reveal something") was affirming that poetic status was less a function of mere imprint than it was of impact. It is in this context, then, that we should understand the significance of the fact that, for the first forty years of his career, Pound's reception was most often a matter of other poets welcoming or, as often, not welcoming his work.

The English poet Edward Thomas was such a one, a poet who regularly reviewed newly published volumes of poetry. He was both among the earliest commentators on Pound's work and also a poet who both welcomed and denied welcome. On May 1, 1909, Thomas wrote to Gordon Bottomley, a friend who was himself a poet, that "since Swinburne nobody except Ellis & Yeats have really faced the difficulties [of writing modern poetry] & Ellis and Yeats have not explained them by seeming to overcome them. . . . But here is Ezra Pound & I think he has very great things in him & the love poems & the "Famam librosque"—in fact nearly all—are extraordinary achievements. I know nothing about him but have an idea he has come from America."[3] Only a month later, writing once again to Bottomley, Thomas had changed his mind: "Oh, I do humble myself over Ezra Pound. He is not & cannot ever be very good. Certainly he is not what I mesmerized myself—out of pure love of praising the new poetry!—into saying he was & I am very ashamed & only hope I shall never meet the man" (187). Thomas would not survive the First World War, and Bottomley too was dead before Pound began to be celebrated as a definitive modernist poet, but by that point so, too, was the poetic scene within which they had once found some public recognition. In 1909, Thomas (1878–1917) and Bottomley (1874–1948) could have imagined themselves as guardians of a distinctly English, or at least British, tradition. Thomas was among the reviewers of the first volume of poems Pound had written in London—*Personae*—pre-Imagist work whose debts to Browning and the Pre-Raphaelites were still very visible, but which nonetheless struck Thomas as sadly "interesting—perhaps promising—certainly distressing" (*Letters*, 185). Rupert Brooke, darling of the Georgian poetic scene, responded in similar terms in a 1909 article in the *Cambridge Review*. If Pound's "assumption of a twisted Browning-esque personality" was "unnecessary," Brooke thought, even more disturbing was his Americanness, his having fallen "under the dangerous influence of Whitman" (166). Similarly, Charles Granville, reviewing *Canzoni* for *Eye-Witness* under the title "Modern Poetry," lamented that Pound had "[cut] himself off from the great traditions. . . . A poet today cannot place his name upon the great roll of British poets if he is indifferent to what has gone before" (247). This early reception, this emphasis on Pound's Americanness as something peculiar and vaguely objectionable, suggests the motivation for Pound's own description, in "What I Feel about Walt Whitman" (1909), of Whitman's "barbaric yawp."[4] If early English reviews of his work didn't exactly force his hand, they suggested the wisdom of forging his own cosmopolitan relationship with American poetic tradition. The forging of this relation was not to be accomplished with essay writing alone but would require years of effort. In truth, Pound spent his entire career working to create the public whose presence he could never assume.

Pound's sublation of this struggle, *Hugh Selwyn Mauberley* (1920), effectually his farewell poem to London, opens with Mauberley's meditation on the consequences of his having been "out of key with his time"—having been born "in a half savage country, out of date." "Sublation" is the word here, because faced with a choice between an American or a British identity, Pound chose to overcome the opposition, setting out to identify a global tradition neither one nor the other, and not so much idiosyncratic as personal. Thomas and Brooke, among others, rightly understood that Pound represented a kind of barbarian at that gate, a most decidedly un-English voice insisting on internationalizing poetic tradition. F. S. Flint, who had been making a name for himself as a keen observer of the French poetic scene, nevertheless spoke for this self-conscious nationalist reaction in observing Pound's "queer exotic hybridity."[5] Twenty-first century readers might celebrate these terms and what they represent, but Flint didn't mean them to be a compliment.

Yeats, "Queerness," and Pound's American Identity

William Butler Yeats's importance to Pound's development has been often remarked and studied in depth, most particularly in James Longenbach's *Stone Cottage: Pound, Yeats and Modernism* (1988). Yeats, too, remarked Pound's "queerness,"[6] although during the First World War he came to depend on it. But for all that he did to help establish the young Pound in London—help from one brilliant outsider to another, perhaps—he played a fairly minor role in Pound's early reception. His 1936 BBC broadcast on Modern Poetry, for instance, made no mention of Pound, although it celebrated Eliot. Shortly before making that broadcast, however, Yeats edited the *Oxford Book of Modern Verse: 1892–1935*, an anthology that, he wrote in the introduction, aimed "to include all good poets who have lived or died from three years before the death of Tennyson to the present moment, except some two or three who belong through the character of their work to an earlier period" (v). Yeats included four of Pound's poems, quoting "The Return" in full in his introduction, and then presenting in the anthology proper "The River Merchant's Wife," a selection from *Homage to Sextus Propertius*, and "Canto XVII." These selections do much more to anticipate twenty-first century estimations of Pound than did Eliot's edition of Pound's *Selected Poems* (1928), both in Yeats's ability to follow Pound's development beyond the early work and in his sense that it would be on *The Cantos* that Pound's reputation would ultimately stand or fall. Yeats felt unable to judge *The Cantos*—to discern how all the heterogeneous elements of the poem relate—until "the whole is finished" (xxiv). But in general, he found that Pound's work displays

> more style than form; at moments more style, more deliberate nobility and the means to convey it than in any contemporary poet known to me, but it is constantly interrupted, broken, twisted into nothing by its direct opposite, nervous obsession, nightmare, stammering confusion; he is an economist, poet, politician, raging at malignants with explicable characters and motives, grotesque figures out of a child's book of beasts. (xxv)

In this view, Pound seems almost a species of Yeats's warning in "Easter 1916," that "Hearts with one purpose alone / Through summer and winter seem / Enchanted to a stone / To trouble the living stream" (1996, 180–82). His art is compromised by his political passion. Echoing in part Wyndham Lewis's attack of 1927, as we'll see, Yeats (1936) felt that "this loss of self-control, common among uneducated revolutionists, is rare—Shelley had it in some degree—among men of Ezra Pound's culture and erudition. Style and its opposite can alternate, but form must be full, sphere-like, single" (xxv). However slight Yeats's impact on Pound's early reception, this emphasis on form would soon enough become important for the New Critics of the next generation.

Yeats's most sustained commentary on Pound's work—"A Packet for Ezra Pound"—was begun in 1928, long after Pound had left London, but Yeats himself thought it important enough to subsequently add to the second edition of *A Vision* (1937); "A Packet," although written earlier, thus appeared after his *Oxford Book of Modern Verse.* He wrote "A Packet" while living in Rapallo, Italy, where Pound had made his home since 1924: "I shall not lack conversation," Yeats wrote: "Ezra Pound, whose art is the opposite of mine, whose criticism commends what I most condemn, a man with whom I should quarrel more than with anyone else if we were not united by affection, has for years lived [here] in rooms opening on to a flat roof by the sea" (3–4). From this personal opening, Yeats offers that the *Cantos* "display a structure like a Bach Fugue" (4). "I find," he continued, that "the mathematical structure" of the poem is in fact "more than mathematical, that seemingly irrelevant details fit together into a single theme" (5). Pound, despite having himself offered similar explanations, was soon grumbling about Yeats: "If Yeats knew a fugue from a frog, he might have transmitted what I told him in some way that would have helped rather than obfuscated *his* readers."[7] But even Pound's grumbling attests to the friendship between them that generally shaped Yeats's account. Section III of *A Packet* relates Pound's complicated relation with the cats of Rapallo—he feeds them, knows their histories, but "has no affection for them" (6). Section IV relates Yeats's failed attempt to find company among the town's small community of English exiles; "I am too anaemic for so British a faith; I shall haunt empty churches and be satisfied with Ezra Pound's society and that of his travelling Americans" (7). But, in this arguably most poetic of essays, Yeats is primarily interested in Pound as a modern exemplar of the deep patterns his *Vision* discovers in history. Yeats's original draft of section V was much longer than the published version, offering lengthy commentary on Pound's verse, and it was to have been followed by a section VI that was in the end not included, and then his poem "Meditation Upon Death," which was. Yeats saw himself as an old man surviving in a hard and unsympathetic world; "A Packet" essays Pound in Yeatsian terms: it makes company with him by observing differences between them.

Pound's Americanness proved no less an issue for reviewers back in the States. Rather anticipating Brooke's response of a few months later, in December of 1908 Ellen Wheeler Wilcox found Pound's poetry "strange, and weird," but nonetheless welcomed him. In Philadelphia, the anonymous reviewer of *A Lume Spento* for *Book News Monthly* (May 1909) complained that Pound "affects obscurity and loves the abstruse; he has apparently been influenced by Whitman." The anonymous reviewer of *Exultations* for the New York *Literary Digest* (Nov. 27, 1909, 958) focused entirely on Pound's fortunes as an American in London. Russian émigré John Cournos—one of the eleven contributors to Pound's *Des Imagistes*—remarked when reviewing *Ripostes* for the *Philadelphia Record*, that Pound's prose "is perhaps [his] chief outlet for his Americanism—and by that we mean American snap, not American English." "Snap," used in this way, itself exemplifies what Cournos was hearing: "snap" as in briskness, vigor or energy; not so much slang as the sound of a people ready to be heard. Even for Cournos, then, Pound's unapologetic American-ness is the chief feature of his work.

Let one further example establish the pattern: reviewers on both sides of the Atlantic regarded Pound's Americanness as a remarkable issue. From his review of *Lustra* in 1917 until his death in 1977, poet and anthologist Louis Untermeyer, like Thomas, Yeats and even Eliot, proved another poet who changed his view of Pound's work over time. In 1917 he scoffed about Pound's having moved "his aesthetic penates to London"; in 1939 he removed Pound from his *Book of Living Verse*—his selections of Pound's work had always, in any case, been limited to Pound's early work. Nevertheless, between 1914 and 1931, Untermeyer maintained an infrequent correspondence with Pound (even visiting him in Rapallo) mostly about which of Pound's poems might be included in Untermeyer's many anthologies. A successful anthologist, Untermeyer was instrumental in shaping the contemporaneous opinions of a broad, middlebrow readership—that same audience that would later be so alarmed by Pound's Bollingen prize. But it was the criticism of poets and writers more sympathetic to modernist experiment that would set the terms of Pound's professional reception.

Among the first English reviewers to celebrate Pound's work in its own terms was journalist, novelist, and socialist-suffragette Rebecca West. She knew Pound casually by virtue of regular visits to the salon of Ford Madox Ford (then still Ford Madox Hueffer); Wyndham Lewis was another such habitué, and it was through Lewis—not Pound—that West became a contributor to *Blast*. Pound's second attempt to spearhead a poetic/artistic revolution, *Blast* managed only two issues before getting lost in the chaos of the Great War, but it marked several important changes over Imagism: it was less patient, noisier and louder, eager to be associated with revolution than with tradition. But West was neither Imagist nor Vorticist. Not only was she not Pound's fellow traveler, she wasn't friendly: Jane Marcus, in her *Young Rebecca*, even suggests that the two of them clashed, particularly after Pound succeeded her as editor of *The New Freewoman*, which he renamed *The Egoist* (8). Nevertheless, West's article (rather than review) in the pages of the *New Freewoman*, "Imagisme," made its literary allegiances very clear. "Poetry," she wrote in a way echoing Pound's own declarative and aphoristic style, "should be burned to the bone by austere fires and washed white with rains of affliction" (Marcus 86). After this short opening salvo, West proceeded by reprinting Pound's "A Few Don'ts" *verbatim*, pausing to admire his determination that the poet should be "as disciplined and efficient at his job as the stevedore" must be at his. This emphasis on Pound's craft would prove a permanent aspect of his reception; sometimes it would be deployed as an explanation for or defense of his difficulty; sometimes, especially after the Second World War, as a means of minimizing his socioeconomic-ideological commitments; sometimes as a sign of his elitism; and sometimes, indeed, simply in admiration of his formal and stylistic accomplishments. West's review is striking in another respect, too. Because West has always been recognized to be, then and now, a defiantly independent thinker, her decision to explain Pound in his own terms deserves special mention. That decision set a pattern that would continue to unfold until after Pound's death: American poet Louis Zukofsky repeated it in his 1931 review of *A Draft of XXX Cantos*, and so too did Hugh Kenner in his 1951 book *The Poetry of Ezra Pound*, which established both his academic authority and Pound's status as a legitimate object of academic study.

Other figures of Pound's socialist acquaintance, most especially A. R. Orage, editor of the *New Age* and later of the *New English Weekly*, were less sympathetic. In July 1918 Orage reviewed T. S. Eliot's *Ezra Pound: His Metric and Poetry*.[8] Sounding that anxious English concern with Pound's nationality and doubting that "even in America anybody [besides Eliot] could have been found to write a book about his work," Orage complained that Pound "always has a ton of precept for a pound of example" (201). His complaints proved, however, a matter of principle, and he closed by admitting—and so returning to his commitments to guild socialism—"that this habit of Mr. Pound's has its good side as well as its somewhat absurd side; there is only a step, you know, from the ridiculous to the sublime." Pound remains poetry's best defense from dilettantes who do not recognize that "poetry should be the practice of 'a learned, self-conscious craft' to be carried on by a 'guild of adepts.'"

Lewis, Eliot, and Hybridity

Most of Pound's earliest champions—and many of his sharpest critics—could be said to belong to such a guild. Wyndham Lewis, after the war, after Pound had left London and their collaborations had effectually ended, proved sharply critical; Yeats, Ford Madox Ford, and of course Eliot—in a special and complex way—proved champions. Lewis's most important commentary on Pound's work came as part of his ambitious critique of modernity, *Time and Western Man* (1927), of which chapters 9 and 15 are devoted to Pound. This is not the Lewis of the *Blast* manifestoes but a conservative critic whose life and work have left him at odds with many erstwhile comrades in arms. Lewis's critique of Pound comes in the book's first part, "The Revolutionary Simpleton," where Lewis denounces what he saw as the Bergsonian glamorization of sensation, a glamorization he fears threatens to create a culture of solipsists. He begins almost apologetically, acknowledging his personal affection for the man: "a kinder heart never lurked beneath a portentous exterior than is to be found in Ezra Pound. Again, Pound is not a humbug even in those purely propagandist activities, where, to my mind, he certainly handles humbug, but quite innocently" (37). But Lewis had been informed "that the good Ezra was breaking out in a new direction. He was giving up words—possibly frightened, I thought, by the widespread opposition to *words* of any sort" (39). He was, Lewis judged, taking to music because "in music the sounds *say* nothing" (39). In other words, Lewis thought, Pound was surrendering meaning to sensation. He also thought, in 1927, that "Ezra's effective life-work is over . . . and of late he has steadily weakened" in his powers (67). From a twenty-first-century perspective, Lewis's attack seems curious—Pound proved more relentlessly didactic after the twenties than he ever had been before—but it reminds us of the hold Enlightenment ideals still had, not just a century ago but, popularly at least, even now. Lewis rejected here his own radical past and aimed to challenge the modernists at their very foundation.

Rather like Blackmur some seven years later, Lewis believed that Pound's creation of personae suggested an emptiness within: "if anyone supposes from these remarks, or if they think I mean, that Ezra Pound is a nobody, he will be mistaken. Yet how he is a 'somebody' is a little difficult to define. Pound is that curious thing, a person without a trace of originality of any sort. It is impossible even to imagine him being anyone in particular of all the people he has translated, interpreted, appreciated" (67). Again anticipating Blackmur, Lewis ventured that "when he writes in person, as Pound, his phrases are invariably stagey and false, as well as insignificant" (68). For all that Lewis reaffirms that he "like[s], respect[s], and, in a sense, reverence[s] Ezra Pound" (68), Pound at last proves another example of the "revolutionary simpleton," a parasite on genuine artists, a would-be poet with no vision of the future.

Eliot, too, was a great defender of tradition, but he understood both its nature and its importance in different ways. Eliot's first published essay on Pound's work was an August 1917 review of *The Noh and the Image.*

Eliot, who was by this time assistant editor of the *Egoist*, in which the review appeared, argued that "translation is valuable by a double power of fertilizing a literature: by importing new elements which may be assimilated, and by restoring the essentials which have been forgotten in traditional literary method. There occurs, in the process, a happy fusion between the spirit of the original and the mind of the translator; the result," he added, and challenging Flint's sense of Pound's "queer hybridity," "is not exoticism but rejuvenation" (102). Eliot noted the presence of Celticisms, presumably the result of Yeats's influence, as well as the "occasional suggestion of Mr. Pound's other influences—of his Provençal mood, or his Anglo-Saxon mood," but felt that these hybridities "give rather an added charm" (103). Eliot was still confronting expectations of a homogenous British tradition a year later when, in a piece titled "A Note on Ezra Pound" published in the pages of London's *To-Day*, he framed a discussion of Pound by taking on Professor Phelps's celebration of Brooke as "something more than either a man or a poet" (10). For Phelps, this something more was that Brooke became a "personality," whereas, Eliot proposed, "the point" of criticism "is to come to conclusions respecting the place of [Pound's] work as a whole in contemporary literature." It is the quality of the writing that matters, not the mobility or attractiveness of the man, and about the question of literary quality Eliot was clear. Most British poets "remained in the age of Wordsworth or in the age of Tennyson"; Pound, by contrast, presents "an organized view of the whole course of European poetry from Homer." His work "is always modern" (5). Eliot's account here anticipates his influential arguments in "Tradition and the Individual Talent" two years later. The critic's job, in his view, is not to assess the mere individuality of the poet but rather his relation to the deep tradition within which his work will find significance, within which his individuality becomes meaningful. Pound's modernity as well as his poetic importance is a matter of his having mastered tradition. It is for this reason, Eliot argued, that the *Cantos* could be "objective and reticent autobiography" without exciting a Brooke-like cult of personality. Here, too, Eliot countered Flint's charge of exoticism; reviewing Pound's career to date, Eliot finds *Cathay* "an absolutely objective work," one which "owes nothing to exotic charm" (8). Eliot also offers possibly the very first notice of "Pound's recent unfinished epic, three cantos of which appear in the American edition of *Lustra*" (6); we know these three cantos today as the "Ur Cantos," the adjective "recent" suggesting no sense that the project was ongoing.

Eliot returned to this argument the next year in a review of *Quia Pauper Amavi* titled "The Method of Mr. Pound" published in *Athenaeum*. His focus this time was on Pound's "historical method," and this review reads like an additional section of "Tradition and the Individual Talent," published the very next month: "Pound has steadily become more modern by becoming, or by showing himself to be, more universal." The present, Eliot elaborated, "is no more than the present existence, the present significance, of the entire past; and when the entire past is acquired, the constituents fall into place and the present is revealed" (1065).

Eliot was not the only poet who celebrated the scholarship that informs Pound's work—in December 1920 Padraic Colum celebrated Pound's success in "fusing his scholarship with his poetry in poems that demand both kinds of equipment."[9] Nevertheless, the expectation that scholarship and inspiration are not necessarily incompatible proved—and still proves—the crucible for many readers. Eliot's contention in "The Metaphysical Poets" (1921) that "poets in our civilization, as it exists at present, must be *difficult*" as the poet struggles "to force, to dislocate if necessary, language into his meaning" remains a matter of contest between elite and popular audiences. This argument took shape in the early period of Pound's reception, 1910–1920, and a century later still shapes his reputation.

Eliot's next sustained commentary on Pound was published in *The Dial* the year after Eliot's 1927 conversion, and represents different stages in both Pound's work and his own. By 1927 Pound was twenty-seven cantos into his "poem including history," and Eliot's poetry had become overtly Christian, "Ash Wednesday" being published that December. Personal relations between these erstwhile comrades in arms became strained after Pound moved to Rapallo and embraced distributionist economics with a fervor no less than that with which Eliot had embraced the Anglo-Catholic church. But this strain was not a break. Perhaps riffing on Maxwell Bodenheim's 1922 review of Pound's *Poems 1918–21*, titled "Isolation of Carved Metal," which was also published in *The Dial* and which opened by remarking "the massive isolation of Ezra Pound,"[10] Eliot called his essay-review "Isolated Superiority."[11] This essay-review took the occasion of Pound's first *Selected Poems* (1928), a selection that Eliot himself had edited, to explain why "Pound has great influence but no disciples. And I think that the reason is this: that influence can be exerted through form, whereas one makes disciples only among those who sympathize with the content" (168). This introduction is the first place we see Eliot deploying the same strategy he would use, more famously, in his introduction to the *Literary Essays of Ezra Pound* (1954): prising apart questions of form and content, declining to engage Pound's political and economic commitments in hopes of finding him readers—hoping to help Pound create the audience he had yet to find. Thus, on the one hand, Eliot acknowledges his own artistic debts to Pound: "I cannot think of anyone writing verse, of our generation and the next, whose verse (if any good) has not been improved by the study of Pound's. His poetry is an inexhaustible reference book of verse form" (168). Eliot's editing reflects this conviction, carefully omitting poems like "Propertius" that suggest Pound's interest beyond aesthetics. On the other hand, and somewhat paradoxically given Eliot's premise, the essay closes with a gauntlet thrown. Having praised Pound's form, Eliot turned to the matter of Pound's content:

> I sometimes wonder how [Pound] reconciles all his interests: how does he reconcile even Provençal and Italian poetry? He retains some mediaeval mysticism, without belief; this is mixed up with Mr. Yeats's spooks (excellent creatures in their native bogs) and involved with Dr. Berman's hormones; and a steam-roller of Confucianism (the Religion of a Gentleman, and therefore an Inferior Religion) has flattened over the whole. So we are left with the question (which the unfinished Cantos make more pointed) what does Mr. Pound believe?" (169)

No part of this business sat well with Pound, who without breaking off relations nevertheless took some years (until 1934 in his essay "Date Line") to answer: "I believe the Ta Hio" (86). Even if Pound refused the distillation of form from content, for Eliot, this review was something of a declaration of independence. Having owed so much to Pound in the first part of his career, close relations with him were no longer easy or socially (or culturally) convenient.

All the same, Eliot remained ready to champion Pound's cause as he understood it. In 1938, he published a rejoinder, "On a Recent Piece of Criticism," to G. W. Stonier, whose "The Mystery of Ezra Pound" sparked an indignation in Eliot that he rarely allowed to be seen in print. Stonier, Eliot charged, felt fit to "dismiss in six pages of frivolity an author who, at the very least, has given thirty-odd years of close study to his art" (91). Eliot took particular exception to Stonier's claims about his, Eliot's, relationship to Pound. Swatting away Stonier's misunderstandings, Eliot explained: "My indebtedness to Pound is of two kinds: first, in my literary criticism (this debt has been pointed out by Mr. Porteus and Mr. Mario Praz); and second, in his criticism of my poetry in our talk, and his indications of desirable territories to explore." Eliot did put a period to this indebtedness, adding that it extends "from 1915 to 1922 after which Mr. Pound left England, and our meetings became infrequent" (92). Nevertheless, Eliot calls Stonier to task over other factual details:

> One good test of criticism is that the intelligent reader should derive some profit from reading it even if he does not agree with the critic's verdict upon any particular author. It should at the least stimulate one to thinking out more clearly one's grounds of disagreement, or bring to one's attention something that one had overlooked. Both Mr. Allen Tate and Mr. R. P. Blackmur have written criticism

> of Pound's poetry containing strictures more serious than anything that Mr. Stonier's petulant levity can adduce. These authors know their texts and have given considerable thought to their judgments . . . (92)

Eliot would, before his death, several times turn his critical eye once more to Pound, but those essays belong to subsequent chapters of this study. For now, we do well to follow his lead and turn to the two academic poet-critics he held up, in 1938, as examples of how Pound might best be read. The old debates about poetry's relations to scholarship would come by mid-century to be conducted by credentialed scholars. Pound was, even in 1938, well on his way to becoming the subject of professional attention.

New Humanism, New Criticism, and the Discontent of Winters

Americans Allen Tate and R. P. Blackmur, and Englishman F. R. Leavis, were all, in their different ways, hugely influential in shaping modern literary study. Each of them, without ever falling into orthodoxy themselves, contributed to the mid-twentieth century institutionalization of what came to be called the New Criticism. This critical discourse was "new" in that it displaced older, Arnoldian, ethics-based approaches to analysis, as well as, in America, the New Criticism's early twentieth-century rival, "the New Humanism." Ironically enough, the "New Humanists" (as they called themselves) drew inspiration from the work of Eliot's teacher at Harvard, Irving Babbitt, particularly from the anti-romanticism that found its fullest and most powerful expression in Babbitt's late work, *Rousseau and Romanticism* (1919). The New Humanists never formed a coherent movement, but critics like Paul Elmer More (*Shelburne Essays,* 11 volumes, 1904–21), Stuart Sherman (*On Contemporary Literature,* 1917), or Norman Foerster (*American Criticism: A Study in Literary Theory from Poe to the Present,* 1928; *Towards Standards: A Study of the Present Critical Movement in American Letters,* 1930), fought against what they saw as the prevailing tendency of modernist thought: the reduction of both literature and society to the play of deterministic materialist or biological forces. The end of this critical project came swiftly and decisively with the publication of Harvey Grattan's *The Critique of Humanism* (1930), which included essays by such formidable critics—and antagonists of the New Humanism—as Blackmur, Tate, Kenneth Burke, Lewis Mumford, Malcolm Cowley, Edmund Wilson, and Yvor Winters. All of the contributors to Grattan's volume subsequently emerged as important critics of modernist literature, despite the fact that several, like the leftist

Wilson or the rationalist Winters, pursued their own ethical programs. Of course, the New Humanists continued to pursue their work after losing this decisive battle, but thereafter lost any real hope of shaping the critical discourse of their age. Their defeat marked the last serious attempt in the United States to establish a non-academic criticism. Criticism, no less than poetry-writing, was to be a professional matter, a business conducted by trained and credentialed professors/professionals.

Distinguishing among critical schools is, of course, easier in theory than in practice, because critics change their positions and preferences. Yvor Winters, among the most influential American critics of the mid-twentieth century, is an important example here. He began his writerly life as a poet of the modernist school—corresponding with and admiring Hart Crane in particular—but by 1930 had reconsidered his early views. Winters's celebratory review of Crane's *White Buildings* in 1927 is remarkable in view of what Thomas Parkinson, editor of the Winters-Crane correspondence, called "his predominantly negative review of *The Bridge* in 1930 . . . and his later and dimmer views of the merits of Crane's work" (xiv). By the postwar era Winters had become a resolute antagonist of modernism, and was championing singularly neo-Enlightenment principles, as the title of his most celebrated book, *In Defense of Reason* (1947), suggests. Winters's early enthusiasm for Crane never extended to Pound. In reviewing Zukofsky's *Objectivists* anthology, Winters found it "symptomatic of the intellectual bankruptcy of the middle generation that Mr. Pound will actively back such a man as Zukofsky" (160). Winters's doggerel "Critiad" (quoted in the above epigraph) appears in the same number as Lytton Strachey's "Doctor, Heal Thyself," a review of Pound's *How To Read* that bluntly proposes that "Mr. Pound does not write well" (555). The "Critiad" praises Pound for his epic energy—for his ability to wake the world—without actually praising Pound's epic. Despite finding that "details and cadences in some of the early Cantos are very lovely," Winters, as Roxana Preda explains in her *Ezra Pound's Poetics and Politics*,

> dismissed the heterogeneity of cultural and historical allusions in *The Cantos* in the harshest metaphors. Pound was a "barbarian on the loose in a museum" and "a village loafer who sees much and understands little" (*In Defense of Reason* 58); his handling of language and technical skill were merely mannerisms which Winters compared to those of Swinburne, who in his opinion had a similar ability to mask insensitivity with rhetoric. As to refinement of emotion, the critic found it severely limited by the scope of the method, which did not allow any sophistication or depth. Winters concluded that since *The Cantos* was the manifestation of a sensibility without a mind, Pound was at his best in the translations, when he could rely on the intellect and subject matter of someone else to give direction and scope to his

> disconnected images. On his own, Pound was therefore incapable of producing serious, lasting poetry. (118)

Winters's hostility to Pound—and really, there is no other way to see it—would in context be surprising except that Winters himself never adhered to the tenets of the New Criticism. As Delmore Schwartz disapprovingly observed in his *Partisan Review* piece "A Literary Provincial" in 1945, Winters always preferred "the correct platitudes of statement," as had "his predecessor," Irving Babbitt (142). Winters's work represented an older humanistic tradition that, three quarters of a century later, contrasts starkly with the New Criticism.

Largely defining itself against biographical, sociological, or New Humanist models, modernist criticism, above all the formalist criticism inspired by Eliot, was almost from the first identified with colleges and universities. John Crowe Ransom, probably unwittingly, gave a simple name to a complex phenomenon with his book *The New Criticism* (1941), the name by which that formalist strain of American modernist criticism has been known ever since. What the New Criticism represented, above all else, was the professionalization of critical activity—an attempt to bring to criticism not just a historical dimension but also the status of scientific inquiry. Ransom and his fellow-travelers worked to distinguish their activities from late-Victorian concerns with ethics as well as from the excitations of consumer culture (hence, in America, the emphasis on the "Agrarian"). The preeminence the New Criticism won by defeating New Humanism was maintained for the next forty years, though tempered and defined more narrowly still (as we will see later) in the national fracas surrounding the award of the 1948 Bollingen Prize for Poetry to Ezra Pound. The judges who awarded that prize, including Eliot and Tate, defended their award to a man who was at the time under indictment for treason in overtly formalist terms; public outcry—virtually all of it from outside academe—was broad and sustained. The New Critics held their own, but did so ultimately by retreating even further not just from sociological issues but also from popular discourses.

In America, the "New Criticism" was initially the achievement of a group of scholars and devotees of poetry who were associated at Vanderbilt University in the 1920s under the name of "Fugitives" (John Crowe Ransom, Allen Tate, Donald Davidson, Robert Penn Warren, and Cleanth Brooks). Basically the American analogue to Russian formalism, the New Criticism stressed the autonomy of the literary work: its elements, qualities, and values were not accessible to philosophical or historical interpretation but only to "explication." Explication involved the meticulous scrutiny of a text for all its layers of meaning, its ambiguities and paradoxes, and its irony and wit. Such extra-literary considerations as the author's life, times, politics, influences, or point-of-view were considered irrelevant. Central New Critical texts included Allen Tate's *Reactionary Essays* (1936), John Crowe Ransom's *The World's Body* (1938), Cleanth Brooks and Robert Penn Warren's *Understanding Poetry* (1938), Cleanth Brooks's *The Well-Wrought Urn* (1947), and R. P. Blackmur's *Language as Gesture* (1952). Their shared assumption was that poetry says things in a complex way that criticism can describe but never duplicate. Thus, a work can only be "interpreted" through the structure of its own language, its imagery, and its ironic self-qualifications. After the Second World War, spurred by contributions from exiled members of the pre-war Prague School like Rene Wellek, the New Critics generated more theoretical justification for their ways of handling text, but in the 1930s and 1940s it was Eliot to whom they most often turned.

Eliot's example is unmistakable in Tate's June 1931 review of *A Draft of XXX Cantos*, titled "Ezra Pound's Golden Ass" (632–34). The *Cantos* present challenges of and for scholarship; Pound has been enormously influential, albeit primarily in terms of form and style. "There is no other poetry like the *Cantos* in English. And there is none quite so simple in form," Tate averred. In fact, the form of the poem is "so simple that almost no one has guessed it, and I suppose that it will continue to puzzle, perhaps to enrage, our more academic critics for a generation to come" (632). Tate's phrase about "our more academic critics" serves, of course, to separate himself from them, himself being a poet. But he is also a New Critic *avant la lettre*: "this form by virtue of its simplicity remains inviolable to critical terms; even now it cannot be technically described": the work, to say it again, can only be "interpreted" through the structure of its own language. It is the form of the poem that matters, not the content: The *Cantos* "are not about Italy, or about Greece, nor are they about us. They are not about anything. But they are distinguished poetry" (632). What's more, Tate continued, effectually paraphrasing Eliot, form does its work best by defeating the attempts of readers to simplify it: "the easiest interpretation of all poetry is the symbolic method: there are few poems that cannot be paraphrased into a kind of symbolism, which is usually false, being by no means the chief intention of the poet" (633). Tate's emphasis on difficulty was shared by other critics, even those less interested in aesthetic questions *per se*. Socially conscious critics like Edmund Wilson saw "all this load of erudition and literature" as "enough to sink any writer"; indeed, Wilson judged in his 1931 book *Axel's Castle: A Study of Imaginative Literature of 1870–1930* that "Pound's work *has* been partially sunk by its cargo of erudition" (110–11). The question had to be met. But the terms of Tate's defense ignored virtually everything that Pound himself wrote about his method and purpose. Like Apuleius's *Golden Ass*, Tate thought, *The Cantos* is "the production of a world without conviction" (633): its singular form is a sign of broader cultural malaise. "The words of a dead man / Are modified in the guts of the living,"

W. H. Auden, remembering Yeats, wrote in 1940, but ten years earlier Pound was learning that it happens to living poets as well.

The same month as Tate wrote his review, the poet Zukofsky, also reviewing *A Draft of XXX Cantos*, wrote to defend Pound from such praise. He acknowledged Eliot's emphasis on Pound's form, enlarging on it to note that the poem will always exceed any synopsis we might try to make of it—a gesture Tate and the emergent New Critics would applaud; he defended Pound's scholarship—his use of quotations; he attempted to justify "Pound's use of foreign languages"; and he observed the regular notice still being given by English critics of "Pound's Americanness" (366).

Later in 1931, anticipating Hugh Kenner's *magnum opus* by forty years, Iris Barry published "The Ezra Pound Period," an account of Pound's London years, which sees a special importance in Pound's being American and so not being conscripted into the army: "the belief seems to have grown up that from 1914 to 1918 no one in England had any interest save in making munitions, entertaining wounded soldiers, letting refugee Belgians camp in their parlours, or participating in active service abroad. Actually, to the generation most concerned with it, the war did not seem so very important most of the time. Young men got into uniform and went away; young women were better paid for jobs; but the war was never the whole of life." Despite all this, Barry wrote, there remained "those to whom the name of Pound meant more than that of [Field Marshall] Joffre." A dozen years later, Barry affirmed, it remains insufficiently "recognized what heavy and important work [Pound] did for letters at that time" (161–62). Barry's account was as bold as it was critical, working to keep separate the life of the nation and the life of letters. Marianne Moore made a similar defense of *The Cantos*, and in response to complaints about its obscurity proposed that all *The Cantos'* historical references "are an armorial coat of attitudes to things that have happened in books and in life"—the two spheres being in Moore's mind equally important." Pound's historical allusions "are not a shield but a coat worn by a man" who "serves under Beauty" (191).

In 1934, Zukofsky and Moore both returned to the question of how history enters Pound's *Cantos*. Zukofsky, with the challenges of Eliot's "Isolated Superiority" still on his mind, proposed in his "Ezra Pound: His Cantos" that "Pound has been both the isolated creator and the worldly pamphleteer," but then, as though still considering Moore's defense, he added:

> To put the defences of his own being in order, he has drafted himself into the defense of all innovation which has been a matter of clarifying and making sincere the intelligence. Contrasted with the leavings of transcendentalism and the belated scholasticism around him, he

> has shown a mentality capable of coping with living contemporary force. (8)

In this view of *The Cantos*, Pound's aestheticism is not *removed* from sociohistorical questions but serves rather as a defense against them. William Carlos Williams, in his 1931 "Excerpts from a Critical Sketch," was also exploring how a focus on language, on words, might represent an engagement of life rather than a retreat from it. Pound "uses a poem, words, modes that have been modified by use—not an idea. He uses the poem objectively" (105). In calling his piece "excerpts" Williams here as elsewhere eschews an interest in academic high-seriousness: his occasional essays were deliberately anti-professional. For Williams, the central issue for Pound criticism was "considering [the *Cantos*] in relation to the principal move in imaginative writing today—that away from the word as symbol and toward the word as reality" (107). Williams, Zukofsky, Barry, and Moore all represent, in this way, a resistance to the gathering New Critical Orthodoxy that had yet to announce itself but that was already being felt.

Moore's second essay on *The Cantos* was published in Eliot's *Criterion* (April, 1934) and took a different tack than had her first. "'The heart is in the form,' as is said in the East—in this case the rhythm which is a firm piloting of rebellious fluency" (482). "We have," she found, "in some of [Pound's] metrical effects a wisdom as remarkable as anything since Bach" (483). Moore's contention that not all wisdom is paraphraseable was not incompatible with the nascent New Criticism—though it certainly flew in the face of Lewis's rationalist position—but her defense of Pound's individual genius would shortly come under serious attack.

Blackmur, Leavis, and the End of an Era

Blackmur's "The Masks of Ezra Pound" (1934) made quite clear the obstacles Pound would have to overcome to find space in the New Critical order: "Mr. Pound is neither a great poet nor a great thinker. Those of his followers who declare him the one only belittle him, and when he writes as the other, he belittles himself" (178). Perhaps taking Tate's suggestion that the *Cantos* are not about anything, Blackmur maintained that "the content of [Pound's] work does not submit to analysis; it is not the kind of content that can be analysed—because, separated, its components retain no being" (178). Nevertheless, these statements were not meant so much as an attack as a clearing of the desk; Pound's poetry is "superficial," he explained, in a very particular way: Pound's "surface is a mask through which many voices are heard. . . . Mr. Pound's work has been to make *personae*, to become himself, as a poet, in this special sense a person through which what has most interested him in life and letters might be given voice" (179). Such a surface, "such a mask," he continued—channeling Eliotian notions of tradition—"consumes more critical than naively 'original' talent; as may be seen when in *The Cantos* Pound demonstrates his greatest failures when he is most 'original', where he has not remembered to be a mask" (179). As Blackmur proceeds, we learn that the textual difficulties of "Mauberley" or of *The Cantos* "are not difficulties in the substance of the poem, but superficial, in the reader's mind" (182). Readers need professional guidance.

Blackmur, an autodidact whose work eventually won him a position on the faculty at Princeton University, wrote with authority—and at length (35 pages): "The Masks of Ezra Pound" was the most sustained discussion of Pound's work yet published; what's more, being published in *Hound and Horn*, it had broad middle-brow circulation. The argument that Pound matters most when he is least himself cut both ways: it celebrated Pound's engagement of deep literary tradition precisely as it devalued a poet then still very much in his prime.

Reception history is, especially in its early stages, caught up with the processes of reputation building, separating from it only once the latter has reached a certain level of public recognition. In the second decade of the twentieth century, Pound was at the center of sometimes roiling storms, fighting to be heard, jostling with other contenders, the terms of his struggling often changing rapidly—twelfth-century Troubadours to Imagism to Vorticism to the Ideogrammic method, etc. We might say that reception history proper begins when the terms and questions of a poet's significance settle down—although of course these terms are always subject to change over time: it is, after all, the primary business of reception history to chart these changes. The story of Pound's reception really begins with Eliot's "Ezra Pound: His Metric and Poetry" and gathers significance following Eliot's "Isolated Superiority" and such academic responses to it as Tate's or Blackmur's. The terms of Pound's reception did not, however, always unfold the same ways in America as they did in Britain—but in both countries it was Eliot who established the criteria by which Pound's status was to be considered.

In Britain, the first important academic response came from F. R. Leavis. Perhaps ironically, Leavis had begun his career with a PhD on "The Relationship of Journalism to Literature" and began lecturing at Cambridge in 1927 (Bell 4). It was, however, his publication of *New Bearings in English Poetry* (1932) that established him as a voice to be reckoned with. Leavis's book acknowledges Eliot's authority, particularly on the question of Pound, and his chapter on Pound essentially works as a riposte to Eliot's "Isolated Superiority." "Poetry," Leavis began, "matters little to the modern world. That is, very little of contemporary intelligence concerns itself with poetry" (5). Leavis was right, of course, but then again this fact was essentially the point of departure for Pound's entire career—Pound's goal early and late being to restore to poetry its ancient cultural centrality. In Leavis's view, a view clearly shaped by Eliot, "Mr Pound's main concern has always been art: he is, in the most serious sense of the word, an aesthete" (140). But Leavis's sense of Pound as a latter-day aesthete is tempered by his sense of the significance of Pound's national origin—twenty years after Pound's appearance in London it remained for British critics a matter for reflection: "Mr Pound is not an American for nothing. What we have in *Mauberley* is a representative sensibility. . . . His technical skill is now a matter of bringing to precise definition a mature and complex sensibility. The rhythms, in their apparent looseness and carelessness, are marvels of subtlety: 'out of key with his time' is being said everywhere by strict rhythmic means" (143). And so, for Leavis as for Eliot, Pound's aesthetic achievements were historically important and a sign of his modernity: "Mr Pound's regeneration of poetic idiom is more than a matter of using modern colloquial speech" (149).

But if Pound is to be seen as important, the question remains *how* important. If the modern world cares little for poetry, as Leavis began by affirming, then how and why do aesthetic accomplishments matter? Here Leavis found little help from the usual authority: "Mr. Eliot does seem to have limited very drastically the kind of importance that can be attached to the *Cantos*—more drastically than comports with the effect of his allusions to them in the *Introduction* [to *Selected Poems*]" (152). Leavis's recourse was to compare Pound's use of allusions with Eliot's: "When Mr. Eliot in *The Waste Land* has recourse to allusion, the intrinsic power of his verse is commonly such as to affect even a reader who does not recognize what is being alluded to. But even when one is fully informed about Mr. Pound's allusions one's recognition has no significant effect: the value remains private to the author" (155).

We quote from Leavis at such length to demonstrate the establishment of historical opinion. Leavis was not a New Critic, but independent as he might have been, and individual as his conclusions certainly were, the questions that he chose to argue had already—and recently—been established for him. Leavis closes by contending that *The Cantos* "are Mr. Pound's *The Ring and the Book*" (156), which is to say that they are ambitious but generally unread. He explains that he believes his criticism of *The Cantos* is necessary as "the most hopeful way of getting *Mauberley* recognized for the great poem it is" (157). But "great" in what way? By the early 1930s critics and reviewers alike were reading Pound through Eliotian lenses, and that orthodoxy would spell trouble for Pound as he continued to work ever further on the peripheries of the modernism he had done so much to imagine into existence.[12]

The years of the Second World War understandably saw a decline, especially in Britain, of literary-critical activity, but in the United States the position assumed by Tate and other neo-classicists continued to stimulate discussion. After becoming chief poetry critic for the *Nation*, in an essay called "The Talk of Ezra Pound" (1940), poet and man of letters John Peale Bishop returned to Tate's proposal that "there is no other poetry like the *Cantos* in English"—that it is a poem developing around conversation and taking the "simple" form of "Menippean satire." Enlarging on Tate's anti-academic position and explicitly making of *The Cantos* a matter for polite conversation, Bishop offered that "what is best in conversation is the marginal comment, the text itself being taken for granted among listeners . . . only a boor would think of bringing it in." Consequently, Bishop found *Cantos LII–LXXI* (aka "the China Cantos" and "the Adams Cantos") inferior to the poem's earlier sections, concluding: "How sound Pound's position may be as an exponent of Social Credit, I cannot say; what can be said is that his concentration on economics has simplified his morality, which was already a little too simple" (639). Writing for the *New Republic*, the poet Randall Jarrell also responded to the suggestion of conversation, and also found the recent cantos wanting: "Mr. Pound has a fine feel for anecdotes that carry the quality of a person or an age, but I should prefer to see a collection of his favorites in some more appropriate form." For Jarrell, *Cantos LII–LXXI* fail as poetry precisely because they fail the conventions of polite conversation: "the versification of these cantos is interesting: there is none. The prose is an extremely eccentric, slangy, illogical, sentence-fragment, note-taking sort of prose—but prose." Worse still, these cantos are impolite because they are preachy—didactic. Within this genteel, elite conversation, the matter could seem little more than regretting that a fellow member was embarrassing the club. But events outside the club's smoking room would soon require a goodbye to all that.

Two serious warnings were sounded by American women, themselves both established poets. Louise Bogan, poetry editor for *The New Yorker*, sounded the first. In November, 1940, responding to what she saw as "Pound's long and rather insolent cultivation of opacity and ambiguity," Bogan nevertheless concluded that although "it would be easy to become hilarious at all this blueprinting" in *Cantos LII–LXXI*, Pound remained "in many ways a great figure" (76–78). Bogan, even before America's entry into the war, noted Pound's fascism but nevertheless thought the real issue was that he had become the victim of his own method. Didacticism had spoiled his aesthetics. Eighteen months later, and six months into the war, that same question held different significance. In April, 1942, the Chicago poet and colleague of Harriet Monroe, Eunice Tietjens, published her scathing dismissal, "The End of Ezra Pound." Like Jarrell, she credited Pound for his youthful service to poetry, but charged that he had never matured beyond that—and concluded by denouncing him as a traitor. A major fight lay ahead. This fight would be no gentlemen's quarrel, and no matter for elite culture alone; it would affect not only the fortunes of Pound's reception but also the very status of poetry in America. This donnybrook would be picked by a critic who saw himself in the tradition of populists like Whitman or even Frost—someone uninterested in Eliot and entirely unpersuaded by Pound's own sense of his work.

Notes

[1] On the emergence of academic culture, see Litz and Rainey, 59.

[2] See Kenner, *The Pound Era*, 150.

[3] R. George Thomas, ed., *Letters from Edward Thomas to Gordon Bottomley*, 184–85. The Ellis to whom Thomas refers was Edward John Ellis (1848–1916), today chiefly remembered for co-editing with William Butler Yeats a three-volume edition of William Blake's poetry. The first of Thomas's mixed reviews of *Personae* was published in *The Daily Chronicle* on June 7, 1909. It matters here to remember that the *Personae* of 1909 is not to be identified with the volume of collected poems called *Personae*, first published in 1926 and repeatedly expanded over the next half-century, culminating in the edition of 1990, co-edited by Lea Baechler and A. Walton Litz.

[4] Pound's "What I Feel about Walt Whitman" was not published until 1973, in William Cookson's edition of *Selected Prose 1909–1965.*

[5] Flint 28–29. Thomas would never change his sense that Pound represented an "exotic," un-English presence: see "Exotic Verse," in *New Weekly,* May 9, 1914, 249.

[6] In a letter to Lady Gregory, December 1909, Yeats called Pound a "queer creature, Ezra Pound, who has become really a great authority on the troubadours" *Letters*, ed. Alan Wade (London: Hart Davis, 1954), 543.

[7] Pound, letter of April 1937 to John Lackay Brown, quoted in Warwick Gould's "The Unknown Masterpiece: Yeats and the Design of the *Cantos*," in Gibson 58.

[8] Orage's review, "Readers and Writers" appeared under the initials R.H.C. in the *New Age*, July 25, 1918, 201. It was reprinted in Homberger, ed., *Ezra Pound: The Critical Heritage* 140–41.

[9] Padraic Colum, "Studies in the Sophisticated," 52–54. See also, for another example of the contemporaneous quarrel over poetry and scholarship, Dudley Fitts, "Music Fit for the Odes," *Hound and Horn* 4 (Jan.-Mar. 1931): 278–89; and Eda Lou Walton, "Obscurity in Modern Poetry," *New York Times Book Review*, April 2, 1933, 2.

[10] This was Bodenheim's fifth and final review of Pound's work.

[11] Eliot, "Isolated Superiority," *The Dial* 84 (Jan. 1928): 4–7. The article was reprinted in Erkilla, ed., *The Contemporary* Reviews, 167–79. Further references are to this reprint.

[12] In 1970, Michael Hamburger, writing anonymously in the *TLS*, reviewed Eliot's relation to the New Critical orthodoxy, submitting that "[t]he leading critics of the following generation—F.R. Leavis, Allen Tate and the late R.P.

Blackmur—read Eliot with great attentiveness and wrote about Pound with him very much in mind. Mr. Tate reviewed *A Draft of XXX Cantos* in 1931 with the suggestion of going Eliot's argument one better, proposing that *The Cantos* 'are not about anything. But they are distinguished verse' (*Nation*, 632). A year later, Dr. Leavis set forth certain areas of respectful disagreement with Eliot in *New Bearings in English Poetry*: the early verse was uninteresting, Dr. Leavis demurred, while the *Cantos* were 'little more than a game—a game serious with the seriousness of pedantry.' [. . .] Dr. Leavis was mainly concerned to emphasize the importance of 'Mauberley' and in this happily followed up a hint in Eliot's introduction to Pound's *Selected Poems* in 1928" (925).

2: A Prize Fight and Institutionalization, 1948–1951

It is necessary to see Pound under two aspects: as he worked upon poetry and as he worked upon the public.

—John Berryman, "The Poetry of Ezra Pound"

Reconsidered Passion

"HISTORY," T. S. ELIOT ONCE HAD WRITTEN, "has many cunning passages, contrived corridors." And it "gives too late / what's not believed in, or if still believed, / In memory only, reconsidered passion."[1] Between 1941 and 1951, between his first regular broadcasts over Rome radio and Hugh Kenner's establishment of "Pound studies," Pound saw his stature and status changed radically by forces over which he himself no longer exerted control. It was an experience virtually without precedent in literary history: Pound, still furiously active as a writer, became the nearly helpless witness to his own canonization. When his Bollingen Prize—endowed by Paul Mellon, but administered by government agency—was announced (February 20, 1949), Pound received a long-awaited formal tribute. But "a man situated as [was] Mr. Pound," as the Fellows' public announcement delicately put it, was no longer capable of defining the terms of his own recognition.[2] Perhaps no writer is; perhaps without the New Critical principles on which his award was predicated, Pound would have received no recognition at all, or at least for some time to come. Be that as it may, after his award, Pound "became his admirers"—and in ways rather different than those imagined by Auden.[3] This is not to say that Pound himself changed either personally or artistically, but that his work assumed a different kind of public presence. The energetic iconoclast became the professors' poet; the reformer who had so often pitched his appeal to those excluded from university education came to depend on the academy for the audience that was at last, mostly, prepared to meet him.

By no means sudden, this transformation was still incomplete even a decade later. But the Bollingen controversy conceived for Pound a new pattern of reception, becoming a battleground decisive in the New Critics' establishment of institutional authority. Their victory, however, exacted a price paid both in the terms by which Pound gained academic acceptance as well as in the terms whereby a suspicious public was persuaded of its inability to judge literary matters. In awarding Pound, the Fellows in American Literature of the Library of Congress compromised much of what *The Cantos* stood for, and occasioned a *rite de passage* that marked a generation of poets and critics.

Indicted (July 26, 1943) and arraigned for treason (November 19, 1945), but found mentally unfit to stand trial (February 13, 1946), Pound excited considerable public antipathy.[4] The pitch of public feeling over his case had an almost definitive impact on his subsequent critical reception; for even if Pound's disgrace had no part in motivating the Bollingen Prize, it informed the language of its justification—a justification demanded not only by the public but very nearly by Congressional investigation. The Bollingen Prize for Poetry was itself implicated in that public suspicion. The prize had been established only the previous year, in 1948, when the Bollingen Foundation acted on a suggestion of Allen Tate's and gave the Library of Congress money to make an annual award of $1,000: "to be awarded annually on the basis of a recommendation by a jury of selection consisting of the Fellows in American Letters of the Library of Congress." An "honorary and advisory group appointed by the Librarian of Congress," the Fellows in 1948 comprised Conrad Aiken, W. H. Auden, Louise Bogan, T. S. Eliot, Paul Green, Robert Lowell, Katherine Anne Porter, Karl Shapiro, Theodore Spencer, Allen Tate, William Thorp, and Robert Penn Warren. The gift stipulated that "the prize is awarded to the author of the book of verse which, in the opinion of the jury of selection, represents the highest achievement of American poetry in the year for which the award is made. The jury may, however, decline to make a selection for any given year if in its judgment no poetry worthy of the prize was published during that year."

In awarding the first Bollingen Prize to the *Pisan Cantos*, the Fellows had anticipated trouble. Formal discussion of the award for 1948 began at their annual meeting in November, and reduced the number of nominations to four. That night, Huntington Cairns—trustee for the Bollingen Foundation—gave a dinner for the Fellows. As he later recalled, "I said that I hoped the prize would attract a little attention, and Tate said, 'Will it attract attention!' We were sitting at a big round table, and they all looked at one another in silence. Then Tate told me that the leading nominee was Pound."

Final balloting, conducted by mail in February, resulted in ten decisive votes for Pound: Paul Green abstained, and Karl Shapiro cast the only negative vote. When informed of the Fellows' judgment, Librarian Luther Evans forecast that the "reaction would be, for the most part, emotional rather than intellectual; public conscience would be outraged; the progress of poetry would be arrested for a generation; international relations, particularly with Italy, would be embarrassed; confidence in the

Library of Congress would be seriously impaired; their faculties would be suspected, their motives rejected, their principles deplored; Congress, inevitably, would intervene." In spite of this forecast, the Fellows persisted in their choice, although their public statement bore the impress of Evans's warning:

> The fellows are aware that objections may be made to awarding a prize to a man situated as is Mr. Pound. In their view, however, the possibility of such objection did not alter the responsibility assumed by the Jury of Selection. This was to make a choice for the award among the eligible books, provided any one merited such recognition, according to the stated terms of the Bollingen Prize. To permit other considerations than that of poetic achievement to sway the decision would destroy the significance of the award and would in principle deny the validity of that objective perception of value on which civilized society must rest.[5]

This statement, repeatedly recited in the months that followed, was initially a successful prolepsis. It identified the imposition of a strictly aesthetic criterion, "the objective perception of value," with the very foundation of civilization. That it said "civilization" and not "culture" reflects the emphasis of Eliot's contemporaneous work; in no way did it identify civilization with democratic values, but that point was missed by the many newspaper accounts. *The New York Herald Tribune*, for instance, in an article titled "A Poet's Prize," submitted that "this emphasis on an objective criterion of beauty and excellence, akin to a belief in an objective truth, is fundamental to a free and rational society." In this and other early responses, the Fellows' defense of artistic freedom almost imperceptibly was translated into a defense of democratic principles. Subsequent responses would not make the same error. In the highly charged exchanges of 1949, claims about the poem as autonomous aesthetic object were often recognized for the polemic they have always been.

Pound had won an award, although not in the terms he would have wanted. He had won a victory, but a victory of an unfamiliar and uncomfortable kind. He had won an audience, but one with which he hardly knew how to relate. Nor did the development of this new audience make his work less marginal to the general readership he had long imagined. Pound's new circumstances merely joined one kind of marginality to another. For prior to his Bollingen Prize, even at the height of his economic preoccupation, he stood for craft and technical mastery, defending poets from the demands of unsympathetic editors, critics, and readers: he had been, in other words, the poet's poet. His sometimes embarrassed embrace by academe after the Second World War in one sense then meant little more than a shift in professional audience. Here too, however, his case entailed broader historical changes. As Gail McDonald and James Breslin have shown, the development of New Critical professionalism related closely to the modernist insistence upon poetic rigor. Pound's "hardness," in all senses, became a sign of his professional expertise, and served after Bollingen to distinguish him from soft-minded amateurs and poseurs. Pound would earlier have welcomed the distinction, and sometimes still did. Again, as Litz and Rainey have observed, Pound tended to distinguish between "experts" and amateurs more than between "professionals" and amateurs, often preferring the lover of the art to the professional. But in his uncertain condition after having been remanded to St. Elizabeths, having been judged mentally unfit to stand trial, Pound was less able publicly to speak for himself. As a poet, the prestige accorded to the *Pisan Cantos* brought him new license. As a critic, however, he was pinned down by hostile and friendly fire alike. After Bollingen, Pound increasingly gave over critical activity: it was Eliot, not Pound, who was responsible for *Literary Essays* (1954), and Noel Stock who edited *Impact* (1960), and neither collection presented new material. The distinction between professional and amateur, like the scholarly representation of modernism it ultimately enabled, left Pound increasingly unqualified to speak about his own work. The Bollingen controversy had formalized the disjunction between the middle-class audience of the weekly reviews and the increasingly specialized readers professing literature in institutions of higher learning.

Many of those who supported the Fellows in their decision took to calling the controversy *l'affaire Pound*, alluding to the infamous *l'affaire Dreyfus*. The comparison is perhaps hyperbolic, but not inappropriate. Although coverage by the mass media had cooled by the publication of Hugh Kenner's *The Poetry of Ezra Pound* (July 13, 1951), academic attention had not (Sutton, 1963; Schulman, 1974, Bloom 1987). When William Van O'Connor and Edward Stone, for instance, published their *A Casebook on Ezra Pound* (1959) more than ten years later, they could still anticipate academic interest sufficient to adopt their casebook in freshman English courses. For O'Connor and Stone, Pound remained sufficiently "controversial" to warrant their collection, yet was removed enough in time to permit disinterested appraisal. Thirty-five years after that "casebook," the debate about Ezra Pound continues to excite partisan passion. Indeed, some recent reviews suggest that the professional audience expects new studies to address the relation of Pound's poetry and politics. The Bollingen controversy remains a part of "Pound" as institutionalized object of study.

The Ongoing Case of the Case that Won't Go Away

The manner and method of that study have changed, but in ways that still contest the ground chosen after 1949 by Eliot, Tate, or Berryman.

Pound's advocates held that ground, but not so as to be able to leave it behind them. More recent arguments, like those of Jerome McGann or Robert Casillo, assert the bearing of Pound's politics on his poetry, but they displace the site of its relevance to within the text itself rather than insisting that the actions of the man cannot be separated from those of the poet. Those arguments must, however, figure later in our account. Here it suffices to note that a half-century later, the terms of Pound's Bollingen prize continue to inform scholarly and critical discussion of his work. Between 1948 and 1951, Pound became the focus of a larger contest about the relation of poetic to political activity, as partisans on both sides never tired of observing. As it changed the terms of debate regarding the relation of poetry and politics, *l'affaire Pound* arguably emerges as one of the defining issues of twentieth-century intellectual life.

The Bollingen controversy was a flash point where many and sundry forces converged. The acrimony owed as much to long-simmering resentments as it did to immediate disapproval of Pound's particular award, or even of his alleged treason, fascism, or anti-Semitism. On the one hand, the controversy afforded an opportunity for middle-class readers to express their resentment of Pound's and of Eliot's elitism and its concomitant internationalism. On the other hand, this popular feeling was exploited and further incited by those literary figures who had been denied stature by modernist criteria for a quarter-century. The Bollingen controversy, as most parties to it recognized, marked the exasperated backlash of middle-class culture to the academic culture that now proposed more to lead it than to serve it.

Pound, Eliot, and other self-consciously "modernist" writers had long and overtly disdained popular understanding. That disdain was, in both Pound's case and Eliot's, ironically caught up in the pursuit of cultural authority. Both poets took a variety of steps to reach beyond the comparatively small audience available to poetry in their early careers: both turned their hand to drama, Pound first but Eliot more successfully; both, although under quite different circumstances and in decidedly different ways, began careers as radio broadcasters; after 1930 Pound turned his hand to a succession of popular primers, and Eliot to a successful career as public lecturer on not only literary but also religious, moral, and cultural issues. Most importantly, both undertook the definition of "culture," actively attempting to shape their audience and the conditions of their own reception. In the process, Pound and Eliot embittered those poets like Frost and Williams who resisted not only their internationalism but also their attempts to resituate the audience for new poetry. It would be one of Frost's more resentful followers, Robert Hillyer, who would whip up a public previously more puzzled than provoked into a patriotic fury.

That infection of nationalist feeling either confused the issues, or underscored them starkly and emphatically, depending on one's position towards Pound. In either case, public indignation quickly raised the stakes for which all involved were striving. While public controversy over the fate of poets has ancient precedent, nothing in American or even English poetry has since so compelled national attention. That such public interest seems to us now unlikely, to say the least, marks the pyrrhic quality of the victory won by Pound's adherents. Their determination to do battle is understandable, and their line of defense—given the previous quarter century of literary-theoretical development—perhaps inevitable. Both sides recognized how thoroughly modernist critical praxis was tied to the perception of an international modernist-literary tradition.

Pound and Eliot's internationalism, their status as cosmopolitans and expatriates, contributed to the explosion of public feeling over Pound's award. It was, of course, related to the elitism that pervaded even modernist gestures towards the public, or in Pound's case at least towards an idealized or imagined public. Pound's support for Mussolini during the Second World War, and the notorious radio broadcasts that followed from that support, lent themselves as justifications for the sometimes indiscriminate attacks upon modernist standards that took shape in 1949 and after. Although indicted, Pound remained legally innocent, since he had never stood trial, but under the prodding of nationalist voices like Carl Sandburg's or Hillyer's, as well as of the mass media (for whom it all made good copy), Pound was popularly regarded as a traitor. For the general public the question was whether Pound's politics obviated the worth of his poetry. In that circumstance, his receipt of the Bollingen Prize was bound to arouse public indignation.

As Karl Shapiro remarked when he soon after chose to break the secrecy of the Fellows' ballot, the Fellows' statement of opinion was a successful device in placating opinion: "the newspaper editorials I saw all rejoiced in 'the objective perception of value on which any civilized society must rest' and I heard one radio commentator remark benignly that 'this could never happen in Russia.'" Shapiro believed that "what appeased the journalists," whom one might have expected to be looking for a scandal, "must have been their belief that Pound, despite his unintelligibility to them, is on the side of beauty or 'technical excellence.' The Fellows and the newsmen meet at the point where an unspecified technical excellence is accepted by the lay readers as successful (i.e., 'beautiful') poetry."[6]

Shapiro determined to prick the public conscience, and the editorial approbation of the *Baltimore Sun* provided him with a suitable opportunity. In a letter to the editor, Shapiro broke ranks both with other modernist poets as well as with the other Fellows and challenged the principle upon which the award to Pound depended. Referring to the Fellows' statement of justification that "to permit other considerations than that of poetic achievement to sway the decision would . . . in principle deny the validity of that objective perception of value on which any society must rest," Shapiro "vehemently" denied that "the objective perception of value" was either possible or desirable.[7] He denied, moreover, that Pound himself respected such a principle. The presumption of objectivity in deciding questions of value was a mistake, Shapiro said, that owed directly to New Critical precepts. "Pound's technical mastery of his craft is," Shapiro concluded, "indisputable, but I do not think the Bollingen prize or any other prize should be awarded on such skimpy grounds as dactyls and images."[8]

On February 28, three days after Shapiro's denunciation, Albert Deutsch wrote to the *New York Post* that he found something "unholy" in the act "of honoring a man who had broadcast fascist propaganda." Clearly the fellows had swatted a hornet's nest. However, two journals that were regularly venues for political debate swiftly addressed the issue and for a while checked the development of an all-out donnybrook. In *Politics* Dwight MacDonald offered "Homage to Twelve Judges," and in *Partisan Review*, John Berryman's "The Poetry of Ezra Pound" praised Pound as a poet even while disparaging the results of the "New Criticism."[9] Noting and dismissing the genteel view of *The Cantos* as being "conversation," Berryman contrasted Eliot's and Blackmur's view that Pound is all manner and no matter with the views of earlier critics like Edward Thomas that "the thought dominates the words and is greater than they are."[10] In fact, Berryman believed increasing dominance of academic criticism caused "*Personae* [to be] the last volume of Pound's that was widely judged on its merits" (392). Subsequently, reviewers and critics succumbed to Eliot's incantations. The problem with Eliot, Blackmur, or other advocates of New Critical technique is that they are "content to consider in isolation originality of either manner or matter without regard to the other, and with small regard to degree . . . Until we get a criticism able to consider both originalities, in degree, Pound's achievements as a poet cannot be finally extricated from the body of his verse" (394). That the importance of Berryman's essay is underestimated now must owe in large part to its having been lost in a flood of polemic. Like Shapiro, and like many of Pound's antagonists, Berryman attributed much of the then-current confusion to the dominance of New Criticism, while at the same time defending and even praising Pound's poetry.

That same issue of *Partisan Review* also included a sharp editorial by William Barrett. Barrett neatly appropriated Berryman's defense, citing its very appearance as a sign of the editorial belief at *Partisan Review* "that independent aesthetic judgment must be the continuing task of criticism," but submitting that "Mr. Berryman deals chiefly with the earlier and middle phases of Pound's career, and does not touch upon what Pound's subject matter became in recent years."[11] Granting, then, the distinction between "Pound the man" and "the value of the particular book, *Pisan Cantos*," Barrett quoted from cantos LXXX and LXXIV in order to demonstrate their anti-Semitic quality. His next step, however crucial to his position, is nevertheless critically debatable. Barrett writes:

> our problem would be much easier if this were a dramatic poem, in which this odious human attitude was expressed by one of the characters with whom the author need not be in agreement. But *The Pisan Cantos* is a lyrical poem, or group of lyrical poems, in which Pound is expressing Pound, and this ugly human attitude expressed in the lines above is one that the poet seeks to convey as his own to the reader. (346)

The question of genre has been, more than once in the history of Pound criticism, hotly debated; Barrett's description assumes much, and flatly denies Pound's description of the poem as an epic. Barrett's identification of *The Cantos* as lyric is ineluctably tied to his judgment that Pound's inclusion of the hateful and ugly is ironic and irredeemable: ironic because Barrett supposes the aim of lyric poetry to be expressive of the beautiful; irredeemable because the failure to achieve that aim vitiates any technical accomplishment. But it was his conclusion that occasioned the most subsequent response. Drawing on Berryman's indictment of the New Criticism, Barrett charged that recent "critical attitudes" were morally irresponsible. By contrast, he affirmed that "every particular literary judgement brings us in the end to some question of principle." He concluded by inviting his readers to regard his concerns as an open question: "how far is it possible, in a lyric poem, for technical embellishments to transform vicious and ugly matter into beautiful poetry?" (347).

Barrett put that question directly to the Bollingen Fellows, offering them a forum in the next issue of *Partisan Review* (May 1949). Only three of them—Auden, Shapiro and Tate—chose to respond, but Barrett solicited opinion from four other prominent critics to amplify his case. All of them had reason to resist New Critical precepts: Robert Gorham Davis was an academic long concerned to relate literary to social praxis; Clement Greenberg was the leading critical champion of modernism in the arts, though on this issue it was his outrage as a Jew that most shaped his decision; and critic Irving Howe and novelist George Orwell were both left-wing literary and social critics for whom questions of art were inextricably caught up with questions about the culture that produced it. To these voices, Barrett added his own further comments. The responses were printed alphabetically, with Barrett acting as final respondent.[12]

Auden began by positing a binary opposition wherein all critics assume either that art is cathartic (aims to purge bad feelings) or mimetic (aims to reflect reality). In the first view, Auden explained, Pound's work should be suppressed; in the second, it fully deserves the award because his representation of evil exemplifies his integrity and artistic responsibility. In its appropriation of Aristotelian terms, Auden's argument aspired to defuse Barrett's charge by refusing his enunciation of lyric purpose. More fundamentally, Auden represented the whole controversy as understandable in terms of basic, simple critical disagreements: a matter for calm deliberation rather than inflamed feeling. Auden closed by suggesting that, even if judged dangerous to the public, *Pisan Cantos* should be awarded before being suppressed.

Davis supposed that the Pound award "is most profitably taken as a problem in aesthetics," but noted that the award owed to the dominance of New Critical ideas and proposed—a month before the attacks by Robert Hillyer—that "nearly everyone in America who is serious about literature is involved in one way or another." Davis's claims in fact prefigured Hillyer's, since he associated the New Criticism not only with "snobbery" and an energetic quest for "prestige," but also with anti-Semitism. Auden had tried to dismiss this aspect of Pound's work by submitting that it was unfortunately "a feeling that all gentiles at times feel," but Davis attributed Pound's anti-Semitism to a very particular source. Linking Pound and Eliot here, Davis underscored Eliot's attraction to the proto-fascist anti-Semitism of Charles Maurras and the Action Française. As evidence for the inherent anti-Semitism of *Pisan Cantos*, this connection was utterly insufficient; nevertheless, it set a portentous precedent and clouded broader recognition of the import of the New Critical underpinnings of Pound's prize.

The question of Pound's anti-Semitism figured more immediately in the response of Clement Greenberg, who wrote to support Barrett's critique: "As a Jew, I myself cannot help being offended by the matter of Pound's latest poetry; and since 1943 things like that make me feel physically afraid too." Unlike Davis, Greenberg did not quarrel with the Fellows' "aesthetic verdict," but he did question the primacy of aesthetic issues in the Pound affair. Indeed, he allowed that he was not necessarily against the award itself so much as the Fellows' unsatisfactory explanation of their verdict.

Irving Howe, George Orwell, and Shapiro all took surprisingly moderate positions. Howe considered whether the aesthetic issue could in this case remain paramount and introduced a new paradox: "while believing in the autonomy of aesthetic judgment, I believe in it so deeply that I also think that there are some situations when it must be disregarded." While not wishing to see Pound prosecuted or censored, Howe yet regarded any award as an immoral social act. The only way, he thought, of taking literature seriously is to love it less than life. Orwell's argument was somewhat more temporizing. He professed himself ready to accept the Fellows' distinction between life and art so long as the public did not mistake an award for aesthetic integrity as the recuperation of evil ideas or opinions. Shapiro too weighed in more calmly than his letter to the

Baltimore Sun might have led one to expect. Barrett's "extension of the official statement of the Fellows makes it clear," Shapiro wrote, "that we are dealing with the *pons asinorum* of modern criticism"; that is, Barrett's extension demonstrates how difficult even the enabling precepts of contemporary criticism are for the non-specialist. Nevertheless, Shapiro reiterated his two reasons for opposing Pound in the Fellows' balloting: first, he could not as a Jew honor an anti-Semite; second, he maintained that Pound's "political and moral philosophy vitiates his poetry and lowers its standards as literary work." Shapiro also repeated his conviction that Eliot's presence in particular pressured the Fellows "to dissociate art from social injunction."[13]

Tate's contribution was wholly different in tone, being angry and out of temper. He accused Barrett of cant and vulgarity, as well as of a dishonorable insinuation in charging with anti-Semitism "the group of which I am a member." Tate, with a bravado perhaps as gentile as it was genteel, then challenged Barrett to a duel. In the next issue of *Partisan Review*, Tate offered "Further Remarks on the Pound Award," in which he countered the contention that "a vote for the *Pisan Cantos* was a vote for 'formalism' and a vote against 'life'" (666–68). There Tate reiterated the Ruskinian belief that "the health of literature depends upon the health of society, and conversely," and maintained that "the specific task of the man of letters is to attend to the health of society not at large but through literature." The dramatic assumption implicit in Tate's apparently unprepossessing "conversely" indicates the degree to which the controversy was, at this stage, still being conducted in literary-intellectual circles; it was after all an assumption that he shared with both Pound and Eliot. Over this point, Tate did not even pause, but continued to explain that his vote for Pound was determined by Pound's service to letters, and was made facing "the disagreeable fact" that Pound had performed this service "even in passages of verse in which the opinions expressed ranged from the childish to the detestable. In literature as in life nothing reaches us pure." Tate's contributions to the Forum as well as his "Further Remarks" unmistakably represented a kind of elite privilege, seeking to appropriate for the Fellows the right to indignation and moral outrage.

Barrett's response to the forum made a show of alarm at Tate's attitude and protested that this was a public and not a personal issue. After praising Davis, and disagreeing with W. H. Auden's comment that "a work of art cannot compel the reader to look at it with detachment" ("The Question of the Pound Award," 513), Barrett took note of Dwight MacDonald's "Homage to Twelve Judges." MacDonald's perception that the award was "the brightest political act in a dark period" struck Barrett as extreme. He declared MacDonald's position "bohemian," and felt that it urged liberalism "to countenance things that deny its own right to exist." Finally, Barrett applauded Shapiro for making "a much better statement of the question of form and content in a literary work than I did in my Comment," and proposed to resign his part in the discussion.

All told, those voices critical of Pound's prize had won a modest victory. Subsequent letters, from self-professed "laymen" to intellectuals like Babette Deutsch, enlisted in Barrett's cause. Only Tate came off looking extreme and unreasonable. He would have his chance to improve on his performance though; for however satisfied Barrett was with the discussion, it would prove more an initial skirmish than the decisive engagement. Other forces, aggressively hostile to Pound, his prize, and the New Criticism that justified it, were already in motion. For them, the discussion in *Partisan Review* had remained entirely too polite, and their determination to turn intellectual check into moral crusade would ultimately reverse Pound's fortunes. In the ensuing clashes, the New Critics were able to identify themselves with that disinterested culture the alternative to which was anarchy.

Storming the Ivory Tower

The energy for this gathering storm would come not from such intellectual voices as gathered in *Partisan Review*, but from that perennial American obsession with conspiracy which was in the first years of the Cold War particularly strong. In the summer of 1949 the disgrace of Alger Hiss and Senator Joseph McCarthy's list of communists in high places were only months away. The House Un-American Activities Committee had recently been given permanent status; and US Representative George Dondero (R-Michigan) had already launched his campaign against artists who do not "portray our beautiful country in plain, simple terms that everyone can understand." The "difficulty" of modern art, Dondero claimed in an interview with Emily Genauer, was a consipracy "to foster communism in this country." Apparently having no knowledge of Stalin's enforced aesthetic of socialist realism, Dondero maintained further that "modern art is communistic because it is distorted and ugly, because it does not glorify our beautiful country, our cheerful and smiling people, and our great material progress. Art which does not portray our beautiful country in plain, simple terms that everyone can understand, breeds dissatisfaction. It is therefore opposed to our government, and those who create and promote it are our enemies" (ibid.). Threats of the kind perceived by Dondero gave New Critical arguments about aesthetic autonomy an immediate political value, helping entrench the New Criticism within the American academy. The willingness, even eagerness of opportunists like Dondero to stifle the arts in the name of freedom drove many academics who might otherwise have taken issue with Pound's award behind New Critical defenses (quoted in Végsö 93).

Karl Shapiro experienced these threats first-hand, and in a manner that may well explain the moderation of his views after his letter to the editor of the *Baltimore Sun*. As Shapiro later remembered, shortly after his letter to the *Baltimore Sun* he received an edgy phone call from New York. The caller identified himself as Albert D. Parelhoff, and said that he wished to interest Shapiro in writing "an article for the *Saturday Review of Literature* about Pound and the Prize, in as much as he had cast the one vote against it." Shapiro was interested enough to consent to an interview in his office at Johns Hopkins. When Parelhoff arrived, however, he pressed his "evidence" that a fascist conspiracy had motivated not only the giving of Pound's award but also the very existence of the foundation. It was no accident, he implied, that "Bollingen" was also the name of Carl Jung's home in Switzerland. Shapiro recalled that Parelhoff "showed me papers purporting to prove that Jung was a Nazi, explaining the name Bollingen, and suggesting that the donors of the Prize were political sympathizers of Jung. [Parelhoff] wanted to enlist me to attack them and the 'political principles' he believed lay behind the Foundation. I told him flatly that I wouldn't write an article, so he went away, and it was then that the *Saturday Review* got Robert Hillyer."[14]

Hillyer was less circumspect than Shapiro, and—as William Meredith noted in a letter of July 4, his "personal animosity, his dishonest methods," consequently undermined legitimate concerns with the aestheticism of the Fellows' premises. Hillyer, then President of the Poetry Society of America, had already inveighed against the principal targets: in a forum in the *Saturday Review* some three years earlier, he had attacked Pound; and in a review of William Van O'Connor's *Sense and Sensibility in Modern Poetry* (*Saturday Review*, March 19, 1949) he had attacked Eliot and the New Criticism. But armed with Parelhoff's conspiratorial evidence, and finding ammunition in Shapiro's and others' reservations about critical "objectivity," Hillyer felt prepared to attempt something on the scale of a literary revolution. For him, the Pound question seemed to offer a last chance to restore critical credibility to popular verse of the old American fireside tradition. Capitalizing on whatever circumstance afforded, Hillyer's two-part invective, "Treason's Strange Fruit" and "Poetry's New Priesthood," was published and editorially supported by the *Saturday Review*. Norman Cousins and Harrison Smith (editor and president of the *Saturday Review*, respectively) predicted that, "if we read the signs of the time correctly, the Bollingen Prize given to Ezra Pound will eventually set off a revolution of no mean dimensions" (21).

Hillyer made three general charges, two of which were incredible enough immediately to open his position to New Critical counterattack. First, he reiterated the protest of Barrett and others that evaluative and aesthetic questions are not finally separable—that it was impossible to honor the poet without honoring the man—which point Hillyer affirmed in the tone of the innocent describing the emperor's new clothes—as though it were impossible *not* to see this. Then, like Davis, but more recklessly, Hillyer implicated the New Criticism with a shadowy fascist conspiracy for which the Bollingen Foundation was only a humanist front.

Journalistic smear rather than argument, Hillyer's invectives ignited a firestorm of protest against everyone concerned with the Bollingen prize. Most of the ensuing letters, published in the *Saturday Review* and elsewhere, were from middle-class readers for whom any notion of recent critical activity was "new." Other magazines like the *Catholic World*[15] or *Time* picked up the tone of Hillyer's charges; *Time* even called its piece "That's All, Fellows," alluding to the bit that closes Warner Brothers' "Looney Tunes." Generally, the popular press exulted in what seemed to be a cutting down to size of both elite and academic pretensions, and pronounced the case evidence of what happens when the judgment of value grows too far removed from common sense. This level of animation was too much for Aline Louchheim, herself Jewish and an established art critic for the *New York Times* and elsewhere; Louchheim protested in the *New York Times* (September 4, 1949) that public insistence on the judgment of "the common man" risked much, since art is after all an uncommon thing. But Hillyer and his supporters were then at the high-water mark of their fortunes. Even some academics like Leon Edel or F. Leighton Peters, not to mention genuinely popular writers like William Rose Benét or James Michener, added to the throng of voices thanking Hillyer for his "detective work." The New Criticism and the new poetry had made many and various enemies.

Nevertheless, most intellectuals deplored Hillyer's tactics and worried over his demagogic sweeping away of principle. Shortly after Hillyer's second invective, Smith and Cousins found themselves having to accede to requests that they print a statement dissociating the Bollingen Foundation from the Fellows—the alleged link between them having been so important to Hillyer's allegations. On July 30, following one letter from Paul Green and a second from all the other living jurors, Smith and Cousins agreed in print "to accept without further question" that the decision had been "arrived at wholly by democratic procedure." Moreover, they added, "it has been proved to our satisfaction that the [Bollingen] Foundation had nothing to do with the award beyond the donation of the prize and its own name" (22). But when Margaret Marshall collected eighty-four signatures from other writers, poets, and intellectuals on a letter of protest and then submitted that to the *Saturday Review*, Smith and Cousins balked. After weeks of evasion, they agreed to print the letter only on the condition that the letter be accompanied by a list of all those writers who had been approached but had refused to endorse it. Consequently, this letter was not published until December, and then in the *Nation* rather than in the *Saturday Review*.

By that time, other important expressions of support for the Fellows and the principle upon which their decision was based, although often not for their decision itself, had already countered Hillyer's offensive. At the end of June, Librarian of Congress Luther Evans published the Librarian's Annual Report. Hillyer had questioned whether it was "proper or legal" for such a group as the Fellows in American Letters to exist, "appointed privately, even secretly, yet speaking openly under the authority of the American Congress." Who, Hillyer demanded to know, appoints such fellows "that so many come from the exponents and idols of the 'new criticism'?" Evans responded:

> With respect to the jury, it was of record that the organization of the Fellows of the Library of Congress had resulted from a proposal made by Mr. Allen Tate, who had served as the Library's Consultant in Poetry in English in 1943-44, during the Librarianship of Mr. Archibald MacLeish. Mr. Tate had himself been largely instrumental in establishing the group which had held its first meeting in May 1944. Their duties were (and are) to advise the Librarian on the development of its collections and the promotion of its services so far as they are related to American literary materials. They have received no compensation for their efforts in the interest of the Library except reimbursement for expenses incurred in attendance at annual meetings. The appointments of the Fellows have been made, of course, by the Librarian of Congress.

After this explanation, Hillyer's charge of conspiracy increasingly came to look like the vituperative hysterics of an embittered and defeated man. But although Evans's report put to rest further questions about the Library's involvement in the Fellows' deliberations, Hillyer's charges had caused the public sensation he desired. Representative Jacob K. Javits of New York, responding to a letter from none other than Norman Cousins, had already called for a Congressional Joint Committee on the Library of Congress. A committee was duly formed, chaired by Senator Green of Rhode Island. In the end, a Congressional investigation of the conspiracy "detected" by Hillyer was finally avoided, but not before the Committee unanimously agreed (August 19, 1949) that henceforth the library was to dissociate itself from all prizes and awards.[16] This decision would have far-reaching consequences. It not only withdrew government sponsorship from the Bollingen Prize for poetry, but also from the Elizabeth Sprague Coolidge Medal for "eminent service to chamber music" and from three prizes endowed by Lessing Rosenwald in connection with an annual exhibition of prints. It would be nearly twenty years before the American government would again risk awarding artistic achievement.

Unfortunately, the decision also provoked a new salvo from the *Saturday Review*; in a piece titled "End of Controversy," Harrison Smith laid responsibility for this ruling on the Fellows, rather than acknowledging that it resulted from Cousins' letter to Javits (23). In fact, poet-critic Mark Van Doren had warned Smith beforehand that any Congressional investigation would, in the current political atmosphere, produce results that even Hillyer would regret (62). Smith was prepared to concede little more than that further prosecution of his cause need be more circumspect. Unwilling to sacrifice the public interest Hillyer had generated, Smith and Cousins selected a new champion to execute new tactics. Peter Viereck was young and already accomplished: war veteran, Pulitzer prize-winning historian with academic credentials, and a Guggenheim fellow in poetry. Viereck had also, as his essays for the *Saturday Review* and *Atlantic Monthly* demonstrate, learned the techniques of modernist polemic. The title of his piece was "My Kind of Poetry." First, recognizing the value of the conservative mantle which Eliot flourished so ostentatiously, Viereck proudly described his own poetic technique as "conservative," by which he meant traditional. Second, however democratic his attitude towards readers, Viereck had internalized Pound's and Eliot's insistence on professional rigor. Thus, he proclaimed to the readers of the *Saturday Review* his "passionate conviction that the time is now ripe for a frontal assault on obscurity as inartistic—provided the assault is not allowed to play into the hands of those who want a pretext for being lazy about poetry" (7). Whose hands he meant was not entirely clear, since he also affirmed the need for poets and readers to make "sincerer efforts at mutual understanding." Poets must be professionally responsible—but to readers as well as to their craft—and readers evidently were to continue writing letters to the *Saturday Review* in order to help keep poets responsible.

Viereck's sincerity and fair play would cause no such stir as had Hillyer's invectives. When, for instance, in an October 1949 article for *Atlantic Monthly* that he called "Parnassus Divided," Viereck reviewed *Pisan Cantos* together with Hillyer's epic poem *Death of Captain Nemo*, he preferred the appreciation of prosody to the prosecution of polemic. Smith and Cousins's dogged perseverance in their cause thus gained them no new ground. Nor did Viereck's moderation win them new support. Throughout August and September, their continued support for Hillyer provoked repeated counterpunches from poets, critics, and intellectuals whose anger was drawn by Hillyer's methods and fixed by the recognition of his aim: to make Pound's award an opportunity to undermine the developing ascendancy of modernist poetry and New Criticism. Hillyer hoped at last to persuade the public that the best verse of the time was indeed that which appealed to popular audiences in the popular press. Unable to influence intellectual or artistic circles, Hillyer had chosen instead to exploit their distance from "lay" understanding. Since he published his invectives in a widely circulated journal devoted to middle-class diversion, while the Fellows and their supporters relied on smaller organs of "serious" intellectual exchange, he seemed at first within reach of his ambitions. Initially, the Fellows found it difficult to reach the inflamed public on any satisfactory scale. Their best bet—wagered by Evans, MacLeish, Marshall, Winters, and the Bollingen Foundation itself—was merely to enjoin the *Saturday Review* to print their clarifications and protests.

Hayden Carruth and the Courage of *Poetry*

Only that fall did the editorial office of *Poetry* magazine devise a better means of recovering public sympathy. Hayden Carruth had not been editor there for very long, but short experience at *Poetry* had quickened his sense of the financial pressures on the arts in America. The magazine that had been so vital in the development of American modernism, and that had persevered through economic depression and war, lay now in imminent jeopardy. After four unsuccessful fundraising campaigns, Carruth foresaw one of two fates for *Poetry*: foreclosure, or the securing of long-term institutional support. At last he approached the Bollingen Foundation, which responded cautiously. Months went by, but on the very day on which he had "previously decided to tell the printer to stop work," Bollingen made the Modern Poetry Association of Chicago the first grant in history ($82,500) from a benevolent association to an independent periodical. The sum, non-renewable and given only on condition that its source remain undisclosed, kept the magazine in business. As a result of that support, Carruth was even more outraged by the indiscriminate manner of Hillyer's campaign than his intense commitment as a poet and an editor would otherwise have made him.

Carruth no less than Hillyer envisioned a long-term objective: the reshaping of that middle-class poetic sensibility that in 1949 still left not only Pound but even Eliot potentially vulnerable. Working not only with members of his own staff but also with others like Tate, Carruth produced a 72-page pamphlet entitled *The Case Against the Saturday Review of Literature*. Published in October by *Poetry* as a special issue, it was distributed to subscribers and sold for a dollar. Given the body of its contributors and the clarity of their arguments, augmented by an authority on this issue that *Poetry* was especially positioned to carry, the pamphlet ended Hillyer's run as someone who needed to be answered. Thereafter, the still-continuing debate turned on the relation of poet to poem, on the question of Pound's fascism, and on the dependence of Pound's prize on New Critical precepts.

Carruth's pamphlet responded to the glaring inequality of distribution between those arguments against the Fellows and those for them. That is, the attacks were being published in middlebrow publications with mass circulation while the defenses were being made in much more elite organs. At the request of Luther Evans, the Fellows themselves had replied in writing to Hillyer's attacks. Their response, which was circulated by the Library as a mimeographed press-release back in mid-August, was originally intended for the Congressional Joint Committee. In the event, that proved unnecessary; but this near-miss clarified the dangers of widespread popular misperception. Because the press had quoted the statement only in brief excerpts, and because the reply "could scarcely have reached more than one person for every ten who read the attacks in the *Saturday Review*," Carruth reprinted it with four "annexes" (by Tate, Léonie Adams—secretary to the Fellows, Evans, and the original announcement of the award), essays by Malcolm Cowley, Aline B. Louchheim, and himself, an editorial from the *Hudson Review*, and letters of counterprotest from Archibald MacLeish, Mark Van Doren, William Meredith, William Van O'Connor, Cleanth Brooks, and Yvor Winters.

The full statement of the Fellows considered the dependence of Representative Javits's apprehensions on Hillyer's unfounded allegations, and took care to refute them. The statement denied that the Bollingen Foundation was linked in any way with Carl Jung; that Eliot had exerted an undue (and fascist) influence on the jury's deliberations; and that the award itself was a fascist action. The statement closed by emphasizing the distinction and diversity of the jury, and by maintaining that the jury is properly "representative" of "the wish of the American people in a matter of this kind." The annexes marshaled other arguments towards the same ends.

Carruth's choice of essays, however, engaged further, aesthetic, issues. Malcolm Cowley's "The Battle Over Ezra Pound" affirmed "that the Fellows were trying hard to perform their double duty as citizens and men of letters." That double duty emerged as apparently conflicting duties, but to Cowley this was no dilemma: "the real questions about their choice are literary rather than political; or rather the literary and the political questions are so intermingled that by answering the first we also answer the second" (34-35). Such confidence as Cowley's has since proven a consistent feature of Pound criticism, although the tone and mode of that intermingling remain as hotly disputed as ever. While Cowley himself found the *Pisan Cantos* "the weakest of [Pound's] books," and regretted that the award restored him from an obscurity he had brought upon himself, he nevertheless defended the basis of the Fellows' decision:

> Today there is a war in which the battle over Ezra Pound is merely an episode. The little American republic of letters is under attack by pretty much the same forces as those to which the Russian writers have already yielded: that is, by the people who prefer slogans to poetry and national self-flattery to honest writing. Hillyer has gone over to the enemy, like Pound in another war. Worsted in a struggle among his colleagues and compatriots, he has appealed over their

> heads and under false colors to the great hostile empire of the Philistines. (38)

The double duty occasioned no dilemma, then, because the Fellows' duty to art—to maintain the independence of aesthetic from political issues—overlapped with their duties as citizens.

Aline B. Louchheim's "The State and Art" also distinguished "liberty" in its aesthetic and political contexts, and defended the Library's decision to surrender the awards before compromising the principles that brought those awards their distinction. Less elevated in tone, but more fiery in its indignation, the editorial from the *Hudson Review* charged Hillyer, Cousins, and Smith with the mean-spirited attempt to write off genuine work merely because it exceeded their understanding (*Case against the Saturday Review*, 38–42). But Carruth's "The Anti-Poet All Told," reprinted from *Poetry* (August), amplified two salient features of Cowley's essay. "The Anti-Poet All Told" framed its arguments by first asserting the precarious position of poetry in modern society, and then that the battle over Pound was merely the latest engagement in the ongoing war all real artists wage against philistinism: "though observedly in our old and insuppressible want for security of mind, we have been taken unawares by the drastic assault on contemporary poetry which the award has incurred, we ought to have known that the enemies of poetry would choose well their opportunity to attack and summarily to condemn the literary achievements of their own epoch" (47). "The enemies of poetry," Carruth warned, allowing his antagonists no greater dignity, are against that constant innovation which is so essential a part of any vital "tradition," and so are "against life."

Lillian Robinson and Lise Vogel pointed out a half-century ago that "whether it is invoked evangelically or pejoratively, 'modernism' suggested an overriding emphasis on the autonomy of the work of art and its formal characteristics, on the permanence of modal change, and on the independence of critical judgment." These emphases incited the polemics of both sides of the Bollingen controversy. Those critical of the Fellows' decision, like Barrett and Hillyer, attacked the Fellows' attempts to insist upon the autonomy of art and the divorce of critical judgment from questions of moral or social value; those defending the Fellows emphasized the necessary independence of critical judgment. But Carruth was the first of the Fellows' adherents to predicate his defense on arguments identifying modal change with cultural vitality, or as Carruth absolutely asserted, "life." This argument would figure prominently in Pound's final transformation into an academic subject, ultimately providing a major underpinning for Hugh Kenner's identification of "the Pound era." Although unwilling to go so far as E. E. Cummings ("a poet's only illimitable country is himself"), and acknowledging that Pound was "a most troublesome case," Carruth nonetheless defended Pound as a most faithful poet (49). He also observed that the poetic revolution Pound wrought was over forty years old: on top of everything else, Hillyer was too late. Modernism, what Carruth referred to as "the experimental process, the exercise in poetic faith," had arrived.

It was not the enemies of poetry, however, but the Modern Poetry Association that exacted from Carruth a personal price for his contribution to the Fellows' defense. For all the modernist and avant-garde poets she published, *Poetry* founder Harriet Monroe had always resisted identifying her magazine with Pound's and Eliot's internationalism. Influential friends of Monroe's like Marion Strobel still figured in the Modern Poetry Association during Carruth's tenure as editor, and they remained anxious to preserve Monroe's legacy. Soon after the publication of the uncompromisingly defiant *The Case Against the Saturday Review of Literature*, Carruth was fired and replaced by the more moderate Shapiro. The decision was symbolically rich.

Still, while *The Case Against the Saturday Review of Literature* discredited Hillyer, it did not win the field for the Fellows and their adherents. Rather, as the subsequent forays of the year's end made plain, it stabilized the lines of opposition. December brought, on one side, the tardy publication of Margaret Marshall's open letter printed in the December 17, 1949 issue of the *Nation* and a special Pound number of the *Quarterly Review of Literature* published the same month;[17] from the other side came Robert Gorham Davis's "The New Criticism and the Democratic Tradition," published in the *American Scholar* (Winter 1949–50). The Pound number of the *Quarterly Review* was edited by D. D. Paige, who was then at work on the forthcoming *Letters of Ezra Pound 1907–1941*. Paige announced his aim "to establish certain axes of reference—axioms, if you will," for "Pound's forty years' labor" (103). As a volume, then, the Pound number purported to subordinate evaluative or critical matters to those of appreciation and exposition. That move was in itself a sign of the times.

Some of Paige's contributors were Pound's old friends and cohorts; some were poets paying homage; some were young academics asserting their special expertise. It was an odd conjunction of critical kinds, joined together by the focus of each on Pound's integrity as poet or as literary critic. Indeed, the volume offers a model for what would become the characteristically eclectic mix of *Paideuma: A Journal Devoted to Ezra Pound Scholarship* (1972–). Wyndham Lewis contributed a "Portrait of a Personality"; John Senior a short poetic ode to Pound's vision offered in a pastiche of his style in "Mauberley"; Marianne Moore a brief testimonial to Pound as "preceptor by example"; Harold Watts a very academic analysis, which we will examine in chapter three; Richard Eberhart a review of *Pisan Cantos* that opened by declaring his lack of interest in

Pound's life, political beliefs, or social pronouncements; and Ray West an examination of "Ezra Pound and Contemporary Criticism," citing Mario Praz to establish Pound's anticipation of the techniques of "close analysis" then being executed by Brooks, Warren, Eliot, and Leavis. The number closed with a previously unpublished ode of Pound's and, all told, consolidated the claims advanced by Carruth's *Case* by insisting on the professional terms appropriate for the evaluation of Pound as poet or literary critic.

Conversely, Davis's "New Criticism and the Democratic Tradition" also proposed to establish a proper context for the evaluation of Pound, but for Davis—an early critic of the awarding of the Bollingen Prize to Pound—that context was primarily political. Expanding on his observations in the *Partisan Review* forum of May, Davis asserted Pound and Eliot's ties to the anti-democratic arguments of Count Joseph de Maistre and Charles Maurras. Although erring in details of Pound's biography, and tending to conflate Pound's views with those advanced by Eliot in his *Criterion* editorials, Davis's was an academically responsible argument. He asserted that the debates over Pound's award demonstrated the fundamental antagonism of New Criticism to democratic humanism, but unlike the partisans of the previous summer, Davis wanted no witch hunt; he sought rather "a new assumption of cultural responsibility by the intelligentsia" within the terms of "democratic society." His essay is then to be distinguished from the brawls of June and July 1949 not so much by its general critique as by its manner and motive of argument. The controversy had withdrawn to academic quarters.

"When is a maverick an enemy?"

A month after Davis's essay, the *New York Times Book Review* offered a "progress report," in the form of a piece by David Dempsey and titled *L'affaire Pound*, on the controversy surrounding Pound's Bollingen Prize. It concluded that the "verdict" was still out, despite Congress having abolished all Library of Congress Awards. Three things, however, it held to be beyond dispute: "1) modern poetry was undergoing its most searching examination; 2) poetry was all the more alive for its battering; 3) Ezra Pound was the catalyst of the year" (8). These conclusions testify to the consequences of the strategies employed to the integrity of the award. Behind the third point is Eliot's seminal distinction between poet and man: "The mind of the poet is the shred of platinum. It may partly or exclusively operate upon the experience of the man himself; but, the more perfect the artist, the more completely separate in him will be the man who suffers and the mind which creates; the more perfectly will the mind digest and transmute the passions which are its material."[18] Pound, in the *Times* account, was merely the "catalyst" in the furor, and not the object of contention. The real subject of controversy was the nature of modern poetry in general and the relation of modern poetry to society.

This somewhat revisionist view of the controversy, this attempt to salvage from it some constructive good, has since remained the preferred tone for continuing discussions. MacLeish's *Poetry and Opinion: A Dialogue on the Role of Poetry* (1950) provided an influential example that such detachment had become possible. MacLeish transformed the previous mayhem quite literally: that is, he changed the form or genre of negotiation and attempted the detachment of Socratic dialectic. Affirming that, "though the defenders [of the Prize] easily demolished their adversary, they failed to establish a position of their own," MacLeish hoped to establish "an acceptable theory" of "the function of poetry" in society (ii). His answer was familiar: poetry, perhaps poetry alone, can reveal the underlying coherence of life. It was not an answer likely to convert the offended public, but as an experiment in genre—Socratic dialogue instead of critical essay—it was an important milestone.

Nevertheless, while the controversy may have assumed some small dignity, it was nowhere near the end of its course. In April of 1951, for example, the editors of *Commentary* maintained that the controversy was "still very much alive." They perceived, however, that the issues involved had changed. At the outset, the question was "whether a poet who in his work expressed fascist and anti-Semitic views . . . was a suitable recipient for a prize." But as the controversy broadened out so did the implications, drawn differently by the opposing sides: "the opponents of the award in many cases used the occasion for a general attack on the whole body of modern poetry, while the supporters of Pound responded with an uncompromising aestheticism that in fact has often ceased to be aesthetic and bordered on the political."[19] The politics of New Critical formalism have fomented debate ever since. By contrast, the optimism of the *New York Times Book Review* that "poetry was all the more alive for its battering" did not survive the fifties. It seems in retrospect another instance of liberal voices affirming a false parallel between aesthetic privilege and democratic process, not unlike the early patriotic editorials that praised the Bollingen Prize judges for their defense of freedom. The kind of privilege that the controversy won for Pound in particular and for poetry in general comes at the cost of public indifference.

In 1955, reflecting on the tenth year of Pound's incarceration, Samuel Hynes noted in *Commonweal* that Pound's confinement seemed "wryly symbolic" to "citizens antagonistic to modern poetry": "the modern poet in the madhouse where he belongs." But Hynes himself believed the case "a reflection of an apparently insoluble modern dilemma, of the way in which individual freedom and the common good have come to be seen as antithetical" (251). The case asks questions, Hynes submitted, but offers no answers: "when is a maverick an enemy? should an artist allow political considerations of any kind to influence or control his mind? does the artist operate under the same restraints which govern the thought and conduct of other men?" (251). Hynes' last question can and has been reframed as a question about the nature of poetic license, and as such that question remains central to the continuing evaluation of the Bollingen controversy. Do poets have special license to operate beyond ordinary sociopolitical constraints because they are harmless fools, or because they are seers?

As Dwight MacDonald suggested in the *Nation* forum, the explanations of Donald Davie and Karl Shapiro represent the range of critical response to this question (198). Shapiro's reassessment in 1960 is particularly interesting. Entitled "Ezra Pound: The Scapegoat of Modern Poetry," it gives no sense of how events had pressured him to readjust his emphasis. Shapiro describes his opposition during the Fellows' balloting without mentioning the role that he subsequently undertook to turn back Hillyer's reckless assaults. He was one of the four jurors who, as "the Committee for the Fellows," carefully composed the statement for the Joint Committee of Congress; and his contribution to Barrett's forum was, as we have seen, judicious and balanced. But in 1960, with the political dangers of 1949 gone but the bad memory of a troubled time still very present, Shapiro resumed his outspoken opposition. The controversy was, he asserted, brought on by the assumption that poetry was of terrific cultural import—that it was in fact the very "hand maid of history":

> It was this self-important attitude that led to the infamous Bollingen Prize award to Pound in 1948 [*sic*], when under the leadership of Eliot, a group of his followers presented a prize to Pound (at that time under indictment for treason) in the name of the Library of Congress. I was myself a member of that group and narrowly escaped being pressured into voting the prize to *Pisan Cantos*, which among other things, contained Pound's wildest anti-American and racial outburst (by that time fused into the same thing). Eliot's criticism had by 1948 so far penetrated the critical mentality of his followers that they dared ignore the plain English in the poems for what they called their magnificent artistry. (82)

Shapiro's sense of narrow escape would seem retrospectively to grant Hillyer much that a younger Shapiro would have denied. Eliot in particular and "modern"—modernist—poets generally had made their own bed. In this essay at least, Shapiro echoes Howe's paradox that the only way to take poetry seriously is to love it less than life.

Perhaps exemplifying Shapiro's sense that modernists overestimate the importance of poetry, Davie draws a very different historical lesson in his *Ezra Pound: Poet as Sculptor* (1964):

> When, in February 1949, the first Bollingen prize for poetry was awarded to *The Pisan Cantos*, and the award was upheld through a storm of protests that followed on the floor of Congress and elsewhere, this was enormously to the credit of American society, but it did nothing to vindicate the exalted reality of living the poet's life. For what it meant in effect was that American society accepted and recognized an absolute discontinuity between the life of the poet and the life of the man. Ever since, in British and American society alike, this absolute distinction has been sustained, and upheld indeed as the basic assumption on which society must proceed in dealing with the artists who live in its midst. Undoubtedly, at the present moment of history it is the most humane, and to that degree the most civilized arrangement possible. Still, the privilege that it extends to the artist is the privilege of the pariah; and it is not at all such a solid or exalted platform as some thought when from that vantage point they fulminated righteously at Russia over the case of Pasternak's Nobel prize. In Russia the artist was found fit to plead, whereas in Britain and America he is found unfit: which conception of the artist is more exalted? (243)

Where Shapiro holds poets themselves responsible for their comparative social insignificance, Davie blames the sociocultural conditions within which modern poets must write. The "privilege of the pariah" is arguably no privilege at all, and jeopardizes all that Isidor Schneider, in a 1945 piece for *New Masses* titled "Traitor or Holy Idiot," had warned would be risked by an insanity defense (13). Davie's is of course the more Poundian perception, and he regards the aftermath of Pound's award as the best that can be made of bad situation. In his view, the choice for modern poetry in 1949 was to risk being silenced, or to guarantee its freedom by fortifying the frontiers of a reduced but defensible domain.

From our twenty-first-century perspective it may not seem much of a choice. The controversy demonstrated nevertheless that, in modern society at least, the public presence of poetry is not distinguishable from the kinds of arguments we make about it. As Peter Russell observed in 1950 in his introduction to the collection *An Examination of Ezra Pound*, the Bollingen controversy developed as "a straight fight between the old and the New Critics, rather than an examination of the merits of Pound's poem" (22). In championing Ezra Pound, the New Critics both responded to and were responsible for changes in the relations of poetry to other discursive forms. Their choice, their distinction between man and poet, left both uncomfortably institutionalized.

Notes

[1] T. S. Eliot, "Gerontion," in *The Poems of T. S. Eliot*, I:32.

[2] "*The Pisan Cantos* Wins for Ezra Pound First Award of Bollingen Prize in Poetry," Library of Congress Press Release No. 542; rpt. in O'Connor and Stone, 45.

[3] W.H. Auden, "In Memory of W.B. Yeats," in *W.H. Auden: Collected Poems*, 247.

[4] See, for instance, "Pound, In Mental Clinic, Wins Prize for Poetry Penned in Treason Cell," *New York Times*, February 20, 1949.

[5] "*The Pisan Cantos* Wins for Ezra Pound First Award of Bollingen Prize in Poetry," 542.

[6] "The Question of the Pound Award," *Partisan Review* 16 (May 1949): 512–22. Contributors: W.H. Auden, William Barrett, Robert Gorham Davis, Clement Greenberg, Irving Howe, George Orwell, Karl Shapiro, Allen Tate. Also in: *Casebook*, ed. O'Connor/Stone (1959).

[7] Karl Shapiro, Letter to the editor, *Baltimore Sun*, February 25, 1949.

[8] Ibid.

[9] Berryman's essay is reprinted in *Ezra Pound: The Critical Heritage*, ed. Eric Homberger, 388–404, and citations are from the reprint.

[10] Edward Thomas, "Two Poets," review of *Personae* by Ezra Pound, *English Review* 2 (June 1909): 627–30, also in Erkilla, 10.

[11] William Barrett, "A Prize for Ezra Pound," *Partisan Review* 16 (April 1949): 345. See also O'Connor and Stone, *Casebook*, 49–53.

[12] "The Question of the Pound Award," 512–22.

[13] On Shapiro's asperity towards Eliot, his further essays on Pound, and an account of his career see also Andrew Gross, 67-73ff.

[14] Quoted in William McGuire, 213. See Karl Shapiro to Léonie Adams, July 26, 1949, quoted by Leick, 28. See also Shapiro's autobiography, *Reports of My Death*, 44.

[15] J.B. Sheerin, "The Pound Affair," *Catholic World* 169 (August 1949), 322–23.

[16] See the more lengthy discussion around the decision of the Congressional Committee in Leick, 30–32.

[17] Special Pound issue of *Quarterly Review of Literature* 5.2 (December 1949), guest editor D.D. Paige.

[18] Eliot, "Tradition and the Individual Talent" (1919), in *Selected Essays*, 7–8.

[19] Quoted from the editorial introduction to the article by Peter Viereck, "Pure Poetry, Impure Politics, and Ezra Pound: The Bollingen Prize Controversy Revisited," *Commentary*, April 1, 1951. https://www.commentarymagazine.com/articles/pure-poetry-impure-politics-and-ezra-poundthe-bollingen-prize-controversy-revisited/.

3: Kenner, Watts, and Professional Attention, 1951–1961

It's only when a few men who know, get together and disagree that any sort of criticism is born.

—Ezra Pound, 1913 Letter to Harriet Monroe[1]

The Pound Wars Get Institutionalized

PUBLIC ATTENTION WAS STILL LINGERING over *l'affaire Pound* in the summer of 1951 when Hugh Kenner's *The Poetry of Ezra Pound* dismissed it for good. It did not do so by overtly hostile gestures, or by presenting incontrovertible arguments about the Bollingen controversy. It was instead silent about Pound's political activities, reticent about Pound's biography, and studiously inattentive to the concerns available to most middle-class readers. It was a splendid performance that never for an instant allowed the relevance of anything besides aesthetic and strictly poetic questions. It was also a performance the reception of which would have been impossible at any earlier moment, let alone in the heat of the Bollingen controversy. *The Poetry of Ezra Pound* was as perfectly the creature of its historical moment as it was the creator of academic discourse on Ezra Pound.

The anxious justifications of Tate, Berryman, and Carruth prepared Kenner's ground, and informed not only what Kenner argued but how. Most dramatically, perhaps, the terms in which the Library Fellows defended their judgment bristle just underneath Kenner's opening, a first chapter entitled "A Prefatory Distinction," which dismisses the passion of the previous two years in two short sentences:

> The *Pisan Cantos* were . . . during a few months of 1949 more "in the news" (for irrelevant reasons) than perhaps any volume of poetry in modern times. They were widely written off as a dead loss, and all sorts of alarming implications were read into their author's receipt of the Bollingen Prize for Poetry at the hands of a committee of fellow poets. (16)

A disarming representation to be sure: the scare quotes around "in the news," and the suggestion that "a committee of fellow poets" cannot but be harmless, render bathetic the indignation and high feeling previously exhibited on both sides of the Bollingen question. *Pisan Cantos* were not merely "in the news," but the basis of Kenner's saying so is evident in that parenthesis tossed off *en passant*: "(for irrelevant reasons)." That is, the parenthesis assumes that the appreciation of poetry has little to do with political apperception, and does not submit this assumption to discussion.

Half a century later, Kenner's "prefatory distinction" comes less easily, if at all. Nevertheless, he could justly say that the *Pisan Cantos* were largely "written off"; even favorable reviews like Richard Eberhart's or J. V. Healy's tended to celebrate isolated lyrical passages. Less positive reviewers, like William Rose Benét, allowed nothing more than that. C. H. Sisson tried to go such reservations one better by praising the volume for its "continuous readability," which quality he attributed to Pound's masterful rhythms. But it is no accident that Sisson also chastised the "obsession" of the average reader with "understanding," about which concept exists, he said, a great deal of confusion. Like most everyone else, Sisson found himself nearly at a loss to describe Pound's content. Few critics other than Pound's antagonists showed much enthusiasm for engaging difficult and dangerous questions about content. Two critics proved exceptional in this regard, proposing models that differed in nature almost as sharply as they stood opposed in method. Harold Holliday Watts got the earlier start, but looked all too much like the confused latecomer in his finish. His contest with Kenner, and the implications of his defeat, are the story of this chapter.

In the contentious history of Pound's reception, Watts's book represents a special case and a specific historical moment: the fortunes of no other study were so profoundly reversed by the time required for its own completion. We will give here primary consideration to Watts's original essays, rather than to the later book, in order to dramatize the consequences of the Bollingen controversy for criticism. Watts's *Ezra Pound and the Cantos* (1952) was not published until nearly a year after Kenner's groundbreaking book, but Watts had begun publishing its chapters as essays in 1947—a crucial two years before Kenner published his first essay on Pound. Initially, Watts's essays attracted respectful notice. No one else had hitherto seemed to command so sure a grasp of Pound's larger purposes. And yet, while Watts's attempt to weigh the whole of Pound's work in a single balance anticipated many features of the revisionist studies of the 1980s, Watts himself would, on the whole, be neglected. For this neglect there are several reasons, as we shall see, but chief among them must be the peculiar way in which Watts internalized Pound's own resistance to the professional compartmentalization of knowledge. Watts reproduced too few of what had become the identifying features of "literary criticism" at a time when the profession of literary study was consumed with policing its own frontiers. Ironically, the displacement of formalist literary theory after the sixties by the varieties of critical theory did nothing to recuperate his reputation, because his Aristotelian and exegetical vocabulary then came to seem too narrowly literary.

Quite simply, Watts's book has dated. Restored to the context of his rivalry with Kenner, however, it demonstrates the terrific impact of the Bollingen controversy on the shape of academic study. Indeed, the increasingly specialized nature of Pound studies in the early fifties in itself bespeaks an academic cutting of losses, an attempt to guarantee intellectual freedom by withdrawing to a reduced but defensible domain. Watts perceived this less clearly than Kenner, and wrote a book for which there could be in 1952 no audience: it had been fractured and scattered by the public outcry over Pound's award. Both Watts's arguments and his method were consequently rendered untimely, an impertinence to lay readers and an unwanted intrusion to academics. By the same token, those readers inclined to regard Pound in primarily political terms felt no need for detailed exposition or nuanced commentary; those readers more favorably disposed towards Pound, or meeting his work for the first time, wanted to regard him primarily in poetic terms. Even Watts's title, which makes the *Cantos* an interest secondary to the man who wrote them, bespeaks his emphasis. Kenner's title, by contrast, identifies the poetry as its principal subject. Lest anyone should miss the distinction, Kenner nailed it down in an aggressively disapproving review of Watts's book. Watts would thereafter never again publish on Pound.

Watts's PhD thesis (University of Illinois, 1932) considered *Art in Fiction: The Intellectual and Artistic Development of Lord Lytton*. The topic may seem an odd beginning for the man who would be the first to expound *The Cantos*, but it should be remembered that Kenner's first book—published in 1947—was on G. K. Chesterton.[2] Moreover, Watts's study of Lytton's intellectual and artistic development anticipated his later work on Pound. Indeed, it was that very combination, and the precedence of intellectual history within it, that would draw Kenner's fire. Generally, Watts's academic writing (he was also a playwright) was exegetical in manner; indeed, by the time that he began writing essays on Pound he had already published his *Modern Readers' Guide to the Bible* (1949). Watts's exegetical proclivities, his tendency to bring to literary study techniques and emphases more usually associated with Biblical hermeneutics, gave to his work an explanatory power new in Pound's reception. The comments of other critics offer ample testimony that this was so. Published in *Cronos* in March, 1948, Watts's second essay on Pound, "Philosopher at Bay," attracted particular attention (*Cronos* 2, 1–17).[3] Robert M. Adams, for instance, borrowed heavily from Watts in the manner of his approach to the Pound question, and even lifting particular phrases. Still young in what would become a distinguished academic career (he eventually became one of the founding editors of the *Norton Anthology of English Literature*), Adams followed Watts in attending to "the philosophy underlying [Pound's] style." And he followed Watts, too, in praising Pound's extra-poetic ambitions: "By the honesty of his word-usage the poet thus undertook to redeem the language and the mind of Western civilization" (206). Adams's purpose, of course, was to champion Pound, but at the same time he was also endorsing Watts's particular approach to Pound. Adams dubbed Watts "Pound's expounder" (209) and in another borrowing from Watts's language argued for the need to construct "an arch" over the *Cantos.* Adams's approval was soon joined by more established voices. Of particular importance was Lloyd Frankenberg, the author of *The Pleasure Dome: On Reading Modern Poetry* (1949). Reviewing both *Cantos I-LXXXIV* and *Pisan Cantos* for the *New York Times Book Review* in August 1948, Frankenberg, too, quoted from "Philosopher at Bay" (14). The title of Frankenberg's review, "Ezra Pound—and His Magnum Opus," distinguishes between man and poem, but Frankenberg, too, saw Pound's greatness as *philosophical* in nature. Watts's work was already making an impact and, by the outbreak of hostilities over the Bollingen Prize, he seemed well on his way to acquiring professional authority.

No strong beginning was ever more wholly disappointed. By the time he published his work, seven years after his first published study of Pound, the controversy had utterly transformed the context in which any book on Pound would be received. If the questions Watts set out to answer remained pertinent, the way in which he asked and answered them did not. Decidedly academic, and unlikely to invite the attention of lay readers, Watts's book was at the same time poorly calculated to appeal to the growing but defensive academic audience for Pound. What Watts offered was literally an "exposition" since, as he explains in "The Devices of Pound's *Cantos,*" he aimed to consider Pound quite apart from, or "out of," his "position near the heart of the most influential form of modernist experimentation." His real interest was in *The Cantos* as "a poem with a 'programme'" (50). Still less germane to Watts's work than Pound's *modernist* credentials were Pound's *poetic* credentials: "*The Cantos* cannot be regarded as a poem that exists for the glory of art; it is *im*pure poetry, calculated to deflect a stream of human events from a bad channel to a good one" (34). Watts proposed that the revolutionary potential of Pound's language was not poetic, but political. This approach makes sense, given Watts's propensity for exegesis, but by 1952, the furor over Pound's award had rendered such a project threatening to the academic interests that had invested so much in Pound's defense.

Watts does not seem to have recognized how public events were changing the cultural disposition of literary criticism. His essay, "The Devices of Pound's *Cantos,*" for example, identifies rhetorical devices and explains *what* they do and *why* without ever attending to them as *poetic* qualities. Pound's *Cantos* are, under Watts's gaze, a locus of locutionary strategies without being a poem. By Watts's own admission, his language is "barbarous" but nonetheless "quite precise" (161). An exegete bent on demystification, he proceeds as though all in *The Cantos* that was primarily poetic was but another rhetorical device to attract and then hold attention. Even though he had done the work for "The Devices of Pound's *Cantos*" or for his review of *The Cantos*, "Points on the Circle," also published in 1949, before the public reaction to Pound's Bollingen Prize reached fever pitch, he made no substantial revisions before publishing them in *Ezra Pound and the Cantos*. This was a crucial error. Watts held back from the Bollingen controversy, and appears to have decided simply to let it play itself out before publishing his study. When he did publish the book, not only "Devices," but also his earliest essay on Pound, "Means to an End," retained their identities as individual chapters. For that matter, "Philosopher at Bay" was incorporated into the "Reckoning" that closes the volume. Tellingly, only his review of the *Pisan Cantos*—"Points on the Circle"—does not constitute a recognizable part of the book. In other words, his one publication treating the section around which the controversy most immediately raged is the one that Watts believed least integral to his argument. During the two and a half years that separated the appearance of *Ezra Pound and the Cantos* from the publication of his most recent essays on Pound, Watts published an exegetical study of Yeats,[4] but offered no revision of his work on Pound.

It would seem then that Watts either underestimated the effect of the Bollingen controversy on the academic reception of Pound's work, or decided quietly to resist the gathering momentum of new critical emphases on poetry as autonomous discourse. If the latter, then one must conclude that Watts lacked polemical skill, for his book offers no preface to make explicit any critical or theoretical determinations. Instead, his first chapter ("Mr. Pound's Pilgrimage") refers only briefly to *l'affaire Pound* in the course of executing a typological troping of Van Wyck Brooks's *Pilgrimage of Henry James*, in which troping James's journey through physical space provides a figure for Pound's "rather devious travels taken in time" (7). Watts's approach had its supporters. Indeed, even the "beat" poet Lawrence Ferlinghetti, with political commitments very different from Pound's, welcomed Watts's book and called it "exceptionally fair." In fact, where Kenner would blast Watts for dwelling too much on politics, Ferlinghetti found Watts's weakness to be his "lack of [any] consideration for what Pound was actually doing in Italy." In calling for a stronger judgment of the poet as well as the poem, Ferlinghetti was proudly out of step with academic tendencies. No other reviewer seconded his response.

In publishing a book begun seven years before, Watts did nothing unusual; but in this instance, history had shifted the ground underneath him and transformed into mere irony what had been offered as instigation. He opened his argument by asserting the precedence of temporal over spatial dislocations (shifts in the *Cantos* across centuries as opposed to shits across cultures and continents) without recognizing the epoch-marking critical dislocations of his own time. That he reprinted the earliest of his essays, "Means to an End," without revision itself speaks volumes. The title identifies a central feature of Watts's approach to Pound: his conviction that the poetry of *The Cantos* functions merely as a vehicle to bring the reader to Pound's ultimately more significant goal—to redeem "a world in most areas hag-ridden by capitalist democracy—more generally, by usury and its maleficent effects" (25).[5] In Watts's thesis, Pound's long poem "is part—and the crucially important part—of a life-long struggle to alter the world as he conceives it" (25). Watts undoubtedly figured that his affirmation that poetry was "the crucially important part" of Pound's "struggle to alter the world" demonstrated his appreciation of it. It was in 1947 a bold step, especially from an academic, to propose that there was anything redeemable—let alone praiseworthy—in Pound's critique of modernity. But to describe in 1952 Pound's poetry as "a part," even "the crucially important part," of Pound's work was bound to attract professional derision. *Pisan Cantos* had been awarded for their excellence as *poetry*, and the Library Fellows defended that award by avowing Pound's politics or anti-Semitism as only having an adventitious relation to that same excellence. By contrast, Watts affirmed that "*The Cantos* cannot be regarded as a poem that exists for the glory of art; it is *impure* poetry, calculated to deflect a stream of human events from a bad channel to a good one" (34). Watts was not unselfconscious about his method. Some readers will find, he acknowledged, in a direct allusion to the New Critics, that his "approach is one that violates 'the integrity of the poem'; I hope, however, it enables me to show others that the integrity is there" (60). Nevertheless, in presenting Pound as a visionary or reformer first, and poet second, Watts unwittingly was playing into the hands of Pound's detractors.

Watts himself thought otherwise. Persuaded by Pound's condemnations of usury as a cancer eating at the heart of Western culture, Watts believed that he could make a compelling case by representing Pound's thesis in a more systematic and philosophical language. Watts's approach in this sense too was diametrically opposed to that adopted by Kenner, Davie, and most of the critics who followed them. Watts developed philosophical paraphrases for recurrent Poundian themes and motifs, writing of "motive forces," "devices of disavowal," or even "nominalism vs. realism"; Kenner, wherever possible, used Pound's own language. Each approach poses its own risks: Watts's substitution of sometimes ugly philosophical jargon for Pound's often resonant phrases risks obfuscating formal and generic transformations; Kenner's approach risks sacrificing the distance necessary to critical understanding—risks producing a criticism that works like a tape loop, like something almost tautological.

Watts in any case ran into trouble, particularly in "Philosopher at Bay." Early in 1948, when the editors of *Cronos* sent Watts's manuscript to Pound for comment, Pound managed little more than exasperated ejaculations ("nuts!") in the margin—leaving it to Dorothy Pound to send a few curt sentences explaining that "my husband is too ill to enter into abstract discussion—largely irrelevant," and that "he has never argued about his poetry." Watts's editors published Pound's marginal responses along with the essay,[6] and although the exchange between the perhaps overly earnest scholar and the unamused poet generated little readerly response, it anticipated in its small way the fracas of the following year. Speculation about Pound's philosophy and politics is, Dorothy adjured, "irrelevant." It was precisely the word Kenner would use in laying to rest popular questions three years later. But in Pound's case, especially given his own history, the answer carried an uncomfortable tone that suggests Pound recognized already that critical matters were out of his hands.

"Philosopher at Bay" opens by distinguishing Pound's rhetorical "techniques" from the "techniques of confusion" developed by "usurers" (or by "whatever group or force that, in our judgement, threatens our culture with disunity and decay") in order to cloud definition. Watts discusses the technique of *The Cantos* "as an application—not an imitation—of the Chinese ideogram to the writing of poetry in English," as he discusses "the heart of Pound's thought on his method," without engaging closely any of Pound's poetry. Watts disposes exactly as his title proposes. His Pound is a philosopher, engaged in an age-old struggle between "realism" and "nominalism" (4). This way of framing Pound's poetic activity establishes critical perspective at the cost of losing contact with Pound's actual texts. Watts's language can be clumsy in its abstraction, and less clear even than Pound's own sometimes willfully metaphorical figures. For example, Watts calls the Poundian practice of suggesting identity through historical and formal change "time-binding." Pound's own term was "subject rhymes" (*Selected Letters*, 210). Any critic is free to depart from his subject's critical vocabulary, but in this and other instances, Watts's decision seems less a critical decision than a function of his having redacted *The Cantos* into a chapter in that ancient contention between realism and nominalism. Watts considers "the actual effect of the poem" not aesthetically, but in terms of "general yet comprehensible statements." As Kenner wrote in his review of Watts's *Ezra Pound and the Cantos*, "Gold in the Gloom," Watts "operates at an incredible remove from the words of the poem" (128).

In publishing "Philosopher at Bay," the editors of *Cronos* expressed their relief that "here at last was an unbiased study, putting in clear light and sharp focus the various ideas which led both to [Pound's] *Cantos* and to his political actions." Watts, they believed, had "ably" completed the first careful examination of Pound's "works." The sense of unbiased examination in Watts's study is a function of the "remove" he maintained from Pound's language. Even so, Watts was by no means unbiased; he advocated what he took to be Pound's position, and wrote in a manner that bespoke his confidence that any thinking reader who came to understand the poem would respond as he himself had. This universalizing of his own perception was not unique to Watts; Kenner did it too. But Watts's confidence that "we" experience a poem in the same way that "we" do a philosophical treatise was an equivocation that other critics refused to allow. To undervalue that crucial difference would be to re-enter the arena of *Saturday Review*-style combat.

Kenner Wins the Field

D. D. Paige's review of Watts was withering. To be sure, Paige already had some skin in the game: in 1950 Norton & Norton had published his edition of the *Selected Letters of Ezra Pound*. In other words, Paige had already demonstrated his commitment to allowing the poet to speak in his own words. Little surprise, then that he blasted "the vulgarity of Prof. Watts's perception" (66) and rejected Watts's commitment to "reading the poem as an anatomizing of usurious and non-usurious civilizations" (69). Finally, Paige judged, "Watts's arid constructions" conceal rather than reveal the riches of the poem" (73). Kenner leveled similar charges, avoiding making an occasion of the publication of Watts's book and deferring his objections until reviewing Pound's translation of *The Great Digest and the Unwobbling Pivot*—thus effecting an opportunity to dismiss Watts's approach in the context of praising Pound's enduring poetic power. Arguing that "the parties to the Bollingen dispute" might have seen things differently had they been aware of Pound's translation (first published in 1948), Kenner chastises Watts for knowing no better even "though his book is dated 1952" ("Gold in the Gloom," 128). "Watts has done some things right," Kenner allows: Watts was the first academic to affirm in print that *The Cantos* offer a sustained and serious purpose. Indeed, there was boldness in the mere gesture of claiming for Pound the dignity of a "philosopher" held at bay by a system unwilling to face its own corruption. But Kenner dismissed Watts for not bringing "adequate equipment to his task" ("Gold in the Gloom," 129). That dismissal amounts to an assertion of territorial prerogative; Watts was not *without* critical equipment, but worked from methodological presuppositions that were at odds with New Critical delineations of literary criticism. These can be simply stated despite the fact, as John Paul Russo observes, "that the New Criticism was 'no monolith' but an inconsistent and sometimes confused movement":

The High Modernist aesthetics of Hulme, Eliot, and the early Pound furnished its poetic canon and elements of its basic theory: the poem as object, craft and technique, economy, precision, complexity, anti-personality, anti-romanticism. Then I. A. Richards gave many of these ideas their exact theoretical shape. He "academicized" them; added topics of his own (contextualism, emotive and referential language, attitude, "belief," tenor and vehicle of metaphor, "tone," the "speaker"); and in the later chapters of *Principles of Literary Criticism* (1924) and *Practical Criticism* (1929), he inaugurated the famous "close reading" method (Russo, 199).

No "close reader" himself, as Kenner noted, Watts declined to treat the poem as object, or turn the techniques of close reading to the economies of Pound's poetic techniques. His criticism aimed to situate poetry in philosophical and political contexts. Like the Pound of the 1930s, Watts was eager to tackle the big questions. He believed he had written a book that could help readers see "that the 'truth' about Ezra Pound and the *Cantos* is—wholly or in part—the truth about matters that ought to be our first concern: the estate of poetry in our culture, the role of language in that culture, the sort of belief needful if that culture is to survive and unfold, the conditions under which belief of any sort is arrived at." He was no less convinced that a demonstration that "the writing of the *Cantos* is at least as much communication as expression" would help Pound's case and establish the social credibility of modernist poetry (*Ezra Pound and the Cantos,* 93). But by 1952 almost no one interested in Pound was pleased to see his poetry brought forward as "'evidence' in any dispute between Ezra Pound and the United States government" (92). Watts's timing could not have been worse.

For one thing, the trick had been tried before. In 1950, the English poet, writer, and translator Peter Russell had edited a collection of essays in honor of Pound's sixty-fifth birthday: it was a book whose very design announced Pound's participation in a glorious tradition.[7] By this time, Russell was already campaigning tirelessly on Pound's behalf, having launched the quarterly review *Nine* and founded the Pound Press—which in 1953 would publish the second edition of *ABC of Economics.* It is, nevertheless, important that Russell was not an academic. His tribute to Pound, revised and enlarged in 1973, would be among the last important collections without a scholarly sponsor.[8] This is not to say that Russell's volume, in assuming the highly serious purpose of evaluating Pound's work, excluded academic contributions; both Marshall McLuhan and his student Hugh Kenner are there to be counted. But Russell includes them among an impressive array of eminent poets and writers: Eliot, Hemingway, Wyndham Lewis, and Allen Tate. Russell's introduction recounts Pound's biography and career up through the Bollingen controversy, a career in which Russell saw "single-mindedness" and "genius" in its dedication to poetry. In his view, the gravest loss in the

Bollingen controversy, besides the embarrassment it caused "academic circles," was that it devolved into a "straight fight between the old and the New Critics," rather than offering genuine "examination of the merits of Pound's poem" (22).

One of the ways Russell tried to break up that "straight fight" was to include pieces written before it started. Hemingway's piece, for example, dated from 1925, and Edith Sitwell's from 1934; Greek poet George Seferis's note to his translation of *Three Cantos* first appeared in 1939; Eliot's essay had been published two years before the Bollingen prize. But to these contributions from celebrated writers, Russell joined a dozen fresh essays, all of which had been written amidst the clamor of the previous year. In fact, Russell had planned his tribute to Pound before the trouble began: Brian Soper's and Wyndham Lewis's essays both date from 1948, though Lewis's essay already turned on the distinction between man and poet. Lewis had been out of touch with Pound between 1939 and 1946, according to Lewis's biographer Jeffrey Meyers (297), but seized the opportunity "to affirm his loyalty and gratitude" (298) to a fellow writer with whom he shared the opprobrium of having been a fascist sympathizer before the war. And so, as Meyers explains, Lewis wrote "a sympathetic portrait of Pound" based on a chapter in his autobiography of 1937, *Blasting and Bombardiering*, which was published in the *Quarterly Review* before being reprinted in Russell (Meyers, 298). Lewis's harsh judgment of Pound had mellowed considerably since "The Revolutionary Simpleton," and he now referred to the drier portions of *The Cantos* only as "deposits" of "often quite dense matter, like volcanic dust" (257). The simile at once bespeaks Lewis's perhaps grudging respect, and also his difference from Russell's New Critics and their professional concerns.

Russell showed a talent for selecting contributors, and several of the younger figures he included were shortly to emerge as authorities on Pound: Kenner, of course, and McLuhan, as well as D. S. Carne-Ross and G. S. Fraser. McLuhan's essay in some sense figures the mood of the others. Tweaking Eliot in virtually Eliotic terms, essentially the celebrated terms of Eliot's "The Metaphysical Poets" (1921), McLuhan ventured that "The Senecal or Jonsonian vigour and precision of Mr. Pound's critical writing has been too much the foil for the urbane sinuosities of Mr. Eliot's prose—a fact which reflects on the twentieth century reader and not on these writers" (165). After Bollingen, many critics thus re-enacted the modernist hostility of 1914 to the common reader.

Russell aimed to offer fair-minded "examination": "Pound cannot but command the respect of all liberal-minded people who examine his work fairly." "Examination" was generally the word of the day, and Russell was eager to announce his volume as "exegetical rather than critical" (Preface, 6). His assertion of *scholarly* detachment was something new in Pound's reception, but reviewers remained unpersuaded that the collection on the whole managed any such thing. Robert Peel, writing in the *Christian Science Monitor*, regretted that while "most of the [Bollingen] controversy has been on the level of a pot-house brawl," most of the essays in Russell "are adulatory, some discriminatingly, some abjectly" (7). Sol Stein complained that many of the essays were badly written and that "these errors in style are more excusable than some of the substantive errors one finds in the book" (184). Stein found still less excusable the apologetics of Max Wykes-Joyce or John Drummond for Pound's fascism, and charged Russell with having "failed in his editorial discretion by permitting such remarks" (185). The result, Stein thought, was a "whitewash."

It was a sign of how small "Pound Studies" still was that Marshall McLuhan not only contributed to Russell's *Examination* but also reviewed it, in an essay-review published in *Renascence* that also discussed D. D. Paige's edition of *The Letters of Ezra Pound* and Archibald MacLeish's attempt to put the Bollingen controversy into perspective, *Poetry and Opinion*. Objecting to the presence of celebration where examination was announced, or to the mixture of personal testimonies and lay praise with professional critical discourse, McLuhan comments only on the academic contributions. Frankly, McLuhan proposes, Russell's *Examination* "might have been more useful if done on the chatty lines of the Eliot birthday volume. Pound has never had the serious critical attention which will eventually come to him, and he doesn't get it here" (200).

Russell's own position on the relation of Pound's politics to his poetry was complicated. His introduction closed by praising Pound's "remarkable" dedication as a poet; but earlier Russell submitted that "to try to separate the poetic essence from the didactic substance of the [*Cantos*] would be valueless pedantry, or at best, adolescent romantic aestheticism" (17). This opinion, so wholly out of key with the affirmations of Pound's supporters, distinctly marks Russell's English perspective and his relative remove from the feverish nationalism so prevalent in early-fifties America. Robert Gorham Davis in particular called him to account on this issue, finding in Russell's position evidence that "after the long religio-critical hiatus of the forties, it is now proper, as in the thirties, to tie up literature with social reform" (18). Davis was, not surprisingly, grateful for the invitation, and resumed his attack on Pound's anti-democratic program.

In Davis's view, the "unfortunate dialectics" of the Bollingen controversy had made Pound "the hero of anti-liberalism as well as of anti-philistinism." The gross injustice of Hillyer's attack had helped create a "Pound vogue," as a result of which younger critics—rushing "into the vacuum caused by the restraint and reticence of some of our best critics"—were now re-examining politics under Pound's "genial but exacting guidance." This last phrase was from Henry Swabey's essay, and Davis invoked it ironically, regarding its praise as "the exact complement of what the *Saturday Review of Literature* was doing in its original attacks on the Bollingen award." The terms of this re-examination should, Davis concluded, "be hit just as hard" as Hillyer had been, "in the name of both politics and poetry."

Richard Chase's review (*Partisan Review*, September 1951) followed the others by almost a year, appearing in fact some two months after the publication of Kenner's *The Poetry of Ezra Pound*. The delay suggests the deliberation of the review, and the appearance of Kenner's book may have prompted Chase's determination to address some of Russell's more partisan tendencies. Chase began by numbering Pound among "that great company of American 'intellectuals' of which Charles Augustus Lindberg . . . is one of the best known examples": "he believes the good society could be achieved, if it were not for the Forces of Evil, by factual practicality, the skill of craftsmanship, and avoidance of 'abstraction' and the supernatural. If he is not actually a professor or a preacher, he would like to be" (587).

Very likely Chase's emphasis on Pound as an American type aimed to dress down Kenner's affirmation, in his essay in Russell's collection, "New Subtlety of Eyes," that "if [Pound] has never ceased to be a midwestern American, he has also never ceased to be a contemporary of Mencius, Guido, and Arnaut Daniel" (98). The exception that Chase took to the claim that Pound's more "dubious views" were merely "incidental" to his poetic accomplishment also responded to Kenner's comparisons of Pound with Milton (Kenner, "Subtlety," 92). In fact, Chase insisted, Pound's politics in *The Cantos* are "radical and central." Kenner is after all the principal object of Chase's attention. When dismissing "Pound's followers' . . . presumptuous claims for his alleged affinity with Dante," Chase distinguishes Kenner in order to claim that, despite the greater sophistication of his work, Kenner too was incapable of disinterested judgment. When dismissing the praise for Pound that rested on perceptions of his mastery of form, it was again Kenner who drew special notice. Anxious about the attractiveness of Kenner's "theological jargon," and working to identify him as merely another of "the young Poundians," Chase nonetheless admitted Kenner's pre-eminent claim to having been the first to give Pound serious—professional—critical attention. Russell's volume on the whole fared less well. Chase granted only its value to criticism as an object lesson: "these essays should teach us anew to eye with suspicion the claim that a work of art projects a 'world of articulate forms'" (589).

Watts may have been innocent of that claim, but he was no longer the one shaping the conversation. In retrospect, the generally hostile reviews of Russell's volume should have served as a warning. If he noticed the warning he did not heed it. In preparing his book he would make no changes to his arguments; he would not even reframe them. His case for Pound's political position as humanist vision made no acknowledgment that other scholars had joined the argument. What John Lucas called "the Pound revival" (63)—but what might more properly be called the creation of Pound's first broad audience—seems to have escaped Watts's notice. He attempted to bring intellectual detachment and far-reaching intellectual-historical context to the study of Pound, without assessing the immediate context for his own study. Kenner was more attentive. At least, he operated within that rarefied critical domain sanctioned by Eliot and the New Criticism. His contribution to Russell's volume had been praised by McLuhan for its comparisons between *The Cantos*, *Paradise Lost*, and the *Prelude*. He had also been blasted by Stein for an inability "to weave quotations into his prose," but his inclination to cling closely to Pound's language would remain one of the most distinctive features of his book. In fact, Kenner used Pound's language for much more than illustration: he used it in the way a minister relies on scripture; he used it to generate authority and to write as though speaking for many; he used it to give his prose cadence and resonance.

A Hierarchy of Values for Pound Studies

Kenner's *Poetry of Ezra Pound* avoided Watts's and Russell's errors, impressing reviewers as establishing at last a proper field of academic study. Reviewers on both sides of the Atlantic considered it to be an advance that Kenner offered "exposition rather than 'criticism,'" and as such presented "a first rate contribution to the study of modern poetry."[9] John Lucas's review in the Winter 1952 issue of *Furioso* similarly found the question of exposition the crucible of Kenner's "notable effort"—"the first full-length one-man" study of Pound. Lucas recognized that each of the four parts of Kenner's book approaches *The Cantos* in a distinct way: "through Pound's critical essays, through Pound's early verse, through a complex process of direct analysis, and through an oversimplifying set of undeveloped suggestions." The last, Lucas acknowledged, Kenner appended "against his better judgment," reducing "what he has to say on the subject to a series of lists and diagrams." Nevertheless, Lucas warned, "what the reader will *not* find is textual explication"; but then "for every one who will resent the lack of it . . . there should be half a dozen who will recognize that it is the very nature (maybe the prime virtue) of the *Cantos* to require each reader to do his own work" (65). While most readers would likely resist so demanding a task, Lucas avowed that Pound did not write for them, and neither did Kenner.

This praise for Kenner's discrimination of audience displays more than a trace of the academic retreat from the public forum dominated by the

Saturday Review of Literature and its like. Three of the four approaches offered by Kenner's book—through Pound's critical essays, through his early verse, and through a "direct analysis" of Pound's poetry—resolutely insist upon some initiation into the poetry; the fourth, presented as a guilty afterthought, makes Kenner's only acknowledgment of readers for whom the fullest commitment of sustained study could be felt as anything other than a religious conversion. Kenner's book had capped the Bollingen controversy by making Pound into a suitable academic subject, and by charting that subject so as to offer courses for further study.

Kenner also sought to transform the controversy, the question of the relation between poetry and politics. He was not alone here—other critics like Robert Peel ("The Poet as Artist and Citizen," 7) had offered very similar language—and his success was less absolute: more in keeping with Poundian propositions of the 1920s and 1930s, but still admissible in New Critical courts. Granting literature its own integrity, and an endurance beyond temporary topicality, Kenner maintained that it was nevertheless "a weapon against bloat and rot" and an agent of social hygiene. Although drawn like most of Kenner's arguments from Pound himself, this argument was deployed in a manner somewhat alien to Pound's own concerns. In arguing that literature was any culture's principal means of preserving the ability of language to register meaning, Kenner intended to reconcile the intrinsic concerns of New Criticism with the calls from humanist conservatives, and from society at large, for social accountability—from both poets and critics. "The poetic is," Kenner submitted, "an exacter speech than the prosaic, whether the material be passion or economics" (*The Poetry of Ezra Pound*, 204). This transformation purposed to reconceive Pound's relation to questions of "value," to make him their champion rather than their pariah. Quite plainly, Kenner asserted that "the main matter of the *Cantos* is to establish a hierarchy of values" (248). But Kenner's transformation made this case only by sublimating Pound's often-voiced ambition to effect real and immediate political change.

This sublimation of political desire was in keeping with New Critical claims about the transformations of immediate experience typically accomplished by the genuinely poetic. But Kenner's insistence on the *poetic* nature of Pound's language elsewhere yielded important results, as when he inveighed against literal-minded attempts to narrativize *The Cantos*, to search in them "for a subject matter, a plot, a line of philosophic development such as it has been Pound's principal achievement to dispense with" (252). Kenner's alternative explanatory models evidently made Pound the poet for the atomic age, invoking Pound's own kinetic metaphors to alert readers to the "mutual irradiation" (276) of the various cantos, and to "reverberations running through the text" (279). Actually, Kenner acknowledged the metaphoric nature of the latter phrase, but only to offer Pound's theory of "the Great Bass" as a more exact model.

Such reliance on Pound's own highly figural language did not please all of Kenner's readers. The anonymous reviewer in the *Listener* (December 20, 1951), while allowing that Kenner was "a sensitive and intelligent critic" whose "book should open up the exciting terrain of Pound's verse to many readers," yet complained that Kenner's "exposition is spoilt by unreasonable dogmatism and historical inaccuracy" acquired "through relying on Mr. Pound himself." M. T. Wilson, in an equally mixed review, found Kenner at his best when showing how Pound's juxtapositions function as a means of discrimination. But "when moving from texture to large-scale Structure," Wilson judged, Kenner fails to prove that it matters much whether motifs appear in one canto as opposed to another: "in fact, [the form of *The Cantos*] emerges as a series of juxtaposed planes, fields of force, loci of intersection, multi-dimensional constructions, shifting tonalities, radiant tensions, and so on through the irritating jargon by which Kenner says little more than somehow things are related to other things" (210–11).

Arguably, even mixed reviews like Wilson's bespeak the high expectations Kenner was able to raise; certainly they testify to his success in focusing attention on the *Cantos* as poetry. That his book would prove a milestone in this regard was granted even in hostile reviews. Lucas mused that "there has been nothing during the years following World War II to match the Pound revival"; W. P. M., no doubt thinking as well of Watts, found his review an occasion to grumble that "the publication of *Pisan Cantos*, the award of the Bollingen Prize, the republication of the earlier *Cantos* and of *Selected Poems*, following upon all the publicity, irrelevant to his poetry . . . have aroused what promises, or threatens, to be a spate of books about the man and his work" (72). W. P. M.'s perspective is curious in that it manages both to quote Kenner's assertion of the "irrelevance" of the public controversy to Pound's poetry and yet see the events of the previous three years as a steady rise. True enough, the efforts of James Laughlin at New Directions, as well as of the editors at Faber and Faber, had published or republished not just the *Cantos* and *Selected Poems*, but also *Patria Mia* (1950), D. D. Paige's *The Letters of Ezra Pound* (1950). Kenner's collection of Pound's *Translations* was forthcoming, and Eliot's selection of Pound's *Literary Essays of Ezra Pound* would follow soon after (1954). But there had been nothing inevitable about this success, and what some reviewers like Ronald Bottrall saw as Kenner's determination "to defend every line that Pound has written and every sentiment that he has uttered" led frequently to the perception of a Pound "cult." In other words, most reviewers believed that Pound's growing reputation was not so much altering public discourse about poetry as it was making a separate peace among the converted.

To his credit, Kenner attempted something more ambitious. However much some readers found his critical vocabulary of "radiant tensions" a private and irritating jargon, Kenner developed these as a corrective to the increasingly mechanistic efficiency of scholarly analysis. In particular, discoursing on "The Moving Image," Kenner addressed the inadequacy of the critical models developed by Richards and, more pointedly, Empson. The difficulty of Pound's poetry, Kenner affirmed, differs in kind from the kinds of difficulty respected by academic analysis: while "the criticism stemming from Empsonian dissection of symbol clusters has made everyone familiar with intellectual complexity, this order of complexity . . . bears no *necessary* relation to the inherent voltage, to the value of the work in question as a human product" (64). Although Kenner's mixture of organic and kinetic metaphors might exemplify the occasional confusions of his language, it leaves no doubts as to its aim. Kenner wishes to establish a poem as a contained dynamic, or process, as opposed to conceiving of it in terms of static relations and fixed structures. In this way, the complexity of Pound's poetry ceases to be the sign of some pedantic obscurity and becomes a sign of its vitality. Scholars who, as Wordsworth wrote, "murder to dissect" are precluded from the outset of detecting any signs of life; hence "Empsonian methods find no handles by which to take hold of Pound's verse." "This is not," Kenner offers, "to be ungrateful to Empson, who has forged analytical tools of the utmost value"; but "one cannot be grateful to the obfuscators who have confused the dialectical-rhetorical analytics of Messrs. Empson and Richards with the 'new criticism' instigated by Mr. Eliot" (65).

It has to be noted, however, that the harshest critic of what Kenner wrought was Pound himself. Pound had early on advised Kenner to use what Walter Baumann would later make the title of his book, "The Rose in the Steel Dust." Kenner's more generic title left him more room to pursue his own perceptions, but Pound complained—in a letter to Patricia Hutchins quoted in Humphrey Carpenter's biography of Pound—"I usually find my own simple statements more comprehensible than the eggsplantation by flatchested highbrows. H. K. definitely AIMED at Yale grad/school etc. and frankly said so" (799). In a letter to Huntington Cairns, also quoted by Carpenter, Pound was more charitable: "Kenner has read the text and does not talk nonsense, if you MUST get all yr/ information at 2nd. hand" (799). He remained uncomfortable in having his writing mediated by academic authority, and in having that mediation mark him as a necessarily erudite subject.

Robert Lowell complained to Pound that Kenner "seems to have read no one except you and Eliot and Dr. Leavis (his style is barbarous earnest parody of you and Leavis)" (Carpenter 799). But on the whole Lowell's reaction of these poets was at odds with other reviewers. Generally, Kenner was praised for bringing professional rigor to the evaluation of Pound. His purpose was to make a case for Pound's poetry as poetry: to submit that "rationalized rhetorical analysis" abets the lifeless scholarly orthodoxy that in America made common cause with Saturday reviewers against the New Criticism, against modernist poetry, and against Pound. Kenner's strategy here thus anticipates those grumblings about "the Pound cult"; Pound is not for Kenner a special case for criticism but a test case, and it is not Pound who needs academe but academe that needs Pound. By emphasizing Eliot's role in the formation of New Criticism, Kenner argued the value of academe schooling itself in the poetry of the modernist masters. In the process, Kenner championed the vitality of New Criticism as much as he did the vitality of Pound's poetry. This association of the New Criticism with Eliot and of Eliot with Pound implies both Pound's prestige and the necessity of Kenner's approach.

A Particular Kind of Critic

For T. S. Eliot, needless to say, the demonstration of Pound's critical seriousness took a different series of steps. A series of distinctions, to be precise: Eliot distinguished between man and poet, and between poet and critic. Pound, Eliot affirms, is a particular *kind* of critic, whose preoccupation is not with understanding but with craft. This demonstration is the primary work of his edition of *Literary Essays of Ezra Pound*. More than the convenience it proposes to be, *Literary Essays* dramatically redacts Pound's work and career, either eliding or de-emphasizing Pound's tireless essays at changing the world. "Pound's literary criticism is the most contemporary criticism of its kind," Eliot affirmed (Introduction, x) "but the limitation of its kind is in its concentration upon the craft of letters, and of poetry especially" (xiii). As Michael Coyle proposes (1995), this idea of Pound's work would be ironic from any quarter, but coming from Eliot and his more than thirty years' experience of Pound's unmistakably extra-aesthetic tirades, it is especially striking. No argument in Eliot's career was bolder—or more successful. "For forty years now *Literary Essays* has been the only one of Pound's critical books to remain consistently in print; and between 1954 and 1968 it was the only serious collection still in print in either Britain or America" (15). Eliot accomplished his redaction with unprecedented agility, with a touch so light and familiar that forty years later we still hardly notice its pressure. We don't notice because the frame of *Literary Essays* has in large part become the frame through which we view the sprawling and heterogeneous body of Pound's prose. The process begun by the Fellows in American Literature of the Library of Congress in defending their award of the Bollingen Prize to Pound here assumes its classic form, a form reproduced in most Pound scholarship through the seventies.

Eliot directed his edition of *Literary Essays* at a broad readership, but his critical criteria were decidedly academic. Despite his protest about the "limitation" of Pound's "concentration upon the craft of letters" it was

Eliot's edition that established for Pound's work that peculiar valency. What Eliot did was to locate within Pound's own writings concerns and features sympathetic with the position aggressively assumed by the Library Fellows. In this way, Pound and Eliot became the twin patriarchs both of modernist poetry, which transformed history into works of art, and also of modernist (formalist) criticism, which transformed works of art into comprehensible and comprehensive tradition.

An exacting sense of tradition and an interest in demonstrating its living presence in Pound's work also conditions the kind of scholarship first brought to bear on Pound's poetry by John Hamilton Edwards and William Vasse's *The Pound Newsletter*. The first issue appeared in January 1954, and the last in April 1956; ten issues were published altogether, the substance of which was collected and expanded into Edwards and Vasse's *Annotated Index to the Cantos of Ezra Pound* (1957). Although Edwards and Vasse's work has since been carried on, perseveringly, diligently, and often creatively by Carroll F. Terrell and all of the scholars associated with *Paideuma*, the first publication of the *Pound Newsletter* demonstrated Pound's re-creation as academic subject. It had, after all, been just a few months since the publication of George Williamson's *A Reader's Guide to T. S. Eliot*. Edwards and Vasse were not necessarily motivated by Williamson's example alone, but Williamson's book was a sign of the academic institutionalization upon which the *Pound Newsletter* patently sought to improve. The newsletter was however just that—a newsletter, usually between thirty and forty mimeographed pages. Like the more visually elegant *Paideuma* after it, each issue of the *Newsletter* presented regular departments—"Notes and Queries," "From the World Press," "Work in Progress," "Bibliographies." Edwards and Vasse intended "from the beginning to work toward a meaningful end, and to make that end a useful point of departure for further studies" (issue 8, 1). The scope of their success cannot be measured merely by the publication of their *Annotated Index*; although their *Annotated Index* has since been replaced by Terrell's *Companion* it was they who modeled such annotations as a valuable and ongoing project for Pound studies, and readers and scholars of Pound's work have ever since found such a forum indispensable. The very look of *Paideuma*, with its recurring departments and features, attested to the enduring model Edwards and Vasse created.

The distinction between man and work so fundamental to Eliot's representation of Pound, and so generally implicit in the work of the *Pound Newsletter*, also informed the next collection of essays dedicated to Pound, edited by Duke University professor Lewis Leary and called *Motive and Method in the Cantos of Ezra Pound*. Leary's entry into Pound studies, published in 1954, is particularly interesting because he was by training and habit an Americanist, having published about such poets and writers as Philip Freneau and Nathaniel Tucker. The title of Leary's Pound book might seem to suggest the kind of concerns treated by Watts, but such is not the case; the four essays comprising the volume take up the traditionally biographical concerns of "motive and method" and deploy them to show that Pound "built the *Cantos* on classical themes" (jacket blurb); Leary's term "motive" in particular has less to do with biographical motivation than it does with poetic *motifs* or elements. In this respect, the volume demonstrates an even more deliberate purpose than does Russell's. What Leary did was reprint two of the essays read at the 1953 meeting of the English Institute at Columbia University, Hugh Kenner's "The Broken Mirrors and the Mirror of Memory" and Guy Davenport's "Pound and Frobenius," and annex to them Sister Bernetta Quinn's "The Metamorphoses of Ezra Pound" and Forrest Read, Jr.'s "A Man of No Fortune."

Kenner's essay is particularly metacritical. He insists on the distinction between symbol and motive—"things in the poem" (4)—and executes a kind of Poundian trumping of Archibald MacLeish's famous dictum that "a poem should not mean but be":

> This effect [of a poetic surface undisturbed by the overt presence of a speaker] is the liability of a carefully calculated risk. Pound is determined to dispel at the start the notion that the things in his poem are symbols: that he says what he seems to be saying only as a way of saying something else. Canto I is not an elaborate metaphor. Nevertheless it is not "just Homer." Such a phrase, for one thing, is impertinent. Homer is not just a Greek document, he contains, incarnates, a paideuma. And the Canto, informed by that paideuma, *does* a great deal more than at first glance it *is*, and ultimately is what it does—something surprisingly comprehensive. (4)

While Kenner's prose might seem elliptical, his purpose is not. His aim is to establish that Pound is by no means the creature of formalist or professional attention but its creator. Even Eliot takes a backhanded cuff in the opening paragraph of the essay. In "Tradition and the Individual Talent" (1919) Eliot maintained that the poet, the individual human being, is to the elements of his poem little more than a "transforming catalyst" (*Selected Essays*, 8); Kenner submits by contrast that Pound "will not have us think of him as a medium in which things happen, nor yet as a poet-hero striding and declaiming before backdrops of his own design" ("Broken Mirrors," 3). This is a formula for dialectic: romantic thesis, Eliotic or New Critical antithesis, Poundian synthesis. The burden of Kenner's essay, and in slightly different ways of the other three essays in the volume, is to demonstrate how Pound can be more than mere catalyst and yet not figure in the poem as loquacious hero.

Leary's inclusion of Bernetta Quinn's essay also merits particular notice, because the essay had previously been published—as "Ezra Pound and the Metamorphic Tradition," in *Western Review*. Quinn lightly revised and expanded it for Leary's volume, altering the title to "The Metamorphoses of Ezra Pound." As befitting her theme, perhaps, she later published the essay again, with the original title, in her *The Metamorphic Tradition in Modern Poetry*. Her alteration of the title for Leary's volume is significant because it underscores not only her particular concerns, but also a way of reading Pound that would grow more common over the next decade. That is, Quinn's second title invites overt comparison with Ovid's *Metamorphoses*, and that comparison in and of itself proposes Pound's *Cantos*, first, as a candidate for greatness and, second, as a particular kind of work: a pre-eminently *poetical* work concerned with beauty enduring superficial historical change. In themselves, the reprintings of Quinn's essay in some ways suggest such a metamorphosis; throughout the turbulence of Pound's post-Bollingen reception, her essay continued to speak to his readers. It's hard to resist immediately contrasting her success with Watts's failure.

Quinn begins by announcing her approach as thematic (Leary, 60). But her thematics does not touch on political questions. Explaining that "Pound's interest in the *Metamorphoses* is twofold: artistic and philosophical" (62), Quinn argues that "the underlying use which Pound makes of the metamorphoses of things might best be classified as an epistemological one. . . . We must admit that our version of reality needs constant revision if it is to remain valid" (73). For all the later essays that treat Pound's interest in and borrowing from Ovid, it is this latter assertion that has proved Quinn's most enduring contribution to Pound studies, despite a lukewarm response from Pound scholars; orthodoxy was shaping quickly (Joost, 140–49). The transformation of political issues into ethical issues, discerned not only by Pound's detractors but also by early critics like Watts would become fundamental to the arguments of later critical arguments.

This foundation would more or less endure until the radical revisionists of the 1980s, but its presence in Leary's volume caused a distinct split among reviewers. In a certain sense, estimations of Leary's success turned on responses to Kenner's manner—increasingly distinct as "the method" of Pound criticism. In a generally positive notice, R. L. Cook remarked Kenner's conviction that "the key to Pound's method is viewpoint," and the importance that Kenner attaches to our understanding "Pound's singleness of purpose and doctrine" (104). Reviewing Leary's volume for *Modern Language Notes*, Professor Robert Mayo of Northwestern University praised Leary's volume for its contributions "to our understanding and appreciation of this neglected 20th Century American Epic" (311). Nevertheless, Mayo observed, the volume "will probably win few new readers for *The Cantos*, although it will be welcomed by the faithful." Kenner's essay, Mayo found, in both senses, to be "the leading essay":

able to demonstrate the integral relations of diverse constituent elements, but proving often "oracular in manner." The same observations would follow Kenner for the rest of his career.

Berkeley Professor Thomas Parkinson shared Mayo's sense that the volume would win "few new readers for the *Cantos*," and was hence a squandered opportunity that makes for "a dull book" (8). Parkinson pulled no punches: "The general method of criticism [in the book] is deducible from the beginning essay by Hugh Kenner; discounting Kenner's truculence and brightness as merely personal qualities, his essay defines the approach of the other three. Naturally Kenner's is first in total quality as well as in appearance; he understands the method of Pound criticism because he invented it" (7). But despite his remark about total quality, Parkinson still found Guy Davenport's essay "Pound and Frobenius" the volume's "most useful" essay, because it brings plenty of new information to a little understood topic. Wesleyan Professor Alexander Cowie, writing a year earlier, had been even less impressed with the volume. Cowie contrasted the fidelity of Leary's contributors with the account of Pound in James G. Southworth's *More Modern American Poets*. Southworth, who was overtly writing for "the general reader," judged the *Cantos* "a colossal failure." The difference between Southworth's and Leary's sense of audience is almost the precondition for their opposed views of Pound, and they represent the still discernible forces met over the Bollingen award. With regard to the reception of Pound's work, and of modernist poetry in general, general audiences were melting away almost precisely as a solid academic and intellectual audience was forming. This, it might be said, was the real beginning of "the Pound Era."

The signs of its coming are retrospectively evident in John Espey's *Ezra Pound's Mauberley: A Study in Composition*, published in 1955. Indeed, the formalist criteria that inform Espey's book largely mark its substantial contributions to the professionalization of modernist scholarship. Espey calls the book "an experiment in criticism" (7), and most of his reviewers responded to his book in just those terms. But this "study in composition" was not only an experiment in criticism, but was also the first Pound study of its kind. At the time only Watts had devoted an entire book to a single one of Pound's works, and that was to *The Cantos*—Kenner's book treated the *poetry* of Ezra Pound; it wasn't necessarily obvious that any of Pound's shorter sequences would stand up to such sustained scrutiny, even though, as Espey notes, "few modern poems have received more notice than Ezra Pound's *Hugh Selwyn Mauberley*" (13). Espey announced three important questions, the first of which returnedimmediately to the crucial issue raised by the Bollingen controversy: "the relationship between Ezra Pound himself and Hugh Selwyn Mauberley, whether the two are to be identified wholly or in part or not at all"

(13). Espey's second question was of the poem's construction, and his third regarded "the nature of the poem's ultimate base, if indeed one can assume that such a base exists" (13).

Espey proposed to address these questions by subjecting the poem to "detailed scrutiny in relation to the materials from which Pound shaped it," a subjection that he knew would inevitably strike many readers as "source hunting" (13). To this charge Espey could offer no significant defense; he only offered to distinguish "the casual source" from "the source that genuinely informs a piece of writing." He had, in effect, run into the limits of the newly institutionalized New Criticism, but because he worked so conscientiously to train all batteries on the poem itself, reviewers were for the most part sympathetic. The anonymous reviewer for *TLS* opened by declaring that "Mr. Espey has written an excellent commentary," though he qualifies that praise by adding that "it cannot be denied that 115 pages devoted to fifteen of *Mauberley* precipitate an initial alarm; phantoms form of the yet unwritten volumes on the *Cantos* lumbering towards the future" (162). "Lumbering" indeed: by our time whole forests have been cleared. The *TLS* reviewer rightly noticed that the same kind of treatment had yet to come to *The Cantos*. But for all that the review praised the excellence of Espey's "commentary," it faulted him for not being formalist enough. The reviewer questioned Espey's interest in "underlying sexual patterns in the poem," and remarked: "it is not surprising that Mr. Espey 'is struck by the disparity between the astonishing complexity of [*Mauberley*'s] surface and the simplicity of its base.' This is an error of analytical method which the findings of semantics should by now have obviated. Once the reality of 'structure' is understood, the concept of 'base' on which everything else rests should no longer be tenable" (162).

Howard Sergeant, reviewing for *English*, also made special note of Espey's methodology. But Sergeant welcomed the break from aggressive New Criticism and praised Espey for showing no "trace of the critical jargon so popular amongst contemporary American writers" (193). Bernetta Quinn also found the book a kind of test-case for the contemporaneous condition of criticism: "Some of the chapters, such as the first (on textual variation) might well have been articles in one of the learned journals; others are less specialized" (1). Like other reviewers, Quinn found the chapter on Gourmont least satisfactory, but unlike the *TLS* reviewer, she engaged happily Espey's talk about "the foundation" of the poem (2). Among Espey's reviewers, only Bernard Duffy, of Michigan State University, declined to grow excited over the book's claims to critical experiment. "This is," Duffy wrote, "a source and influence study" (601). Duffy is largely right, although in saying so, he passed judgment on Espey's combination of Freudian and formalist critical techniques.

That combination marks Espey's volume as a creature of its times, a book that came of age in the heyday of Lionel Trilling's attempt to temper Matthew Arnold with Sigmund Freud, or Herbert Marcuse's attempt to temper Marx with Freud. Such a combination was almost characteristic of those places in academe where the New Criticism had not triumphed over older traditions. Espey's arguments about the distinction between Ezra Pound, the poet, and Hugh Selwyn Mauberley, the persona, would stand for over thirty years. But the reviewer for *TLS* was right about the immediate implications of Espey's publication. Espey himself claims that "anyone who has mastered the miniature handling of devices and techniques in *Mauberley* is prepared for their larger use in the *Cantos*" (106). Stanley K. Coffman, Jr., of the University of Oklahoma, took his point, recommending that Espey's book "is perhaps less important as 'explication' than as a highly readable introduction to Pound, which fortunately escapes the contentiousness of the usual interpreter's prose" (222). Implicitly submitting Pound's work for consideration as an oeuvre, the totality of which is to some degree inherent in its parts, Espey's work was another crucial step in Pound's constitution as an academic subject.

The next major study of Pound, however, made clear that less academic concerns remained and would remain an indelible part of public interest in Pound. The book was Clark Emery's *Ideas into Action: A Study of Pound's Cantos*, a volume in the University of Miami Publications in English and American Literature series, published in 1958. In the preface to the volume, Emery wrote:

> Taking a hint from Mr. Pound's *ABC of Reading* and *ABC of Economics*, I might have called this collection of essays *An ABC of Ezra Pound's Cantos*. For it pretends to be no more. Literary critics have written excellent studies of the poem—for other critics; scholars have made original contributions to the knowledge of other scholars. It appears time to offer the lay-reader who stands in bemusement before the epic's variegated bulk something in the way of aid and comfort.

Years in the making, Emery's original manuscript had been much larger, having "included explications of over forty cantos." Both Ezra and Dorothy Pound had seen this earlier version and made "corrections" to it. Indeed, even Leary had made "editorial use of portions of [Emery's] unpublished study" (iv). The book had been around. The consequence of its long gestation was that it was published a full ten years after the Bollingen controversy; it's hard to imagine anyone interested in Pound wanting to demonstrate Pound's zeal for changing the world at any earlier moment in the 1950s, when Poundians were (mostly) following Kenner and Eliot's lead and representing Pound as a poet's poet, interested primarily in poetry.

For all his humility, Emery does not notice the irony in his having to popularize the popularizer, but he was all the same among the first critics to take seriously this aspect of Pound's work. Neither is it accidental that this turning to Pound's homiletic or meliorative ambitions should be accompanied by hostility to academe: in his original preface to the book, Espey characterized his book as "an experiment in criticism"; in his preface to the 1974 paperback edition, Espey admitted "that some pages seem to sound a faint note of (deliberate?) parody of the academic style" (6). Emery implicitly recognized the link between the valorization of Pound as visionary poet and the critical circling of the wagons that followed Bollingen, and challenged the increasingly professional standards that regulated as they legitimized Pound's claims to public attention.

Emery is very clear on the question of *The Cantos* as art. Pound's "purpose" in writing the poem is "didactic . . . is, negatively, to show that a civilization does not now exist in Europe or the United States and, positively, to show how one can be produced" (93). In taking this position, Emery of course must distance himself from Watts and his errors, which he does by two principal means. First, Emery characterizes Watts's work as being too aridly intellectual; "Mr. Watts, in *Ezra Pound and the Cantos*, fails to consider . . . the significance of the mythological pattern in the *Cantos*" (109). The key word here is "pattern"—Emery tries to respect what he understands to be Pound's *poetic* structures. Second, Emery follows Kenner's example of retaining wherever possible Pound's own language. Like Kenner's *The Poetry of Ezra Pound*, Emery's *Ideas into Action* sometimes reads like an annotated anthology. Moreover, and again like Kenner, Emery tends to work in a self-consciously Poundian manner: by juxtaposition rather than by argument. Most often his juxtapositions are of selected passages from Pound's poetry and prose, but in his final chapter, where he makes his claim for the value of the *Cantos* as poetry, Emery selects "passages from the *Cantos* which seem . . . to have poetic worth and set them beside well-thought-of passages (from poems late or old) which possess a resemblance of one kind or another" (160). His operative assumption, then, is that, presented in a sympathetic context, Pound's work can speak for itself.

Emery's reviewers divided over his success as a popularizer, and over his success in demonstrating anything about *The Cantos* as a *poem*. Frederick T. Wood objected that for an "ABC" Emery's account was not very lucid—and chafed against what he found to be Emery's constant effort "to assert the claim of the *Cantos* to be considered a great poem" (407). But three years later George Dekker celebrated Emery's work as "a popular but responsible exposition of the main ideas and principles upon which the poem is based" (xiii). Richard G. Landini, in the only other review published at the time of publication, submitted that "despite the prominence of analytical and evaluative study of the poem, before Clark

Emery's *Ideas into Action* little had been written of the poem [*The Cantos*] as poem. Emery has been able to do what earlier critics had failed to do: present a critically and scholarly palatable study of the poem's major patterns without sacrificing its poetic strength and integrity" (49). For Landini at least, *Ideas into Action* "easily assumes a position of preeminence in the context of Pound study" (49). He grants, nevertheless, that "Emery's is not a book for beginners; it will not serve, for example, as supplementary reading to William Van O'Connor's *Casebook on Ezra Pound*" (49).

William Van O'Connor and Edward Stone published their *A Casebook on Ezra Pound* (1959) only one year after Emery's *Ideas into Action*, but Landini is right to observe their different understanding of popularization. In fact, O'Connor and Stone's *Casebook* demonstrates the continuing danger that Pound's work poses for the institution of criticism. Commemorating the tenth anniversary of the Bollingen controversy, O'Connor and Stone's volume purports simply and objectively to present "the case of Ezra Pound, pro and con selections intended to be used as controlled source material for the Freshman English course" (cover copy). In this volume, Pound's poetry figures as nothing more than a short, first appendix (excerpts from his radio broadcasts comprise the second appendix): Pound himself is "the case." It isn't exactly the way that Pound might have hoped to be remembered. The tenth anniversary of the Bollingen controversy was remarked by other writers in other places: Paul A. Olson, H. A. Sieber, James Blish, and especially Nathaniel Weyl in his *The Bollingen Award*—a book brought out by the same publisher who did O'Connor and Stone's *Casebook*. Although Pound had been released from St. Elizabeths and had returned to Italy midsummer of the previous year, the tenth-anniversary discussions showed only that the American public had yet to discover a means collectively to evaluate what remained a perversely embarrassing "national skeleton," as Samuel Hynes put it.

N. Christoph de Nagy's *The Poetry of Ezra Pound: The Pre-Imagist Stage*, published in 1960, seemed by comparison blithely undisturbed by the issue. Certainly it helped that de Nagy wasn't American, but his contributions owed more precisely to what we might call a methodological innovation. No previous study of Pound had so relied on historical context, or had so contextualized history. For one thing, de Nagy focused on Pound's earliest poetry, a body of work not then self-evidently rewarding of lingering attention. But de Nagy largely solved that problem by sustaining a literary-historical approach: he studied Pound's earliest volume with one eye to what Pound borrowed from eminent poetic tradition—the Pre-Raphaelites, Browning, Swinburne, Yeats—and with the other to how the early work "heralds and prefigures" *The Cantos* (148). De Nagy's Germanic method thus sidestepped the entrenched battle lines in America: his work was neither aggressively formalist nor insistent on playing out the political implications of Pound's work. To pursue this kind of literary history might bracket political-historical questions to much the same result as any formalist focus on the text, but at the time de Nagy's very method argued for the importance of considering Pound's work within larger contexts—contexts whose very identification honors Pound.

Lewis Leary and C. Heywood each praised de Nagy's book in spite of certain unevenness in its treatment of Pound's earliest work. Arthur Terry called de Nagy's conclusions "clear and unforced," and judged him "more precise than any previous critic on Pound's early dealings with Symbolism," but like Leary and Heywood, Fred B. Millett found de Nagy sometimes plodding, sometimes given to belaboring the obvious. Still, on the whole the Anglo-American scholarly community was quick to appreciate this contribution from a continental colleague.

Indeed, for all the recurrent polemics evident in such places as O'Connor and Stone's *Casebook*, it was increasingly clear that modernism was already reconstituting the relations between academe and literary-poetical activity. Critics of modernism in general, and of Pound in particular, were already finding themselves struck by the difference created by their own presence. George S. Fraser's *Ezra Pound*, published in A. Norman Jeffares's series "Writers and Critics," offered a prospect view of this process. Unlike most of the early "experts" on Pound, Fraser was already a Scottish critic of growing authority—the author of six critical books, and editor of *Poetry Now: An Anthology* (1956). Comprising three sections and a bibliography, Fraser's *Ezra Pound* treated the man, the work, and the critics. It was a perceptive structure, implicitly recognizing Pound's unprecedented relations with his commentators. Fraser was most interested in the criticism "of those writers who, as themselves creative, could in a sense speak of Pound as equals" (112); but he also paid special attention to F. R. Leavis, Yvor Winters, and Roy Harvey Pearce. Fraser's own circumspectly respectful conclusion was delivered in one complex sentence:

> I think myself that he is an innovator of the utmost importance, a superlative verse technician, a poet with from the beginning to the end of his career an impeccable ear; an explorer of genius; a man bitterly and exactly sensitive to the pressures in a democratic society that kill instinctual life, rather as D. H. Lawrence was; a man, in all his personal relationships, of the utmost generosity of heart; a poet more splendidly and largely concerned than any poet of our time with the disparate yet similar essences of human civilisation; the poet, perhaps, as amateur cultural anthropologist. (113)

Fraser's focus on criticism caught the attention of J. C. Maxwell, who reviewed his book in the *Durham University Journal.* Maxwell noted

Fraser's aim to supply a "little plain man's guide," but found the book rambling and inconsistent. Writing a year later, George Dekker characterized Fraser's work as a "genial, intelligent, but sometimes too casual popularization" (xi). In general, the conjunction of a popularizing intention and a sharp sense of the important mediating role being performed by academic criticism seems to have been unsuccessful, however prescient.

M. L. Rosenthal's *A Primer of Ezra Pound* opens with a similarly broad sense of Pound's importance to the institution of modern letters: "Ezra Pound's career is so interlaced with the whole of modern letters and politics that one might devote many pages to it and never touch on his poetry" (1). Nevertheless, Rosenthal's generally sympathetic account purports to "distinguish Pound the poet from Pound the thinker, propagandist, and literary man of action" (2). Rosenthal's book demonstrates perceptiveness and sensitivity, but in reading his introduction today one is struck by how repeatedly young modernist critics re-inscribed the terms of the Bollingen victory, and in every instance offered that re-inscription as a kind of discovery. These critics were generally energetic, talented, and intelligent, but it is open to question whether the distinction between man and poet owed to a sustained excitement over the new possibilities it opened, or whether—a dozen years after Bollingen—it had simply become a kind of shibboleth whose proper recitation was virtually synonymous with the presentation of professional credentials.

In this sense and in others, Rosenthal's *Primer* contended with Watts's and Emery's model for engaging Pound. In a closing "Envoy," Rosenthal lists almost without comment the previous studies of Pound, describing the lot of them as "valuable"; "but the best commentary on Pound," he maintains, "is his own prose" (52–53). Like Kenner or Emery, and unlike de Nagy, Rosenthal purports only to offer an introduction. But despite affirming the value of Pound's own prose, Rosenthal breaks from Kenner or Emery's habit of essentially juxtaposing big chunks from Pound's own criticism. *A Primer of Ezra Pound* is among the earliest works to show the impress of previous studies. De Nagy's example makes Rosenthal's first chapter on the early poetry not only possible but necessary; similarly, Espey's book stands before the third chapter on *Mauberley*. All of this in a book designed for non-academic readers.

Professor Robert D. Spector of Long Island University praised Rosenthal for not attempting "to find excuses for 'the terrible aberrations of a man of genius,'" but nevertheless concluded that "whatever its merits, Rosenthal's primer unfortunately does little to explain Pound's 'obscurities' to those outside the sacred circle" (6). For Spector, Rosenthal's effort "will only confirm the general reader's suspicion that . . . Pound is a cultural as well a political exile." Ironically, then, this popular primer demonstrates rather than obviates the distance between professional and general readers.

By the end of 1960, Pound was an increasingly regular figure of academic study. The terms whereby he was made subject to such study did not—could not—necessarily have pleased him, but there was no chance of his being swept aside by objections to his "difficulty," both poetic and political. Indeed, the next year his disciple Eustace Mullins published a defense that attempted to make of that difficulty a salient virtue. Although objections to Pound's character and wartime behavior would never disappear, and would sometimes even make their way into academic discussion, Pound's career in the sixties would be very different in tenor than it had been during the fifties. For all the fine work that would be published between Rosenthal's *Primer* and Hugh Kenner's *The Pound Era*, the sixties would be a period less dramatic in engagement. At precisely the time when American streets and campuses became the site of virtually unprecedented public unrest and civic disobedience, Pound's work was withdrawing ever more securely into the hallowed halls of higher learning.

Notes

[1] *Selected Letters of Ezra Pound, 1907–1941*, ed. D. D. Paige, 12.

[2] The choice of topic is not as anomalous as it might seem: Chesterton was a major influence on Marshall McLuhan—perhaps the major influence in McLuhan's conversion to Roman Catholicism while he was at Cambridge; and McLuhan was Kenner's teacher at the University of Toronto.

[3] *Cronos* has an interesting history, having begun life as *The Maryland Quarterly* before moving to Ohio State University in 1947, becoming associated with the *Golden Goose* Press and becoming a venue for Charles Olson and Robert Creeley; see Peter Brooker and Andrew Thacker, eds., *Oxford Critical and Cultural History of Modernist Magazines*, 980–82.

[4] Watts, "Theology Bitter and Gay," *South Atlantic Quarterly* 49 (July 1950): 359–77.

[5] Compare this language to the similar language of Watts's 1947 essay, "Pound's Cantos: Means to an End." There, Watts wrote: "it is part—and to Pound the crucially important part—of a life-long struggle to alter the world as he conceives it: a world in many areas hag-ridden by capitalist democracy, by usury and its maleficent effects." Five years later, "many" became "most"; far from modifying his original stance Watts chose to double-down.

[6] In a prefatory note to Watts's essay, the editors wrote of their pleasure "to find that here at last was an unbiased study, putting in clear light and sharp focus the various ideas which led both to his *Cantos* and to his political actions. In fairness to Pound, the editors sent to him the manuscript for comment." Dorothy's response also included three subsequent sentences which identified where Watts should go to understand Pound's philosophy and views on poetry and politics.

[7] Russell's volume was published in England as *Ezra Pound: A Collection of Essays To Be Presented to Ezra Pound on His Sixty-fifth Birthday*; in America the volume

appeared as *An Examination of Ezra Pound* (New York: New Directions, 1950). The difference between the titles is significant: whereas in England the volume could simply be identified as concerned with "Pound," the American title worked to distinguish its contents from the polemics surrounding Pound's prize.

[8] Peter Russell, "Vingt-Cinque Ans Apres: An Editor's Personal Retrospect," in *An Examination of Ezra Pound*, 1973, 267–304.

[9] See M. T. Wilson, Review of *The Poetry of Ezra Pound*, by Hugh Kenner, 210–11.

4: Sailing after Knowledge, 1962–1971

One way by which a poem might be thought to "contain" history is by mirroring in its own large-scale rhythms the rhythms of discovery, wastage, neglect and rediscovery that the historical records give us notice of.

—Donald Davie, *Ezra Pound* (1965)

The View after Mid-Century

WALTER SUTTON'S EDITED COLLECTION, *Ezra Pound: A Collection of Critical Essays* (1963), sought to balance Pound's reception without speaking to partisan issues. Marking an important moment in what was the still comparatively new field—the volume testified to a new self-consciousness of Pound research as a legitimate area in the profession of literary studies. Included in the popular series "Twentieth Century Views," it did well enough to be reprinted in 1965. Sutton included essays from poets as well as scholars, and from British scholars as well as American. He included, for instance, essays by both Watts and Kenner, an inclusiveness not repeated in any later twentieth-century collection, Watts's opposition to Kenner's more New Critical approach having largely been forgotten along with Watts's briefly important status as "Pound's Expounder." Sutton included Watts even while pointedly declining to revisit the Pound wars of the late forties and early fifties. As his jacket blurb puts it, this volume "reflect[s] the fresh surge of interest in Ezra Pound since World War II," but "does not, however, reopen the Pound 'case.'" If Rosenthal's work holds the impress of previous studies, Sutton's collection overtly displays that body of work as the context for its own activity.

In fact, Rosenthal's chapter on *The Cantos* is the first in the volume to focus on the poem as the place where the question of Pound's greatness will finally be decided. Generally, Sutton's table of contents could serve as an index to this transitional period in Pound studies—to what the jacket blurb calls "a turning point in twentieth-century poetry and criticism." The language of the blurb is meant to apply to Pound but, more trenchantly, the phrase "turning point" applies to changes in literary study. The volume opens by reprinting essays from poet-peers Yeats, Williams, and Eliot, but all subsequent essays are written by academic critics. Leavis's essay is the first of these, but it is immediately rejoined by the already ubiquitous Kenner, whose discussion of *Mauberley* contends with Leavis's assessment of Pound as a one-poem poet (Leavis judged *Mauberley* to be the only poem of Pound's that will matter). Next comes Rosenthal's chapter, and then Forrest Read's essay "A Man of No Fortune," reprinted from Leary's *Motive and Method*. David W. Evans suggests a new context within which to consider *Pisan Cantos*—as "prison poetry"; Harvard Professor of French W. M. Frohock regards Pound as an outspoken critic of Western culture, a révolté; and Watts's chapter, "Reckoning," reappears as a way of distinguishing Pound from the Symbolist tradition. Of the five remaining contributions, one is by a writer and poet, George P. Elliott, and the others by critics who were becoming academic authorities in their own right: Earl Miner, R. Murray Schafer, J. P. Sullivan, and Roy Harvey Pearce. The range of the volume remains impressive, and submits Pound's work to a variety of perspectives. Along with Eva Hesse's, William Cookson's, and J. P. Sullivan's multi-author collections of 1969 and 1970, Sutton's collection almost too conveniently bookends the next decade of Pound scholarship, a period in which Pound scholars declared the vitality of their field almost as often as they took its collective pulse.

The extent to which Sutton's collection was a departure from the norm is underscored by contrast with William Van O'Connor's *Ezra Pound* (1963): published in the University of Minnesota Pamphlets on American Writers series, O'Connor's volume hearkens back to an earlier moment. Certain that Pound was "mad" (7), O'Connor was nevertheless willing to entertain the possibility that he was "not merely . . . a poetic genius" but "a writer who was revolutionizing English and American poetry" (6). He showed himself relatively unimpressed by the "various efforts" to "say what [*The Cantos*] are about" (7) and concluded that "presumably Time will forgive or at least forget" Pound's offenses and errors: "if his poetry achieves a place in the permanent canon of English and American poetry, Time, as Auden says, will lay its honors at his feet" (45). Auden's poetic abstraction of "Time" deliberately avoids historical particularities, and O'Connor's appropriation of that abstraction would imply that critics somehow only serve a cosmic and dispassionate judgment of history: a strange conclusion for one of the editors of the Pound *Casebook*. The only review, by Arthur Terry, Lecturer at Queen's University of Belfast, complained of inaccuracies and dismissed the pamphlet as breezy and anecdotal. But O'Connor's beginning suggests one of the more innovative studies of the year; he began by quoting Pound's broadcast over Rome radio on December 7, 1941—Pearl Harbor Day, an event Pound did not yet know about. Toward the end of the broadcast, Pound began describing what he took to be a Confucian politics.

Pound's deep interest in Confucius, his tendency to invoke Confucius in those moments when his ethical or political position seemed most precarious, is the main focus of L. S. Dembo's *The Confucian Odes of*

Ezra Pound: A Critical Appraisal, published in 1963. Dembo considers what he allows to be "an essentially minor work," but a work that "more clearly than the *Cantos*, defines the achievement and the tragedy of Ezra Pound as a poet, an aesthetician, and an interpreter of the culture that he apotheosized" (1): Pound's translation of *The Classic Anthology*. In one sense, Dembo's work picks up the cue of Kenner's "Gold in the Gloom," a cue offered more than ten years earlier. Kenner had argued that the parties to the Bollingen debate might have seen things differently had they known—or even known *of*—Pound's translation; Dembo's work attempts to demonstrate that difference.

Published in the University of California Press's "Perspectives in Criticism" series, Dembo's book evaluates Pound's version of the *Odes* both as a translation and as, in the words of its jacket blurb, "a reflection of [Pound's] own theories of poetry, morals, manners, and politics." Having served as an interpreter of Chinese for the US Navy, Dembo was able to compare the traditional significance of the *Odes* with Pound's translations. He did not go to the old chestnut that Pound did not know enough Chinese to make these translations accurately, as a true Sinologue might, but outlined Pound's "metaphysical bias" in conceiving them in a certain way, which was both archaizing and deeply American. In his review, poet Charles Tomlinson expressed some uneasiness about Dembo's book being thesis-driven, but concluded nevertheless that "Dembo's case is unassailable: he grants that Pound's translations are 'free' but urges that the lyric core of many of the poems in the Confucian anthology have never before been so successfully exposed" ("Tone," 48).

Dembo's emphasis on professional "criticism" shared the keynote of most Pound criticism in the sixties, and that emphasis came increasingly to dominate older interests in more general explanation. Among the more enduring studies published in this period, George Dekker's *Sailing after Knowledge: The Cantos of Ezra Pound* yet shows many signs of its own historical moment. Like Dembo, Dekker considers Pound's "translator's ethic," although maintaining that this ethic transformed into a consistently workable poetics only in the *Pisan Cantos.* Dekker's work, published in 1963, also resembles Dembo's in its disclaimer of any intention to have written "an 'introduction' to Pound's mature poetry" (xi). Suggesting that, in order of importance, Kenner's *The Poetry of Ezra Pound*, Emery's *Ideas into Action*, Rosenthal's *A Primer*, Fraser's *Ezra Pound*, and Watts's *Ezra Pound and the Cantos* already provided for such need, Dekker affirms a different purpose; his aim, like Dembo's, is "to provide a reliable criticism of the poetry, not an introduction to it." Such an aim meant not only changes in how Pound was to be discussed, but also changes in audience. These changes resulted from the dramatic shifts of the fifties, but it was only in the subsequent decades that Pound criticism, like modernist criticism in general, became—in perhaps every sense of the word, but certainly in the sense Pound most likely would have used—academic.

It was an additional sign of the times that Dekker was the first Pound scholar to have come of age with a certifiable pedigree. Professional structures were in place to enable self-reproduction. As Dekker explains in his preface:

> I first studied Ezra Pound's poetry under the supervision of Dr. Hugh Kenner of the University of California. He has not read this book and would doubtless disagree with much that I have written; yet it certainly owes much to his sympathetic and informed instruction. Dr. Donald Davie, Fellow of Gonville and Caius College, Cambridge, has read the book—several times. . . . It is only just to add that he disagrees with many of my interpretations and judgments. (vii)

As C. Heywood wrote in opening his joint review of Dekker's book and Christoph de Nagy's *The Poetry of Ezra Pound: The Pre-Imagist Stage*, "Pound studies have been gaining ground steadily in recent years" (457). But Heywood was also eager to clarify the kind of study Dekker had written. He found Dekker's book—along with de Nagy's—to be "a departure from the inclusive studies" of Kenner or Rosenthal. Dembo made a similar point in his review, observing that Dekker's book "is not so much a systematic exegesis as it is an attempt to investigate Pound's ideas on knowledge, love, myth and ritual as 'points of entry' into the poem" (89).

Heywood was right to associate Dekker with de Nagy, in the sense that both critics concern themselves with historical context, and neither intends their work as a primer. But Dekker's book differs substantially from de Nagy's in terms of method; Dekker is more given to drawing out the implications of Pound's own phrases ("sailing after knowledge"), and to developing "points of entry" in thematic terms suggested by the work itself, rather than by the larger context of literary history. Dekker consequently reserves his discussion of Pound's poetics until Part II because, he claims, he wishes first to highlight the theme of Eros and thus be able later to "generalize about the poem which one reads, not about the various *a priori* poems which Pound's method encourages his friends and enemies alike to invent" (xiv). He justly assumes, in other words, that technique is inseparable from theme, but joins to that assumption a less fortunate corollary, that *he* can reach a "neutral" or accurate *paraphrase* where others have distorted the text.

This corollary was doubtless easier to make before the impact of critical theory later in the decade, but reviewers bumped up against it nevertheless. Dembo complained that Dekker "is occasionally over subtle and not beyond making certainties out of ambiguities" (387). Heywood flatly maintained that Dekker failed to meet his "own ambitious standard, 'to provide a reliable criticism of the poetry'" (458). W. D. Maxwell-Mahon found that Dekker was at his best when discussing the *Cantos* "from the point of view of their effectiveness as poetic statement," but often risked losing "the reader in a sea of mytho-poetic abstractions." Charles Tomlinson, however, found in Dekker's work the first sign that "the master [Pound] can now be argued with":

> Perhaps the first important result of this relaxation of approach was George Dekker's *Sailing after Knowledge* (1963) which contains some of the closest reading of the *Cantos* we possess. At the same time, Dekker's tone could be stringently though calmly critical of much of Pound. If Dekker's book in itself measured a stage, the conditions of its gestation underlined the distrust Pound still calls forth in academic circles. For it is common knowledge that, only after a prolonged struggle, was Dekker permitted to venture on Pound as a research topic in the University of Cambridge. ("Tone," 46)

Tomlinson's point bears particular consideration. It would have been inconceivable, a decade earlier, for any of Pound's champions to have admitted more than isolated weaknesses. Dekker's study attempts real criticism.

Most of Dekker's topics had been broached before: "Poetic Method and Strategy" (chapter 1) recalls Leary's *Motive and Method*; "Fertility Ritual in the *Cantos*" (chapter 2) draws from the contemporaneous preoccupation of Eliot criticism with Frazer and Weston—as Dekker himself drew directly from Eliot's critique of Pound's "Hell without dignity or tragedy"; Bernetta Quinn had already published on "Myth and Metamorphosis" (chapter 4); and Pound's Odyssean theme had already been treated by Forrest Read. But it wasn't so much the thematics of Dekker's work that marked its importance as the decisively critical context within which he explored those thematics. That difference also marked one of the seminal studies of the following year: J. P. Sullivan's *Ezra Pound and Sextus Propertius: A Study in Creative Translation* returned to the much-contested ground of Pound's status as a translator, but treated it in a manner that changed permanently the very terms of discussion.

The battle had initially been sparked back in 1919 by University of Chicago Latinist William Gardner Hale in his article in *Poetry* entitled "Pegasus Impounded." As Sullivan explains, Hale misunderstood "the aims and methods of the *Homage*," and accused Pound "of making about three-score errors"; from this perception, Hale famously concluded that "if Mr. Pound were a professor of Latin, there would be nothing left for him but suicide" (5–6). Sullivan offers his book as an attempted sublation of the old argument between academic translators and the modern poetic tradition that largely arises from Pound, and to that purpose he brings the tools of sophisticated textual studies to bear. Thus it was that Tomlinson suggested that "the real importance of J. P. Sullivan's *Ezra Pound and Sextus Propertius* lies in his establishment of a decent text of *Homage to Sextus Propertius* and in bringing together that text with the apposite sections from Mueller's edition of Propertius of 1892—i.e. the edition on which Pound based his poem" (47). Thomas Drew-Bear offered similar commendation. Other reviewers, in keeping with the tenor of the time, praised Sullivan's critical detachment. Hugh Gordon Porteus observed that Sullivan was "not preaching to the converted, but addressing his fellow-academicals," and that he "simply provides a practical commentary, as useful for the *Homage* as Mr. Dembo's 'critical appraisal' is for Pound's pseudo-translations of the Confucian Odes." Philip Hobsbaum also praised Sullivan's presentation of Pound's and Propertius's poems on facing pages, but was readier than Porteus to praise Sullivan's victory over "the scholars . . . fighting a rearguard action against . . . creative translation." Sullivan's book remains, more than fifty years later, a nearly definitive work, and in its day helped demonstrate that thoroughgoing critical principles could turn not only against casual prejudice but also against prevailing academic assumptions.

Apostate Dignity

The increasing concern of Pound criticism in the sixties with its own professional status is nowhere more evident than in the many insistent disassociations of scholarly work from "readers' introductions." In this regard, Noel Stock was less singular than emphatic, writing two books about Pound—*Poet in Exile: Ezra Pound* (1964) and *Reading the Cantos: A Study of Meaning in Ezra Pound* (1967)—and editing another, all within a three-year period. Together, these books chart Stock's passage from youthful acolyte to scholarly apostate, a passage that culminated in Stock's *The Life of Ezra Pound* (1970). Biography always holds pride of place in Stock's work, and *Poet in Exile: Ezra Pound* is no exception. At the same time, as poet-critic Charles Tomlinson notes, Stock was developing "a new personality": "not so long ago he was content to write a prose that imitated the worst element of Poundian belligerence," but now he aspired to scholarly dignity ("Tone," 47). Setting the tone for his books to follow, Stock inveighs in *Poet in Exile* against insufficiently professional criticism: "the aim of this book is not to explain Pound's work but if possible to cut through the tangle of opinions, favourable or unfavourable prejudices and the various irrelevancies stemming from Pound and others, which prevent many a reader of goodwill from getting at the best of his work" (vii). Stock saw his book as a restorative to "the disease of modern criticism (or criticism crossed with biography)," a disease which he tellingly took to be a persistently sentimentalized version of literary history. Consequently, Stock framed his object as "eliminating the biographical confusion which overlays [Pound's] essential work" (ix). These statements mark an interesting historical moment that in part preserves pre-Bollingen patterns of critical behavior, and in part could have come only after Bollingen. The idea that biography is a corrective to criticism is an old one, even to the extent that biography can be the key to "reading"; but the alarmed sense that criticism is insufficiently professional bespeaks how thoroughly formalist tenets had come to inform the writing of criticism.

The following year, Stock edited *Ezra Pound Perspectives: Essays in Honor of His Eightieth Birthday*, a volume which included contributions from a handful of scholars like Donald Gallup, Kenner, and Peter Whigham, but which predominantly featured the work of other artists, like Conrad Aiken, Ernest Hemingway, Wyndham Lewis, Hugh MacDiarmid, Marianne Moore, and Allen Tate (who returned to the story of the Bollingen Prize). Offered as a gift to Pound, the book is chiefly remarkable today for its difference of tone from those Stock wrote immediately before or after.

The title of Stock's *Reading the Cantos: The Study of Meaning in Ezra Pound* is portentous, suggesting less perhaps than the book actually delivers, because the book is not about the nature of "meaning" in Pound, but proposes, after all, "the" meaning of Pound's work. Stock begins by challenging the influential celebrations of Pound's work by Kenner, Davie, and Dekker, all of whom Stock finds guilty of supplementing the "deficiencies" of Poundian texts from their own imaginations. Nobody, Stock protests, "has yet shown any signs of understanding" the *Cantos*, and so "our present task is not then to discuss the obscurities of a text in the main already understood, but to work out what the text means" (vii). What Stock understands is that, due to an "inability in the *Cantos* to write sustained passages, or to join the passages together, musically or any other way, into larger units," Pound "does not write poems, but poetry. . . . The *Cantos*, as a result, do not constitute a poem, but a disjointed series of short poems, passages, lines and fragments, often of exceptional beauty or interest, but uninformed, poetically or otherwise, by larger purpose" (116–17). What distinguishes this unambiguous position from earlier attacks on Pound is that Stock's critique presumes to be formal in nature; Stock does not attack Pound's politics or person, but his poetry.

This second of Stock's critical studies of Pound was warmly received by critics unsympathetic to Pound, or to the aggressively academic New Criticism that championed him. Indeed, it received notices in several important organs. Louise Bogan, writing for the *New Yorker*, found Stock's work "long overdue and distinctly refreshing"; Stock exhibits, she said, "a total lack of that glum and dreary pedantry that disfigures so much of the uninspired commentary issuing from the academies yearly, and *en masse*" (134–35). Bogan was not, of course, alone in thinking that any attack on Pound's new status as a canonical writer was necessarily an attack on professional criticism ("pedantry"), and this perception largely explains the divided reception of Stock's work. The opposition was not just between academic and non-academic critics, but also between those in the academy who were sympathetic to Pound and those who were not. Critics on both sides of the latter opposition who regarded Stock's work as flawed nevertheless praised his preservation of professional standards. Reviewing for the *Journal of American Studies*, R. W. Butterfield observed that *Reading* enlarges on the final chapter of *Poet in Exile* (284–86). Butterfield found Stock's approach to be "authoritative," and contrasted it favorably with the work of Stock's fellow Australian, K. L. Goodwin. Although "one may dispute some of Mr Stock's fundamental aesthetic and metaphysical assumptions," Butterfield concluded, one must admire his ability to recognize flaws in *The Cantos* and to account for why they are there. G. A. M. Janssens embraced Stock's book for "documenting . . . what some of the most sensible 20th century critics suspected long ago" (584). Douglas Barbour agreed, and submitted that, "unlike many critics of the *Cantos*, [Stock] concentrates on the poetry and the poem." For Barbour, Stock's arguments about *The Cantos*' artistic failure are "convincing" precisely because he shows himself to be "levelheaded and very well read in the poem and the books that lie behind it" (551–52). For these reviewers, the ultimate criterion remained one of close-reading.

Other reviewers, however, sought something more. The anonymous reviewer for the *New York Times Book Review* appreciated Stock's ability to see failure in *The Cantos* even while acknowledging that Pound could still sometimes be *il miglior fabbro*, but nevertheless concluded that Stock "is short on long views. And when he does make generalizations they tend to be clumsy and unclear." This conclusion approximates the general response to the book. Reviewers from outside the growing circle of Pound scholars welcomed a genuinely *critical* and patient evaluation of his work, but felt that Stock's book was more serviceable than inspiring. As for Pound scholars themselves, Stock's books ultimately drew little engagement, and had little impact on the work of future toilers in the field.

Reaching for Professional Rigor, Again

The reception of Donald Davie, perhaps the greatest of the second wave of professional Pound scholars, was very different: his first book, *Ezra Pound: Poet as Sculptor* (1964), received mixed to plainly unfavorable notices, but was nevertheless eventually established as a landmark study of enduring importance. That it was so established bespeaks in large part Davie's subsequent critical successes, but it also owes to Davie's sometimes pained sense of his own historical specificity. More clearly than anyone before him, he understood that the Pound controversy had changed, perhaps forever, the relation to poetry of readers and critics alike. "Pound has," he wrote, "made it impossible any longer to regard the poet as seer" (*Sculptor*, 242–43).

Nevertheless, within this broader change, Davie regretted that things had not changed more. In the preface to *Poet as Sculptor*, he found it "dispiriting to have to admit that the study of Ezra Pound's writings, if it has moved out of the pioneering stage, has only just done so" (v). What is striking about this opening is that, although thanking Kenner (for his book of fourteen years earlier) and Dekker, Davie still regarded Pound studies as beyond the pale of professional rigor: a sense that he shared with virtually every other contemporaneous Pound scholar. This situation is rather like that which Michel Foucault, in *The History of Sexuality*, described as "the Repressive Hypothesis" wherein "a society which has been loudly castigating itself for its hypocrisy for more than a century, which speaks verbosely of its own silence, takes great pains to relate in detail the things it does not say, denounces the powers it exercises, and promises to liberate itself from the very laws that have made it function" (I:8). The situation here is not of Davie's making, but is rather the continuing function both of the postwar professionalization of literary study, and of the particular way in which that professionalization was instituted. In other words, fifteen years later, the consequences of the Bollingen controversy were still working themselves out, and were still setting the terms by which the study of Ezra Pound could be conducted. Davie's take on Pound differs dramatically from Stock's. And yet, although their understandings of this phrase were mutually exclusive, both of them responded keenly to the perceived need for professional, "non-partisan" criticism.

Like Dembo (whom he does not mention), Davie begins by considering Pound's translations of Confucius, and moves on from there to reconsider the shape of Pound's career. But Dembo's review of Davie's book was resoundingly negative. He charged that the book lacked any "real unifying principle," and "is characterized by a series of arguments" only "occasionally related, and having a common denominator more in an attitude than a point of view" (88). The book offers, Dembo maintained, "little more than the isolated illumination" and is marred by much "that is either merely speculative or ill-reasoned" (89). Finally, however, although regretting Davie's "lack of rigor," Dembo judged that Davie's "comments are at least on the level of critical insight," which even when spurious "are not without a certain interest" (90). Given his severe criticisms, that judgment might seem surprising. It meant, however, that whatever the flaws of Davie's book as a book, his standards were nonetheless suitably professional.

In this conclusion, Dembo anticipated the responses of other reviewers. Gordon Grigsby, for instance, shared Dembo's sense that *Poet as*

Sculptor "at its worst, is piecemeal and thin," but nevertheless valued both Davie's "helpful specific insights" and also his "effort at a balanced view" (423–24). Edward Lucie-Smith similarly felt that Davie managed real criticism, avoiding the pitfalls of either damning or revering his subject (569–70). Sister Mary Cleophas pointedly observed Davie's virtues by contrast with much else that passed for "criticism" in the wake of Bollingen: "Florid, turgid, verbose are a few of the more uncomfortable adjectives that could justly be ascribed to some of Pound's nervous critics. In contrast, Professor Davie, who seems to be wholly devoted to Pound's poems, never indulges in the shrillness of those who seek to defend or to denigrate the expatriate American" (455–57). Whatever the implications of Cleophas's adjectives, Hugh Kenner, writing in *American Literature*, framed his praise very differently, implicitly proposing that critical detachment paradoxically brought the critic closer to the language of the poem. "Uneven but benevolent," Kenner called Davie's work, and commended him for having "learned his virtues from Pound himself." Kenner's appreciation for Davie's distinguishing Pound's "concrete actual" from the post-symbolism of Yeats and Eliot echoed Charles Tomlinson's review of a few months earlier. Indeed, this insight of Davie's came to be the most widely praised aspect of *Poet as Sculptor* (see, for instance, P. Le Brun's mention in a review of Goodwin and Stock, discussed below). But Tomlinson's praise went further, expressing his gladness that Davie "conveniently forgets the too absolute implications of his title and goes on to write a book which presents the most challenging account of Pound's oeuvre since George Dekker's" ("Tone," 49). In the most substantial review of *Poet as Sculptor* apart from Dembo's, Christopher Ricks established its importance as a historical occasion. "Davie's praise of Pound is far more convincing than anyone else's, for two reasons. First, that he actually discusses how Pound uses words and rhythms" and, second, because he is reluctant "to exculpate Pound, technically or morally." Ricks does offer that Davie is, if "not soft, softish" on Pound, but concludes that "the terms on which Mr. Davie correctly asks us to discover what is best in Pound, are by their nature an implicit admission of Pound's drastic limitations" (610).

Davie's book generated a great deal of discussion, but its terms remained demonstrably those set by what we might call "the treaty of Bollingen." The issue of professionalism informed both positive and negative reviews of Davie's book, and those who most praised it did so on the basis of his attention to formal detail. Those formalist grounds would not be available for the work of the Australian K. L. Goodwin, who sought another basis for gauging Pound's importance besides that offered by the Bollingen judges. *The Influence of Ezra Pound* set out to test the wide "belief that Pound has been the chief influence on American poetry this century, and one of the chief influences on British poetry," but ironically enough his attempt itself proved of little influence. Dembo gave it a grudging and qualified nod, submitting that Goodwin is "essentially a literary historian" (i.e., not a critic) and that the book must be "taken on its own terms." But P. Le Brun found much of the book "overstated," and dismissed "the final part" of it as "diffuse and marred by a parade of flimsy evidence" (235–38). R. W. Butterfield, in a review ostensibly of Noel Stock's *Reading the Cantos*, blasted Goodwin, finding his book void of "fresh insights" or "new information," "unexciting," and in its conclusion "a shambles." More pointedly, Butterfield attacked Goodwin's "apparent ignorance both of much recent critical writing upon Pound and of important areas of American poetry and poetics" (285). Butterfield's attack itself underscores the extent to which previous scholars had professionalized Pound studies, and the charge told on Goodwin because his book professed scholarly detachment.

In effect, Goodwin essayed to investigate Pound's relation to poetic tradition by looking for his impact on other writers. Meanwhile, other scholars took up the impact of earlier writers on Pound. In his second book on Pound, *Ezra Pound's Poetics and Literary Tradition: The Critical Decade,* N. Christoph de Nagy wrote the first study of Pound's prose: his subtitle "the Critical Decade" refers not only to the important decade wherein Pound's poetics developed from his last pre-Imagist volume (*Canzoni*, 1911) to that of *The Cantos*, but also to the fact that in that same period Pound emerged as a distinct and powerful critical voice.

Despite its venturing into uncharted critical territory, this book received less attention than did de Nagy's previous book. In the first of only two reviews, John Espey observed how de Nagy's topic was prepared by Eliot's introduction to *Literary Essays of Ezra Pound*, but suggests that no other critic had taken up this work because of Pound's own dismissal of academic criticism (577–78). Despite one or two cavils, Espey found that "de Nagy's omissions are minor, however, and his new monograph will become a standard reference." Reviewing for *English Studies,* Wallace Martin noted de Nagy's careful distinctions among the different kinds of criticism that Pound wrote, and praised de Nagy's demonstration "that Pound's poetics possess an unsuspected degree of coherence," as well as an acumen that establishes him as "a literary critic" deserving a "place alongside the better-known critics of the century" (86). From these reviews, one might have anticipated that the book would indeed "become a standard reference" (de Nagy, 578): that it did not testifies to the sea-change that would overtake critical discourse in the next decade.

In the meantime, Richard Ellmann's *Eminent Domain: Yeats Among Wilde, Joyce, Pound, Eliot and Auden* offered still further evidence of the increasingly important position of Pound studies in the academy. Ellmann's book explicitly locates Pound in the "eminent domain" of canonical modernism, relegating him neither to the role of unheeded Jeremiah in the wilderness nor to that of the crack-pot in the asylum. Ellmann's study of "influence," the "guilty acquisitiveness of talent," takes a wholly different approach to the matter than had Goodwin, as W. K. Rose remarked to Goodwin's disadvantage (415–16). Rose found Ellmann's chapters on Pound and on Auden "the most rewarding" of the book, "for almost obverse reasons": Pound and Yeats were very intimate, while Auden and Yeats "hardly knew each other." Ellmann's success owes to his "not forcing the issue" but setting up "a dialogue between two contrasting but related poetic attitudes" (416). Louise Bogan observed "the recent run on Pound," but nevertheless offered warm praise for *Eminent Domain*, which she found to belong "to that rare category of critical writing that provides continuous entertainment as well as varied insights from beginning to end" (134–35). The extra-academic appeal of Ellmann's writing remained, however, exceptional in Pound studies, and Bogan shared Rose's gratitude for Ellmann having resisted "the ugly jargon of so much American criticism" (Rose, 416).

Walter Baumann's *The Rose in the Steel Dust: An Examination of the Cantos of Ezra Pound* was brought out by the same press that had published de Nagy, but it is a book very different in kind. For one thing, Baumann explicitly set out "to find some of the reasons for the predominance of negative criticism of the *Cantos*," most of which strike him as having dismissed *The Cantos* "before even its basic scope is taken into consideration" (13). Such a goal might have expected cheers from other Pound scholars, but the method of Baumann's demonstration struck many as inadequate to the task. In contradistinction to de Nagy's inclusive, Germanic-style survey of a large body of work, Baumann purports, in Dembo's words, "to indicate the central themes that make the *Cantos* in general a unified poem. Pound's vision" (576). Baumann's purpose is to uncover in these themes a riposte to other critics who find the poem uneven and celebrate only particular lyrics. But, pointing out that Baumann himself implicitly proceeds in the same way, explicating only Cantos IV, LXXIV, and LXXXII, Dembo concludes that while "explicating the explicable is worthwhile, . . . the assumption that everything in the *Cantos* is justifiable or explainable in terms of a great, hidden theme is one that can turn the critic into an alchemist" (567). Dembo's reservation anticipated the breakdown of formalist assumptions that was, even in 1967, already beginning. It would, however, be another fifteen years before published studies began to reflect the limits of praxis. In the meantime, monolithic and masterful, Kenner's *The Pound Era* would push modernist-formalist precepts further than they had ever been tested before, striving for a model of unity that could take in the extraordinary complexity of Pound's *Cantos*. And before that apocalyptic brilliance would come an anticipatory wave of publication. Pound studies seemed at last securely institutionalized, but the very process of that institutionalization was to undermine the critical models on which it depended.

In the remaining four years prior to the publication of Kenner's *magnum opus*, no less than ten book-length studies were published in the United States and Britain. These years were, in certain respects, prefiguring a golden age of Pound Studies: the hostile voices of the early fifties had either been silenced or proven (for academic audiences, at least) to be irrelevant to the concerns of scholars; the new, theoretically-charged voices that would challenge the very rules of the game had yet to be raised. The reservations of a few voices like Dembo's might have been accepted as family squabbles—and for all intents and purposes were just that, insofar as these disagreements no longer held the attention of readers outside "Pound Studies."

The comparative security of Pound studies as professional business is evident from the appearance of studies that reverted to such unmistakably extra poetic concerns as Earl Davis's *Vision Fugitive: Ezra Pound and Economics*. Indeed, Davis returned to paths untrodden since Watts, as Davis's series of proleptic defenses acknowledges. Basically, Kenner's disapproving shadow is in the early parts of the book everywhere to be seen. Kenner is the only Pound scholar mentioned in Davis's acknowledgments:

> Professor Hugh Kenner criticized an early version of this book with microscopic intensity, and his notation of weaknesses and faulty exegesis was of great assistance. He has generously allowed me to thank him for his criticisms, and he asks that no one be allowed to get the impression that he is responsible for anything said in the book. (xiii)

If this gratitude for so reluctant a sanction seems over the top, later evidence suggests why. Davis avers that "the main theme running through *the Cantos* is [Pound's] economic interpretation of the meaning of history" (26), and does so after suggesting that it is "typical of the trend of modern criticism that a writer of the capacity of Kenner has found it more interesting to describe . . . technique . . . rather than concentrate on what Pound is trying to say" (6). In effect, Davis returns to the postwar conflict over the proper emphasis of criticism, form or content. His technique is no more sophisticated than had been Watts's, and later attacks on formalism by critics versed in poststructualist theory would soon render his work obsolete. Nevertheless, the historical moment had changed sufficiently so that Pound studies could admit if not really welcome his presence. Davis's dissatisfaction with formalist orthodoxy not surprisingly extended also to the question of audience; his foreword begins by addressing "what audience does the critic write for? Will it be specialists in the field covered, or some part of the general public, or a combination of readers with varied kinds of interests" (vii). Davis settles for the last.

Reviewers, however, did not find that settlement adequate. Joseph Schwartz faulted Davis for making "almost no attempt to relate Pound's ideas to their final expression in the poems. . . . *Vision Fugitive* is clearly not a work of literary criticism, and I doubt if it would be regarded as a significant book in economics" (46). Marion Montgomery was only marginally more accepting. Observing that a study of Pound's economic arguments "was long overdue," he nevertheless found the book "insufficient": "this study clearly represents much labor, but it displays too little of the art and scholarship demanded by its subject" (508). Montgomery at once wanted more discrimination among related ideas and a more conscientious attempt to examine how those ideas inform the poetry. Michael Hamburger, the reviewer for *TLS*, expressed similar disappointment. Although praising Davis's "refusal of mystification," and appreciating his suggestions of similarities between "Pound's ideal economic system and the New Deal," the reviewer nevertheless found Davis guilty of his own kind of apologetics: the nature of Pound's hatred for Roosevelt and even for Keynes "speak for themselves . . . Pound's rhetoric was a contradictory mixture of doctrinaire rant and populist optimism" (*TLS*, 925–926). It was thus to be Davis's fate to have described a scholarly project that readers denied he had himself realized.

This review from *TLS* bears special mention, because in and of itself it suggests much about the rapidly expanding field of Pound studies. The anonymous critic tackled quite a job, reviewing no less than eight recent books about Pound—one of them Eva Hesse's collection of essays by several hands—and two new editions of works by Pound: all of this at a time before it was customary for every assistant professor in the United States to publish at least one book for tenure. Hesse's *New Approaches to Ezra Pound: A Coordinated Investigation of Pound's Poetry and Ideas* comprised fourteen essays, not including her introduction; her volume was followed less than a year later by William Cookson's special issue of *Agenda* "In Honour of Ezra Pound's Eighty-Fifth Birthday"—a collection of eleven pieces by friends and critics sympathetic to Pound, and, about the same time, J. P. Sullivan's collection, *Ezra Pound: A Critical Anthology*. Sullivan's collection was more academic than Cookson's, but less so than Hesse's, his thirty-eight entries joining new essays with short reprints from Pound's contemporaries, like W. B. Yeats, F. S. Flint, or T. S. Eliot. Hesse's book attracted the most reviews, and the response of Bernard Duffy, writing in the *South Atlantic Quarterly*, characterizes all: "Hesse's work, despite the broad claim of its title, is essentially a collection of essays on Pound reflecting the critical trends of the 1960s. In that sense they are 'new,' but in no sense that I can discover, except that of their assembly here, are they much like a 'coordinated investigation of Pound's poetry and ideas'" (298). Duffy seemed to want a single narrative to the volume, regretting the very nature of the book as an academic collection. Some forty years later, the kind of book that Hesse edited has become a staple of academic exchange; indeed, presses approach scholars asking them to produce just such volumes—ones that can exemplify contemporary critical trends. In other words, their heterogeneity becomes a selling point. Despite Duffy's concern, in retrospect it is clear that, more so than Sullivan's more traditional collection, Hesse's book was groundbreaking. Duffy himself observed that Hesse's collection was "symptomatic of [the] *academic* concern" that now invested and invested in Pound's work. It managed both to take stock of the state of the profession and served as a harbinger of things to come. That second aspect of Hesse's book was not recognized in 1969, but virtually everyone saw that the profusion of new books about Pound represented big changes both for Pound studies and for academe in general.

Academic Subdivisions

Inevitably, perhaps, with Pound having been established as a legitimate academic field, that field began to subdivide into special areas. Between 1968 and 1969, four books appeared on the "young" Pound—a Pound in whom both greatness of achievement and enormity of error still lay off in the distance. We might note first Wai-lim Yip's *Ezra Pound's "Cathay"* (1969), which had been listed in *Dissertation Abstracts* at the end of 1968. It proved a mostly well-received study which, reviewers noted, helped amplify the case made earlier by J. P. Sullivan for Pound's value as a translator. L. S. Dembo, however, was impatient with Yip's apparent unfamiliarity with previous Pound studies—Yip wasn't apparently aware of where and how his work related to Sullivan's. That kind of objection would become increasingly familiar in the years ahead. The other three books to address Pound's early work were more focused on his "poetics"—much the critical shibboleth of the day. The earliest of these was Thomas H. Jackson's *The Early Poetry of Ezra Pound* (1968). Joseph Schwartz, writing for *Spirit,* commented tellingly that Jackson examines Pound's early poetry "only in order to discover Pound's poetic theories; the work is not an explicit examination of the poetry for its own sake" (44). That last prepositional phrase suggests something like an exposed nerve, but Schwartz nevertheless regards Jackson's book seriously, even if he is somewhat suspicious of Jackson's effort (an effort developed further in the next two decades by scholars like George Bornstein, Robert Langbaum, and Thomas Parkinson) "to see Pound as a kind of romantic poet" (45). Other reviewers were struck by Jackson's emphasis on Pound's "relationships" to other poets. John Fraser, in the *Dalhousie Review,* opened by declaring that "this is a first-rate book on an unpromising subject" (563). Although most of the poetry on which Jackson writes "is bad," Fraser noted, "he is not out to resurrect it." In other words, Fraser sounds the same note as Schwartz, but in a different key altogether. For Fraser, the issue is that Jackson's thorough examination leads to dubious conclusions; Jackson shows that Pound's "poetics" is "an absolute witches brew of questionable assumptions and procedures." In thus arming Pound's detractors, Jackson failed to attract the support of many of Pound's friends. Wallace Martin leveled a less interpretive charge, the charge that accounts for Jackson's comparative absence from future debates: Jackson made no reference "to any book on Pound published in the last ten years," not even to scholarship he must have known. In particular, Martin complained, "Jackson discusses many topics previously and more adequately discussed by de Nagy" (172). If Pound scholarship is to continue its development, Martin counseled, it is crucial for scholars to know the work of their predecessors.

Hugh Witemeyer's *The Poetry of Ezra Pound: Forms and Renewals, 1980–1920* fared better, and established him among the important Pound scholars of the next generation. Merle Brown was perhaps the least enthusiastic of his reviewers, submitting that "the main usefulness of Witemeyer's book lies in the information it gives about the early poems which Pound rejected from [his two volumes of 1908]" (414). Brown's major complaint, of a kind with Schwartz's complaints about Jackson, was that "Witemeyer makes no effort to distinguish Pound's poetics and criticism from his poems. In fact he treats many of the early poems as "criticism in new composition." Thirty years later, this aspect of Witemeyer's book seems prescient—as well as being in keeping with Pound's own sense that the creation of a new work is the best form of criticism. Dembo noted the inescapable comparisons that must be made between Witemeyer's book and de Nagy's, but appreciated Witemeyer's being "much less ponderous than de Nagy and [that] he is able to bring into sharp focus the patterns underlying Pound's criticism and poetry" (112). John Espey, distinguishing between criticism and scholarship, declared that "Hugh Witemeyer's study is clearly part of the advancing Pound scholarship, for it meets the work of the poet on its own terms, which is not to say that Mr. Witemeyer is in any way lacking in critical insight" (403). For Dembo, the basis for Witemeyer's success lay in his aspiring to "more expository than judicial" aims: that, primarily, is the difference between scholarship and criticism. Bernard Duffy exercised similar distinctions in his review for *South Atlantic Quarterly.* Of the six new books about Pound published in the last year alone, he noted, "all are symptomatic of academic concern"; some of these authors are "interpreters," some are "exegetes," but all are academic—all are *scholars* (298).

This same tone informed contemporaneous reviews of Herbert N. Schneidau's *Ezra Pound: The Image and the Real.* As Leon Surette notes, Schneidau's study was "a J. Hillis Miller-inspired examination of Imagist rhetorical theory and practice" that introduced many of the concepts and persons Surette himself would discuss at length in his *Birth of Modernism*, published much later, in 1993 (10). At the time, however, reviewers showed considerably less interest in Schneidau's intellectual warrants than they did in his professionalism. In their reviews, Kingsley Weatherhead and Elizabeth Wright all returned to a common theme of late-sixties reviewers of Pound studies, pausing over Schneidau's interest in Pound's poetics and taking that interest as a sign of the maturity of Pound studies. This same emphasis was noted by Leonard Casper, who wrote an approving review, opened by observing that twenty years had passed since the Bollingen furor, and that the time had come when, "properly manipulated, Pound could easily be recovered . . . as a prophet who pulled down the vanity of Western pretensions. Schneidau, however, has preferred understanding Pound to judging or using him" (301). Casper could not but approve, but he clearly held some regret for a road not taken. Like everyone else, Frederick Sanders praised Schneidau's emphasis on Pound's poetics, and judged his book the best of the recent spate of studies devoted to Pound's early development.

In that comparative judgment Sanders included Daniel Pearlman's lyrical *The Barb of Time: On the Unity of Ezra Pound's Cantos,* a book for which he nonetheless expressed genuine admiration. Sanders's omnibus review of contemporary Pound scholarship, "The View from the Dinghey," is itself a notable accomplishment of contemporaneous Pound scholarship. Steady in tone and sober in perception, Sanders was conscious that his facing a stack of *nine* books—only four of which were also among the eight books reviewed in the *TLS* review of the previous summer—to review was itself a sign that the nature as well as the quantity of Pound studies was changing. His comments about Pearlman gave him an opportunity to reflect broadly on how new professional techniques were enabling critics to essay Pound's accomplishments in ways unavailable to an earlier generation. What this meant is clear in what he says about *The Barb of Time:* "Mr. Pearlman . . . is quite aware of the case that can be made by critics who take what he calls a 'disintegrative' view of the poem. . . . [His own] view is 'integrative'. He asserts that meaningful structural patterns, thematically united are there to be discerned" (449–50). Pearlman's stress on integrative pattern not only contended with those critics who treated Pound's work in convenient piecemeal: it might also, in retrospect, be seen as a caution against another kind of source study contemporaneously represented by K. K. Ruthven's *A Guide to Ezra Pound's "Personae" (1926)*. This isn't so much to say that Pearlman did not welcome that kind of source identification as that his book implicitly cautions against the uses to which such identification might be put.

Where a critic like Davis tried unsuccessfully to contextualize Pound's engagements of economic theory, Pearlman aimed to discover in *The*

Cantos the form given to timeless wisdom. Indeed, some reviewers complained that Pearlman showed little consciousness of the contemporary context in which and for which he was writing. The *TLS* reviewer, Michael Hamburger, found Pearlman's approach programmatically antihistoricist and suggested that Pearlman takes Pound so "seriously as a thinker on religion, Western culture, the Renaissance, and ethics in general" that "sometimes it is hard to tell if Dr. Pearlman is merely describing Pound's view of things, or his own" (926). Writing for *Thought*, Leonard Casper saw Pearlman's work in more positive terms, noting that whereas other attempts to discern the unity of *The Cantos* typically took narrative form, Pearlman pursues only a "thematic" unity. Casper hoped that Pearlman would entice other critics back from the "minute observation of the trees long enough to reconsider the forest" (615). A. K. Weatherhead, in *Criticism*, strikes a similar note. For Weatherhead, Pearlman's great strength lay precisely in his not surrendering "the attempt to see [*The Cantos*] whole," and his resisting the lately popular impulse merely to swim "back to the wreck, as it were, only to salvage the ship's biscuits or the carpenter's tools" (359). Weatherhead's metaphor invites pause and suggests that by the late sixties many readers felt that the great postwar critical project had run aground, individual readers—like so many Crusoes—being left to salvage from it whatever they could. Perhaps in this way, Schneidau granted that Pearlman's study "is one of the most ambitious of the recent Pound studies," but sounded a generally consensual view in finding that the book "is disappointing in these claims" (598). Schneidau avers that "by accepting challenges to show the 'form' in the kaleidoscopic *Cantos* Pearlman gives away much to his opponents, and possibly dissipates some of his energies." After all, Schneidau asks, could anyone show the "true structure" of *Canterbury Tales*? Classifying Pearlman's book as an "apologetic" (a perhaps inevitably recurring charge in the history of Pound criticism), Schneidau considers that its arguments are at last "Procrustean," trimming the unruly heterogeneity of *The Cantos* to suit its own integrative model.

Although Pearlman's own reading of fundamental time patterns in *The Cantos* would not itself set the precise terms of critical argument, his book in a certain way summed up the critical progress of the previous decade and revealed the major critical context of the next. *The Barb of Time*, as Thomas Whitacker remarked in *Modern Philology*, was among the first studies to make a persuasive case for "major form" in *The Cantos*. Moreover, it moves beyond identifying aspects of *The Cantos* that seemed ready-made to meet prevailing academic tastes and standards, and suggests instead that in failing to appreciate the scope of Pound's achievement the academy was failing itself. That other critics like Schneidau blamed Pearlman for not living up to his own ambition only testifies to how quickly things were changing. It was only a short step from here to the magisterial and sometimes even condescending reprimands of Hugh Kenner's magnum opus—and to the thunderous reception that met his claims about "the Pound Era."

The last major book to be published prior to *The Pound Era* was Christine Brooke-Rose's *A ZBC of Ezra Pound* (1971), a book that—as the review in *TLS* by Eric Homberger observed—attempted to offer a non-academic reader's guide to *The Cantos* (624). Brooke-Rose believed that it is unnecessary for new readers (who she calls "reader initiates") of Pound to have a particular grasp of his facts and conclusions; rather, she proposes, the understanding of Pound's method is the only necessary guide. Thus, the title "ZBC": the order of individual details almost doesn't matter. That Brooke-Rose's position was implicitly rejected by Pound scholars is evident from the appearance of *Paideuma* the next year, and both Edwards and Vasse's *Annotated Index* and ultimately Terrell's two-volume *Companion to The Cantos* (1984). Moreover, Brooke-Rose cites the Parisian thinkers of the day—Kristeva, Derrida, and Lacan—rather than the panoply of thinkers proffered so often by Pound himself, and by his advocates: Agassiz, Frobenius, Douglas, Confucius, etc. So it was that Homberger opened his *TLS* review by submitting that "Christine Brooke-Rose writes a highly personal mixture of criticism and advocacy. In both cases she arrives at fundamentally conventional conclusions by a most remarkably idiosyncratic path" (624). Brooke-Rose's modest aim was to orient readers to the dazzling textures of *The Cantos* by providing contemporary intellectual reference points. She was in one sense at least Pound's true daughter, in that she imagined a non-academic readership. By contrast, Hugh Kenner's *The Pound Era*—also published in 1971 by the University of California Press—worked to reorient the contemporary world by showing the recurring presence of Poundian motifs. Kenner's text is dense, its manner paratactic and its size (606 pages) rivals that of *The Cantos* itself. But Kenner in 1971 still occupied the ground he had staked out in 1951: the proper way into Pound's work was through the halls of academe. The study of Pound is best left to professionals. Thirty years later, there is a kind of irony in the fact that it was Kenner who caught the attention of the intellectual world. But, as we will see, catch that attention he most certainly did.

5: The Pound Era and Its Monumental Companion, 1971–1985

One way by which a poem might be thought The most prevalent critical assumption among sympathetic readers of the Cantos has been that their significance and form are hidden in an iterative and kaleidoscopic pattern for the assiduous and intelligent to discover. This assumption stems from Pound himself, but it was first articulated in Hugh Kenner.

—Leon Surette, *A Light from Eleusis*

The Pound Era

THE CONFIDENCE THAT FORTY YEARS AGO enabled Hugh Kenner to announce "The Pound Era" is almost unthinkable today. While it was Kenner's *The Poetry of Ezra Pound* (1951) that had first found the terms to successfully present Pound as candidate for academic status, *The Pound Era* (1971) attempted to define modernism with Pound at its very center. What is remarkable is not that Kenner failed, but that he came as close as he did to realizing at least part of his ambition. The twenty years that separated his two books is less than half of the time that separates *The Pound Era* from our own moment, but in many ways academe has changed less in these forty-plus than it did in the twenty years following the Bollingen controversy. *The Pound Era* was published at precisely the moment that poststructuralist criticism was beginning to shake the foundations of the Anglo-American academy, and though Kenner's paratactic presentation at the time struck many as partaking in that disruption of New Critical hegemony, it had in fact nothing to do with it. For all his stylistic pyrotechnics, Kenner was decidedly old school, still adhering to formalist insistences on the hegemony of the author's *text.* For all of his contextualizing forays into science, art, economics, and history, the emphasis of Kenner's title was on "Pound" and not on "the era."

Two decades into the next century Kenner's book still remains the benchmark against which all others are measured. Thus, in 2008, when reviewing the latest in a succession of unsatisfactory literary surveys of modernism for the pages of the *New Yorker* (which in 2007 had a decidedly un-academic circulation of 1.062 million readers), Louis Menand still closed with a reference to *The Pound Era.* Menand claimed that

"Kenner's title was deliberately ironic: the point of 'The Pound Era' is that a Pound era never happened. The hopes of the pre-war avant-garde, the artistic excitement of the years between 1908 and 1914, when the modernist movement spread throughout Europe, died in the trenches and the camps" (127). That the dreams of the pre-war avant-garde died, as Menand puts it, succinctly gathering the catastrophes of two world wars together in one phrase, "in the trenches and in the camps," is well said. But it would have been news to Kenner that Pound's dreams were irrecoverably lost. For Kenner, the point was that although we have yet to realize the impact of Pound's work, that realization would eventually and necessarily follow. Pound is, Kenner famously affirmed, "very likely, in ways controversy still hides, the contemporary of our grandchildren" (*The Pound Era*, 558). But Menand's critical revisionism is no more dramatic than Kenner's own. Indeed, *The Pound Era* established revisionism as the dominant tenor of Pound Studies.

Other unsympathetic reviewers like W. W. Robson or Michael Rosenthal also refused to concede Kenner the rightness of his title. Arguing the British standpoint in the *Partisan Review*, Robson resented the laurels being taken away from Eliot: not an "era" he maintained, but a "cultural milieu":

> Quite apart from the hostility aroused by his behaviour during WWII, Pound has never been generally accepted by the British cultural establishment as a considerable author in his own right, and Mr. Kenner's apparent claim for him might be more provocative over here than in America. [. . .] His attitude to Pound is one of almost complete acceptance; he seems to feel that exposition and explanation are enough to deal (by implication, no doubt) with the familiar adverse criticisms of Pound—formlessness, fragmentariness, sciolism, a truculent crankiness bordering on and sometimes shading into insanity. Mr. Kenner does not exactly deny these charges; nor does he offer an apologia for Pound's sins and follies as a man, but he banishes them to a remote periphery. (140)

It is all too easy to forget that Kenner's book was the apotheosis of twenty years of intensive scholarship. It was Kenner who institutionalized Pound studies in 1951, but he himself waited another twenty years before publishing a second book on Pound. It is, finally, unlikely that *The Pound Era*—at least as the critical phenomenon it was widely taken to be—could have been possible at any earlier moment. Robson may have been unaware of Kenner's previous books devoted to Eliot (1959, 1962), Joyce (1956), Lewis (1954) and Beckett (1961, 1962). His title did not simply express the admiration of an acolyte, but was the result of an evaluation process that had taken him twenty years since the publication of his first book on Pound in 1951. But Robson's review was significant in the invocation of "general culture"—the idea of the cultivated reader seemed to be still strong on British soil—it was in fact the same kind of reader envisaged by Cookson's magazine, *Agenda*, which was started at Pound's instigation in 1959. Robson felt that Kenner's book was too academic and left interested non-professionals outside his circle. This hypothetical common reader had to be the true target of any critical book. Robson concluded: "If Mr. Kenner's approach is the right one, Pound will remain a reader for aficionados only, whereas Eliot's best work seems to have already become part of general culture" (141).

Robson's assumptions about the identity of the Poundian critic/scholar as somehow derived from the poet's own personality and intellectual interests would haunt the era and re-appear in various reviews of Kenner's and Terrell's work during the 1970s. It was not that Kenner, as had Noel Stock before him, came to question his early admiration for Ezra Pound. On the contrary, that admiration had evidently and even programmatically grown. But whereas in 1951 Kenner had done as much as he could to allow Pound (as perceived by Kenner) to speak for himself, so that *The Poetry of Ezra Pound* was in large part a sequence of long quotations, in 1971 Kenner felt able to speak not so much for Pound as in his *own* Poundian voice. *The Pound Era* is written in an often dramatically paratactic style, with a kind of epic sweep worthy of the *Cantos* themselves. Michael North observes as much in *Reading 1922: A Return to the Scene of the Modern*, though he attributes Kenner's paratactic jumps to an "interest in science and technology [that] made it possible to link modernist literature with other disciplines advanced by experiment" (10). But it's hard not to see Kenner's style as an imitation of Pound's. It's not just the paratactic leaps but also a taste for the dramatic reveal and Romantic double irony. Kenner used the full implications of the ideogrammic method for his book, including the power of the vignette as luminous detail, leaving the interpretation to the latitude of the reader. One of these, on Eliot and the Stilton cheese (440–42), fully illustrated what in Kenner's opinion had happened to Eliot when he ceased to let Pound influence him and chose rather to obey the demands of the British establishment, which he represented so well.

These features inform Kenner's writing at its best, and also at its worst. Consider the closing three sentences of the chapter "Douglas." After suggesting analogies between the "Social Credit" economics of Major C. H. Douglas (which became one of Pound's causes after the First World War) and the writings of Thomas Jefferson, and after distinguishing these from the programs of the Fabians (in one deft parenthesis), Kenner closes: "Against which, *usura*. And by 1933 it seemed possible to suppose that Benito Mussolini understood these notions. Perhaps he did, in a way" (317). Kenner's own style here borrows strategies from Flaubertian "free-indirect discourse," moving without signposts from inside

Pound's head to outside. Historical retrospect ("by 1933 it seemed possible") merges with apologetics presented as objective judgment ("perhaps he did"), only slightly qualified in view of a dictator's crimes ("in a way"). As creative writing this is skillfully done; as critical writing, it is irresponsible. As a fusion of the two genres, it is, well, Poundian. If Kenner's fundamental moves are indeed today unthinkable, that is, of course, a tribute to his boldness of conception as well as to the strength of his convictions. A critic of exceptional power, and a stylist whose like appears in academe but rarely, other critics might (and did) follow his lead, but none could match his success.

Kenner's courage, skill, and ingenuity in writing so successfully in a style modeled on Pound's own, what Albert Gelpi called "Vorticist criticism" (502), created the first "classic" of Pound scholarship and the first complete textbook for the Pound student, roles that are unchallenged today, more than forty years later. But Kenner was not one to rest on his laurels. After the publication of his almost universally celebrated book, he began exchanging letters with a professor at the University of Maine, Carroll F. Terrell, discussing the desirability and possible qualities of a journal dedicated to Pound studies. In an extended tribute that Burt Hatlen published in *Paideuma* in 1997 with the title "Carroll Terrell and the Great American Poetry Wars" he pointed out the nature of his colleague's interest: facts and sources, rather than interpretations were what the times needed. Terrell initially thought that a journal dedicated to Pound would put "the facts" together in about ten years. However, the journal would naturally include criticism, which could not be reasonably extracted or separated from the documentary scholarship. Ten years—that was indeed a conservative estimate! *Paideuma* would be Pound's dedicated journal for thirty years, from 1972 until 2001. In Burt Hatlen's words, "Terry's journal would carry on the project initiated by Kenner's book—the project of persuading the literary world that Pound's poetry is central to our culture" (53). In view of this statement, the journal was defeated by the times. After the turn of the millenium, Hatlen conflated *Paideuma* with *Sagetrieb,* the journal dedicated to poetry in the Pound tradition, and opened it up to modernist studies in general, acknowledging that an author-based journal had no future. But *Paideuma* had an excellent run and accumulated a treasure trove of Pound research over the years.

Kenner and Terrell intended not only to offer a key to reading Pound, but to interpret modernism with Pound at the center. Their key would unlock not only the short period of brilliance in pre-First-World-War London, but the whole modernist era more broadly conceived, from Imagism to the Beats. Kenner proceeded to write on American modernist writers who chose staying at home over cosmopolitanism and exile. Since Pound's work was his criterion of value, Kenner was perhaps inevitably condescending towards the localist brand of American modernism and expressed it clearly in his follow-up book called *A Homemade World*. Terrell would take an interest in the Objectivists, but did so because he became convinced that their talents drew life from the Poundian fountain. Together, albeit in their very different ways, the two scholars would open a new era for professional Pound studies, close the door on the past, and restart them on a more solid foundation.

A Companion to The Cantos of Ezra Pound

Terrell supplemented his journal with energetic conference organizing and in-house publishing of Pound scholarship at the University of Maine at Orono, where he was employed. Whereas Kenner had been claiming that Pound was the primary modernist, giving students an axis for understanding the whole palette of changes and variants of modernism, Terrell's interest was more focused. If Pound is the father and initiator of both his contemporaries and his followers, what are his sources exactly, and how should scholars read him professionally? The existence of the "Explicator" section from the first issue of *Paideuma* onwards tells us that even if the actual project of creating a Companion to the *Cantos* was born at the 1975 Pound conference in Orono, Terrell had felt the need for such a work from the start and initiated the journal to gather about him the necessary body of knowledge to write it. He even mentions in his preface that since 1972 he had wanted to supplement Vasse's *Annotated Index* with glosses on the post-Pisan cantos. The 1975 conference was a catalyst, the right point in time when Terrell felt he was ready. As indeed he was. With immense commitment and discipline, he sat down to write the book and to coordinate the occasional assistance of other contributors, like Hugh Kenner, Eva Hesse, David Gordon, John Nolde, Ben Kimpel, and T. Duncan Eaves. By 1981, the first volume was ready, by 1986, the second volume was available. After ten years' work, the *Companion* stretched the resources of print culture to the limit. In his introduction, Terrell pointed out what the two volumes, hemmed in by the constraints of the 800-page ceiling he had set himself, had not been able to include: extensive quotations from sources, variant readings, detailed glosses, uncertain dates of composition (x).

Reviewers of the *Companion* did not hold back their criticism. While generally recognizing that the work was fundamental and supremely useful, they pointed out errors, doubted and questioned just about everything. Often the *Companion* was lumped together with other guides, like Cookson's *A Guide to the Cantos* (1985), which addressed a different reader—namely the general public that Kenner's reviewer W. W. Robson had had in mind, at least for the UK. By comparison with the *Companion*, Cookson's *Guide* fell flat—few commentators could see its use, although the benefit of a reading guide in handy format, containing just the minimal annotation required for a more informed general reader, should have been obvious.

In a review of both Terrell's and Cookson's volumes in the *Sewanee Review*, William Harmon issued the most trenchant rejection. His upfront praise for the *Companion* was transparent enough to leave the devastating criticism plain to see:

> Carroll F. Terrell deserves to be dubbed "Blessed" or "Venerable" for his work on Pound. We seem to be aimed at a stupendous variorum *Cantos*, which will be, in a technical sense, as unreadable as a variorum Spenser. For now—and this may be one of those blessings in disguise I've heard so much about—all we have is Terrell's heroic two-volume *Companion to the Cantos of Ezra Pound*. Benefit number one is that it wipes out any need for any other index or guide. Benefit number two is that it collects in fairly handy form most of what is important in the way of explanation. Benefit number three—maybe controversial—is that it undermines our confidence in Companions (and, as Harry Truman said, if you want a friend in this life, get a dog).
>
> By that smart remark I mean that we have here 10,000 glosses, and at least 5,000 of them involve what looks like an error of some sort on Pound's part. These are not incidental flyspecks, nor are they something Pound started lapsing into when he lost his mind the first time. They seem to be built in to the fabric of the work, almost as if saying aloud and repeatedly, "This 'Ben' or 'Muss' or 'M.' cannot be drained into a pan labeled 'Benito Mussolini, 1883–1945, and so forth.'" So many of Pound's exotic references work less as tourist traps than as booby traps that I think he must have meant for them to be that way and that no *Companion* will ever be even approximately correct. With poems other than *The Cantos*, Pound had ample opportunity to correct errors, but he seldom did so. I think that a warning label ought to be put on all guides, indexes, and companions, lest readers think that that is the only way to read. Poems ideally ought to be celibate and isolated: if they need companions they're either archaic or just plain bad. But we have Terrell's *Companion* now, and there's no use complaining about it. Reviewers and correspondents will surely be flooding *Paideuma* with corrections. (633)

While Harmon himself went on to identify errors, as was to be expected, he had more political objections that seemed well-taken—Terrell's "tap-dancing" tendency to excuse Pound's use of terms like yidd, kike, goyim, and wop, and the gliding over their pejorative implications. Other reviewers, like Anthony Woodward, also noticed that "even Pound's wildest or nastiest vagaries tend to be smooth-talked into an unobtrusive corner"

(127). Terrell, no less than Kenner, left himself wide open to accusations of partisanship. Testimonies and comments about him stressed his friendliness, his energy, and his will to action as modeled on Pound's personality (McDowell 74).

Harmon concluded that what readers should strive for is a poetry liberated from scholarship: "The center of Pound is poetry, on its own, free of biography, ideology, and annotation; away from that center the reader encounters a phalanx, all marching to the beat-beat-whirr-pound-thud of an indifferent drummer" (639). Other reviewers, like Jim Powell, while being far more charitable, suspected that the poem is irreducible to its exegesis: after every allusion had been clarified and all the sources studied, the poem would continue to have zones of shadow that would not be amenable to explication. That was another way of saying that the *Companion*, while being the result of a laudable intention, missed its target, that the very idea of explication through annotation was misguided.

Peter Makin, in *Modern Language Review*, clearheadedly observed that the *Companion* was a work in progress, a body of knowledge that no sooner published will need to be updated. While correcting a few errors he had discovered, Makin did not lump them together, but distinguished among Terrell's contributors: Hesse and Gordon better than Grieve, the translator from Greek better than the one from Latin. For Makin, corroborating Powell's observation, "the worst fault is a recurrent imprecision of thought: thought about what the poem's words mean, thought about what the reader needs to be told in order to make him understand them, thought about the meanings of the words the commentator himself is using" (435).

Finally, Sally Gall in her review questioned the very ideology that had stood at the foundation of Terrell's activity as an annotator: his interpretation of *The Cantos* as a great religious poem. Gall warned readers about glosses that looked "overly long or skewed" (595). While it was evident that every scholarly project of this kind had to have a unifying ideology behind it, it was not obvious that Terrell's integrative theory about the *Cantos* was the right one and thus produced an accurate balance of information across the whole *Companion*.

The critical objections to the *Companion* were right: indeed, we should not read a poem with annotation in hand, should not constrain it with a unifying theory, should not freeze it to our state of knowledge at a particular time. However, in view of the value we assign to it today as the fundamental textbook on *The Cantos*, these criticisms look like the protests of people used to candles when electricity was installed. The light is too bright: too much information, some of it unnecessary, too much detail, most of it disturbing to the quiet reading which should be alert only to the beauty of the verse. The light was harsh indeed but it instantly proved indispensable and divided two eras of scholarship as sharply as a knife. To subsequent generations, studying *The Cantos* without the *Companion* looked like the Dark Ages indeed.

The Classics of Scholarship in the 1970s

And yet. Scholarship had been possible in the candle-lit era, and Kenner's two books on Pound were not the only classics that the pre-*Companion* period produced. Other scholars, while focusing on a part or area of Pound's output, were also grand scale—the 1970s saw much work done that was totalizing in its ambition, aiming at a definitive statement either on the whole, or on parts or periods of Pound's oeuvre. James J. Wilhelm's *Dante and Pound: The Epic of Judgment* (1974), Ron Bush's *The Genesis of Ezra Pound's Cantos* (1976), Leon Surette's *A Light from Eleusis* (1979), Wendy Flory's *Ezra Pound and "The Cantos": A Record of Struggle* (1980), Massimo Bacigalupo's *The Forméd Trace: The Later Poetry of Ezra Pound* (1980), Michael André Bernstein's *The Tale of the Tribe: Ezra Pound and the Modern Verse Epic* (1980) were systematic studies aiming at total and thorough explanations of *The Cantos.* In time, they built up the scholarly canon, the books that a novice must read in preparation for service in the Pound studies temple. While Kenner gave the necessary entry and mapped out the scholarly domain, these later studies provided instruments and keys for interpreting Pound's major poem. They were and still are the classics of scholarship: level-headed, informative, and illuminating in the ways they order the vast material of *The Cantos* and cut paths into it. What separated them from the ideologies and issues of the 1980s was the critical trust that the text was *there*, completed, and available for analysis. Pound's death in 1972 had ended scholarly and editorial attempts at correcting errors and providing a definitive edition that could in principle be sanctioned by the poet. New Directions and Faber then unified their editions of *The Cantos* in 1975 and stopped modifying the text. Kenner, who had been involved in the editorial revision process for two decades, could draw the conclusion that the dream of the definitive edition was over—what professional readers could aim for after 1972 was only a *Variorum.* The 1980s would indeed re-open the text and relate it to the vagaries of publishing and the specific qualities of the print medium. But during the seventies, the trust that the textual issues were closed underlay major works of interpretation that would not have been possible in this form otherwise. The text of the poem was indeed not complete—the so-called Italian Cantos 72–73 were still missing (they would be included in the New Directions edition in 1986). But this lack was not allowed to change the critical perspective on the others.

The trust that *The Cantos* could be explained through a single idea, whether this idea is the metaphor of "Eleusis" (Surette), or the concept of the epic (Bernstein), or "record of struggle" (Flory) would be radically challenged in the postmodern era. Their approaches derived from the notion of the integrity of the text and Pound's own affirmations of the unity of his poem. In 1981, Richard Taylor would start the project of the *Variorum* edition, thus insisting on the importance of re-opening the text. But until then the respite offered by the temporary closing of the textual question permitted the writing of important studies using the New Directions/Faber 1975 edition as it stood.

Although "objectivity" and "neutrality" were standard academic requirements during the period, scholars allowed personal attitudes and evaluations to come to the fore in their texts. Surette's open criticism of sections of *The Cantos* and Flory's evident compassion for Pound's plight gave these authors a textual substance and reality that was their own and separate from Pound's own personal and political choices. This was especially valuable, since in spite of the magnitude of their interest in Pound, these critics could not be accused, as Kenner and Terrell had been, of being Pound's re-incarnations, or fellow travelers. This was indeed a positive turn, a sign that the partisanship derived from the disastrous Bollingen event could be left to the past.

Politics, Again

All through the 1970s the scholarly community continued the general non-involvement policy with regard to Pound's political attitudes and activities, focusing their attention on the poetry and gliding with minimal friction on the slippery stones of Pound's fascism and anti-Semitism. The formalist stance, the attention to aesthetic, philosophical, and historical matters was almost universal. According to the bibliography compiled by Volker Bischoff, *Ezra Pound Criticism 1905–1985*, out of the 1,742 items published on Pound from 1970 to 1980 (books, articles, reviews, dissertations), only 31 dealt explicitly with Pound's fascism. Among these, three items stood out: William Chace's *The Political Identities of Ezra Pound and T. S. Eliot* (1973), Leonard Doob's edition, *"Ezra Pound Speaking": Radio Speeches of World War II* (1978), and John Lauber's article in the *Journal of American Studies*, "Pound's Cantos: A Fascist Epic" (also 1978).

Chace's book was praised by all reviewers for offering a valuable guide to the political thought of both poets as well as for the truth and moderation of its analysis. It was observed that Chace tended to favor Pound over Eliot, to make the former appear more "alive" and interesting. But Chace had done everything right: he was "unhesitant" and "unflinching" in his insights, connected Pound's attitudes to his upbringing, historical context, and prevailing currents of political and historical thought. Still, Walter Sutton remarked in a review published in *American Literature* that one side effect of the book was to make the reader aware that the very Americanness of both poets precluded them from having fascist political "identities" in the strict sense of the word:

> Despite the authoritarian bias of both Pound and Eliot and despite their sympathies with European reactionary and totalitarian thought, especially in the 1930s and 1940s, it is obvious that neither could be called a fascist in the literal sense. Though Pound foolishly idealized Mussolini and lent his voice to the stream of racist propaganda that disgraced the age, he was intellectually and temperamentally incapable of the subordination and discipline required by a totalitarian ideology. His cranky and essentially anarchistic individualism, recognized by Mr. Chace, can best be understood in the context of the tradition of the 100% Americanism that he imbibed with his mother's milk. (285)

Another of Chace's reviewers, J. P. Dougherty, concurred in this assessment and went even further to say that for both poets, politics in general was not a commitment to the real world but rather an eccentricity, an intellectual game, a "macrocosmic fabulation," a poet's politics.

But this assessment was ever harder to defend after Leonard Doob's 1978 publication of Pound's radio broadcasts, "*Ezra Pound Speaking*." The "macrocosmic fabulation" was put out there in the world, first on the air, then printed in a collection with critical apparatus and index—it was ugly indeed. Scholars and readers had been hitherto able to read just fragments of this vast corpus, some of them severely mangled by the effects of static combined with the sometimes ludicrous incomprehension of the transcribers. The scholarly response to the collection was surprisingly exculpatory: Richard Sieburth's review, especially, did not even consider the speeches as what they obviously were—real-time politics on Pound's part—but instead sought to discern the poetical effects that listening to his own voice had upon the refinement of his Uncle Remus persona and the composition of the *Pisan Cantos*. William Harmon in the *Sewanee Review* acknowledged the overwhelmingly anti-Semitic tenor of these texts but complained about the errors in the index and in the references to people in the critical apparatus. And Daniel Pearlman, who had made it his purpose to comment on Pound's anti-Semitism in the speeches, while being very clear about the irreconcilability of the poetry with the politics, remarked that the "hysteria of the time," the hatred that both the aestheticist elite and the "mob" felt towards the middle class, found a convenient scapegoat in the Jew. That Pound had also fallen prey to this current of the times was a tragedy.

Of all the texts that Pound ever wrote, one could have expected that the speeches were at the heart of a darkness that could not be forgiven or explained away, and yet it was. It was not that the scholars whose souls had been won over by the beauty of the verse had lost their moral compass. But all of them shared a baseline belief from which their assessment of the speeches derived. That basis of agreement was that the poetry needed to be rescued and the beauty understood. That was a ground to stand on even for critics like Surette or Bacigalupo, who openly criticized not only Pound's politics, but his poetry as well. What Frederic Morgan, the editor of the *Hudson Review* wrote in the wake of the Bollingen controversy still stood true thirty years after:

> Pound's anti-Semitism . . . is never given thematic importance or elevated into a structural principle; rather it takes the form of occasional slurs and contemptuous references. I find these slurs offensive, and I resent them; I should expect any civilized person today, Jew or not, to feel the same way. But whatever Pound's personal opinions may be, I do not find anti-Semitism central to his work. The slurs are there, real and not to be condoned, but occasional and peripheral. There is much more in the work, and more centrally located in it, that is valuable and beautiful. We read a writer, after all, for the good that is in him; no one who is willing to exert the intelligence which a careful reading of the *Cantos* requires will be taken in for a moment by the slurs, unless he be already a confirmed anti-Semite. Pound's work will continue to be valuable despite this fault, just as the work of other major writers (Dostoevsky is one who comes to mind has survived the same or similar ones). (Quoted in Jarman 361–62)

However, the times were changing, and a profound division split critics not only on the "marginal" issues of Pound's speeches, correspondence, or articles in the press, but rather on the very foundations of the palace, *The Cantos.* It was in this context that the British *Journal of American Studies* published John Lauber's article on the *Cantos*, subtitled "A Fascist Epic." Lauber argued the very opposite of the generally accepted point of view expressed by Morgan. His argument was that anti-Semitism and Fascism were not mere contingencies in the poem, but underlay its entire verbal structure. In other words, *The Cantos*, in whose beauty and significance supporters strongly believed, was structurally fascist, something that only Bacigalupo had asserted, but not entirely substantiated in his book *The Formèd Trace*. Lauber insisted on the figure of Mussolini as the most important hero of the poem and dwelt at length on the *Eleven New Cantos*, which he saw as an extension and development of Pound's infamous pamphlet *Jefferson and/or Mussolini*. The *China Cantos* were the elaboration of the political theory of fascism, with the basic confrontation between the adepts of Confucius and Lao Tze reflecting the conflict between the fascists as supporters of good government and the Jews who radically undermined it. The later sections of the cantos, *Rock-Drill* and *Thrones*, did nothing more than bring further support to Pound's political views of the 1930s, to the value of one-man rule. Pound was never "saved" by regret, remorse, or recantation, continuing to defend fascism in his poetry of the 1950s. Lauber's arguments have never been properly refuted to the present day. In retrospect, his discussion of fascism and anti-Semitism in *The Cantos* was prophetic, since it announced one important current of the 1980s: anti-Semitism would be the topic of the decade in Pound studies. The hard shell of the book containing the rebellious poem would be prised open to allow the flowing of the writing into its time and historical context. Scholars would no longer assume the ugly words were unhappy or tragic contingencies: they would turn them against the poem itself.

6: Pound Studies and the Postmodern Turn, 1980–1990

> *Those who practise deconstructive criticism typically see themselves as taking part in an activity which has much more to do with political change than with the "understanding" (much less the "appreciation" of what has traditionally been called "literature").*
>
> —Richard Rorty, "Deconstruction" (1995)

The Theoretical Turn: Derrida against the Traditionalists

As THE GRAND PROJECTS of explaining and interpreting Pound's major works were unfolding in the 1970s in the framework set by Kenner and Terrell, their critical certitudes would be challenged by the new emphasis on theory in American universities. This theoretical turn would have a major impact on the discipline of Pound studies, which at the beginning of the 1980s was in the process of creating and consolidating its canon of scholarship. Jacques Derrida's destabilizing influence was making itself felt not only in avant-garde philosophical circles, but also within the whole spectrum of the humanities. Its origin could be located in the symposium held at the Johns Hopkins University called "The Languages of Criticism and the Sciences of Man," organized by Eugenio Donato and Richard Macksey in 1966. Derrida's paper, delivered in French, was the legendary "Structure Sign and Play in the Discourse of the Human Sciences": it was translated and published in the volume of conference proceedings *The Structuralist Controversy* in 1970. Derrida's prestige and influence thereafter continued to grow, popularly mediated by gifted teacher-critics like Paul De Man, J. Hillis Miller, Geoffrey Hartman, Edward Said, and Joseph Riddel, who adapted his ideas from philosophy to literary criticism. A steady stream of translations and two new journals, *Diacritics* (launched in 1971 at Cornell) and *Glyph* (1977–1981, published by Johns Hopkins) opened the field for what came to be known as poststructuralism, a concept that in its narrower sense pointed to Derrida's work as it was published and translated, but in its wider acceptance referred to theory-oriented critical texts, including discussions of "fathers" such as Nietzsche, Heidegger,

Saussure and Freud, and "sons": Foucault, Lacan, Deleuze, Baudrillard, and Lyotard. By 1980, poststructuralism was fully established and yielding its critical fruits in new, theoretically informed perspectives on literature, posing the radical provocation of the new method of deconstruction to all traditional approaches.

Derrida's critique of the philosophical tradition initiated by Plato, which he called "metaphysics of presence," or "logocentrism," proposed to destabilize the primacy of the spoken word as privileged vehicle of truth, arguing that the latter is never fully *present* to consciousness but rather endlessly deferred from one signifier to another in a play of differences never reaching the moment of plenitude (complete overlapping between verbal expression and meaning). In this sense, spoken language has in it the nucleus and germ of writing, the locus of the speaker's absence: in writing, the absence of the originating consciousness who had put pen to paper made evident the illusion and deferral of "presence" (defined as the presence of truth to consciousness). Derrida asserted that the primary instrument of this illusion is phonetic writing—its ability to transcribe and mimic speech creates an illusion of the precise naming of the real, which he called "logocentrism." Derrida made it his philosophical task to expose and deconstruct this philosophical shibboleth: he made a place in his pantheon of luminaries for Fenollosa and Pound, who had been among the first to question its primacy:

> It was normal that the breakthrough was more secure and more penetrating on the side of literature and poetic writing: normal also that it, like Nietzsche, at first destroyed and caused to vacillate the transcendental authority and dominant category of the epistémè: being. This is the meaning of the work of Fenellosa [*sic*] whose influence upon Ezra Pound and his poetics is well-known: the irreducibly graphic poetics was, with that of Mallarmé, the first break in the most entrenched Western tradition. The fascination that the Chinese ideogram exercised on Pound's writing may thus be given its full historical significance. (*Of Grammatology*, 92)

Derrida was particularly interested in Fenollosa's own critique of phonetic language and its effects on thought and philosophy, as Roxana Preda detailed in her *(Post)Modern Ezra Pound: Logocentrism, Language, and Truth* (26–49). In the endnote to this passage, he proceeded to consolidate his point by quoting from the *Chinese Written Character as a Medium for Poetry*, insisting on Fenollosa's description of Chinese poetry as a script. Derrida's deconstruction of the connection between phonetic writing and the non-linguistic referent, and his favoring of alternative scripts like the ideogram, had the potential to make Pound's *Cantos* a privileged locus for studying pure textuality, a stage where the philosophical illusion of phonetic writing's advantage (telling the truth about truth in the clearest and most objective way) is challenged by the mystery of the ideogram, seen as a primal, non-arbitrary, natural writing relying on metaphor and interpretation, hence on deferral and provisionality of meaning.

Derrida thus encouraged his readers to take pleasure in following the textual play of signification and not try to limit it by assigning it either textual borders like beginnings and conclusions or a center outside itself. He made it a point to understand writing as a figural play that is independent of the origin and goals of meaning. Textuality was distinct from the conventional limits assigned to it, be they a certain genre, or the idea of "book" itself.[1]

Derrida thus questioned not only the idea of an outside, non-discursive center called "meaning" or "truth," but also modes of knowing such as the idea of origin, which served as a starting point for knowing and investigation. He argued that origins were caught in the mechanisms of language, which ever deferred them out of grasp. Ideas of endings were similarly elusive. If the margins and centers of texts were questioned, so was the authorial consciousness that produced them. Writing was by definition "absence": when a text was finished, it detached itself from its authorial "father" and could not be interrogated through an appeal to its moment of creation or to the consciousness that produced it. Writing, thus separated and estranged, stood on its own. An appeal to a virtual presence of authorial intention was an attempt to provide an arbitrary ground for the play of *différance*. The "critic," who was left without a validating presence of the author or even an illusion of it, was thus free to interpret without forever trying to approximate what the author may have intended. The origin of writing was lost and irretrievable: interpretation had no outside validity but stood on its own; hence Derrida's invocation of a sense of "play" and "jouissance" in writing in and for itself. Questions of correctness understood as reconstruction of "truth" or authorial intention were bracketed out—critical writing had the degree of autonomy that a literary text normally had. The difference between critic and author was undermined and effaced—both were writers, both produced texts, and a critic's prose was no less interesting and valuable in and for itself.

In order to adapt his own writing to the fundamental dislocation he proposed, Derrida practiced a new, decentered way of writing, using an array of non-concepts that would later consolidate into a jargon: "arché," "trace," "différance," "dissemination," "logocentrism," and of course, his most productive creation, "deconstruction." This last term was to be used as a pivot of decenterment: its proponents would use it to grasp a textual thread that had been marginal and neglected in order to unravel the settled meanings of a text and turn the tables on established interpretations.

Soon after Derrida's first interventions, the protests of the "traditionalists" made themselves heard in a series of confrontations with the Yale critics who were his privileged mediators in the US. Among the most widely acknowledged of these was M. H. Abrams's riposte to J. Hillis Miller in his essay "The Deconstructive Angel" of 1977. In that text, Abrams succinctly recapitulated the traditionalist position:

> 1. The basic materials of history are written texts; and the authors who wrote these texts (with some off-center exceptions) exploited the possibilities and norms of their inherited language to say something determinate, and assumed that competent readers, insofar as these shared their own linguistic skills, would be able to understand what they said.
>
> 2. The historian is indeed for the most part able to interpret not only what the passages that he cites might mean now, but also what their writers meant when they wrote them. Typically, the historian puts his interpretation in language which is partly his author's and partly his own; if it is sound, this interpretation approximates, closely enough for the purpose at hand, what the author meant.
>
> 3. The historian presents his interpretation to the public in the expectation that the expert reader's interpretation of a passage will approximate his own and so confirm the "objectivity" of his interpretation. The worldly-wise author expects that some of his interpretations will turn out to be mistaken, but such errors, if limited in scope, will not seriously affect the soundness of his overall history. If, however, the bulk of his interpretations are misreadings, his book is not to be accounted a history but an historical fiction. (426)

Abrams's first point reasserted the importance of the "center," understood as "something determinate" which is the outside point of reference of the literary text, a meaning that is the primary duty of the critic to understand and reveal. The second point stressed the importance of the author and his intentions. The critic's duty is to recapture and be faithful to both. Abrams also pointed out the utter separation between author and critic, a separation that is visible in a spectrum of differences: linguistic skills, purpose of writing, and order of importance. The critic is definitely not the author and should not assume he is producing "writing" on a par with the author. The third point dealt with the issue of the objectivity of interpretation and status of error. It matters whether the critic understands the author correctly or not. While any interpretation should be allowed a margin of error, its validity rests on correct, unbiased understanding. In order to hold on to the possibility of "truth" we must allow for the possibility of "error," and not just infinite play.

Pound Scholarship between New Criticism and Poststructuralism

Abrams called practitioners of these assumptions "historians." In Frank Lentricchia's account of the parties in his *After the New Criticism* (1980), the conservative positions were much more eclectic, consisting of "traditional historicists, the Chicago neo-Aristotelians, . . . Stanford moralists, myth critics of the Frye type, old line Freudians, critics of consciousness (such as were left), budding structuralists, and the grandchildren of the New Critics" (159), who all found themselves confronted with a theory that ran counter to all their epistemological certainties and attacked the very foundations of any intellectual pursuit aimed at truth and knowledge.

If we place Pound criticism of the pre-deconstruction era in the traditionalist camp, we would be hard put to find its place in Lentricchia's list. Were "Poundians" to be included into the New Critical tradition? Were they writing from a historicist standpoint or were they rather rooted in hermeneutics? While it would be incautious to assign Pound studies to a unique paradigm, since Pound scholars were methodologically eclectic and proceeded from unarticulated theoretical positions, it would also be useful to point out some coordinates of tacit agreement in the traditionalist (Poundian) camp. These points of agreement are spelled out in Abrams's points quoted above: first, a strong reliance on a pivot of meaning outside Pound's texts that served to critique the poet's work: when for instance Flory chose to entitle her study *The American Ezra Pound* (1989), she selected such an outside focus of interpretation by arguing that in spite of a life spent in Europe, Pound had stayed fundamentally faithful to his American roots. The center, pivot, or focus of interpretation could be "error" (Froula, 1984); "epic" (Bernstein, 1980); or "influence" (Beach, 1992).

Generally speaking, Poundian critics were intentionalists: they believed their mission was to recapture Pound's intentions in his writing; further, to understand his emotions, his preferred associations, even his unarticulated, unconscious desires. Reading authors like Eastman (1979), Froula (1984), Casillo (1988) and Flory (1980, 1989), we realize at once that the vocabulary of intentionalism is ubiquitous and unchallenged. All these authors were in no doubt about what Pound thought and felt.

Third, traditionalist Poundians believed in validity—they were not writing because they conceived themselves to be creative writers, but rather because they wanted to contribute to a better understanding of Pound's literary work. Their writing was not the outcome of unfettered imagination but the result of research, discovery, and understanding. Validity was established by recourse to primary texts, whether published or in manuscript. Kenner's *The Pound Era* had furnished a model of how intentionalism could brilliantly produce an influential critical work that was at the same time a piece of creative writing. But Kenner's stylistic aplomb was never followed and remained an exception to the general practice. Academic writing was distinct in its own domain and did not aim at turning itself into art.

The sum of these assumptions made Pound scholars resistant not only to deconstruction but also to the still-reigning paradigm of New Criticism and its critical method of "close reading." Certainly, reading for detail was desirable and fruitful, but the way it was applied and theorized by the New Critics did not quite fit Pound's work. Rooted in I. A. Richard's influential manual, *Practical Criticism* (1929), the fundamental assumption of the method was that poetic language was qualitatively different from discursive literal language. As Stephen Matterson has written, poetic idioms made use of the full spectrum of verbal manifestation, like the sound of the words, their powers of suggestion, ambiguities, and ironies—and this complete use of language made poetry autonomous from the world and supreme over a separate domain with a truth of its own (167). The mission of criticism was to describe this spectrum of differences and concentrate on illuminating such truth as only poetry could convey. It was ordinarily not envisioned that the method should build bridges to discourse, historical context, and authorial intention. These were irretrievable and irrelevant to understanding a poem. The New Critics believed in the autonomy of the aesthetic, and their formalist analysis was meant to recognize and enforce the division between poetry and non-poetry. This separation between poetry and history had been the argument that saved Pound's life and justified the decision taken in the Bollingen controversy. On the other hand, this kind of assumption was well-suited to the short lyric poem, in which a sophisticated, detail-oriented analysis could reveal a sense of structured, unsolvable ambiguity. Ultimately, the truth of poetry was never direct and univocal, but hopelessly enmeshed in and irretrievable from the web of interpretation that was seeking to draw it out. Close reading as understood by the New Critics had a few assumptions that poststructuralism would only need to develop and radicalize, but not deny. The result of "close reading" as a method was an aporia, an irony, a locus of undecidability. Like deconstruction, it had programmatically to abstain from using information external to the poem, like say, an author's letters, journalism, or diaries in order to "decide" or "conclude."[2]

Like deconstruction, New Critical close reading was anti-intentionalist, assuming that "design or intention of the author is neither available nor desirable as a standard for judging the success of a work of literary art" (Wimsatt, 3). If the poet succeeded in materializing his intention, it should be regained from the internal evidence of the poem. In his essay "Intentional fallacy," Wimsatt recurred to the example of Eliot's *Waste*

Land to argue how allusions and intertextuality could be successfully incorporated into a poem so that further exegesis beyond what Eliot himself put in his notes should be unnecessary. But an evaluation of Eliot's intentions, a reconstruction of the moment of writing, or a recourse to external evidence from letters and diaries were not to be regarded as providing standards against which the poem should be judged.

Finally, because the New Critical quest for unity of structure was focused on short lyrics, it invariably ran into problems when extended to long poems. The New Critics left out of their view not only Pound's *Cantos* but also Williams's *Paterson* and Hart Crane's *The Bridge*. Whenever they wrote about Pound, New Critics discussed theoretical issues like the notion of "structure" or "thought," or else concentrated on a few lines of verse and broke their relation to the context of the full poem.

This state of affairs explained not only the uniformly negative criticism that Pound got from the New Critics like Yvor Winters, Richard Blackmur, and Allen Tate, but also the confused critical scene, which could only provide a very limited sense of theoretical orientation to a scholar writing about Pound. The first obvious reason was that the autonomy of the aesthetic did not apply to Pound's poetry after the Malatesta Cantos. By quoting from Malatesta's letters and insisting that they should be regarded as poetry, Pound had broken the wall between poetry and prose, and a further wall between literature and discourse. It was clear that Pound, while being well aware of the truth of poetry ("Man gittin' Kulchur had better try poetry first," *GK* 121), never meant to keep it apart from the historical or political truth available in non-poetic, "non-literary" documents. His *Cantos* show again and again how the borderlines between "the truth of poetry" and philosophic, political, and economic truths are porous and frangible. Moreover, the aim of New Critical analysis—showing how the poetic contradictions resolved in structured ambiguity and irony—was difficult if not impossible to achieve with a poem such as *The Cantos,* where the accumulation of details could not be subsumed to a unified resolution, not even one marked by irony and paradox.

A "traditionalist" critic's intuition was that primary fidelity was owed to the assumptions operating in Pound's work as available in his texts. A Pound critic had to describe, interpret, and explain his author on his own terms, as revealed in the interaction between his criticism, the poem in question, and life. And Pound's convictions about the nature of interpretation changed over time. He used dramatized voices and personae that were supposed to be reconstructions of other poets, imaginary voices out of the past (letter to Schelling, July 8, 1922, *SL* 180); he compiled anthologies that were meant to present the manifestation and recurrence of literary ideas and techniques; and he described his music writing as an act of criticism (Dateline, *LE* 74). However, by the time of *Guide to Kulchur*

(1938), Pound had revised the view that the poet has to be utterly distinguished from the texts he produces: the goal of critical understanding was to recapture authorial intention and reconstruct the way it worked:

> How to see works of art? Think what the creator must perforce have felt and known before he got round to creating them. The concentration of his own private paideuma, whereof the shortcomings show, my hercules, in every line of his painting, in every note of his melody. (114)

Pound's declaration of the primacy of intentionalism was much more congenial to professional academics than his earlier experiments in critical method: masks, anthologies, and music were elusive and called for further interpretation, where no secure haven was possible. Even if his literary intentions were similarly elusive, the work of investigating a poet's private world was established and had a tradition in literary studies.

In spite of close attention to Pound's text, "traditionalism" in Pound studies was not close reading of the New Critical type. It had to go beyond the poetic text to configuring the artist's *paideuma*, assess its relation to its sources, to Pound's life, and to the historical context: it had to be historicist and contextual, hence committed to intentionalism as Pound had described it. At the same time, it had to aim at understanding extremely complex poetic structures objectively. Even if Eliot had included in the *Waste Land* its own exegesis in order to make his poem self-sufficient in relation to its sources, Pound had not done the same in *The Cantos.*

Moreover, Pound studies were committed to the traditional tools of the trade in literary studies and did not particularly see the need for theory, or philosophical methodologies. A close, detail-oriented reading of the text, archival research, the study of context and biography, the points of view provided by genre, the collation of poem and sources, all these were methods provided by the discipline of literary studies. Traditional Pound studies resisted the wave of deconstruction as they had implicitly resisted New Criticism. The requirements of the poststructuralist approach, consisting in a close reading of theoretical texts, familiarity with the major philosophers in the poststructuralist pantheon (Nietzsche, Heidegger, Husserl, Hegel), and successful application of deconstruction to Pound's texts were paths rarely followed, as we will see below. The main allegiance to a historical approach as summed up by Abrams, in what Christopher Carr called the "ascendancy of historicist assumptions in Pound studies" (478) would stand, though as we shall see, it was hotly contested. Throughout the theory wars of the 1970s and the so-called Culture Wars of the 1980s, Pound scholars continued to attempt to develop methodologies suitable to the heterogeneous and dynamic engagement of history that was, in one way or another, always a salient feature of Pound's work. Even works that were aware of the theoretical challenges of poststructuralism retained a generally intentionalist orientation, as with Massimo Bacigalupo's *The Formèd Trace* (1980), Wendy Stallard Flory's *Ezra Pound and "The Cantos": A Record of Struggle* (1980) and *American Ezra Pound* (1989), Reed Way Dasenbrock's *Literary Vorticism* (1985), or Christopher Beach's *ABC of Influence* (1992).

From "Book" to "Writing": The Textualist Turn and the Question of Error

Derrida's theory of writing, affirming the dissemination of meaning and the impossibility of assigning origins and endings to textual play, did not radically dislocate Pound studies from their historicist assumptions. Nevertheless, questions initiated in Derrida's writings percolated into the traditionalist domain, creating self-reflexive and self-critical stances from which it was possible to look back on the work already done and outline new positions that were informed by theory and could be fruitful for the interpretation of Pound's work.

A first line of reflexive awareness, visible in Christine Froula's study *"To Write Paradise": Style and Error in Ezra Pound's Cantos* (1984), concerned the agonistic scene that had emerged in the preceding decades, particularly manifested in the demand for definitive, error-free editions of Pound's poetry. John Espey's text of *Hugh Selwyn Mauberley* (1955, revised 1974) and J. P. Sullivan's of *Homage to Sextus Propertius* (1964) were textbook instances where negotiations with Pound as to the correction of textual errors had been inconclusive and unsatisfactory (Froula, 144–45). But this competitiveness between critic and poet came to a head in the desire to establish a definitive, author-sanctioned, error-free edition of *The Cantos.* This activity had started in the 1950s and ended in 1975, when Laughlin and Kenner agreed to stop making corrections to the text (Eastman, 28).

Although scholars tried to correct errors in active dialogues with Pound, they found that he often did not authorize obvious corrections. Despite Pound's having repeatedly and in various contexts declared the necessity of further editing so that error should be eliminated, his approach was inconsistent and eclectic, authorizing some corrections and rejecting others. After publishing *Thrones* in 1959, Pound lost control over his poem, whereas scholars, publishers, and other specialists asserted their knowledges and concerns on his text in what looked like serious competition between the critic and his author.[3] In asserting and arguing about Pound's errors of scholarship and/or judgment, whether political, literary, or linguistic, traditional Pound scholarship eroded his textual authority in significant ways. Only after waves of corrections had been incorporated and after unauthorized changes that had slipped into the poem in the printing and publishing process had been silently accepted by the poet in the last decade of his life, even Kenner came to realize the slipperiness of validity and intentionality as critical approaches to texts.

While firmly anchored in literary historicism, Kenner was instrumental in opening the door to studies indebted to poststructuralist views. In his introduction to Barbara Eastman's *Ezra Pound's Cantos: The Story of the Text 1948–1950* (1979), Kenner, while acknowledging the importance of gauging Pound's intention, questioned the notion of "deliberate and final" intention, pointing out that intention was elusive and even if found, could not be acted on. From the privileged position he enjoyed as scholarly adviser to New Directions, Kenner recounted the process of printing Pound's *Cantos* (which had existed in two different versions in the Faber and New Directions editions from 1933 to 1975), showing how often Pound sanctioned a printing error in an already published text, how he changed his mind, how he allowed other people—printers, critics, editors, translators, publishers—to intervene in his poem, how he refused to correct an error because that would spoil the sound and rhythm of the line, etc. In his introduction to Eastman's book, Kenner also provided a clear review of the limitations of print technology and also of the inability of the printed medium and book form per se to do justice to the poem, or to Pound's intentions for that matter:

> Thus in the Faber text we find a thematic ideogram placed at the end of each of the ten "China Cantos" *except* 52, 54, and 61. The one at the end of 53 has been there all along. The others were added at the time of *Seventy Cantos* reprint (1950) obviously by the author, and the three China Cantos that lack a terminal ideogram all finish at the very bottom of the page, so that there was no place to put one. In the New Directions printing by contrast (the one now shared by Faber) we may discover the ideogram at the end of 52 that Faber had no room for, and the one that has always terminated 53 and no more. The explanation for this is that Faber started printing by offset 20 years before New Directions did, indeed embarked on this new fluidity just when the author was finding ideograms especially salutary. He sent them a set for incorporation, and they incorporated what they could. New Directions in those days were still printing from plates of earlier printings, and if they received the ideogram list likewise they could see no way to do anything about it. (xii)

Starting from the laudable premise of arriving at the best possible text, scholars had often gone over and against the poet's writings and corrected for the New Directions editions of 1970, 1971, and 1972 beyond what Pound could or would authorize. Eastman's *Story of the Text* records the more than two hundred alterations in the collected American editions after 1968 made by scholars and publishers *after*

Pound had ceased taking an interest in the poem. As Froula noted in *To Write Paradise,* these changes eroded Pound's authority and created additional problems in the text (146). The *implicit* rationale of Eastman's book was to present these alterations so that future scholarship might reverse them, if necessary. The printing and editing history of *The Cantos* had destabilized the poem, imposing on it a certain view, namely that its authority should rest in conformity to and not divergence from Pound's sources.[4]

Looking back on the scholarship of those years, Froula pointed out that in spite of the effort to "stabilize" the text in a final version, the poem is still fluid due to the impossibility of settling Pound's intention and origin of writing. She observed on the nature of these scholarly corrections:

> The danger of mistaking deliberate divergences for errors and the impossibility of simulating Pound's eclecticism regarding corrections render a policy of correcting the authorial errors in *The Cantos* unsound. Further, they show that the "corrections" Pound's editors have tended to advocate and, in some cases, have actually made far exceed the limits of editorial authority as it is ordinarily conceived. Most important, they imply a misunderstanding of the part of the editors that involves much more that the errors in the text. [. . .] The errors which Pound wished *not* to correct must be understood as part of his "intentions" for his poem, in relation both to his aims for the poem at the outset and to the final achievement that the words on the page constitute. (*To Write Paradise*, 151)

The wish to correct, she maintained, was the result of a certain unease not only with Pound's textual errors but also his political ones. It was derived from the wish to impose a correct reading of history and to see the poem as an objective reflection on its *established* realities, not as the production of a hero/poet immersed in historical uncertainties and provisionality. Froula proposed a view of Pound's poetics in which fragment and error were not excessive, unwelcome supplements, but rather constitutive of his vision of history and his own writing.

Although Froula herself was indebted to an intentionalist point of view in suggesting that Pound was aware that his reading of history was fraught with lacunae and error, her vision of *The Cantos* owed its strength to the idea that Pound was writing against the assumptions of genre, and against the epic itself, as conceived in the West:

> The history which the poem includes does not fall away like a scaffolding as a transcendent meaning emerges from it. . . . [That kind or meaning] never does emerge from Pound's epic, not because the poem is unfinished or a failure but because the history of which it is made never did, in fact, redeem itself into a conventional story, a

> form in which "it all coheres." But the failure to resolve into a story, paradoxically, *is* its story. The poem is the history and the history is the poem: a record of a world without epistemological certainty, which offers no rest from wandering—a world in which error is all. (*To Write Paradise*, 154)

For Froula, the "collaborative and the contingent" relation between writer and reader established in the history of publishing *The Cantos* gave a warrant to interpret the text as fluid, not definitive, authoritarian, and "sacred." The variants she isolated in her review of the printed editions made it possible to see the poem as a "track of a human being in time" (3). Thus Froula located the "center" of the poem not in its particular meaning or telos but in the process of its telling itself, in the very process of writing. She thus turned the tables on the arch-fiend, "error," which had been the nemesis of important scholars like Kenner, Hesse, Davenport, and Achilles Fang. Error, defined at root as "wandering," was the figure with which to understand the *poem as product of an erring consciousness* without the redemption of a "paradise" understood as final closure that should resolve conflicts, redeem the poet, and end his work. History was not plotted into a certain type of story, and it contained no resolution.

The theoretical side of Froula's study was informed by poststructuralism and was the first to consistently apply a view derived from Derrida and Hayden White to Pound studies. Since the book's reviewers were traditionalists, they did not like that part at all, nor did they understand that the very poststructuralist view they deplored ("She hails from Yale," commented one reviewer)[5] had been the foundation and rationale of her case study, a genetic analysis of Canto IV, which everybody approved of. Hers was an attempt to go to the very origin of the poem, the beginning of beginnings—Pound's fourth canto, composed at the same time as the later discarded *Three Cantos* but the first to achieve a near final form in 1919. She found that like Gertrude Stein, Pound was "beginning again and again": the "origins" were multiple, extended over a period of ten years (1915–1925). The writing itself was accompanied by a profusion of outlines and sketches and by reflections published in various articles in the press. Moreover, Canto IV, published before *The Waste Land*, looked like a new form, never done before—in this sense, it could be considered the beginning of a modernist poetics in English.

Froula's approach was different from Ron Bush's *The Genesis of Ezra Pound's Cantos* (1976), which had studied Pound's revisions from the *Three Cantos* onward in order to ascertain the poet's changing horizon of intention, the "becoming" of his method. While Bush's study was oriented towards Pound as a thinking, creative artist, Froula's book shifted the ground towards language and figural discourse, stressing the impact that the critical revisionary program had upon the text. Bush had respected the limits imposed by the concepts of book or periodical publication and did not question them, limiting his analysis to Pound's revisions in print. But Froula, even though similarly focused on questions of textual emergence, undermined the foundation of the poem as printed artifact, showing how it dispersed in a chaos of beginnings: multiple manuscript versions, outlines, notes, scraps, and comments. She focused on manuscripts in relation to published versions, showing how porous the borders between them were. And whereas Bush's book aimed at reconstructing the changes of Pound's intentions throughout the process of (published) revision, Froula questioned the whole apparatus of scholarly appraisal of intentionality from the ground up.

Steeped in the plurality of beginnings, Froula considered not only the impossibility of finding a point of origin, but also of determining the closure of the poem. Her book was a milestone in a series of studies investigating the question of endings: these had started with Alan Durant's chapter on *The Cantos* in his *Identity in Crisis* (1981), continued subsequently in Ronald Bush's article "'Unstill, Ever Turning'" (1994), Peter Stoicheff's *Hall of Mirrors* (1995), and Preda's *Ezra Pound's (Post) modern Poetics* (2001). These studies described the textual instability and tenuous authorial position in *Drafts and Fragments*, as well as the profusion of revisions of the poem at New Directions from 1972 to the 1990s. The question of Canto 120, the insertion and positioning of the Italian Cantos 72 and 73, the indecision as to what truly constituted the ending of the poem to coincide with the ending of the book that contained it was a strong vein of criticism nourished by the poststructuralist emphasis on textuality and the inability of the "book" to control the poem's writing energies. In *Of Grammatology* Derrida had challenged the familiar relationship between writing and the print medium:

> The idea of the book is the idea of a totality, finite of infinite, of the signifier; this totality of the signifier cannot be a totality, unless a totality constituted by the signified preexists it, supervises its inscriptions and its signs and is independent of it in its ideality. The idea of the book, which always refers to a natural totality, is profoundly alien to the sense of writing. It is the encyclopedic protection of theology and of logocentrism against the disruption of writing, against its aphoristic energy, and, as I shall specify later, against difference in general. (18)

If Derrida had theorized the insufficiency and limitations of the codex in philosophical terms, Kenner pointed out these limitations and their effects on *The Cantos* as we know it. Froula's study in its turn brilliantly exemplified an era in which it had become possible to think of *The Cantos* as independent from the book designed to contain it.

Scholars could study the poem genetically, from manuscript to setting copy; it was possible to conceive that a *Variorum* edition, listing the line variations in all published versions of the poem, would be possible in a non-print medium. Grand unfinished projects like Ron Bush's genetic study of the *Pisan Cantos* and Richard Taylor's *Variorum Cantos* were started in this decade.

Seeing *The Cantos* as the poem of an erring, ever wandering consciousness, as Froula did, was symptomatic of an era in which critical attention was shifting from the deciphering of authorial intention to the study of a textuality independent of it. Though her own position was perceived by contemporary reviewers as a hybrid, making it possible for them to accept the genetic study and discard the theory, her critique was a way of affirming the poem's success against the traditional desire for unity, closure, redemption, and finality. Most notably complemented by Stoicheff's study of endings, *Hall of Mirrors* (1995), Froula showed that the text of *The Cantos* overcomes both the limitations of the print medium and the historical trends of critical desire.

Poststructuralist Readings and the Shift to Rhetoric

Froula's incursions into poststructuralism were compensated by the solidity of her genetic study and thus forgiven; nevertheless, Pound studies were confronted with new critical approaches whose commitment to theory was not hybridized with a conservative historical method. The most important re-alignment these created was to shift the ground of criticism to textuality and analysis of rhetoric, renouncing the reconstruction of authorial intention. A second shift, joined to the first, was to dismiss what was perceived as the unwarranted division between Pound's poetics and his politics: the analysis was meant to reveal the necessary link tying Pound's aesthetics to his fascism and anti-Semitism, moving these topics from a position of marginal invisibility to the center of interest.

This criticism was made by "outsiders," scholars, who, although they wrote and published about Pound, did not consider themselves "Poundians." From their position on the margins, they were outspoken in their rejection of received opinions and approaches current in Pound studies. In 1981, for instance, Durant openly criticized the tradition assuming that the study of the poem's relation to facts would bring us nearer to understanding it as supreme expression of what Pound intended. Durant started from Pound's politics, remarking that scholars had failed to notice how his literary prescriptions were bound to flow into his political theories:

> In addressing the question of the success of Pound's writing, and in particular of his long and unfinished poem the *Cantos*, available commentaries continue in a reluctance to pose contingent questions as to the theoretical conditions for that success or failure. Effectively *an unacknowledged complicity with Pound's founding aesthetic principles* (often to do with notions of precision in language, and tissues of necessary relations obtaining between bodies of facts) *has substantially vitiated many of these criticisms.* This can be quite clearly seen in referential or cartographical approaches, which seek to elucidate the *Cantos* by explaining allusions in the poem to an extra-linguistic world.
>
> What damages this kind of project is the ease with which it moves from the written page itself to an external circumstantial world and back again, *as if by learning to see through the language of the poem the world, its culture and its history will become transparently available to the reader.* (Durant 2–3, italics mine)

Durant affirmed that the willingness of Pound studies to adjust their critical methods to Pound's work, accept his "facts," and follow his instigations made them accomplices to his worldview, vitiated as it was by fascism. What Durant proposed was an investigation of the relations between poem and culture—not so much in terms of adherence to facts as in terms of the figural play of the text. The first step was to "dislodge" the traditionally privileged question of "intention," replacing it with the concept of "reading," a move that Kathryn Lindberg would also later make in her 1987 study *Reading Pound Reading.*

The concept of "reading" was a basic shift from retrieving the lost scene of the writing origin (the poet's intention) to interpret forms of writing. A shift from the conscious intention of a particular writer, then, to a form of subjectivity in relation to language and therefore to an analysis of his rhetoric seen as independent of his mind or volition: Durant argued that Pound's conception of language necessarily spilled over into a particular (fascist) cultural perspective, a phenomenon that was not adequately dealt with by a historical approach. Using Lacan's theory as a frame of reference, Durant chose to follow Pound's use of metaphor and metonymy, adopting the non-intentionalist assumption that the text itself has all the information a critic might need to assess not the poetic achievement per se, but rather the contradictions between declared intention and poetic result.

> What is crucial about Lacan's contribution to that theory [Freud's] is that the unconscious appears not simply in the substance of what we say or omit to say, but in the disposition of metaphor and metonymy in the very constitution of our discourses. The application of such a theory to literature displaces an analysis of the represented

> symptoms of great writers . . . by an examination of their discursive organization. (Durant 8)

Durant's rhetorical move, then, was to separate his own criticism from Pound's work, to refrain from the hermeneutic adaptation of scholarly work to the author. He refused to let Pound set the rules of the critical game and adopted the mediation of a particular theoretical discourse to look at Pound's poetry from the outside. This significant rhetorical move, of interposing a philosopher as mediator, was adopted by other scholars following the theoretical turn during the 1980s. Notable examples are Peter Nicholls's *Ezra Pound: Politics, Economics and Writing; A Study of "The Cantos"* (1984), which looked at Pound's work through Marx; Jean-Michel Rabaté's study *Language, Sexuality and Ideology in Ezra Pound's "Cantos"* (1986), which used Heideggerian and Lacanian readings; and Kathryne Lindberg's *Reading Pound Reading: Modernism after Nietzsche* (1987), which sought parallelisms between Pound's critical reading and Nietzsche's practice.

Whereas Froula's Derridean approach had been deplored by her reviewers as a theoretical supplement spoiling an otherwise excellent book, these studies were universally praised in very short reviews that did not go into any sort of detail. Reviewers did not question the books' theoretical mediation and its usefulness, but their resigned non-involvement and dignified praise left these studies in an implicit theoretical ghetto.

It became obvious as the 1980s progressed that one of the aims of theory was to dislodge and criticize those Pound critics who had adapted their work to Pound's aesthetics and who had neglected to give an adequate account of his fascism and anti-Semitism. What remained to be done was to tie rhetorical and political analyses more strongly together and move both from the margins of literary concerns to the center.

Reading Robert Casillo's preface to his *Genealogy of Demons* (1988), we see that he followed Durant in attacking Pound scholars for the neglect of and complicity to his policies. He accused them of turning a blind eye to the

> deeply disturbing contrast in Pound's thought and works, a contrast thus far beyond the comprehension of his critics: Pound the imitator of Dante and Cavalcanti, his mind filled with images of light, beauty, and benevolence, passing judgment on the world from his "Thrones" of justice; and Pound the violent anti-Semite and fascist, whose hatred and fear of Jews finally reduces them in his mind to the demonic status of germs and bacilli, invisible carriers of plague and disease, a swamp, an enormous "power of putrefaction" (SP 317) and profanation preying invisibly on the body of the West. (Casillo, 1988, 3)

In order to redress the situation, Casillo first systematized Pound's reading, looking for structures of metaphor he could use in his analysis. Second, he assumed the task of demonstrating the limitations of the critical tradition that had explained Pound chiefly on the poet's own terms—for this he used René Girard's study *Violence and the Sacred* (1977) as a theoretical pivot that should mediate and at the same time institute the necessary distance between Pound and himself; but more importantly Casillo sought to demonstrate that the anti-Semitic apparatus belonged to the deep structure of Pound's worldview and vitiated everything he wrote. Fascism/anti-Semitism and Pound's poetic work had to be integrated and reflect on each other. Since Hillyer's articles during the Bollingen controversy, Casillo's book remains to this day the most ferocious and thorough attack on Pound's political and literary reputation. Whereas the Bollingen polemic could be dismissed as political journalism heated by the war suffering and the passions of the day, Casillo's book drove its points home by thorough scholarly argumentation that had much greater staying power.

But Casillo's measuring the poetry and the politics by the same standard could have just one result. After he was finished, Pound could not look at the sun as a human being, much less as a poet, but only as an anti-Semite. Though Casillo's study purported to be an objective look, its relentless searching for metaphors of anti-Semitism in Pound's work left nothing untainted and opened the critic to a questioning of personal motives. This became evident in the published controversy Casillo had with Reed Way Dasenbrock in the pages of *American Literary History* in 1989. Dasenbrock's review of *Genealogy of Demons* was a call to reason, fairness, and balance. While agreeing with Casillo that Pound scholarship had been largely apologetic, he defended the previous generation of scholars by historicizing: from 1945 to the moment of writing, the first generation had been concerned to keep the poet alive and further to establish his literary position in the canon. During the 1980s, the scholarly task had changed—to understand, within that consolidated position, Pound's good and bad. Dasenbrock pointed out that the tradition had not been silent on Pound's politics: his own study *The Literary Vorticism of Ezra Pound* (1985) had revealed the homology between the middle cantos and Pound's admiration for Mussolini; Peter Nicholls's study *Ezra Pound: Politics, Economics and Writing* (1984) had analyzed Pound's fascism at length, whereas Michael André Bernstein's *The Tale of the Tribe: Ezra Pound and the Modern Verse Epic* (1980) had provided a political analysis of the late cantos.

Dasenbrock then proceeded to delineate the objections he had to Casillo's argument, observing a certain neglect of history in Casillo's approach and pointing out that Pound's anti-Semitism developed late, and erupted as a consequence of the Nazification of Italy after 1938. By that date, Pound had already produced about half of the cantos: to see the work before that time as equally tainted or as manifesting a hidden anti-Semitism was, Dasenbrock proposed, a scholarly sleight of hand.

Finally, Dasenbrock expressed his sense of a metaphoric overkill in Casillo's prose that damaged his stance as objective scholar and pointed in the direction of a personal resentment:

> But correction can often lead to overcorrection, and there is more than a hint of that in *The Genealogy of Demons*. Casillo seems determined, not just to correct the record, but to paint it as black as possible. The avenging fierceness with which he tracks down all of the unpleasant aspects of Pound's thought makes his book seem nearly as obsessive as Pound's anti-Semitic diatribes. His reluctance to admit any mitigating factors can be seen in his dismissive treatment of Pound's later recantation of his anti-Semitism, which to my mind in the way it informs *Drafts and Fragments* deserves much more consideration than the two pages Casillo gives it. Even if Casillo is right and anti-Semitism stands at the center of *The Cantos*, an end to that anti-Semitism stands at its end. [. . .] Ultimately, I fail to see how Casillo's attitude toward Pound is really an improvement on the older apologetics. The one refuses to face what is less than admirable in Pound's achievement, but the other refuses to face anything that is admirable. We need to see Pound steadily and see him whole. (1989, 238)

Casillo attempted to defend himself against Dasenbrock's charge that his argument lacked a historical dimension, but six months later Lawrence Rainey's review of *The Genealogy of Demons* would recapitulate Dasenbrock's criticism, particularly Casillo's "synchronic" approach and his rhetorical misuse of metaphor. Rainey even pastiched Casillo's prose to show that mimetic scapegoating did not lie at the root of Pound's poetry but rather at Casillo's very own scholarly prose. But Rainey's principal move was to spell out his major criticism of Casillo's analysis—the rhetorical tribunal, the absence of the historical dimension, and the forcing of metaphoric interpretation to the point of absurdity:

> Though it offers many instances of local insight into psychological and metaphorical structures in Pound's work, it is constantly vitiated by arguments that seem forced and belabored, by a tone of ingenuous moralism and strident denunciation, and by a remarkable disinterest in the historical dimensions of fascism and anti-Semitism in the Italian setting in which Pound lived and operated. In the final analysis it says little about the historical questions that it purports to consider, and even less about the ethical questions that it proposes to address. It is a disappointing work. (1989, 560).

In spite of the bad reviews that Casillo's work received from Pound scholars, his book remained a gashing wound in the political awareness of the community. It was a book firmly anchored in a decade in which Pound's anti-Semitism was chosen by criticism in the deconstructive vein as the main point of accusation against Pound the poet. Arguably, it did more than any other book to awaken scholars to their duty to face Pound's political commitments unflinchingly and at every turn. The days in which scholars could just withdraw into a congenial "innocent" or "politically unproblematic" period of Pound's work without saying a word about his politics were now past. Flory's *The American Ezra Pound* (1989), Redman's *Ezra Pound and Italian Fascism* (1991), Rainey's *Ezra Pound and the Monument of Culture* (1991), and Surette's later work (1998, 1999, 2011) were bound to show awareness of and relate to Casillo's position. The scholarly landscape was irrevocably changed.

Deconstructing *The Cantos*

Casillo's book, while grounded in Girard's theory of sacrificial violence, was not written in the deconstructive mode. However, the range of arguments Casillo presented and his focus on anti-Semitism would have been inconceivable outside Derrida's and De Man's deconstructive ideology critique. The overcoming of humanism and the argument that language, rather than "man," should be the supreme framework of reference for criticism led to a politicization of analytical practice. As Richard Rorty has pointed out:

> Those who practise deconstructive criticism typically see themselves as taking part in an activity which has much more to do with political change than with the "understanding" (much less the "appreciation") of what has traditionally been called "literature."
>
> The latter term has traditionally borne a humanistic sense, one which presupposes that "great" poems and novels are repositories of enduring moral truths which correspond to something essential in human beings as such, regardless of their historical epoch or their linguistic repertoire. By contrast, deconstructionists wish to replace this sense with de Man's description of "literature" as "the persistent naming of a void," the perpetual discovery of the blindness which made previous insight possible, and of the new blindness that made it possible to cure the old. Literature ceases to be a place where the perturbed spirit can find rest and inspiration, where human beings can go to find their own deepest nature manifested, but rather an incitement to a new sort of perpetually self-destabilizing activity. Deconstructionists hope that such activity, carried over into politics, might succeed in overcoming the blindness of the bourgeois democracies to the cruelty and injustice of their institutions. (1995, 193–94)

Rorty points out here that the hope of the deconstructionist brand of close reading is to engender political awareness and the dismantling of the linguistic foundations of unjust institutions. According to another definition, that of J. Hillis Miller, deconstruction looked for the loose stone that would pull down the building, a set of contradictions in a marginal, neglected zone of the text.[6] The "loose stone" to pull down not only Pound's *Cantos*, but his poetic work as a whole, was found soon enough. If for Robert Casillo, "anti-Semitism" was the most important "loose stone" to ruin the poem and its author, for other practitioners of deconstructive criticism like Andrew Parker, Richard Sieburth, and Maud Ellmann, it was "usury."

Andrew Parker's essay, "Ezra Pound and the 'Economy' of Anti-Semitism" (1983) took as its starting point the divorce between literary criticism and ideological analysis in the "Pound industry" (as Casillo would call it. In the rhetorical figures of Pound's economic system Parker sought "certain 'excessive' figures ('usury' and 'Judaism') which motivate (as well as undermine) both the 'economy' of this system and of the poetry in which it is inscribed" (104). The basic rhetorical move of deconstructive analysis was to follow the flow of metaphors in Pound's work, especially important figures such as "usury" and "the Jew" and to show how their use undoes or destabilizes everything Pound had to say on those subjects, and ultimately his poem itself:

> Although Pound would attack Judaism as a consequence of its tendency towards "excess," it is for this very tendency that Judaism has become adopted as the "unofficial religion" of much contemp,orary French writing. As posed by deconstruction, for example, "excess" would be a property of all written texts, a product of the inability of any form of discourse to master fully its own rhetorical status. If this "excess" by which writing is distinguished can be understood (provisionally) as "an experience of the infinitely other"—that is, as an encounter with textual elements which remain irreducibly peripheral with respect to a presiding (authorial) consciousness—we might then infer that Judaism conveys a rhetorically similar experience, for it forms an analogous, unassimilable "excess" on the margins of the dominant (Christian) culture. Just as the textual sign both differs from and defers perpetually that which it represents, so may Judaism be viewed as a religion of difference and deferral, as an ethos of absence and loss conditioned by the hope for a Messiah who "always already" remains yet to come. The writer and the Jew, by extension, would each become "nomads," exiles displaced from any univocal origin; adrift in a play of language without fixed arché or telos, both are condemned to modes of interpretation which foreground endless metonymic succession (in which sign and referent never coincide)

> rather than ultimate symbolic identity (in which the one incarnates the other). (114)

In Parker's argument then, Pound had attempted to eradicate the "nomadic" play of rhetoric in the same way that he sought to "purge" himself of "the Jewish poison": he had proposed to avoid abstractions and seek in the ideogram a natural, motivated, visually rich linguistic sign reconnecting language to referent; he had cultivated precision, not dissemination; he had abjured monotheism and looked for a Christianity infused by a "natural" pagan spirituality; and looking for alternatives to a money system based on the fetishism of gold, he had found in stamp scrip a kind of money that would wither and die like plants or food. However, for deconstructionists, oppositions are always "inhabited by that which each was intended to eradicate": Pound's precision bred excess, his just economy created usurious writing, his anti-Semitic stance created the author as Jew. In Derrida's view, writing itself is excessive, marked by supplementarity and deferral, therefore Pound's insistence on precision, with its ramifications into an economy of signification and sexuality was rooted in a failed logo- and phallocentrism. Indeed, Pound seems to have anticipated the tenor of the deconstructive critique in *The Cantos.* Though the passage from canto 99 below was not quoted in Parker's essay, it maps in miniature what Parker and later Maud Ellmann perceived as Pound's animus against writing, as well as Pound's own inability to go beyond it. *The Cantos,* in their view, was inhabited by rhetorical excess, supplementarity, and "paltry yatter":

> But their First Classic: that the heart shd / be straight,
> The phallos perceive its aim.
>
> Tinkle, tinkle, two tongues? No.
> But down on the word with exactness,
> against gnashing of teeth (upper incisors)
> chih, chih!
> wo chih^3 chih^3
> wo^4 wo ch'o ch'o, paltry yatter
> wo$^{4-5}$ wo$^{4-5}$ ch'o$^{4-5}$ ch'o$^{4-5}$
> paltry yatter. (XCIX/722)

The "economy" of Pound's poem was thus "broken up" by its hostility towards writing conceived as excess, which he associated with Jewish "otherness." He was thus entangled in an aporia he was unable to resolve, that of trying to write against writing. In a second rhetorical move, Parker's deconstructive analysis projected this aporia against Pound himself and showed that Pound was marked by Jewishness. That led him to comment at length on Pound's name, following the biblical ramifications of the original namesake "Ezra"—a nomad and a forger (120)—a move that Richard Sieburth would complement by commenting on the economic connotations of Pound's name as signifier of a unit of measurement or monetary value.

Parker's article remained exemplary both for the rigor of its deconstructive reading and for its thematic condensation. In particular, his demonstration of Pound's hostility to "writing," understood in Derridean terms as excess, supplementarity, and deferral, was to provide a ground of agreement for ulterior deconstructive critique. Durant had shown how Pound's wish for closure and resolution went against his own poetic method in *The Cantos*; Parker demonstrated how the idea of Jewishness, which Pound sought to purge from his own text, was integral to it and to himself.

In this context, Richard Sieburth's article "In Pound We Trust: The Economy of Poetry/The Poetry of Economics," written in 1984 but published in 1987, starts from the accepted idea in deconstructive criticism that Pound's poetic language is actually usurious. By acknowledging Parker, Rabaté, Casillo, and Nicholls as fellow travelers, Sieburth provided an ambitious overview of Pound's poetic career as a succession of stages of poetic economy. Organizing his essay as a survey of Pound's work in chronological order, he showed that Pound's poetry is not simply usurious within the verbal excesses of *The Cantos*, but also in the archaizing rhetoric of his early poetry:

> Skillful though it may be, the gilded fin-de-siècle glamour of this kind of poetry runs the twin risks of rhetorical inflation and narcissistic sterility, for rather than providing a medium of exchange, rather than articulating reciprocity (or allowing for difference), its language repetitively celebrates its own parthenogenesis—word begetting word, gold begetting ever more gold, precisely the sort of self-reflexive, fetishistic creation ex nihilo that Pound would later denounce as usury. Pound's poetry forever skirts the dangers of this sort of post-Symbolist solipsism. His abandonment of his early troubadour manner in late 1912 for the modernist poetics of Imagism entailed more than the mere rejection of the aureate archaisms of his first collections of verse. It represented a fundamental attempt to get his poetry off the gold standard, to defetishize the signifier, as it were, to establish a poetics whose economy would be based on the direct exchange between subject and object, language and reality, word and world. The poetry he was now after, as he noted in connection with his famous haiku "In a Station of the Metro," would try "to record the precise instant when a thing outward and objective transforms itself, or darts into a thing inward and subjective." (1987, 146)

In retrospect, structuring the essay in the chronological order of Pound's ideas and pronouncements in matters of economy, language, and usury is an essential merit of Sieburth's article and its main corrective to what deconstructive analysis presupposed: "the erasure of history" (Ellmann 1987) and the subordination to rhetoric. Sieburth located Pound's imagist doctrine as a first effort to counter excess with an aesthetic of precision that imposed on the reader a synecdochic economy. The word charged with meaning would thus make language economical and efficient: understanding would proceed in a flash and would be direct and intense. Rhetorical figures may block or redirect the reader's understanding of meaning: in a similar manner, usury clogs the circulation of money and goods in a society.

Sieburth's analysis recapitulates the moves of deconstructive criticism along the figural route that has by now become familiar: following from Pound's allegiance to a natural language and instantaneous access to a meaning outside writing, to the animus against usury as deferral and blockage, and further to the perceived solution in stamp scrip, which Pound considered a counter-usury mechanism, Sieburth moves predictably towards the reasons why Pound's poetic efforts are a failure. The reasons this time are economic: Pound allowed the arbitrary nature of money: the fact that its value lay not in the intrinsic value of gold but rather in the "writing" or "stamp" on the notes. Hence his fear that anybody could play on the symbolic gap between monetary sign and value and his hope that fascist state money would close this gap.

Moreover, Sieburth asserts, Pound had privileged distribution over production: following Clifford Hugh Douglas, against Marx, Pound had implicitly abjured the idea that value would be created by new production. He had read, taken notes, recapitulated privileged texts of the literary tradition and thus turned *The Cantos* into an excess and supplement to that tradition. What is more, Pound did not consider distribution as a political act so much as a technique that any political system could potentially employ. Translated to the poem, says Sieburth, distribution as a technique opens the way to disseminative rhetoric, which is held together by our trust in Pound's person and name. Or to put it differently, *The Cantos* is based on credit: meaning is deferred in continuous writing, which the reader has to accept by trusting that the author, in the end, will pay his debt in an ultimate revelation.

> Indeed, Pound's work is permanently haunted by the possibility that poetry might very well be as chrematistic or self-engendering as usury. For if poetry can be made out of nothing more than "a mouthful of air" (as he liked to quote Yeats), what then distinguishes it from the money that banks create ex nihilo? And if usury is akin to false-coining, what guarantees that poetry might not also succumb

> to the inspired counterfeitings of fiction or the golden deceits of catachresis? And if usury is based on money reproducing money, that is, on the narcissistic reduplication of the same, does this not also implicate the very workings of poetic language as rhyme and repetition—like begetting like, reiterative figures of the same? And if usury profits from the price of time, does this not in a certain sense mirror the very temporality of a poem like *The Cantos*, written on credit and including its own history within itself by an ongoing structure of deferral and delay? (Sieburth 1987, 172)

Sieburth does not allow the last lines of *Drafts and Fragments* to point to anything else but silence. His analysis, geared as it is to finding Pound's lifework an aporetic failure, is bound to argue that the credit is misplaced and the poet is a deluded usurer. The very logic of deconstructive analysis does not allow Sieburth to concur with Froula (whom he does not mention) that Pound's redemption and implicit resolution—his "paradise" had been found in the Pisan hell, in a transcendence revealed in the present moment, in an intense, spiritual attention to the minute details of actual living. For Sieburth, Pound never pays his debt to the reader: the lines "Do not move / Let the wind speak / This is paradise" do not redeem the poem. They instead point to the "bankruptcy of his enterprise, to the collapse of its economy, as the poet now withdraws his words from circulation and renders them back unto silence" (Sieburth 1987, 172).

As deconstruction opened the door to questions of linguistic "economy" it also threatened to shut the door on questions of history and of the relation of text to its historical context. With this move, Pound critics applying deconstructive method could destabilize every certainty of Pound's own convictions and, by extension, the position of traditional historicist criticism itself. It was Parker who first articulated the implicit competition between deconstruction and historical analysis. Following Derrida, Parker affirmed that even if recent deconstructive criticism had privileged rhetorical over historical analysis in a refusal to submit to the criterion and methods of history as a last instance, Derrida's own writing practice refrained from establishing another pair of oppositions. According to Parker, rhetoric and history were both marred and invaded by one another—a separation and a working opposition was not possible.

Still, rhetorical analysis of Pound's figural universe took precedence over history in the general deconstructionist practice, if not in Derrida's own; this is shown in one of the star essays of the 1980s, Ellmann's "Ezra Pound: The Erasure of History" (1987). As expected, Ellmann takes in stride what Parker, Casillo, and Sieburth had argued: Pound's writing is a kind of usury; his dissociations only appear to be operative, but are in fact invaded by their opposites; his poem is a rhetorical failure and a fascist one to boot. Yet Ellmann's essay is not argumentative along established academic lines, but is rather a deconstructive overwriting of Pound's cherished dissociations. As Ellmann says: "For his discriminations crumble every time he sets them up: and his writing stutters on its own delusions, unable to progress or to retreat. This essay investigates his blindness with the perspicuity of his own idiom, as if obsession could observe its own finesse" (244).

In a sense, Ellmann's essay marks an endpoint and culmination of the whole project of deconstructive criticism applied to Pound's work. One reason is that it makes good on Derrida's effacement of the author-critic position. "The Erasure of History" is a pastiche of Pound's style, a collage of figures—as such, it is performative and not argumentative, its power rests in the persuasion achieved by its own rhetorical ingenuity, not in an appeal to the validity of argument. While Ellmann addresses aspects of Pound's ideology of history in the first part of her essay, her main focus is usury as trope, and this warrants a nomadic meandering through Pound's whole oeuvre. The method superficially resembles Pound's own: taking quotations from his work and juxtaposing them in new ways. The meandering is not logical or chronological: in this sense, it imitates the poetic moves of *The Cantos*. But Ellmann's mock-academic pastiche has its own purpose and rationale: the concluding paragraph of the essay merits full quotation, for it showcases the culmination and perversion of political analysis done as deconstructive critique:

> He would sign his name in speech, in rhythm, on the air, rather than in any medium corrupted by the usury of writing. But his names are both compounded in all that The Cantos denounce. Pound himself is the infected currency; and Ezra is the other face of the same coin, the face that belches into hell. In the end, the blank of Ezra subsumes the blank of truth, for the text is truly created out of nothing—out of the ruins of the excremental pound. (259)

Here Pound was called to yet another tribunal and once again found guilty. The apologetic character of traditional historical criticism had found its ugly double in Ellmann's academic-credentialed smear. Her article would be the logical culmination and the impasse of deconstructive criticism in Pound studies. Her "argument" was a rhetorical sleight of hand meant to dishonor and call names.

Out of this dark place there had to be an exit.

Notes

[1] For the conflict between "writing" and "book" see Derrida's *Of Grammatology*, trans. Gayatri Chakravorty Spivak, 6–26; for a discussion of the metaphysical privilege of phonetic writing, see his "The Pit and the Pyramid," in *Margins of Philosophy*, 69–108; against genre, see his "Force de loi: Le Fondement mystique de l'autorité/Force of Law: The Mystical Foundation of Authority," 919–1045;

against borderlines, see his *Memoirs of the Blind: The Self-Portrait and Other Ruins*, 1993.

[2] See Jerome McGann's corrosive criticism of New Critical assumptions from the position of historical and textual criticism in "The Text, the Poem and the Problem of the Historical Method," in *The Beauty of Inflections*, 111–32.

[3] Froula described the case of John Espey, who silently corrected errors against Pound's wishes in his edition of *Hugh Selwyn Mauberley* (Froula, *To Write Paradise*, 145).

[4] "While Pound's approval was obtained for many of these corrections, the inaccessibility of the documents necessary to editorial work, the lack of a considered editorial policy and of methodical procedures, and the unmanageable extent and complexity of the poem conspired against this unsystematic attempt to establish the texts of *The Cantos*. Consequently, the changes made by the New Directions committee cannot be presumed to be authoritative, but instead constitute newly problematical readings which must be examined critically in any future attempt to edit the text of the poem" (Froula, *To Write Paradise*, 146).

[5] In his review of Froula, Anthony Woodward looked on her theoretical sections with scorn: "The second half of the book is an unconvincing attempt, with some fleeting moments of plausibility, to fit Pound to the current contortions of postmodernist deconstruction" (594–95). See also the reviews by Lawrence S. Rainey, Peter Makin, and George Bornstein.

[6] "Deconstruction as a mode of interpretation works by a careful and circumspect entering of each textual labyrinth . . . The deconstructive critic seeks to find, by this process of retracing, the element in the system studied which is alogical, the thread in the text in question which will unravel it all, or the loose stone which will pull down the whole building. The deconstruction, rather, annihilates the ground on which the building stands by showing that the text has already annihilated that ground, knowingly or unknowingly. Deconstruction is not a dismantling of the structure of a text but a demonstration that it has already dismantled itself." (Miller 341)

7: Reading Pound in the New Millennium, 1990–2016

To theorize concepts of "text" purified of the material complexity in which cultural works are located is to imagine the nonexistent or the unimportant. Theory advances not when it codifies empty abstractions, but when it facilitates fuller accounts.

—Lawrence Rainey, *Monument of Culture*

The Emergence of New Modernist Studies

The explanatory ebullience of Pound studies in 1970s, driven by Kenner's *The Pound Era* and Terrell's *Paideuma,* was cut off by the theoretical and political turn of deconstruction, whose ideological critique was strongly felt all through the 1980s. Understanding in detail and structurally relating what Pound had written in his poetry, early and late, ceased to be the priority of the day. The second volume of Terrell's *Companion to The Cantos of Ezra Pound*, published in 1984, proved to be not only the summing up of the scholarship produced by a whole generation, but the swansong of an era. Source hunting, clarifying allusions, and literary interpretation had become suspect: political facts and attitudes had been swept under the carpet for the sake of aesthetics; Pound scholars were (not innocently) promoting a poet whose moral values were appalling, whose politics was totalitarian, and whose economics was mad. An emphasis on the literary meant a turning away from the ugly truth: no amount of poetic innovation could justify anti-Semitism after the Holocaust. The feeling that Pound had not been properly punished, that he had had it easy at St. Elizabeths and cheated the system of its rightful retribution was running like a silent undercurrent in the detailed ideology critique of the postmodern era. The turn away from purely literary interpretation in the 1980s meant a reorientation towards theoretical tools that could be best used to face up to the scholar's responsibility: to chastise Pound as an anti-Semite, to dismiss his work as fascist.

More generally, postmodernism had critically conceived modernism as part of a binary opposition, and the inferior part at that. Modernism was bad: formalist, essentialist, elitist, fascist, or at least authoritarian, difficult, even abstruse, conservative of cultural values, in short genteel and anti-democratic.[1] Modernism was genteel because it was committed to

Eurocentric high culture and to the imperative of preserving and contributing to it; racism and sexism had continued, unquestioned; elitism, exclusions, and inhuman politics had been promoted beyond reason. In such a view, Pound could be nothing else than the dark heart of modernism, the poster image of evil. His career, ideology, erudition, and poetic practice summed up everything that was wrong with modernism.

Yet, as Michael North has noted, despite its tarnished image, "modernism, as a movement and as a collection of works, has turned out to be more durable than the postmodernism that was supposed to replace it" (2014). This much became ever clearer around the turn of the millennium. Gradually, as academics were letting go of deconstruction as a critical method, they also let fall the interest in a postmodern cultural era. Postmodernism as a concept dissolved into history, whereas modernism stayed and flourished. Scholars whose theoretical awareness was awake to the change drew attention to this paradox. Rainey, who had been among the first to critique postmodern theoretical assumptions and turn towards a methodological New Historicism, stated it bluntly in 2005: modernism as seen by postmodernism was "dispiriting, a travesty which eviscerated modernism of its wild opacity and reduced it to little more than a collection of the most reactionary political views [. . .] But since then, the climate has changed again. Postmodernism . . . is waning in prestige" (xxvi). Looking back on the decade in her article "Pound's New Criticism" (2010), Rebecca Beasley concurred, observing that the theoretical goal of the new approach was to dismantle the "straw-man modernism that featured in the postmodernist, anti-modernist and historical avant-garde polemics of the 1970s and 1980s" (649).

However, the survival and flourishing of modernist studies for the past decade and a half have shown several postmodern ideas to be positive and fertile. The first one, derived from François Lyotard, enjoined scholars to distrust grand metanarratives and attend to small stories, thus opening the way to a pluralism of perspectives in which no single one could determine a central view of the field. The strongest underlying idea of modernist studies in the new millennium was that, as Michael Coyle put it in his 2005 article "With a Plural Vengeance: Modernism as (Flaming) Brand," "there can be no one master narrative, no single key" (20). Apart from Lyotard's immensely fruitful idea that overarching metanarratives should be distrusted in any field of knowledge, and further, that margins rather than centers should receive privileged attention, Richard Rorty's antifoundationalist meditations on conceptual revolutions were remarkably prescient as to what would happen after postmodernism itself withdrew into the past: in his 1982 book, *Consequences of Pragmatism*, Rorty maintained that there is no unshakeable foundation to our concepts; it is rather the discussion around them that creates, figures, and refigures them in time (148, 169).

Inclusiveness and historicity thus became the preconditions of a reconceptualization of modernism along pluralist lines that burst open the boundaries of the academic canon to include what previously had been neglected or disparaged: women artists, writers of color, ethnic modernisms, queer modernisms, and "the others"—modernisms outside the English-speaking world. Giving up the canonical criteria of value (restricted as they were to the work of dead white males) meant seeing them in a specific context and history permeated with questions of race, gender, sexual orientation, and ethnocentrism. This was a move in consonance with the times: in 1998, on the threshold of the new millennium, modernist studies found their renaissance by means of establishing the Modernist Studies Association (MSA), which took it upon itself to become the institutional framework through which modernism could be re-conceptualized, in the US and internationally. The MSA chose *Modernism/modernity* as its periodical, a journal whose senior editors, Lawrence Rainey and Robert von Hallberg, had committed to an interdisciplinary study of modernism at its launch in 1994. The success of the MSA led modernist scholars in the UK to follow suit and create the British Association for Modernist Studies (BAMS) in 2010, with *Modernist Cultures* (started in 2005) as its flagship journal.

The pluralization, even atomization of interests, as well as the flattening out of hierarchies became evident within the organizations meant to contain and channel the new forms of scholarly expression. Pound's position in the new landscape thus became a topic of constant renegotiation. The 1990s and 2000s continued the turn of the 1980s away from his literary output and away from the mode in which both he and Eliot had conceived their own value for literature—as literary innovators and cultural diagnosticians—towards other fields of interest: race and gender studies, the market and institutions, popular culture, and new media. Therefore, in order to understand the main orientation of critical work focused on Pound for the last two decades and a half we have to see it as negotiating its production with what came to be known as New Modernist Studies (Latham and Rogers 149). Diverging from Kenner's canonical view was paramount: Pound was not a central modernist, not even a privileged one: he became one author among others in a non-hierarchical area of study marked by pluralism and inclusiveness. Pluralism meant that modernism was not to be defined by a resort to a very few star players and their aesthetic, moral, or political scale of values: Eliot, Pound, Joyce, and Lewis (the men of 1914). The canon, which in Kenner's generation was focused on these key writers, was exploded from within. If in the 1970s scholars thought they would find the textbook of modernism in Pound's poetic practice and critical work, that belief disappeared by the turn of the millennium.

The sum of ways in which the new perspective diverged from that of the older generation became evident in a group of articles on Hugh

Kenner published in *Modernism/modernity* in 2005 (volume 12.3). These were meant as a taking stock and re-evaluation of Kenner as prime mover in the forming of the modernist canon. Marjorie Perloff's essay was a landmark evaluation. She stressed Kenner's brilliance, eccentricity, and individualism, which led him to seek difference, not conformity to a school or trend. She conceded that Kenner's studies on Pound, Joyce, and Beckett had invented "modernism"—a selective version, dwelling on "constatation of fact" (a Poundian value), "internationalism," and conjunction of literary innovation with technology and the arts. Moreover, she saw in his choice of writers a "self-consistency that we find only in the great critics—in for example, Walter Benjamin or Roland Barthes" (468).

It was recognized by the other commentators that Kenner, whom one of them, Gerald Bruns, called the "Newton of Modernism" (477) had left a fraught inheritance, one still speaking to new generations of scholars with its initial brilliance, but also one marked by a set of evaluations and dismissals that hurt, even insulted. Two of his major errors were spelled out by Christine Froula in her contribution: the first was Kenner's assumption that Pound's *Cantos* had to be "corrected" in relation to its sources. Froula had objected to that in her book, "*To Write Paradise*," pointing out that Pound never assumed an impeccable scholarly authority and that his error-laden poetry had to be taken as he wrote it. Now she restated that "error, chance, fallibility, divagation are interwoven in Pound's epic 'record of struggle'" (473). Kenner had initiated a program of corrections at New Directions that had not been approved by the author, who was too ill at the time; Kenner had thus introduced into the text a new dimension of error.

Kenner's second fault was the disparagement of the Bloomsbury group, particularly of Virginia Woolf in what was adjudicated as his weakest book, *A Sinking Island*. Froula reviewed Kenner's positions on Woolf with scorn, remarking: "Who wouldn't wish that this well-known Canadian mathematician and conjurer of fantastic great men lost in Time's mists had quit while he was ahead?" (474).

Aware of the mounting criticism aimed at him as a creator of restrictive views on modernism, Kenner defended his position in the essay "The Making of the Modernist Canon" (1984) arguing that a canon was not a mere author list in a curriculum, but a story. He recounted his own tale of discovery, resting on his personal experience: the visits he had made to prominent modernists—T. S. Eliot, William Carlos Williams, and Wyndham Lewis—at Pound's instigation in 1956. As readers of his essay, we come to realize how Kenner had developed that initial experience by adding Joyce and Beckett, and separated Williams's position, thus elaborating his fundamental distinction between international modernism and local modernisms. Kenner had also intuited a shift of prestige in the use of language (a shift from British to an "international" English), and consequently a shift in taste. It was on the basis of these lived experiences that he elaborated his distinctions of value among modernists. Perloff was right—Kenner's work hung together, was anchored in his personal life, and was a highly individual response to the critical fashions of his day, Leavisian impressionism and American New Criticism.

But now it was time that Kenner's list of brilliant modernists be interrogated and expanded, his criteria of value be decentered: a new generation of scholars corrected and supplemented his internationalism by attention given to modernists anchored in the local and marginal (starting with studies on Dorothy Richardson, H.D., even William Faulkner, and Wallace Stevens); his attention to modernism and mechanics would be replaced by controversies around the impact of newer technologies (displacing the mechanical with the digital, the linotype with the internet); his disparagement of British modernism would be compensated for, with a vengeance, by the spread of Virginia Woolf studies in the UK and the world. Finally, his attention to selected individual authors would be the most contested terrain of modernism studies as newly conceived: a new "thematics," to use Reed Way Dasenbrock's useful concept ("Saladin" 63), would become the imperative of the day. Authors had to step aside to serve as arguments for significant topics and revaluations of modernism—their works were drawn in to illustrate a practice, ideology, or strategy: they were significant to the extent to which they contributed to a modernist discourse, institution, or medium.

Pound studies were thus radically challenged to shift their focus from author to theme. After the 1990s, and particularly after Kenner's death in 2003, Pound scholarship has been increasingly included in books that are not exclusively dedicated to him. In practical terms, this trend ended Kenner's bid for a "Pound Era." To new scholars in the field Kenner did so much to open, it was important to consider Pound's work in the context of other writers and poets. For these scholars, Pound was less often *the* key poet from whom the streams of innovation originated than someone who along with other modernists was involved with libraries and archives, little magazines, museums, and publishers; someone who along with other writers held politically conservative or fascist views; someone who along with others was involved in imagism, or wrote long poems. All through the 2000s, we observe an increasing reluctance on the part of scholars to dedicate a monograph or a PhD dissertation to the work of a single artist—more often than not, s/he was placed in a group: Pound was studied in this manner, along with other authors. Sometimes, his name would show up in the study's title alongside other poets,[2] but this became an increasingly unpopular practice. The names of actual writers disappeared from the titles of monographs and collected volumes to make place for the new privileged protagonist: "Modernism." Defining and discussing modernism became the priority of the day. Pound had an important place in such accounts, but in order to assess his importance, the interested reader had to go to the table of contents and/or to the index.[3]

This contextualization sometimes meant a turning away from the immediately literary, this time not so much towards ideology critique and theory, but towards a more sociological, historicist view, contextualizing the emergence and transmission of texts. The canon was rethought in relation to its "others," particularly in relation to the institutions of modernism: the museums, the little magazines, the publishing houses, the grants and literary prizes. This led to a certain ideological bent, where Pound was seen primarily as a patron, a mediator, or a cultural manager of modernism. After the turn of the millennium, turning away from the literary meant considering Pound's role as a researcher, manager, patron, supporter of artists, literary agent, journalist, and propagandist. During the past two decades, then, Pound has been seen by the community of new modernist scholars less as a poet, and more as an ideologue, a facilitator and an influencer—always in correlation with his peers, his time, and his environment. It is only in the past three years that this ideological focus began to be tempered by an interest in Pound's major poetry in books and projects on *The Cantos*: the digital "The Cantos Project," started by Preda in 2014; Michael Kindellan's book-length study, *The Late Cantos of Ezra Pound* (2017); the collective volume edited by Richard Parker, *Readings in "The Cantos"* (2018); and the *Glossator* number on *Thrones* (Cantos 96–109), May 2018.

Material Criticism, the Social Text and the Institutions of Modernism

The reorientation of Pound criticism towards a social dimension was anticipated by Michael North's book *The Final Sculpture: Public Monuments and Modern Poets* (1985) and began in earnest with the work of Jerome McGann's *The Textual Condition* (1991) and Rainey's *Ezra Pound and the Monument of Culture* (1991) and *Institutions of Modernism* (1998).

McGann was among the first to signal dissatisfaction with the theoretically inflected mode of reading texts prevalent in the 1980s, putting the insights he had gained as an editor of Lord Byron (1983–1992) into his textual criticism, which became more obviously concerned with what he called "bibliographic codes" (that is, the material support of the poem: paper, binding, illustrations, etc.). He thus initiated a reorientation towards the social conditions governing the emergence of literary works, which he described in *The Textual Condition*:

> Texts are produced and reproduced under specific social and institutional conditions, and hence [. . .] every text, including those that may appear to be purely private, is a social text. This view entails a corollary understanding, that a "text" is not a "material thing" but a material event or set of events, a point in time (or a moment in space) where certain communicative exchanges are being practiced.
>
> [. . .] Texts always stand within an editorial horizon (the horizon of their production and reproduction) [. . .]
>
> Briefly, the editorial horizon forces one to reimagine the theory of texts—and, ultimately, the theory of literature—as a specific set of social operations. To the extent that recent theoretical work in literary studies has left its social dimension unexplicated, a reasonable "resistance to theory" will be raised. (21)

McGann's analysis insisted that the material support of Pound's *Cantos*, whether the poem was published as a luxury edition, a mass circulation one, or in a periodical publication, cannot be separated from its overall interpretation of the poem. Pound's decision to market his first sixteen, then thirty cantos in deluxe, illustrated editions resulted in a composite meaning derived from the poems in combination with the illustrations, paper quality, binding, etc. McGann's focus on Pound's early cantos (which he called "Pre-Raphaelite Cantos") did not aim to offer an explanation why Pound gave up book illustration and deluxe marketing—but Miranda Hickman's articles of 1997 and 1999 in *Paideuma* did just that.

Lawrence Rainey's work on Pound showed a profound agreement with McGann's view of the text as social, which became evident from his first book, *The Monument of Culture: Ezra Pound and the Malatesta Cantos* (1991). For Pound studies, it was a landmark publication from the methodological point of view because it marked a turning away from the ideological textualism of deconstruction towards the idea of social text; it was a first application of New Historicism and Geertzian thick description to Pound studies. Implicitly, it was a beginning for New Modernist Studies as well. Though Rainey's title promised an analysis of the *Malatesta Cantos*, it disappointed every expectation in that respect, since it did not offer any interpretation of the poems per se, but concentrated on the context and transmission of Malatesta's story not only to Pound, who researched it in detail, but also to his contemporaries, who had their own versions to tell. Rainey's method broke with the primacy of the finished literary object, effacing the border between published text and manuscript, indeed giving far more attention to drafts and materials ancillary to poetry composition than to the completed work:

> The materials documenting Pound's composition of the Malatesta Cantos are [. . .] unique for their extent, integrity and complexity. [. . .] The materials are massive—more than 700 pages comprising

> 180 documents, including over 60 drafts and draft fragments. They are also heterogeneous—roughly two thirds of the material consists of "nonliterary" documentation: train schedules, journals, lists of books, bills and account statements from booksellers throughout Europe, call slips from libraries in Paris, Rome, and Bologna, transcriptions taken in archives in eleven different cities, reading and bibliographical notes from an array of secondary sources, marginalia and submarginalia entered in Pound's own copies of books, letters of enquiry and administrative records, drawings and epigraphical transcriptions, photographs of epistolary seals . . . and the list goes on. It testifies to the radical interpenetration of the authorial and social worlds and to the impossibility of distinguishing rigorously between literary and historical documents. (8)

Though some reviewers, such as Joseph Kronick, protested against the utter lack of comment on the actual cantos (588), Rainey's methodology shows a clear instance of how author-oriented scholarship flowed into New Modernist Studies. Rainey's book was the prototype for a new methodological approach, effacing the borders between the literary text and the surrounding historical environment, foregrounding problems of textual transmission, disregarding the focus on the textual primacy of the poem as a work of art to a dialogue between surrounding practices of writing and research. For better or for worse, Pound was the key channel of transmission from an old author- and text-oriented scholarship to a new historicism concentrating on the context, writing practices, new media, and changed environments of the poem. His work would acquire an important role in the comprehensive agenda of New Modernist Studies, which aimed to overturn the idea of the autonomy of the literary vis-à-vis practices of modernity; in other words, the critic did not focus on the poem as finished work of art, but rather, on the writing practices and living experience of its author in time. The era heralded by Rainey's book would strive to show that modernism was heavily involved with modern life, technologies, assumptions, and popular culture, an involvement nuanced by the modernists' own practice of deploring, say, newspapers, publishers, and capitalism, yet using their methods, playing their games, swimming with the flow. The chief aim of the scholarship of this period, wrote Rebecca Beasley in *Ezra Pound and the Visual Culture of Modernism* (2007), was moving "beyond the exaltation of formal experiment for its own sake and conducting a sustained interrogation of early twentieth-century cultural production" (3).

Within that aim, scholars took up a wide variety of specific topics and approaches. Rainey himself proceeded to connect Pound's work to questions of marketing, advertising, and patronage in his *Institutions of Modernism* (1998); Catherine Paul inquired into Pound's "exhibitionary method" grounded in his reading at the British Museum in her *Poetry in the Museums of Modernism: Yeats, Pound, Moore, Stein* (2002); Miranda Hickman explored the relationship between Vorticism and Fascist culture in Pound's cantos of the 1930s in her *Geometry of Modernism: The Vorticist Idiom in Lewis, Pound, H. D., and Yeats* (2006); Beasley researched the role of visual cultures in Pound's early work in her *Ezra Pound and the Visual Culture of Modernism* (2007); Robert Scholes argued for Pound's centrality in the interaction of modernism with little magazines, even calling him "founder of the modern periodical studies," in his *Modernism in the Magazines: An Introduction* (2010); and Robert Spoo argued that Pound was the only modernist to have elaborated a copyright statute (2013).

The New Modernist Studies were an effort to turn away from authors towards material practices: if modernist writers had been heretofore seen as autonomous vis-à-vis the capitalist structures of modernity, scholarship now proved that they had been aware of and actively used them. Though Pound was a magnificent case study for this approach, scholarly attention was not focused on him, but on his participation along with other writers in the institutions and practices of capitalism: cultural institutions like museums, archives, libraries; writing practices, like editing and translation; publication venues, such as little magazines, independent publications, small presses, etc. The Modernist Studies Association codified this orientation in the way it presented itself on its website and in its conferences. On the "About" section of its website, the MSA made clear, in a text first posted ca. 1998, its emphasis on interdisciplinarity and historicity as opposed to what it is now as the more inward-looking tendencies of traditional, single-author and/or literary societies:

> Single-author societies still dominated the professional field, and there was little opportunity to respond to the impulses of what we might loosely call cultural studies.
>
> The early MSA refused to be merely a gathering place wherein individual societies could pursue their several projects. It aimed rather to represent the dynamic relations among fields too often reified as separate and unrelated and to facilitate the development of more supple—and ultimately more complete—historical models.

In their calls for papers for their annual conference, the MSA organizers put it even more bluntly. Panels and roundtables on a single author were "strongly discouraged." Author societies could not participate.

Yet, scholars working in interdisciplinary, culturally oriented approaches found Pound everywhere they chose to look. Even when considered in a group, he was central: his innovations, opinions, actions had to be and were acknowledged in any general arguments on modernist practices.

Refusing to Kneel: Pound-Centered Scholarship

The scholarly community found itself divided, as it had been since the close of the 1970s, between academics following the trends of the day and the fewer and fewer scholars stubbornly persisting in a single-author approach based in the author's own assumptions about his work. This exclusive interest in Pound was of course not absolute: prominent Poundians like Leon Surette, A. David Moody, Ronald Bush, Tim Redman, Ira Nadel, and Richard Sieburth, to name just a few, were also doing critical work on other writers, but their author-focused perspective remained constant. In this approach, "Poundians" or "Poundistas" differed from most other scholars of modernism by refusing to go with the trend. They had ignored deconstruction in the 1980s, even in the face of outspoken criticism. Now they refused to subordinate their interest in Pound to a more sociological and eclectic approach to modernism. They stuck to a historicist, explanatory project focused on the poet, recognizing that this approach was not exhausted and that new interpretations based on published and archival sources and documents made it still relevant.

But this commitment took severe blows as time was wreaking havoc on the scholarly structures and channels created by the previous generation. The benevolent protector of the Pound community, Terrell, died in 2003, in the same year with Kenner and Cookson. It was not evident at the time what this meant for Pound studies. Terrell's longtime friend and collaborator, Burt Hatlen, was still working to maintain the institutional structures that Terrell had created at the University of Maine: The National Poetry Foundation (NPF, 1972), The Ezra Pound Society (1979), and the two periodicals, *Paideuma* and *Sagetrieb*—Hatlen took care of them all, but recognizing the changed situation at his university and beyond, he worked to adapt and simplify his workload. He realized that an author journal like *Paideuma* had reached its limit in the new scholarly context of New Modernist Studies. *Sagetrieb,* on the other hand, was founded on Kenner's idea of a modernism anchored in Pound studies and had a rather narrow focus on poets in his tradition. Hatlen could not run both: he decided to discontinue *Sagetrieb*, turn *Paideuma* into an annual, and open it up to modernism as a whole. The result was that articles on Pound became few and relatively far between in that periodical after 2005, when these changes became operational.

The Poundians had lost their journal and their society was almost invisible since it had always been indistinguishable from the NPF. The community was thus only loosely held together by the bi-annual conference organized by an informal group outside Terrell's university: William Pratt (University of Miami), Walter Baumann (University of Ulster), and starting in 2005, John Gery (University of New Orleans). The conference locations were various: in the 1970s and 1980s, they were held mostly in the UK; after 1990, locations in Italy, France, UK, USA, and China were decided at the end of each conference. This group succeeded in maintaining the event against increased difficulties and lack of institutional support. Through continuous effort, individual conference organizers found opportunities for publication, printing a number of conference proceedings in handsome collective volumes—this too was an uphill struggle: just one volume was published in the 1970s and one in the 1980s; during the 1990s there were two volumes; but during the 2000s there were seven; and in the 2010s there have been four. However, the restricted print runs and high price of these volumes, the minimal number of reviews they received and the scant coverage they got in the *MLA Bibliography*, as well as their focus on one author did not endear them to the community of modernism scholars at large. Their impact was strongest among author-oriented readers, not new modernist scholars.

Indeed, the mirror that the *MLA Bibliography* provided for Pound research was defective, to say the least, a situation that was opaque to scholars of modernism at the time. Recent research for the online *Bibliography of English Language Scholarship on Ezra Pound* (Henderson/Preda 2015–) has shown that the *MLA Bibliography* covers only a very small fraction of publications on Pound, particularly since, given the current bias against single-author studies, the name of the author under study is not evident in the book title or even in its chapter headings.

Established Pound scholars like Leon Surette, Ira Nadel, and Lawrence Rainey contributing to the new discourse in modernist studies, showed themselves to be more permeable to the practices of the times. One possibility was to study Pound in a group with other writers, as Surette did in his *The Birth of Modernism: Ezra Pound, T. S. Eliot, W. B. Yeats, and the Occult* (1993) and *Dreams of a Totalitarian Utopia: Literary Modernism and Politics* (2011) and Rainey did in his *Institutions of Modernism* (1998). Another possibility was to respond to the multiplicity of themes circulating in New Modernism Studies with collective volumes. Ira Nadel in his *Cambridge Companion to Ezra Pound* (1999) and *Ezra Pound in Context* (2010) chose this path, which allowed engagement with a great variety of topics, providing opportunities for the intersection between Pound studies and New Modernist Studies broadly conceived. What *Ezra Pound in Context* achieved for scholars, *The Ezra Pound Encyclopedia* (Tryphonopoulos and Adams, 2005) achieved for students and the interested general public. Short articles from over one hundred contributors made the *Encyclopedia* the first hub of information on all topics of interest concerning Pound's life, work, and significant others.

For Poundians, themes and topics tailored on the single author approach differed from those of the larger circles of New Modernism, since they were tailored on Pound's special interests and life and not on cultural institutions and practices of modernity as a whole: monographs dealt with Pound and the occult (Tryphonopoulos, *Celestial Tradition* 1992); Neoplatonism and medieval philosophy (Liebregts, *Ezra Pound and Neoplatonism* 2004; Byron, *Ezra Pound's Eriugena*, 2014); economics (Marsh, *Money and Modernity*, 1998; Surette, *Pound in Purgatory*, 1999; Malm, *Editing Economic History*, 2005; Desai, *The Route of All Evil*, 2006; Preda, *Ezra Pound's Economic Correspondence*, 2007); Chinese culture and art (Qian, 1995, 2003, 2008, 2015; Xie, 1999; Jin, 2002; Lan, 2005; Wang, 2013; Nadel, 2015) and of course right-wing politics (Redman, 1991; Surette, 2011; Feldman, 2013; Marsh, 2015).

Apart from works of critical interpretation, Pound studies found themselves in a period of consolidation, buttressing criticism with a much stronger editorial activity. Pound's creative writing came to be related more intimately with his translating and editing. The Garland edition of *Ezra Pound's Poetry and Prose: Contributions to Periodicals* (11 volumes, 1991) edited by Lea Baechler, James Longenbach, and A. Walton Litz enabled researchers to read Pound's periodical publications, whether poem, article, or review, in chronological order. These contributions had been scattered in a great number of locations (the Beinecke archive at Yale contributed about half the material), and having them together in one book was a tremendous service to scholarship. Litz was a true champion of archival studies and changed forever the ways in which Pound's poetry would be seen. Never again could his poetry be considered as "autonomous" from his criticism and journalism. These volumes created the awareness that Pound's work must be understood integratively, as Baechler, Longenbach, and Litz wrote in their preface, "as parts of a single, developing argument [. . .] a rich autobiography, a vivid record of the most extraordinary poetic life this century has witnessed" (ix).

The fundamental work of connecting the published poetry with Pound's contributions to periodicals in the Garland volumes thus provided a point-by-point contextualization of the poetry, a contextualization that was further refined by the publication of numerous volumes of correspondence. Most of these documented a one-to-one relationship, either personal (letters to Dorothy during their courtship and in captivity), or with fellow artists (Joyce, W. C. Williams, F. M. Ford), editors/publishers/magazines (the *Little Review*, *The Dial*, Alice Corbin Henderson, Stanley Nott), and politicians (Cutting, Borah, Tinkham). In the 1990s, which were extremely prolific in this field, there were ten volumes published, more than in any other decade.[4] All these volumes were important for throwing light on Pound's activity, whether literary, political, or economic. However, none was more fruitful for research than "*I Cease Not to Yowl*," the letter-exchange with Olivia Rossetti Agresti published by Tryphonopoulos and Surette in 1998.[5] This volume was eye-opening on Pound's anti-Semitism and right-wing politics in the St. Elizabeths years, surely an insight that Pound aficionados would have gladly done without, as Surette noted in the volume's introduction (xi). The critical apparatus of the volume benefitted from extension and supplementation in Archie Henderson's *"I Cease Not to Yowl": Reannotated* in 2009, which increased it to 782 pages. The two volumes provided a basis for a renewed interest in studying Pound's later years in more detail: Alec Marsh's *John Kasper and Ezra Pound* (2015) and *The Glossator* issue (a collection of commentaries on each canto of *Thrones*, 2018, edited by Alexander Howard) would have been difficult to conceive without the wealth of facts and the richness of insight into Pound's thinking that the annotated correspondence with Agresti provided.

Editorial activity in the new millennium was especially valuable for establishing the foundations of Pound's work in musical composition. Prime movers in this area were Robert Hughes and Margaret Fisher. Their collaboration resulted in the publication of the unfinished operas *Cavalcanti* (2003) and *Collis O Heliconii* (2004) in editions combining the score and libretto with essays on the work. After Margaret Fisher's study *Ezra Pound's Radio Operas: The BBC Experiments, 1931–1933* was published in 2003, she and Hughes tackled Pound's composition *Le Testament de François Villon*: first the performance scores of 1926 and 1933 (2008), then the facsimile edition of the Pound/Antheil score of 1923 (2011). Hughes had performed the opera in 1971 and recorded it on LP in 1972. Now he strove to recuperate the old recording by transferring it from vinyl to CD, publishing first a compilation of Pound's musical compositions, *Ego Scriptor Cantilenae* (2003), and then the full *Testament* in 2012. This activity of publication, performance, recording and interpretation laid the foundations for studying Pound as a composer, a new interdisciplinary field that now awaits further development.

Editorial activity in the 1990s and 2000s was not limited to Pound's contributions to periodicals and to his music compositions, but extended to his poetical work as well. This work took several directions. One of them was to publish luxury editions: a notable example is *Shakespear's Pound: Illuminated Cantos* (1999) which published fragments of cantos of the 1930s together with artwork by Dorothy Pound (née Shakespear) from the archives. Another example is the facsimile edition of six notebooks of *Drafts and Fragments* (2010), prepared by Glen Horrowitz, a bookseller who had sat at Pound's feet at St. Elizabeths.

Further notable editions were *Personae,* prepared by Baechler and Litz for New Directions in 1990 as well as Sieburth's *Pisan Cantos* for New Directions and *Poems and Translations* for the Library of America, both published in 2003. Crossing the boundaries between published poem and manuscripts were Bacigalupo's *Canti Postumi* of 2002, republished as *Posthumous Cantos* in 2015. This edition included selections of canto drafts arranged along the phases of poem composition and chosen, according to the editor, on "criteria of quality, accessibility and documentary interest" (xii). Continuing this line, Haun Saussy, Jonathan Stalling, and Lucas Klein's *The Chinese Character as a Medium for Poetry: A Critical Edition* (2008) put the magnifying lens on Pound's editing of Ernest Fenollosa's essay—it is the only critical edition of any Pound text to date.

Pound Research in the UK

At the start of the 1990s, the situation of Pound research in the UK was frail: a bleak diagnosis was provided by Michael Alexander, co-editor, with James McGonigal, of *Sons of Ezra* (1993), a volume that explored Pound's influence on British poetry. In his review of *Studies in Ezra Pound* by Donald Davie (1991), Alexander remarked:

> Over the years the English resistance to Ezra Pound has taken different forms. I have heard objection taken to his nationality, and to his name; to his amateur scholarship; to his obscurity, his economics and his egotism; then to his politics or his racism; more rarely, to the lack of unity of the *Cantos*. I can report that new objections to this poet are being made; to his sexism, his logocentricity, or even his phallogocentricity. The latter may sound an obscure disease, but it has recently been found to be widespread among writers, and is dangerous, especially to the eye. It can be caught by reading long poems, though works of criticism are safe. Safest of all are the long works of theoretical literary criticism. (64)

Alexander's sarcasm against the theoretical approach to Pound's political sins, typical of the 1980s, is obvious and unmistakable. His association with William Cookson's magazine, *Agenda*, gave the magazine one of its most serious scholarly commentary in Poundiana. As long as Cookson was alive, Pound had an established place in *Agenda* because Cookson considered the poet to be the founder of the magazine. Looking back into issues of the 1990s, we see that Cookson continued to follow Pound research, to publish reviews of important publications, and to relate Pound's oeuvre to British poetry. Cookson's book publication venture, Agenda Editions, published translations of poets whom Pound valued: Villon (by Peter Dale), Dante (by Laurence Binyon), and Catullus. This policy was a natural outcome of a forty-year editorial practice of publishing original poems by, translations of, or critical essays on poets whom Pound considered important in the magazine. Cookson characterized it as a "shoe-string operation, never supported, except for individual books, by any external funding" (*Agenda* 33, no.1 [spring 1995]: 6). This was not strictly correct, since he had received funding from the Arts and Humanities Council and later, just before he died, from the Lottery Fund—but funding was intermittent, not based on the permanence of a university press, or even of a commercial press of high prestige, as Eliot's *Criterion* had been.

Cookson found steady collaborators in his co-editors, first Peter Dale and then Patricia McCarthy. The last issues of *Agenda* to have a strong Pound presence were the forty-year anniversary issue in 1999 (37, no.2, Autumn-Winter 1999) and the Sheri Martinelli number of the following year (38, no.1–2, 2000–2001). When Cookson died in January 2003, in the same year with Terrell and Kenner, McCarthy took over the magazine. For her, Pound was not the object of lifelong love and permanent interest as he had been for Cookson—the new editor oriented the magazine towards a reflection of contemporary poetry across the world. It was a timely move, in consonance with the orientation of general poetry research. Pound disappeared from the periodical.

The discouraging statements that Alexander was making in 1991 seemed to come true as Pound's staunchest admirer and unconditional promoter in the UK went to his grave. But during the following twenty-five years, Alexander's bleak view of a decline in Pound studies in the UK has received a few correctives. In November 2006, a group gathered for the first time at the University of London's Institute of English Studies. The purpose of its members was to read and discuss *The Cantos* on a regular basis, one canto at a time. They organized a schedule where speakers would moderate two hours of close reading once a month. As an attempt, it may seem modest; yet, the Cantos Reading Group persisted, and in 2018, it is still going strong. The group is open to scholars, students, and non-academic *afficionados* alike. Officially, it is a classroom, but an open one: a place for people who feel that keeping *The Cantos* alive across the boundaries that separate the university from the wider public is the test and indicator of a poet's real survival and significance.

The key figures of this spot of liveliness are Helen Carr and Richard Parker. Parker, especially, has been vitally interested in the moderators' readings, which he has recently gathered into a volume; beyond that, he was interested in the transmission of Pound's specific poetics to the contemporary British avant-garde. The latter was a necessary work, since Pound's influence on American poetry, particularly on Charles Olson and Robert Duncan had already been well documented by Christopher Beach in his *ABC of Influence: Ezra Pound and the Remaking of the American Poetic Tradition* (1992).

In 2014, Parker published *News from Afar*, outlining Pound's reception among contemporary poets in the UK, a volume departing from Alexander's earlier collection, *Sons of Ezra* (1995). For Parker, the key mediator was Eric Mottram, poet and professor at King's College London, who had absorbed Pound via his interest in Olson's *Maximus Poems* and his correspondence with Robert Duncan. Parker was no defender of Pound's politics and economics the way Cookson had been, but made clear the spectrum of literary methods which a politically oriented avant-garde could learn from the older poet and effectively use to write on politics today—Pound's use of rage, sarcasm, and invective offered possibilities for the affirmation of a *littérature engagée*. Further, Pound's translations from Chinese in *Cathay* showed the way for translation experiments by contemporary poets. Moreover, his knowledge-driven poetic practice offered methods which could be adapted to new content, for new syntheses. The novelty of Parker's collection was that it did not include just academic essays, but also samples of creative work, from a piece of political rant by Keston Sutherland, and translations from Chinese poetry by Harry Gilonis to avant-garde poetic experiments by Tony Lopez.

Helen Carr, on the other hand, produced the most detailed and useful account of the imagist revolution in her *The Verse Revolutionaries* (2009). Other high-profile scholars like Moody with his monumental biography *Ezra Pound: Poet* (3 vols., 2007–2015), Beasley with her *Ezra Pound and the Visual Culture of Modernism* (2007), and Bush with his stream of articles on the *Pisan Cantos* were producing work that was in active dialogue with the needs of their time, making the UK a distinctive force field from which new research on Pound irradiated.

Pound's Politics: Research for the New Millennium

The political lessons of the 1980s derived from the deconstructionist ideology critique were thoroughly internalized in the New Modernist Studies. Pound's fascism and anti-Semitism were beyond controversy, a matter of grounded knowledge that permeated everything Pound wrote and all the activities he was involved in. If scholars were inclined to be charitable, they stressed Pound's good side—his help for fellow artists, his energizing involvement in little magazines, his early Vorticist period—but even then, they took care to draw the lines forward to his fascism of the 1930s and 1940s, to stress his authoritarianism, racism, and gender bias.

A variant of this charitableness was to emphasize, as did Marjorie Perloff and Charles Bernstein, that there is a fundamental tension between Pound's politics and *The Cantos*—the collage form of the poem had a way of escaping control, its cultivation of the fragment made it impossible to subsume under the idea of a coherent (fascist) totality, and its sheer heterogeneity eluded the reign of the "right" word. Bernstein's polemic essay "Pounding Fascism" (1992) owed a lot to the De Man-ian critique that posited spots of blindness and incommensurability between Pound's intention and ideology on the one hand, and the rebellious, ungovernable poetic texture of his poem on the other. Bernstein's main insight was the radical conflict he saw between Pound's poetics of fragmentation and his totalizing fascism:

> I do not, however, equate Pound's politics with Pound's poetry. *The Cantos* is in many ways radically (radially) at odds with the tenets of his fascist ideals. In this sense, Pound has systematically misinterpreted the nature of his own literary production; refused, that is, to recognize in it the process he vilified as usury and Jewishness. This blindness to the meaning of his work, to how in significant ways it represented what he claimed to revile most, contributed not only to the rabidness of his dogmatism but also to the heights of magnificent self-deception and elegiac confusion that is *The Cantos* at its best. (122)

The intensity of his polemic and the idea that *The Cantos* is permeated by Jewishness or that the author is blind to the qualities of his own work directly locate this essay in the tradition established by the poststructuralist critiques of the 1980s like those by Robert Casillo, Andrew Parker, Richard Sieburth, and Maud Ellmann. Unlike them, however, Bernstein did not damn the poem to perdition, but affirmed its independence from the poet. Moreover, Bernstein's scorn was directed at the privileged position of the Eurocentric canon in universities, which had made it possible for Pound to be himself canonized, instead of being marginalized and forgotten. For Bernstein, there was an underlying complicity between conservative education and the ideas of "culture" that had enabled Pound's literary survival. His solution to this impossible conundrum was a multiculturalist agenda that would dissolve the cultural foundation of Pound's poem and thus interrupt its transmission.

But even here Bernstein could not simply damn Pound together with a Eurocentric canon, since he was aware of how the poem had eluded that as well, toward an inclusion of non-European cultures:

> In contrast, the success of *The Cantos* is that its coherence is of a kind totally different than Pound desired or could—in his more rigid moments—accept. For the coherence of the "hyperspace" of Pound's modernist collage is not a predetermined Truth of a pancultural elitism but a product of a compositionally decentered multiculturalism. (122–23)

Bernstein's ambivalence towards *The Cantos* at the start of the 1990s, his indecision as to whether to damn the poem as promoting a conservative Eurocentric idea of culture, or rather to save it as initiating a "decentered multiculturalism" gives us an implicit permission to like and study the poem despite everything that a postmodern critique might say about its fascism. The poem denied and surpassed the poet, and it is here that Perloff concurred. Her review of the third volume of Moody's biography *Ezra Pound: Poet*, published in the *TLS* in 2015, reiterated a variant of this point of view, namely that the poem surpassed the poet and that

Pound's "unconscious habits" won out in his literary composition despite any of his particular political or literary ideologies:

> The brilliant "phalanx of particulars," drawn from Ovidian myth, Eleusinian mysteries, and the uncannily detailed remembrance of actual names, dates, incidents, menus, headlines, war dispatches and the *bons mots* of friends, as well as pronunciation games (as in the reference to the Oxford college Magdalen, "rhyming dawdlin"), and especially the revolutionizing of the poetic line and the printed page, creating a field of force that transformed twentieth-century poetry—it is these almost unconscious poetic habits, rather than Pound's overt allegiance to Neoplatonism or to the Confucian Idea of inner order, that make his writing so unique. Not the allegiance to the "Great Crystal" but the fulfilment of the early axiom "Dichten = condensare," exemplified on page after page of the *Cantos*: this was Pound's genius. (2015)

Other scholars were not so charitable. In his work on the Malatesta Cantos, *Ezra Pound and the Monument of Culture* (1991), Lawrence Rainey invoked Clifford Geertz's method of thick description to create his historical narrative and to suggest that the temporal limits of Pound's fascism are malleable and can be pushed further back. The origins of the poem coincided with those of Fascism, since Pound had researched for the Malatesta Cantos in Italy in 1922 before the March on Rome and published them in the summer of 1923, after the event. Bearing in mind that these cantos were the stimulus behind the composition of *A Draft of XVI Cantos* as a whole, and further, that the Malatesta Cantos reverberated in Pound's whole poem with some one hundred references, Rainey argued that *The Cantos* is inextricably interwoven with the origins of Fascism and cannot be separated from it. What fascinates most in Rainey's book is his treatment of time: it is a homogeneous present, in which isolated acts of reading and writing are placed in new contiguities with a view to creating causalities. Pound's research and writing of the Malatesta Cantos were thus placed next to Mussolini's March on Rome, though the two were not causally connected. Apart from that, Rainey drew a line of necessity between the Malatesta Cantos and the so-called "Italian Cantos" (72 and 73) which Pound would write twenty-two years later, in 1944–45, though there can be no sense of destiny connecting the two. Rainey's absorption with drafts and refusal to go into an interpretation of the final Malatesta Cantos did not help drive home his political point that he viewed them as a first manifestation of Pound's fascism in his poetry, or that they are indeed the prefiguration of the propagandistic Italian cantos.

That same year, 1991, Cambridge University Press brought out Tim Redman's *Ezra Pound and Italian Fascism*, the impact of which is still registering. Most of the contemporary reviews refrained from evaluation, preferring to offer descriptions of Redman's argument: Pound's fascism developed out of his Social Credit apprenticeship in London in 1918 and mutated to a "felt-wing fascism" in Pound's interactions with Italian politics and society up to the Second World War. Redman chose not to discuss *The Cantos*, but focused on Pound's prose. This attracted a very strong attack from Casillo in the *Modern Language Review*: Casillo had refuted the argument that Pound was attracted to left-wing fascism in his *Genealogy of Demons* (197–203), and viewed Redman's book as an attempt to sanitize and defend Pound. In Casillo's opinion, cutting the politics out from a discussion of the poem was a disastrous choice that weakened or even nullified Redman's argument. Casillo attacked Redman's premise that Pound's fascism had evolved out of his economic education, implicitly attacking the establishment of Pound scholarship, as he had done in his book, published three years before:

> Like most critics, Redman views Pound's fascism one-sidedly as "economic" (p.78): Pound hoped that Mussolini would implement financial and monetary reforms similar to those proposed by Douglas and Silvio Gesell. Such an interpretation would detoxify Pound of the worst elements of fascism. Redman does not understand Pound's attraction to fascism's organicist social theory and its ideal of a hierarchical, functional, non-class, and corporate society. (186–87)

Unfortunately for Casillo's objections (whose mordant tone had been previously criticized by Dasenbrock and Rainey), subsequent scholarship would reinforce Redman's findings (Surette, *Ezra Pound in Purgatory* [1999]; Preda, *Ezra Pound's Economic Correspondence* [2007]). Pound's economic correspondence, in particular, provided tangible proof that what attracted the poet to Mussolini's regime was not the integration or rather effacement of the individual within an organic state, but the opportunities that the political experiment of Fascism presented for the implementation of Douglasite distributive justice. Pound's correspondence with Odon Por, in particular, made clear that they were both involved in a common effort to persuade the regime to adopt Social Credit and Gesellite measures. Pound thought that Fascists would be more amenable to Douglasite arguments, especially because liberal political structures in Italy were recent and weak. Hence Mussolini's *senso storico,* his reorganization of political representation along vocational lines, and his banking reform of 1935 were positive signs in Pound's eyes that Douglasite and Gesellite measures would take hold in the end, that Mussolini was moving slowly but surely towards them, or a close interpretation of them. Pound never relinquished this goal and proposed Gesell's "vanishing money" to Mussolini just two months before the dictator fell from power in July 1943 (Moody, *Ezra Pound: Poet,* III: 58–59). Looking back on his efforts, Pound wrote in the *Pisan Cantos*:

"No longer necessary," taxes are no longer necessary
in the old way if it (money) be based on work done
inside a system and measured and gauged to human requirements
inside the nation or system
and cancelled in proportion
to what is used and worn out
à la Wörgl. Sd/ one wd/ have to think about that
but was hang'd dead by the heels before his thought in proposito
came into action efficiently (LXXVIII/501–2)

and

you can, said Stef (Lincoln Steffens)
do nothing with revolutionaries
until they are at the end of their tether (LXXXIV/560)

Indeed, the economics angle would prove fertile in subsequent research on Pound's politics: Marsh's *Money and Modernity* (1998), Surette's *Pound in Purgatory* (1999) and *Dreams of a Totalitarian Utopia* (2011), Desai's *The Route of all Evil* (2006), and Preda's edition of the *Economic Correspondence* (2007) were landmark studies elaborating the economic underpinnings of Pound's support for Fascism. But none of these involved a thorough discussion of economics in *The Cantos* as a whole, nor did they seek to argue that the poem was Fascist. This became even more evident in the ways scholars handled the "Italian Cantos" (LXXII-LXXIII). For Rainey, these cantos were a direct reverberation of the Malatesta sequence across a span of more than twenty years, expressing the same ideology and the same wish to represent Fascist ideals. For other scholars like Bacigalupo (1984, 2005) and Patricia Cockram (2000) these cantos were a deliberate departure from Pound's general poetic practices in the poem and were considered separately from the rest.

New discussion threads on Pound's politics took another route and revealed a fraught relationship with the *aesthetic* ideologies and practices of Fascism. Michael North (1991), Miranda Hickman (2006), Catherine Paul (2005, 2008) and David Barnes (2010, 2014) are notable examples of that discursive field, discussing how aesthetic features of Fascism such as monumentality, the hero cult, the idealization of the Roman Empire, nationalism, and the big Fascist exhibitions of 1932 and 1937 were reflected in Pound's work. Other interesting new threads in the political discussion were brought onto the stage by Matthew Feldman's research. His book *Ezra Pound's Fascist Propaganda* (2013) enriched both the archival basis of the topic and the detail in the narration of historical facts. Additionally, his work branched out into Pound's involvement with broadcasting, which can be very well accommodated within the New Modernist Studies on radio (Feldman 2014; see also Dinsman 2015). Another new and interesting direction that Feldman followed was Pound's political legacy, his value as a model for subsequent fascisms in the US and Italy (Feldman 2014, see also Mangiafico 2012).

The year 2015 was especially important for illuminating the politics of the 1950s and the role that Pound played in them. Two books shared the field: Marsh's *Ezra Pound and John Kasper: Saving the Republic* and the third volume of Moody's biography, *Ezra Pound: Poet*. Though differently calibrated, these monographs considerably enlarged the field in which Pound's politics was presented and discussed, showing that Pound's anti-Semitism was particularly virulent in this period and his politics veered towards the American extreme right. The question of Fascism was thus decentered and re-contextualized within the framework of the American conservatism and racism of the 1950s. However, the split between Pound's allegiances, attitudes, opinions, letters, and the cantos that he was writing at the time was evident. Though both scholars had focused on this period of Pound's life for many years, they did not propose to prove that the later cantos bore the colors of the extreme right. That project might yet be realized in the future, but for the time being, the poem and Pound's political ideology are still treated separately.

In the second volume of *Ezra Pound: Poet* (2014), Moody argued that Pound had a personal, eccentric involvement with Fascism: his juxtaposition of Mussolini with Jefferson, his defense of the American constitution, and his belief that Confucian philosophy is the foundation for good government and peace were enmeshed in his loyalty to Fascism but overlooked in his indictment for treason and most arguments concerning Pound's political activities. Nonetheless, it is too early to tell whether the argument for eccentricity is going to make an impact against the much simpler "there can be no doubt that Pound was indeed a Fascist" (Perloff 2015).

The Conservative Revolution: *The Cantos* Research and Digital Culture

> *Technology tended to engulf people gradually, coercing behaviour they were not aware of.*
>
> —Hugh Kenner, *The Mechanic Muse*

All through the late 1990s and 2000s we may observe the decline in the number of studies on *The Cantos* and, most of all, the disappearance of a whole genre of scholarly work—the monograph on the poem as a whole.

If a few years like 1983 or 1991 had been miraculously rich in publications (five monographs on the poem in 1983; four in 1991),[6] for the nineteen years between 1997 and 2016, there were just seven monographs in all, and none in the last four of those years. Book-length studies, like Liebregts's, *Ezra Pound and Neoplatonism*, or even collective volumes like Rainey's *A Poem Containing History* became scarce, yet the work on the poem continued, albeit low-key. Prominent scholars published articles in collections or series, rather than a full monograph: Baumann gathered his articles in *Roses from the Steel Dust* (2000); Bush wrote mostly on the *Pisan Cantos* (eleven articles between 1995 and 2013); Bacigalupo published the *Canti Postumi* (2002), translated as *Posthumous Cantos* (2015) and he also translated *A Draft of XXX Cantos* into Italian (2012); finally, in Nicholls's broad palette of article publications, an acute reader could discern an interest in *Thrones* (Cantos 96 to 109). The poem was rarely seen alone and even less in its entirety: scholars chose to focus on a single cycle (Stoicheff, *The Hall of Mirrors: Drafts and Fragments and the End of Ezra Pound's Cantos*, 1995; Malm, *Editing Economic History: Ezra Pound's "The Fifth Decad" of Cantos*, 2007; Ten Eyck, *Ezra Pound's Adams Cantos*, 2012), or compare the poem with epics or drama (Shioji, *Ezra Pound's Pisan Cantos and the Noh*, 1997, Henriksen, *Ambition and Anxiety: Ezra Pound's "Cantos" and Derek Walcott's "Omeros" as Twentieth-Century Epics*, 2007; Flack, *Modernism and Homer: The Odysseys of H. D., James Joyce, Osip Mandelstam, and Ezra Pound*, 2015). This trend continued in the dissertations of the 2000s and 2010s: grouping Pound with other modernist authors, and *The Cantos* with the epics of Homer, Olson, Williams, Seferis, etc. was the practice of the day.

Moreover, the contemporary situation inherited the unfinished great projects started in the 1980s: Taylor's *Variorum Edition of Ezra Pound's Cantos* and Bush's *Ezra Pound's "Pisan Cantos": A Genetic and Critical Edition*. Kenner's *The Pound Era* and Terrell's *Companion* were still the gates and pillars of Pound scholarship, more than thirty years after publication. The sense of a rupture and estrangement from *The Cantos*, an obscure need to return to the unfinished project of understanding the poem seemed to trickle down into the interstices of the reigning sociological and historicist approach to Pound studies.

In this same period, however, digital culture began to make itself felt ever more forcefully. From the very first website uploaded at CERN by Tim Berners-Lee in 1991 to the world wide web as we know it, digital culture impacted modernist studies in thousands of ways and Pound studies with it. But there was a privileged domain in which the concept of hypertext, coined by Ted Nelson in the 1960s, and that of the internet, created by Lee, impacted the Pound scholarly community most, and that was in the research on *The Cantos*. The development of digital interactive platforms, first within institutions and then for individuals, made it conceivable that projects and dreams, which for at least two decades had been hitting the walls of the print medium, could thrive in the digital.

1997 might be seen as the year in which the importance of the digital medium for Pound scholarship became unmistakable. In 1997, Pound scholars showed real interest not just in the digital publication of work, but more importantly, in theorizing the possibilities of hypertext as applicable to *The Cantos*. A first instance was proposed in the two articles published in *Paideuma* 26, no.2–3 (Fall-Winter 1997) by William Cole ("Pound's Web: Hypertext in the Rock-Drill Cantos") and Patricia Cockram ("Hypertextuality and Pound's Fascist Aesthetic"). Both these articles used "hypertext" as a methodological concept that mirrored principles of formal organization within *The Cantos*. Cole's article clarified how the notion of hypertext reformulates the poem's method as a network of nodes and links, giving a contemporary color to what Pound called the ideogrammic method, subject rhyme, and luminous detail. Cockram's contribution was a meditation on and warning against the model of power underlying hypertext. A generation before, in his *The Mechanic Muse* (1988), Kenner had compared modernism with the linotype machine, whose complex, unnatural logic was geared towards maximum functionality and visibility (9–15). Now Cockram warned that despite the illusion of convenience and freedom that hypertext promised, readers were not actually empowered, because the programming behind the text was invisible, ever changing, and impenetrable to the uninitiated (160–61). Cockram's warning has lost nothing of its edge at this moment of writing, twenty years after the article publication.

Hypertext, understood as blocks of text connected by links, was indeed a useful conceptual tool in thinking about *The Cantos,* offering a suggestive image of Pound's working method and textual organization. Nevertheless, a more fruitful line of inquiry was in thinking about *the model of reading* that hypertext offered: a freedom to cross Pound's sequences as a surfer crosses the flow of the wave: to traverse the poem from link to link, from node to node. Readers thus become aware of the changes of context that each particular reading instance affords and of possible choices and alternate routes within the poem. Redman's article "An Epic is a Hypertext Containing Poetry" (1997) explained it best: readers would find a quotation or a name—clicking on it would bring a page explaining it and including another significant name, which could also be clicked on for an explanation—the reader would thus find further instances where the name occurs in the poem and would check them out. But such simple glossing of references in the poem would not be spectacular and a true departure. This would emerge when

> the addition of electronic paths would transport us to other cantos. Notes on Sigismundo and Isotta would lead us to the Malatesta

> Cantos, to photos and drawings of the Tempio and a discussion of its place in early renaissance architecture, or to photos of its sculptures and the relation they bore to Hermetic philosophy. A hypertext, then, is an electronic text that allows the reader to traverse it in a number of different ways. It can take two forms, a read-only hypertext, where readers would discover paths already embedded by the creator of the hypertext, and a read/write hypertext, where readers could add their own links and screens. (141)

There was a certain enthusiasm in this period for creating an electronic instance of *The Cantos* like a huge network where a reader could skip around from gloss to gloss, link to link; each reading could thus be unique and produce different results, even if the starting points of the journey were the same. Apart from the freedom in choosing readings, interactivity and continuous updates of the critical apparatus were also strong reasons why the digital glossing of the poem, with its provision of active links, was a desirable goal.

These were dreams and speculations on paper. In reality, copyright restrictions were in place, forbidding the digital display of the whole poem; moreover, the technology of the 1990s was not advanced enough to handle *The Cantos*: Taylor's account of his *Variorum* Project saga proved this in the clearest terms ("Tragi-Comical History," 2005). Several one-canto prototypes were published on the internet at various times. The first was "Kybernekia," Ned Bates's website at the University of North Carolina-Greensboro in 1997. This was a website dedicated to Canto LXXXI, including annotations linked to it. The model was simple: the reader could find the poem on one webpage; annotated words and phrases were marked in blue, to signal they were links. The gloss was on a different page; the model was thus a simple route of away and back, not much different from the experience of reading the poem with Terrell's print *Companion* and perhaps even inferior to that, despite the illustrative material and the possibilities for correction and supplementation of the gloss. At least a student reading Terrell could have the *Companion* open on the table together with the poem: the eye indeed goes from poem to gloss and back, but it is not absolutely necessary to keep turning a page for every gloss.

Kybernekia's model was fruitful: Jeff Grieneisen annotated Canto XXXI in 2004 along the same lines; another example was Canto XLV, published in the digital magazine *Flashpoint* in 2008. These webpages have meanwhile disappeared from the web, but their principle was the same: poem text on one page, gloss on another. The situation began improving after 2009, when a number of cantos were uploaded on the "Genius" platform, a website dedicated to song lyrics—glosses appeared on request, on the same page as the poem, which was an improvement.

Definitely less attractive were the commercial ads cluttering the pages.[7] However, all these practical applications were done as student work, magazine articles, Wikipedia-like community contributions: uncoordinated, contingent, incomplete, provisional, and in many respects amateurish. It was only in 2014, with Preda's upload of *The Cantos Project* platform, that a coordinated effort to follow up on Redman's vision of a professional digital research environment (DRE) was begun. Taking account of *The Cantos* as a whole, providing full access to sources, connecting Pound's poem to his journalism and correspondence were steps toward spanning a bridge over the thirty-five years that had passed since the publication of Terrell's *Companion*. The aim is to create what Terrell himself would have wished, an integrated and updatable system of information on the poem that would include annotations but not stop there (as Terrell had been forced to do by the constraints of print). Instead, it would offer a definite procedure to supplement, connect, and emend the critical apparatus by way of the cooperation of a myriad of scholars.

The establishment of such a DRE on *The Cantos* was made possible by the rise and development of digital humanities after 2010. Universities and research councils were sponsoring them: digital editions, facsimile presentations, archives of correspondence, databases, and bibliographies. These sponsorships are very precious in the digital world, as they insure not only the professional character of interactive platforms, but also, due to teams of IT professionals, their perfectibility, sustainability, and security over time. Signals that the time was ripe for a digital reformulation of scholarship became evident in Preda's proposed return to fundamentals of research, to picking up textual studies on the poem and improving on the print media's possibilities of rendering text.

Digital culture has also made Pound's sources available, as well as the reception of these sources in other professional circles, confirming their value for culture. The internet can now offer digital editions of the books Pound read and used, which are very scarce and difficult to find in the print medium: from Divus's Latin translation of the *Odyssey,* to Ficinus's anthology of Neoplatonists, Paul the Deacon's *History of the Langobards,* the *Li Ki,* to Alexander Del Mar's *History of Monetary Systems* (Chicago edition, all but unfindable in *Paideuma* days). Access to these sources has made it more obvious that Pound's interests, inexplicable to his contemporaries, were not merely exotic or abstruse. Reintegrating these sources into the cultural circuit has shown the service that *The Cantos* provides as a monument in and to the transmission of culture. The Pound Society found its way into the digital age in 2014, initiating large collaborative projects like Henderson and Preda's *Bibliography of English Language Scholarship on Ezra Pound* and Sansone and Bacigalupo's *Online Bibliography of Italian Pound Studies (OBIPS).* Indeed, the society launched its first digital magazine, *Make It New,* and its first digitizing project, the eleven volumes of *Ezra Pound's Poetry and Prose: Contributions to Periodicals* (1991) in 2015.

The fact that Pound had challenged the limits of the print medium was well known to scholars: *The Cantos* presupposed reading several books at once; playing scores; contemplating ideograms and seals; and suspending reading habits in various ways, notably by eccentric layouts and foreign languages. Still, it must have come as a surprise to every scholar of modernism everywhere to see that Jessica Pressman, in a book called *Digital Modernism* (2014), included a chapter consisting of a close reading of a digital-born text (Young-hae Chang Heavy Industries's *Dakota*) and analyzed its reliance on Pound's Canto I, adding that this particular chapter was essential, even the reason her book was written. Even more surprising was Pressman's attempt to revitalize New Criticism and its valorization of close, "slow" reading. Paradoxically, the new digital technologies are not always sympathetic to the poststructuralist theory that sometimes heralded them. To Pound scholars concerned with how outdated, dispersed, and incomplete the present knowledge of *The Cantos* currently is, Pressman's theoretical reorientation intimates that this new era might reclaim old values. Digital editing and glossing has meant taking up the oldest philological pursuits and giving them a new face—and a new lease on life.

Notes

[1] See in this context the list of the oppositions between modernism and postmodernism produced by Ihab Hassan in his *The Dismemberment of Orpheus* (1982) as well as the concept of the "great divide" between high and popular culture in Andreas Huyssen's *After the Great Divide* (1986).

[2] See monographs such as: Daniel Gabriel, *Hart Crane and the Modernist Epic: Canon and Genre Formation in Crane, Pound, Eliot, and Williams* (2007); Rebecca Beasley, *Theorists of Modernist Poetry: T. S. Eliot, T. E. Hulme, Ezra Pound* (2007); Helen Carr, *The Verse Revolutionaries: Ezra Pound, H.D. and The Imagists* (2009); Miranda B. Hickman, *The Geometry of Modernism: The Vorticist Idiom in Lewis, Pound, H.D., and Yeats* (2006); Harold Kaplan, *Poetry, Politics, and Culture: Argument in the Work of Eliot, Pound, Stevens, and Williams* (2006).

[3] Examples are so abundant that only a very few instances can be given here: Rupert Richard Arrowsmith, *Modernism and the Museum: Asian, African, and Pacific Art and the London Avant-garde* (2011); Mark Antliff and Scott W. Klein, eds., *Vorticism: New Perspectives* (2013); Peter Brooker and Andrew Thacker, eds. *The Oxford Critical and Cultural History of Modernist Magazines*, volume 2: *North America 1894–1960* (2012); Daniel Katz, *American Modernism's Expatriate Scene: The Labour of Translation* (2007).

[4] The publication of the volumes of Pound's correspondence was slow at first: until 1980, there were 4 volumes; during the 1980s, 8 volumes; publication then peaked in the 1990s with 10 volumes; in the 2000s the process slowed down to 5

volumes; since 2010, we have had 2 volumes. The numbers rely on Archie Henderson's bibliography of correspondence volumes (Ezra Pound Society, 2016).

5 See a few of the numerous reviews of this volume by Jonathan Morse, R. W. (Herbie) Butterfield, Robert Merritt, and E. P. Walkiewicz.

6 1983: Michael Culver, *The Art of Henry Strater: An Examination of the Illustrations for Pound's A Draft of XVI Cantos*; Guy Davenport, *Cities on Hills: Study of 1–30 of Ezra Pound's Cantos*; Peter D'Epiro, *Touch of Rhetoric: Ezra Pound's Malatesta Cantos*; John Driscoll, *The "China Cantos" of Ezra Pound*; John J. Nolde, *Blossoms from the East: The China Cantos of Ezra Pound*. 1991: Akiko Miyake, *Ezra Pound and the Mysteries of Love: A Plan for "The Cantos"*; Lawrence Rainey, *Ezra Pound and the Monument of Culture: Text, History and the Malatesta Cantos*; Stephen Sicari. *Pound's Epic Ambition: Dante and the Modern World*; Richard Taylor, *Variorum Edition of "Three Cantos" by Ezra Pound: A Prototype*.

7 On the Genius platform, one can find the annotated texts of cantos I, XLV, LXXII, and LXXXI. See https://genius.com/Ezra-pound-canto-i-annotated

8: The Many Lives of Ezra Pound: Biographies and Memoirs, 1960–2015

> *If we think of truth as something of granite-like solidity and of personality as something of rainbow-like intangibility and reflect that the aim of biography is to weld these two into one seamless whole, we shall admit that the problem is a stiff one and that we need not wonder if biographers have for the most part failed to solve it.*
>
> —Virginia Woolf, "The New Biography"

> *[The facts of history] do not speak for themselves, alone, exclusively, "objectively." Without the narrator to make them speak, they would be dumb. It is not objectivity that is the historian's best glory. His justness consists in seeking to understand.*
>
> —J. G. Droysen, *Outline of the Principles of History*

THE BIOGRAPHICAL LITERATURE that has accumulated around Ezra Pound for more than half a century is vast and diverse. Retrospectively speaking, it could not have been otherwise. Pound was a bohemian and a rebel; he insisted on his individual point of view in the face of governments and war; was deprived of liberty for thirteen years without trial; locked up in a mental hospital, he was denied personhood: he was deemed incurably insane, in spite of the steady stream of original poetry and translations from Greek and Chinese that poured from his typewriter in the asylum years. Pound had chosen to fight the world—the world fought back and conquered. From 1945 onwards, his life was turned into a cause célèbre and opinions among academics and non-professionals alike have been sharply divided. There were those whose interest was born of compassion, who witnessed or read accounts of his tribulations as an old man, and looked upon him as a poet of genius whom America had treated unconstitutionally and unjustly. There were others who saw him as a monster guilty of betraying his country in time of war and deserving execution—shooting or hanging, whichever was most practical. In this view, the mental hospital was not only inadequate punishment; it was no punishment at all. Pound had privileges, he received visitors and held court; he even continued his outrageous anti-Semitic rants and placed himself as an *éminence grise* behind right-wing radicalism in the US. The telling of Pound's life has always hinged on his biographers' political and moral commitments, and the writing of a Pound biography cannot but be a political act, inscribing a certain moral position that the biographer makes clear in his text. The biographer's identity is bound to be split: admiration and interest for Pound's poetry and compassion about his plight might be assumed—on the other hand, abhorrence of Pound's anti-Semitism and fascism is also part of it, in many cases the main part. The moral choices have been so dramatic as to create differences of genre. Was the telling of Pound's life a morality tale, a comedy, a tragedy, a mystery, a vindication or a prosecution? Fortunately, biographers have often not simply allowed their attitudes to trickle down between the lines, but have left autobiographical accounts that made clear to readers where they stood. Some were positive, even enthusiastic, like Eustace Mullins or Michael Reck. Some were former enthusiasts who became disengaged from the life and critical of the work, like Noel Stock. Some were ironic, even sarcastic, like Humphrey Carpenter. Some kept up the flame of an admiration born out of lifelong study and commitment, like Wilhelm or Moody. In every case, the biographer left enough traces of himself for the reader to judge and respond to the story he had to tell. As in historiography and fiction, the ultimate achievement of a Pound biography has come to depend on the maturity, complexity, and professionalism of its point of view.

The 1960s: Fluttering about the Ezra Pound Case

Pound's months in a disciplinary training camp at Pisa in 1945, his indictment for treason for the broadcasts he had made in Rome during the war, his hearing, his life at St. Elizabeths, and the efforts of his friends and well-wishers to win him release and freedom were the engines of human interest propelling the emergence of the biographical impulse. Pound's first biographers were people who became interested in him because of this sequence of events, or who visited him regularly in the mental hospital—their interest was not extended to his life as a whole, or to his poetic career, but geared to elucidating the ins and outs of his case.

The first biography, published in 1960, was written by Charles Norman, who was a poet, a soldier, and a Jew (Grimes 1996). Norman's interest in Pound had begun early, after returning from the war. In 1948, he assembled a little book, *The Case of Ezra Pound* that combined a biographical sketch with quotations from the broadcasts and testimonials from W. C. Williams, E. E. Cummings, Louis Zukofsky, Harriet Monroe, and Conrad Aiken. Norman's little book was the first to stage the dilemma of the Pound biographer in the clearest terms: the appreciation for the poetry had to magically happen in spite of the disgust for Pound's politico-economic beliefs and behavior. Norman's solution was to state facts and other people's opinions: he kept silent about Pound's poetry and his own evaluation of it. Understandably, Pound hated the *Case*, which he characterized as "cat shit," and did all he could to obstruct the full biography Norman intended to write. In 1957, while Norman was trying to win both Pound's and his publisher James Laughlin's trust and good will, he was getting a lot of flak and obstruction from both, as they feared negative information coming to light and making Pound's difficulties even greater (Barnhisel 185–88).

Norman's biography of Pound initiated what would become a characteristic of subsequent texts by Mullins, Reck, and Harry Meacham, together with Julian Cornell's documented account: the preponderance of "the case" and how the case was finally resolved; connected to that, an interest in how Pound had got from here to there, from a normal American with a middle-class upbringing to a spokesman for Italian Fascism on the radio. Norman traced this route by writing a series of vignettes that dramatized Pound at various junctures. By presenting his life as a series of scenes and anecdotes, Norman did indeed illuminate Pound's character and offered explanations of aspects of his behavior during incarceration. Two such vignettes from his college years are particularly revealing as examples of Norman's method and what could be achieved by it. By all accounts, Pound was not popular in his college days: his schoolmates quickly saw he was naïve and played practical jokes on him. Once, one of them crept into his bed while another, pretending to panic, poured water on the intruder, drenching Pound's bed. The matter was left as it was until the next day when his mates, expecting a good laugh, asked Pound how he could sleep in a wet bed. He replied carelessly that he had slept on the floor. As he did not complain and did not seem to care, the joke fell flat. Another time, his mates sent him to fetch a doctor for one of them who feigned being sick. They hurried him out in the snow to a fake address ("without socks," Norman says). They expected him to come back quickly. Pound returned hours later with a doctor. He did not complain about anything, so he was asked why he was late. He said that the address was wrong so he had to go on looking for a doctor who would come to the school. He located and asked three doctors before one agreed to come. The doctor of course sent his bill to the fake patient, so the joke again turned against the pranksters. These two episodes show Pound's naïveté and explain a good deal of his aversion to any sort of lie, personal, political, or literary; his generosity towards his friends, whom he did not question even when they did him harm; his intelligence, endurance, and persistence; and finally, his ability to put up with major physical discomfort without complaint—aspects of Pound's personality that every visitor at St. Elizabeths was able to see.

Norman's biography was primarily interested in Pound's life events and did not go into matters of poetry at all. This opened his book to attack, since, as reviewers were keen to point out, Pound was not simply an interesting character, but a poet. Surely Pound was interesting precisely *because* he was a poet in a madhouse. Norman was following the life and the man, hoping to illuminate his personality through the mosaic of vignettes and other people's opinions of him, not through the poems he wrote. But stitching anecdotes together did not give Norman a storyline for Pound's life so much as produce an archive of little stories. Consequently, his biography was generally well received for what it had aimed to do, but was not regarded as "serious": the volume was considered "chatty," a "popular biography," an "indiscriminate marshalling of information" leading to commonplace conclusions (Heringman 65). Another reviewer was even more to the point:

> Readers in search of a fresh and full solution to the enigma of Ezra Pound's personality will not find it in Charles Norman's crowded biography. Mr. Norman has assembled an impressive number of facts concerning the poet and has quoted numerous opinions and impressions of him, but the conclusions drawn from these materials are mainly sentimental commonplaces [. . .]. What is needed is a study that will see Pound complexly in the context of his time, assess the shape, force and intent of his influence, and venture to evaluate his contribution as poet and man of letters. (Baro 286)

Greg Barnhisel, a careful chronicler of the biographies in the 1960s, remarked that the next two attempts were made by devoted admirers and members of Pound's entourage at St. Elizabeths, Mullins and Reck. Although Mullins's book, titled *This Difficult Individual: Ezra Pound*, is routinely classified as a biography, it is not so in the proper sense of the term: it passes very quickly over Pound's life prior to the St. Elizabeths period and is not narrative. Rather, it is a defense and a memoir, a frank apology, and a refusal to blame Pound for fascism or anti-Semitism: as such, it was bound to raise uproar and discredit its author.

Reviewers thought that Mullin's book was inadequately and superficially researched: those who did not want to engage with the complexities of Pound's case, or with a detailed assessment of his politics, pounced on the errors. Moreover, Mullins's book was full of gossip culled from memoirs of people who had known Pound at one time or another and made no attempt to verify this information. However, Mullins made the best use of what he knew firsthand, namely the scenes, atmosphere, and reality of St. Elizabeths. His arguments—that Pound was a political prisoner, that the case for prosecution was shaky, and that Pound should have been allowed his day in court—were politically dangerous in the context of early 1960s America. These ideas, expressed unseasonably early by Mullins, have since become part of the biographical tradition and have flowed into the discourse around Pound's case. Mullins made no secret of the fact that he was writing a defense—a counter-statement to the way Pound's life and work had been attacked by peers and in the press. In detailing the sordid reception of Pound's poetry in the best temples of learning (see his references to Robert Graves's Clark Lectures in *The Crowning Privilege*),[1] Mullins's book documents how writers, critics, anthologists, and reviewers actively sought to ridicule and dismiss Pound's work. Mullins did not back down from defending Pound against the accusation of anti-Semitism by listing the number of Jewish artists and writers the poet had actively helped. And by quoting innocent excerpts from Pound's wartime radio broadcasts, Mullins showed that they were not uniformly anti-Semitic and treasonous. Sincere and open about his intentions, he is at his most persuasive in his description of St. Elizabeths as a living hell; his book serves even today as a radical challenge to hostile claims that the hospital was no punishment, and much better than prison. Nevertheless, contemporary reviews were universally negative, and to this day, Mullins's book continues to be regarded as a biographical embarrassment. Robert L. Stilwell's judgment is representative:

> Through this well-intentioned but grievously marred book, Mullins has undertaken a bristling, full-length, disciple's-eye apologia for the character and career of Ezra Pound. There are many fine, moving details within the author's fusion of biography and polemic; indeed, these pages easily might have constituted the most revealing and cogent account of Pound's sufferings and triumphs yet published. However, Mullins's argument has been hopelessly undercut by childish vituperation, wild statements, specious logic, minor errors of fact, and a prose incredibly flashy and ill-organized. In short, the whole volume casts only a little really dependable light over one of the greatest poets—and one of the most vexed private and public tragedies—of our century. (Stilwell 76)

Michael Reck's book *Ezra Pound: A Close-Up* "was a less developed version of Mullins' project" (Barnhisel 189), but received a better critical reception. Reck divided his book into three parts: the first delineated Pound's life until St. Elizabeths, the second dealt with the asylum years, and the third with Pound's return to Italy. The centrality of the hospital period was only proof of what Reck considered the most important fact—his own experience and acquaintance with Pound (Barnhisel 190). Unfortunately, Reck openly stated that he had taken no notes of his visits and conversations with the poet—this sentence alone should have disqualified the book from consideration as an accurate portrait. But Reck's admiration for Pound's work made him confident that the poet would survive his political choices, like Dante's or Dostoevsky's reputations had outlived theirs. In retrospect, his confidence still strikes us as naïve: the poet has survived, but his reputation remains tainted and his poetic status is still precarious.

The Curiosity of Biographers: The 1970s

For ten years, then, Norman's biography was the only volume that proposed to review Pound's life as a whole in any detail—but being so anecdotal and so little concerned with drawing Pound's poetry into a discussion of his life, it was felt that it was too popular and unserious for academic use. This situation was remedied in 1970 with the publication of Noel Stock's biography, *The Life of Ezra Pound*. Here was a narrative that accounted both for the life and the work in relation. However, the complex discussion that emerged around Stock's biography in the press is still very instructive today.

The first signals of sharp criticism were drawn in the very perceptive, but polite and toned-down discussion in the *Times Literary Supplement* in August 1970, titled "Complete Poet's Poet." The reviewer, who did not have a byline but was in fact Michael Hamburger, outlined Eliot's and Davie's mixed reception of Pound's work and made a crucial observation on the merit and fault of Stock's biography: the work included a mass of detail, yet this accumulation did not contribute to a portrait of Pound's personality. After reading the book, we are still in the dark as to who Pound was and what he was like:

> It must be admitted that Pound poses unusual problems for a biographer, especially for one concerned with a personal, psychological interpretation. There are thousands of articles, letters, poems and anecdotes which surround Pound's life, yet there remains a private person, stubbornly inaccessible. The poems are filled with many voices and "selves" but none gives any real sense of openness, or hint of the complexities of the inner life; no "private" consciousness is revealed in his work. It seems unlikely, out of character even, for Pound to have kept a confessional diary, and we know, when he sat down to write a letter, that he rarely if ever felt it an occasion to unbutton. Mr. Stock writes of Pound's public life. His personality remains elusive, "invisible" even. (925–26)

This distinction was also observed by Al Alvarez, writing for the *Saturday Review*. Noticing the whirlwind of public activities presented in Stock's biography, Alvarez declared that they were the outcome of a writer without a self, "nothing but a 'vortex,' an unappeased, abstract energy whirring on and on without a body to inhabit" (28).

Alvarez was the only voice to formulate the opinion that Pound had no inner life—Stock's other reviewers considered the lack of any insight into Pound's personality to be rather the biographer's fault. Stock had written a biography without a person: this emptiness derived from his lack of interest in his subject matter and his prejudicial point of view. Davenport in the *Hudson Review*, Kenner in *The New Republic,* and Schneidau in the *Nation* all pointed out the trivialization of Pound's life by the accumulation of irrelevant, mundane "facts"; the undifferentiated, deadpan way in which luminous, significant elements of Pound's life were jumbled together with ordinary details in the same paragraph; the lack of elementary curiosity and intellectual involvement in the enigmas and paradoxes of Pound's life. All three reviewers pleaded for ways out of the "granite" of fact toward the "rainbow" of the soul. Davenport asked (like Virginia Woolf before him) whether the biographer's art should not be tempered by that of the novelist. In both fiction and biography, point of view mattered enormously in the type of plot, the perspective on the events, the selection of facts, and most of all, the evaluation of information. Davenport continued:

> But the most curious effect of Mr. Stock's biography is its apparent assumption that Pound is a fairly ordinary man, an enthusiast who sprang hotheaded and half-wild from the University of Pennsylvania, insinuated himself into various grand moments of the century's art, evolved a mad theory of economics, wrote some passable lyrics, botched a long poem called *The Cantos*, got himself jailed for thirteen years, and is therefore eligible to have his life written. (754–55)

For Davenport, Stock's biography gave information on where Pound was on certain dates, yet offered no insight into his intellectual discoveries, no explanation of how he was able to perceive the genius of Eliot and Joyce, no sense of the importance of the grand, dramatic moments of Pound's life.

Kenner's review, "Incurious Biographer," which had been published slightly earlier in the *New Republic*, broadly went along similar lines: for Kenner, the book was a "heavy box of oddments, many of them verifiable and most of them useless" (30). A biography of Pound should try to answer the question of who Pound was: in this respect, Stock had utterly failed. Kenner pointed out what curiosity could have done for the biographer: it would have made him sensitive to the epiphanies that made up the substance of Pound's intellectual life; it would have made him aware of the defining, lively characteristics of the people Pound found interesting; and would have impelled him to follow Pound to the locations that the poet found magical and transformed into poetry. Kenner pointed out that this insensitivity was not simply an intellectual and emotional failing—it was political too:

> Such a life, usefully written, would be a chronicle of acts of attention, and exact of the chronicler a corresponding attention. Mr.

> Stock's inert sentences, his uninspected connectives, his flaccid verbs lying between noun and noun, do not radiate attention. So when Pound about 1939 lapsed for once in his life into a general idea, anti-Semitism—an idea he has since categorically repudiated, though Mr. Stock does not tell us that—the reader of this biography is unprepared to see how uncharacteristic it was, what a symptom of isolation, confusion, rage; and the old myth of a man raging all his life at hook-nosed villains goes un-neutralized. Mr. Stock is candid and judicious on this topic, but cannot prevent the reader from supposing that Pound tended to fall into any folly that was handy. (31)

Kenner's trenchant rejection of Stock's book reflected the contingency that it had been published slightly earlier than his own *The Pound Era*—in which Kenner chronicled exactly such acts of attention and derived the significance of Pound's life from his intellectual and emotional exploration.

Schneidau's review, while criticizing Stock along the same lines, offered yet another way out of the maze of banality and incuriosity: facing the predominance of an emotion, say irascibility or rage, the critic recommended following the thread of its emergence and formulation in Pound's work and letters—in this archaeology, the biographer could better evaluate the rise of prevalent emotions of Pound's life, know and present his interiority in a more plausible way. A similar process, he suggested, might help readers understand Pound's beliefs, with the added benefits of contextualization and parallels with other writers. Schneidau offered the example of Pound's absorbing interest in money as needing to be brought into connection with parallel interests in the works of other contemporaries, say Lawrence.

Yet there was a reason for Stock's leaden approach to Pound's life, and the reviewers all knew it: it was the biographer's own disenchantment with Pound's work over the years. Despite being enthusiastic acolyte working in Australia to propagandize Pound's cultural and political agenda in his magazine, *Edge*, Stock had proved unable to cope with *The Cantos.* By 1966, when Stock published his *Reading the Cantos: A Study of Meaning in Ezra Pound*, his negative opinion of the poem as a ragbag of details that did not hang together was already consolidated. The poem was too disjointed and the fragments Pound collected in it were not subsumed to a "larger purpose" (Stock 117; Barnhisel 243). In the *Life,* Stock continued on the same tack—this could conceivably be the reason why the events of Pound's life were presented in such an emotionally neutral and disjointed manner. Stock's deadpan style owed to his own ambition of delivering the last word on the life and work of a poet whom he had admired in his youth, but with whom he had long lost sympathy. Stock declared:

> Early in his life Pound had dedicated himself to the writing of a masterwork and later decided that it should take the form of an "epic" about history and civilizations. But the trouble was that the "epic" was born of a desire to write a masterwork rather than of a particular living knowledge which demanded to be embodied in art. At no stage was he clear about what he was trying to do and further confusion was added when in the wake of Joyce and Eliot he decided that his "epic" would have to be modern and up to date. Although he had no intellectual grasp of the work to be made he was determined nevertheless to write it. Thus persisting against the virtue of his art he lost any chance he may have had to pause and rethink the whole project and went on piecing together an endless row of fragments. Some cantos and some fragments contain high poetry and there is much that is humorous or otherwise interesting; but in so far as the work asks to be taken as a whole it verges on bluff. (*Life* 291)

Stock rejected Pound's mature poetic work and concluded that his only valuable contribution was to letters in general, not to poetry. Kenner responded to this by pointing out the chasm between Stock's ambition to deliver a book usable for research and the flimsiness of documentation (an aspect also observed by Homberger in the *TLS*). For Kenner, Stock's predilection for paraphrasing from Pound's letters without acknowledgment made for bad style and weak authorship; he concluded that, regarding scholarship, it was Stock's book that verged "on bluff." By writing about an exciting life in a deadpan way, insisting on the trivial, mundane, and irrelevant detail, Stock was therefore offering universities a negative view of the poet, a poisoned chalice. He also offered an easy way of rejecting Pound's work: by adjudicating it as disjointed and meaningless, but beautiful "in places"; by implying that behind the vortex of Pound's literary and economic activities there was no person at all; more damning and influential, by affirming that Pound's importance does not rest in his poetry, but rather in influencing and supporting writers better than himself. All this was especially sad, as Pound had trusted Stock and given him privileged access to his personal papers. No doubt, he was impelled by the scholar's sacred duty to speak his mind and reveal truth as he saw it. But bearing in mind that Stock's biography was the standard reference for Pound's life even as late as the 1990s and is still being quoted today, one wonders how new students of Pound's work could have overcome Stock's dismissive view.

Kenner's poor opinion of Stock's biography was echoed in the policies of the new Pound journal *Paideuma,* which started its long career in 1972, just two years after Stock's *Life* was published. The journal's editor, Carroll F. Terrell, took up the challenge in matters of biography. What was needed were lively snapshots derived from personal encounters with the poet: memoirs, scenes of Pound's life at various times that would dramatize him as a person in context and in vivid relationship to others. Terrell's desire to publish these in his journal seemed a direct response to Kenner's critique of Stock. Something had to be done to counteract the impression of abstract energy, or action without a person, that Stock's biography seemed to evoke. So in the first number of *Paideuma*, Terrell declared that he hoped

> to publish in this spot the memories of people who have known Pound personally. What one remembers most from even a single meeting can sometimes be as valuable as the thoughts of those who have known him for a long time because such memories may distinguish characteristics that old friends take for granted. (103)

The first such memoir did not take long to appear: in the second number of the journal (winter 1972), Terrell published the recollection of Richard Stern, a doctor who visited Pound in Venice in 1962–63. Indeed Stern's account of his visit was everything that Stock's biography was not: a lively, personal account of a circumscribed short period of Pound's life, a memory and a vivid portrait of Pound as an old man. Over the years, *Paideuma* would prove to be a running thread of such snapshots. Interspersed with these, there were memorials by numerous important people in Pound's life, a vivid record of family, friends, disciples, and acquaintances.

By far the most important memoir of the decade was the autobiography of Pound's daughter, Mary de Rachewiltz, entitled *Discretions.*[2] Reviewers reacted very positively to the book, which besides being autobiographical, shone a strong sidelight on Pound from the mid-1930s onwards. With her graceful style, simplicity, and immediacy, De Rachewiltz was instantly recognized as a writer in her own right. Scholars were especially thankful that by illuminating details of her personal life and of her relationship with her father, she gave information that was useful for understanding *The Cantos* and their allusions to lived experience, which otherwise would have remained impenetrable.[3] To quote one of the book's reviewers, Robert Lee:

> What stands out in Indiscretions [*sic*] are the vignettes of Pound's life and Mary de Rachewiltz's own: the childhood glimpses of the patrician father, the patient sessions at the desk working with Pound, the flights through war-torn Italy, the facing of America for the first time, the famous visitors, the return of the mauled Ezra. These form part of a special connection with a large strand in recent cultural history. But perhaps the best value is the use she makes of the Cantos, subtly interweaving sections of that linear odyssey with her own story, thus explicating hitherto highly esoteric passages and at the same time giving us great clues to the contours and processes of Pound's creative design. (183)

The value of *Discretions*, which has stayed on as a foundational text for Pound studies, was acknowledged from the start—not so with the other biography written during the decade, that of the young C. David Heymann: *Ezra Pound: the Last Rower: A Political Profile*. The reason for this biography was ostensibly the disclosure of the FBI files on Pound as a consequence of the Freedom of Information Act. Its mission was to draw a political portrait, but its understanding of Pound's politics did not go beyond fascism. It showed no comprehension of the American underpinnings of Pound's political views, neither had it any use for their Confucian side. Heymann's plot was not merely a recounting of events, but a scheme of Dantean rising: Settings (1885–1939), Inferno (1939–1945), Purgatory (1945–1958), and Paradise (1958–1972). This plot made no sense to reviewers, who failed to see how Pound's poetic life until he was fifty-four could be conceived as "settings," much less how the prisoner camp in Pisa and the American mental hospital could be a purgatory, or how Pound's later years in Italy, spent in deep depression, grave health problems, and extended hospital stays, could be a paradise. Moreover, they could not see the rhyme or reason for yet another introductory volume to Pound. The similarities with the schemas and assumptions of the biographies written in the 1960s worked against the book being taken seriously: here was another volume centered on Pound's case, another biography that made no account of the poetry, another tale that seemed to reduce Pound the poet to Pound the offensive fascist and anti-Semite. Through oversimplification and bias, Heymann gave a skewed image of Pound's economics, and, implicitly, of his politics.

Of all the reviews Heymann's book received, William McNaughton's in *Paideuma* was the most thoroughly critical, pointing out that despite having ample material at hand to incriminate Pound, Heymann chose to invent episodes to make his story even more incisive: first, a fake interview, which McNaughton exposed in *Paideuma* and Kenner in *The Alternative*. McNaughton visited Olga Rudge in Venice—she had just read Heymann's book and denied that Heymann had visited on the day specified. It was not merely a case of bad memory: all the guest had to do was to look around him: the room where they sat did not match Heymann's description, which was taken wholesale from *Discretions* and reflected how it had looked thirty years before. As for the interview itself, Kenner discovered that it was taken from an Italian one, published in Venice (*Historical Fictions* 55).

Then Heymann declared that Pound had been photographed at a Fascist rally in Rome in 1961 (273–74). Yet no scholar after him, Italian, British, or American, could document this claim (Moody, *Ezra Pound: Poet*, III: 447–48). The story reverberated, precisely because of the sheer mechanics of the profession. Moody mapped the spread:

> I find the story first in Heymann (1976) 273–4, with no source given; then in Torrey (1984) 272, citing Heymann as source; in Tytell (1987) 334, probably from Heymann, but without acknowledgment—Tytell places it in 1962, though on May 1 of that year Pound was convalescing with Olga Rudge in Sant' Ambrogio; in Carpenter (1988) 873–4, evidently from Heymann, but without acknowledgment or source; and in Marsh (2011) 214, citing Torrey. The suspicion that Heymann might have invented the story is warranted by the total absence of corroborating evidence. (*Ezra Pound: Poet* III: 611)

Heymann later turned from literary biography to the lives of celebrities. In 1983, when the heiress Barbara Hutton discovered that he had freely spiked her life with factual errors, she threatened to sue, and Random House pulped 58,000 copies of Heymann's biography of her. Journalists ransacking his career found Hugh Kenner's article describing the fake interview with Pound, which in retrospect made the Hutton disaster a plausible, almost natural development. Unfortunately for his reputation, mishaps like these were recounted in his own obituary in the *New York Times* in 2012, tainting it forever.[4] There was obviously a permanent flaw in Heymann's work ethic—he was definitely not the biographer that the professional community was still waiting for. The need for an objective, sensitive, factually correct narrative of Pound's life, which should strictly rely on what could be documented by unbiased research, continued to make itself felt.

The 1980s: An Explosion

The 1980s can be regarded as a period of studied correction to the popular insufficiencies and academic failures of the 1970s. At no other time, before or since, were professional biographers, writers, psychoanalysts, and scholars more eager to present Pound's life story: no less than five biographies were published in this decade: Peter Ackroyd's *Ezra Pound and His World* (1980); E. Fuller Torrey's *The Roots of Treason: Ezra Pound and the Secret of St. Elizabeths* (1983); James J. Wilhelm's *The American Roots of Ezra Pound* (1985); John Tytell's *Ezra Pound: The Solitary Volcano* (1987), and Humphrey Carpenter's *A Serious Character: The Life of Ezra Pound* (1988). To these, we might add James Laughlin's *Pound as Wuz* (1989), which included memoirs of the encounter of a mature poet with a young man who would become his friend and publisher.

During this decade, it became conceivable to differentiate between British and American biographies on Pound; national and cultural differences began playing a role in the points of view, the style of biographical narration, and the readership envisaged. It became evident that the biographies by Ackroyd (1980) and Carpenter (1988), written by professional biographers outside both academia and Pound's inner circle, could provide an alternative, specifically British tale that could reconnect Pound to a non-professional readership.

The British approach addressed a literate, leisured reader, implicitly recognizing that biographies must conform to an old tradition, indeed a genre. This tradition, which had originated in England in the eighteenth century with James Boswell's *The Life of Samuel Johnson, LL.D.* (1791), already had a history of its own, which had been renewed and freshened by Virginia Woolf's theory and practice of biography writing. In her essay "The New Biography" (1927), Woolf pleaded for a compromise between the "granite" of fact and the "rainbow" of inner life, arguing that the unresolvable conundrum of biography writing is a reconciliation between the two into a vivid portrait. This compromise presupposed that elements of fiction writing could flow into biography (emplotment, dramatizations of character, regions of light and shade). A necessary change had to happen to the biographer himself, not only in the way he approached the material, but also in the manner in which he chose to dramatize himself in his narrative. He was given permission to be irreverent, to shake off Victorian constraints of austerity and decorum, to loosen up, make himself conspicuous, judge his author from a position of equality, and laugh a little:

> We can no longer maintain that life consists in actions only or in works. It consists in personality. Something has been liberated beside which all else seems cold and colourless. We are freed from a servitude which is now seen to be intolerable. No longer need we pass solemnly and stiffly from camp to council chamber. We may sit, even with the great and good, over the table and talk. (150)

Woolf was acknowledging freedoms and effacing distinctions, demanding a literary status for the biographer, a liminal territory specific to his genre, in which he was free to claim liberties hitherto unknown. He was

> no longer the serious and sympathetic companion, toiling even slavishly in the footsteps of his hero. Whether friend or enemy, admiring or critical, he is an equal. In any case, he preserves his freedom and his right to independent judgement. Moreover, he does not think himself constrained to follow every step of the way. [. . .] He chooses; he synthesizes; in short, he has ceased to the chronicler; he has become an artist. (152)

Woolf's critique may have formed the background of unspoken assumptions behind the massive and most sustained biographical effort of the decade: Carpenter's 1005-page book, which he called *A Serious*

Character: The Life of Ezra Pound. Maybe, in his nod to Pound's own phrase, he should have adopted his idiosyncratic spelling to make the message clearer. It was not simply the poet, but the biographer himself who was deeply "seereeyus." Carpenter produced the most detailed account of Pound's life to date while adopting a somewhat patronizing tone of easy familiarity that irritated many readers. He was the first and only biographer to refer to Pound consistently by his first name: that produced a leveling of differences, and of course a corresponding increase in the biographer's authority to pass judgment. In the first instance, Carpenter rendered a judgment on the poetry: he thought that *Cathay* was Ezra's real peak of achievement and that what followed was rather a series of disappointments and missed opportunities that he could easily criticize in a phrase, make fun of, or simply pass over. The problem was the evolution of Pound's style: unlike Eliot and Leavis, Carpenter did not put *Mauberley* on a pedestal and was relatively charitable to *A Draft of XVI Cantos*; but by the time he reached the Adams Cantos, the biographer's patience was exhausted: these were proof of "a mind in chaos" (573). In his review of the biography in *The New Republic*, Denis Donoghue called Carpenter's treatment of Pound's poetry a "rigmarole of hiccoughs": just boring interruptions of the comedy of Pound's life. Donoghue observed that towards the end of the book, Carpenter did not even bother to mention new work: *Rock Drill* and Pound's translation of Confucius are passed over in silence (39).[5] Michael Alexander, writing for *Agenda* in 1991, saw this disparaging treatment of a complex poetic work as the symptom of a more general cultural climate in Britain:

> The British and the American literary traditions seem (to me at least) to be growing further apart. Perhaps it is that the *Cantos,* like the *Faerie Queene*, are simply too literary and too ambitious for our stomachs: Humphrey Carpenter's biography demonstrates at length an incomprehension entirely characteristic of modern British culture as to why anyone should want to write or read a long poem. (66)

Apart from a lack of interest in the poetry, there was his judgment on the man: Carpenter alleged that of course Ezra was crazy, he had been warned by so many people, but would he listen? Charles Tomlinson summed it up when he remarked on the biographer's amused and superior attitude toward Pound—he had "difficulty in believing such a desperately foolish man to be capable of the awesome in poetry" (191). Carpenter's main interest was to capture Pound's personality, yet he failed, Tomlinson thought, because the biographer could not fathom Pound's deepest motivations. Carpenter approached his subject with a ready-made point of view that the episodes of Pound's life could only validate. "My sense of the book," Tomlinson wrote, "is that, for all his industrious gathering of information, Carpenter was highly suspicious of Pound before he began to write his life and, long before he had finished it, was heartily sick of him. It is surprising how early in *A Serious Character* the impatience shows itself or is thinly disguised by a playful and condescending sarcasm" (196). The sarcasm was buttressed by Carpenter's informal construction of the reader-biographer bond as a "we": this "we" was, of course, better informed, more moral, and less prone to humbug than Pound's generation had been.

However much we would like to be amused and however much the light tone, the anecdotes, the laughs make going through the thousand-page tome easier, the impression remains that Carpenter had neither the intellectual and aesthetic foundations to judge Pound's mature work nor the common sense to assess his life. And then the haste, as Tomlinson observed:

> Pound's design is not always easy to discern and finally falls apart into fragments—among these, some of the most beautiful stretches of the poem, which Carpenter is in too much of a hurry to look at in any detail. I have already spoken of his impatience and, insofar as it relates directly to Pound's own character, one cannot but feel that it damages the apparent scrupulosity in the large-scale amassing of biographical facts. (Tomlinson 197)

Woolf envisioned modern biography, no less than history writing and fiction, as a genre deeply involving the personality of the biographer and his/her horizon of freedoms and constraints. To become free from Victorian seriousness, to assert oneself, to have a definite voice and point of view, to appeal to readers over and beyond the topic and author, even to make fun of the author and of oneself was liberating and welcome to a biographer. But these factors so attractive to a literate middle-class public made it difficult for Carpenter's work to be accepted by the academic British or American readership that was by then crucial to its commercial or historical success. The reviews were negative; Stock's biography continued to be used, and scholars regarded Carpenter's book with prolonged suspicion, in spite of the wealth of new detail he had provided in a biography that went farther in length and research than anything attempted until then. In his review in *The New Republic,* Donoghue reiterated what reviewers had missed in virtually all biographies to date (1989): no biographer had taken the trouble to understand Pound's inner life and no one had yet presented him as a poet, not as foolish, traitorous, insane, or anti-Semitic. His life was understood as a whirlwind of energy and facts with no relationship to his emotions, beliefs, or imagination. An understanding of Pound's poetry on the part of the biographer played no role in the life presented (38).

For Carpenter, Pound had started as a lazy schoolboy, developed an exaggerated sense of his own importance, became simple/single-minded with rage, and paranoid during the war. His most generous summing up of Pound's character was that he was a trickster figure: "Undisputed as a poet but also a wartime broadcaster for Mussolini. I don't separate the two. Pound was a very American phenomenon—a trickster and full of showmanship, like P. T. Barnum, but I don't think that diminishes him at all. He was funny but, no, I don't think he was wicked or nuts. In the end, an amazing character."[6]

It was apparently not enough to present Pound as a clown. There was the question of Pound's sanity, which continued to haunt the biographical imagination. For Flory, in *The American Ezra Pound* (1989), the fall into insanity was made possible by Pound's attempts to rationalize and excuse his hero Mussolini's incursion into Abyssinia (Flory 82–83). E. Fuller Torrey, a psychiatrist at St. Elizabeths, focused his own account of Pound's life on the insanity question. Starting with Pisa, in order to tell the tale of the nervous breakdown that was at the root of the insanity plea,[7] Torrey demonstrated that the greatest "secret" at St. Elizabeths was that Pound was sane. Torrey's book is demonstrably the first to attempt an understanding of how Pound's inner life worked. Like Norman (1960) before him, his approach to biography was largely anecdotal; but this time, the stories were all made to mean something and were not simply added like beads on a string. With vividness and economy, Torrey analyzed vignettes for accounts of character and described Pound's behavior based on his own observations and witnesses' comments, presenting in detail the circumstances that led to changes of attitude.

It wasn't just his handling of anecdotes and vignettes that connects Torrey's work with that of the biographers of the 1960s; like them, Torrey regarded Pound's "case" and the question of his sanity as of central importance. He argued that Pound's battle with the world had started long before his London period and that the early personal defeats of his American youth played a huge role in the rage and belligerence that he felt later. Torrey showed that a genuine attempt to understand Pound's anger and verbal violence should go back to his student days. Pound's troubled relationship with America was at the root of his tragedy: both the cancelling of his doctoral fellowship and the refusal of the University of Pennsylvania to re-admit him to the doctorate, in 1906 and 1910 respectively, and the ignominious loss of his job at Wabash in 1908 played important roles in his ambiguous expatriate status, his nomadic life, his refusal to return to America, and his constant abrasive criticism of his country. The feeling that America did not respect or even know him did much to explain his hubris as a broadcaster for Fascism; his incarceration as an enemy to the US and madman could not but deepen the chasm between his country and that part of himself in which he felt deeply American. Finally, the lack of recognition for his poetic achievement did much to deepen his depression in old age.

This was a path that American scholars started to follow in earnest. Stock had published a little book on the topic, *Ezra Pound's Pennsylvania*, in 1976. Pound's own memoir, *Indiscretions*, was republished in 1980. Finally, a full volume dedicated to Pound's life before 1908 was published by Wilhelm in 1985: *The American Roots of Ezra Pound*. In itself, the book could hardly be regarded as a *literary* biography, since it covered just Pound's youth before he published his first poetry volume. But as Margaret Moran noted in her review of Wilhelm's book, it was a response to Torrey's hypothesis that the roots of Pound's misfortune had to be found in Pound's American youth (114). *American Roots* was the first volume of a biographical trilogy. It would be five years before Wilhelm would publish the sequel to his American story.

Towards Achievement and Completion: 1990–2018

Over the past twenty-eight years, the landscape of biographical writing has changed again. Since Carpenter's biography of 1988, nothing more has appeared from dilettantes, fans, or professional biographers. Like a line of ships safely arrived into port, the most recent biographies have been written exclusively by Pound scholars with substantial prior critical experience. The longer, three-volume biographies by Wilhelm (1985–1994) and by Moody (2007–2015) have become works of reference for scholarly research. The short biographies, by Nadel (2004) and Marsh (2011) provide points of entry to the beginning student. None of these scholars needed to be reminded that Pound's real life played itself out in his poetic and intellectual pursuits. All of them had the literary life in view and considered Pound's politics and fate as particular to that of a man who defined his life in terms of an artistic and intellectual journey.

Wilhelm's *Ezra Pound in London and Paris, 1908–1925*, the volume to continue what he started with his *American Roots*, appeared in 1990, and the concluding biographical volume, *Ezra Pound: The Tragic Years, 1925–1972* four years later. We may thus perceive the ruling idea behind Wilhelm's trilogy, which presented Pound's life very broadly as a tale of roots, flowering, and decline. For Wilhelm, the central part of the story, that of the London and Paris years, showed Pound in his prime: his maturing as a modern poet from his first volume of verse, *A Lume Spento* in 1908 until the publication of *A Draft of XVI Cantos* in 1925. Wilhelm located the beginning of the tragedy much earlier than would have normally been supposed, namely with Pound's move to Italy in 1924. After an initial taste of paradise in Rapallo, the history of Pound's life was naturally interwoven with the calamities that were to unfold themselves in Europe and lead to war: Fascism, the great crash of 1929, the Abyssinian crisis, Pound's frantic but ineffectual attempts to prevent another war, leading to "Rome and ruin." The peak of hubris in Pound's life, his wartime broadcasting, is placed neatly in the center of the third volume. The first half is devoted to the preparation of this event and the latter half to its consequences.

For the first time in the history of biographies on Pound, scholars were finally getting what they had been clamoring for: a biography of Ezra Pound, the poet. The difference between Wilhelm's second volume and Carpenter's earlier effort was clear: whereas Carpenter wrote the life of a trickster figure who was writing poetry (almost on the side) that occasionally happened to be brilliant, especially in his youth, Wilhelm positioned himself at the other end of the spectrum. His story was from start to finish that of Pound the artist: the "life" is told as much as possible as an effect or reverberation of Pound's poetry and ideas. Wilhelm read the life from the poetry, as far as that was possible. The tone was completely different as well. We sense Wilhelm's sympathy, but also his deliberate restraint. He did use Pound's first name, but only when he referred to his family relationships—that touch lightened the narration without bringing with it an intrusive familiarity and a leveling of the biographer–poet relationship. Wilhelm sought to understand, but not judge more than absolutely necessary. He did that explicitly only in the short three pages of his afterword to *The Tragic Years* called "And Whither Tending?" In those pages he not only assessed Pound's merits and faults, but also the needs and hopes for further research on the poet.

In another departure from Carpenter's style and assumptions, Wilhelm did not establish an "I/we" position that would connect the biographer to his readers in an alliance to judge, be critical, and feel superior to Pound's character and decisions. Rather, by an effort of empathy, he imagined himself in Pound's position in order to give a realistic feel to his life, especially in the difficult moments. Wilhelm's prose is sufficiently transparent to allow the attentive reader to see his underlying questions. These questions are human, generous, and natural—for instance, at the beginning of volume 2, he follows Pound's first weeks in London in the autumn of 1908 in great detail. Pound was penniless and depended on small remittances from his parents to make ends meet. We sense Wilhelm's implicit questions: "What did he live on?" "How did he manage to survive?" "Who or what helped him take root in an alien environment?" The response that Wilhelm found was that people and social rituals kept Pound afloat. Reviewers of Wilhelm's work invariably observed the importance he gave to Pound's social network and the great wealth of information he added by researching the lives of Pound's contacts, who often wrote about him and provided a number of snapshots of the poet at different times. Wilhelm's prose is also clear enough to show that he relied on detailed timelines, which he used for his own tale, but liked to show in and for themselves. One such can be found in volume 2, chapter 19: "A Paris Diary" has a fine granularity that makes it still useful to researchers who want to check quickly where Pound was and what he did at certain times during the Paris years.

But Wilhelm's work was superseded by Moody's monumental *Ezra Pound: Poet*. The first volume, *The Young Genius* (2007), proposed a markedly different structuring of Pound's life story. Unlike Wilhelm, who had stressed Pound's American roots in his first volume, Moody's biography balanced the periods of Pound's life differently: his first volume devotes just sixty pages to Pound's youth in Pennsylvania. The rest of the volume, 360 pages, tells his London story in detail. This in itself reflects Moody's greater emphasis on the English period and is also visible in the work of prestigious contemporary British academics like Helen Carr and Rebecca Beasley, who also focused their scholarship on the London period. Moody's second volume, delineating Pound's Paris sojourn and early years in Rapallo, carries the biography to the brink of war in 1939. The third volume deals with Pound's late period, starting with the Rome broadcasts and their aftermath. The principle is not Wilhelm's root-flower-decline, but rather, as Moody himself pointed out in an interview with the present author published in 2016, "lyric-epic-tragic" (1:40). The first volume presents Pound as a lyrical poet, making his first unsuccessful attempts at epic form; the second volume has the development of *The Cantos* as the epic of the twentieth century at its center; the third volume is a detailed account of Pound's personal tragedy against the background of war, treason, and insanity.

Ezra Pound: Poet is in many ways the greater refinement of a story that has been told many times, but its wealth of detail and sophisticated treatment of its topic has a focusing effect. Events acquire greater precision and outline; characters become more dramatized and vivid; discussions around the issues of treason, madness, Fascism and anti-Semitism attain greater clarity and force. Certainly, Moody could rely on a much larger body of scholarship accumulated as he was researching: for instance, between 1994 (the year in which Wilhelm's *Tragic Years* was published) and 2007 (the year in which Moody's first volume appeared), eleven volumes of Pound's correspondence were published, which could serve as support and documentation.

Moody's *Ezra Pound Poet* makes an integrative statement about both Pound's life and his poetry; it is the only biography yet written that a student or literary critic might consult for its analysis of poems: a few highlights are those of canto IV in volume 1, canto II in volume 2, and canto LXXIV in volume 3. Moody does not stop at the factuality of "what happened"; he rather goes further in evaluating events critically and correlating them to Pound's professional interests and ruling mentality at a given period. In this sense, he goes much farther than Wilhelm, for whom narrating the life was the main purpose. Wilhelm had devoted two books to *The Cantos* before writing his biography,[8] so readers wanting a more detailed interpretation of the poetic work could have recourse to them. Also unlike Wilhelm, who went seamlessly from poetry to life and back,

Moody separated Pound's works into subsections in order to discuss them for their own sake. *Ezra Pound: Poet* is not a simple biography, but rather a Life and Works, a *summa*. Critical appraisals of the poetry, of the musical compositions, and of the criticism that Pound wrote are as important as the narration of the life into which they are embedded.

Moody's approach to biography writing thus differs from Wilhelm's empathetic method. While moved by compassion and fairness, he reserves for himself a certain detachment, the duty to evaluate evidence and judge Pound's life and work in its complexity and diversity, without reducing either to a political statement. As he declared in the second part of the interview with the present author:

> My point is that the biographer has to be as detached as the novelist and the dramatist. There's also an analogy with the French *juge d'instruction,* whose job is to be intent on establishing, objectively and impartially, what can be known about the case and making the best sense possible of the complications and contradictions in the evidence. To put it simply, as a biographer I am caught up in the research and the writing, and am not sympathising with Pound, nor being shocked and offended by his faults. [. . .] While the events are simply tragic, the telling goes beyond the events in seeking to comprehend them, to make sense of them. And, in Aristotle's terms, the pity and horror are purged—I would say, refined into—understanding, "gathering the meaning of things"; and not the meaning of those particular events only but a grasping of some general, or "universal" truth of human experience. (II: 30–31)

Moody's biography has made clear the necessity of a balanced and professional point of view regarding Pound's life: that of a historian who evaluates evidence, is immune to gossip and hearsay, relies solely on documented traces, and has an unwavering commitment to truth, daring not only to say what is known, but also to go against established prejudice with no other weapon than research and impartiality in evaluating its results. The aim of the historian, as J. G. Droysen commented in 1868, is not simply to know the truth of facts, but rather to seek to understand. But this understanding is not limited to the biographical subject—if the enquiry is made seriously and with integrity, it is a coming home to a truth greater than the subject. The biographer arrives at a deeper understanding of experience and of the self. If we follow to the end, we might do the same.

Notes

[1] Mullins 281–82; Graves 127–31. See also Graves's parody of *Homage to Sextus Propertius*, "Dr. Syntax and Mr. Pound," first published in the *TLS* in 1953 and included in *The Crowning Privilege* 216–18.

[2] *Discretions* was a title that responded to Pound's own memoir of his American childhood, *Indiscretions,* written in 1918 as a series of articles in the *New Age* and published as a volume in 1923.

[3] See John L. Brown's review, which emphasized that the value for scholars of de Rachewiltz's account was as much in the illuminating of the life as in understanding of poetry: "The underlying sadness of this chronicle of botched human relations is counterbalanced by a spirit of life-acceptance and of unbounded admiration for the genius of Pound. The *Cantos* became Mary Pound's 'Bible' and she devoted herself with filial zeal to putting them into Italian. In *Discretions*, thanks to her first-hand knowledge of the circumstances of the composition of many of them, she often sheds needed light on the interpretation of the later *Cantos.* It is evident that much of the difficulty of Pound is not of an intellectual order, but is rather a question of the obscurity of personal allusions. Commentators might well puzzle over such a line as, "'Gruss Gott!' 'Der Herr, Tatile, ist gekommen'" (LXXVIII), if it were not for her note that it refers to Pound's arrival in Gais in 1944. The information imparted by *Discretions* clarifies numerous passages which, in their privacy, might otherwise resist analysis" (155).

[4] Margalit Fox, "C. David Heymann, Biographer of the Rich and Famous, Dies at 67," *New York Times*, May 10, 2012. http://www.nytimes.com/2012/05/11/books/c-david-heymann-biographer-of-rich-and-famous-dies-at-67.html?_r=0.

[5] This is not strictly correct. Carpenter takes two paragraphs for *Shih-Ching: The Classic Anthology Defined by Confucius* (787–98) and four paragraphs and a quotation to dismiss *Rock-Drill* (813–14).

[6] This assessment is quoted by William H. Pritchard, in his review "Eztravaganza," *New York Times,* December 18, 1988. http://www.nytimes.com/1988/12/18/books/eztravaganza.html?pagewanted=all.

[7] Torrey quoted Dr. Weisdorf, who examined Pound on July 17, 1945. "The doctor declared that the spell was "transitory anxiety state as the culmination of several weeks in close confinement . . . These manifestations cleared up rapidly as the prisoner was made more comfortable physically" (9).

[8] See James J. Wilhelm, *Dante and Pound: The Epic of Judgement* (Orono, ME: National Poetry Foundation, 1974) and *The Later Cantos of Ezra Pound* (New York: Walker, 1977).

9: Educating the World: Periodicals on Ezra Pound, 1954–2017

Gad, I get the flower of the California school system here every semester, and mod. langs almost totally gone. Not a soul in a 3rd year class who cd translate phrase "idee recue" 'tother day.

—Hugh Kenner to Ezra Pound, November 28, 1952

Beginnings: A Set of Annotations, a Newsletter, and an Index

IT MAY COME AS NO SURPRISE that the first stirrings of Pound studies as an academic discipline were to be found not only in book-length studies, editions, and reviews, but significantly, in periodical publications. To configure Pound studies as an academic discipline, scholars needed a form of organization, such as a society or a dedicated journal, with goals, coordination, data, and communication: in the United States at least, individual academics realized that if universities and students were to cope with Pound's work, especially *The Cantos*, it was necessary to collect information on exegeses published in Europe and America, contact the poet for access to his papers, be tuned to their transfer into libraries and archives, and reach out from one's own isolation to like-minded scholars willing to do foundational work such as bibliographies, annotations, and translations—this was best done by means of a serial that could report on discoveries, networking, and news. This perceived necessity created a very peculiar kind of Pound scholar: one who was willing to be the editor of a periodical, an annotator of *The Cantos*, a bibliographer, and a biographer, all in one: John Hamilton Edwards happened to be all of these. Cookson, Terrell, and Preda, who later shared these impulses, all found themselves fulfilling similar roles, albeit not *all* of them—in this, Edwards was unique. After graduating from Columbia in 1948, he wrote a dissertation on Pound's early life, *A Critical Biography of Ezra Pound: 1885–1922*, which he finished at Berkeley in 1952. Though unpublished, it did not disappear into obscurity, but influenced Torrey's later biography of 1983 (Espey 1990: 529). Pound was not interested in it much, if Edwards's letters are anything to go by. In a reply which has not been preserved, Pound must have given Edwards the "wait till I'm dead" protest. The young scholar replied with great energy and determination:

> Of course the time to write biography is post mortem, but as the mortem isn't post and as things are pressing—that is, as there is a need to indicate what is worth "fighting FOR" and why and how and by whom, and what against—Jesu, seest thou not!—the time becomes now and I'm going ahead and do what I can.[1]

While working on his dissertation, Edwards had also assembled the first bibliography of Pound's works, called *A Preliminary Checklist of the Writings of Ezra Pound: Especially His Contributions to Periodicals*, sent to the publisher on August 8, 1951, as he informed Pound in a letter sent that day.[2] It was published in New Haven two years later and formed the basis of Donald Gallup's own bibliography, whose first edition came out in 1963 (Gallup xi). There is indeed beauty in the way a student's work, made in the heat of a felt necessity, flowed into other scholars' mature books that would be used in academia as standard tools for longer periods. Gallup brought out a second edition of his bibliography in 1983, the same year as Torrey published his biography. If Torrey's work was controversial and replaced by later biographies written by other scholars, Gallup's bibliography is still being used today: Edwards's name is in the first line of Gallup's acknowledgments.

The *Checklist* may have given Edwards a taste of the sweetness of networking, particularly valuable in his Californian isolation from Pound's hub in Washington, an isolation he hated. For his bibliography, he had requested information from several individuals and institutions in the United States and Europe. This might have been the impulse for his subsequent projects, both network-based and both equally uninteresting to Pound:[3] one was the *Pound Newsletter*, ten issues of which he produced between January 1954 and May 1956 at Berkeley. The other was the compilation of the *Annotated Index to the Cantos of Ezra Pound*, a work that Edwards carried out in collaboration with William Vasse, a graduate student who planned a dissertation on Pound and American history. The two projects ran in parallel and ended at about the same time; the *Index* was begun in 1953 and published in September 1957, but was ready a year earlier, as Vasse informed Pound.[4] It is obvious from this timing that Edwards hoped that index and newsletter would reinforce each other: he needed professional networking for the index, and the newsletter was a good way to create it. A parallel editorial collaboration that was begun in March 1953 by E. M. Glenn and Robert Mayo at Northwestern University was a possible model for how things could be done: their newsletter *The Analyst* was started for annotating *The Cantos*. It proceeded canto by canto, appeared three times a year, and consisted of a set of mimeographed pages that could be sent to interested people on a mailing list free of charge. It is conceivable that this is how Edwards was inspired to start the *Pound Newsletter* a few months later in the same format. Using the resources of the university, creating a serial, and setting up network collaboration for the annotated index were the right procedures to get research on Pound off the ground. He first wrote to an initial list of people to sound out their possible interest in such a project. Then, after having received encouraging answers, he sent out the first issue of the *Newsletter* in January 1954. The goal of the serial, according to Edwards's first editorial statement, was to create and maintain a "life of the mind" for its readers, respond to and cultivate a "demand for awareness" that Pound's work had created. Edwards was also keen to point out that he would not go beyond the ten issues he had envisioned from the start. Judging by how regularly he referred in his editorials to the end of the newsletter, Edwards must have been gasping under the burden of producing it. *The Analyst*, for its part, sputtered as a periodical dedicated to *The Cantos* by 1957 and morphed into a Joyce serial, as its editors became more interested in the annotation of *Finnegan's Wake*. All in all, *The Analyst* annotated just eleven cantos in the five years between 1953 and 1957. Two more issues, in 1960 and 1969, contained revisions of the annotations already done. All three attempts at setting up the foundations for coordinated, systematic research—the *Pound Newsletter*, *The Annotated Index to the Cantos of Ezra Pound: Cantos I-LXXXIV* and *The Analyst*—were undertaken at the same time, from 1953 to 1957—but they were limited and went only part of the way toward the goal, as both the energy and the expertise required flagged over time.

Edwards must have been aware of the dispersal of expertise on Pound's work and the sheer need for a forum of shared information: the *Newsletter* attempted to sail on the wave of the present and provide news that was relevant to research, but seldom included bona fide articles. More often than not, it collected comments, notes and queries, bibliographies, letters to the editor, snippets from international publications, abstracts of dissertations, and translations. It published occasional reviews as well as comments on them. Edwards also used the *Newsletter* to publicize the *Annotated Index* and to request contributions. He included first commentaries on the *Rock-Drill* cantos as they were first published in the *Hudson Review*: Cantos 85–87 were annotated by Paige and Cantos 88–89 by Kenner. These may not have encouraged Edwards and Vasse to continue the index beyond 1956 and include *Rock-Drill* in the *Annotated Index* they were compiling. The desire to conclude the project and not go into territory where expertise was most evidently lacking may have been paramount.

In the end, neither Edwards nor Vasse had any sense of success—they felt they had failed their purpose. The "awareness" and "collaboration" had not materialized, at least not as they had dreamed of. Pound was unhappy with this effort—apart from an article on Social Credit, the *Newsletter* had not followed his economic agenda, nor showcased the political knowledge he most cared about. Despite Edwards's best efforts to draw him in, Pound remained conspicuously absent from the pages of the *Newsletter* and did not answer any questions about the *Index* either. This lack of interest could strike us as strange—after all, Edwards's were the sharpest and most determined efforts to make *The Cantos* teachable to students, to create a specialist community, and to make the poet's work clearer to anyone approaching it. One of Kenner's letters to Pound might throw light on this issue: Pound put his faith in little magazines, the medium of small circulation serials that he had used as channels of communication in his youth and tried to recreate and promote among his young disciples in his St. Elizabeths years. Kenner astutely argued against them, but could not dislocate the master from his idea that a samizdat publication was an adequate conduit for his economic, cultural, and political ideas. Referring to Dallam Simpson's little magazine *Four Pages*, in which Pound was eagerly involved, Kenner insisted:

> No one wants ANOTHER "Little Mag" NOW, because there is no public, public as distinct from stray readers . . . Wash. Spec. to hand, wish edtl. wasn't written in Dallamese. And the thing is to build up a PUBLIC, which can't be done by "private jokes," e.g. ref. to del Mar[5] at bottom of p.14 (November issue) or (worse) the "Foreign Intelligence" on p.8. These things convey NOTHING to the uninstructed, or rather convey only irritated sense of lack of coherence in edtl. mind. [. . .] I repeat that the existing publics are sewed up . . . by the quarterlies and other agents of dissolution. [. . .] And the things to do is NOT to cry in the wilderness about the absence of a public, but to build one up. Leavis has built one up. Hell is paved with the gravestones of little mags which had no dynamic except proclaiming their own independence & isolation.[6]

In the same letter, written in 1952, Kenner proceeded to impress upon Pound the fate of the college student and of the tutors who taught them—a picture of desolation: at the time he wrote the letter, Kenner was professor of English at Santa Barbara, while Edwards had just finished his dissertation and was entering the academic labor market at Berkeley. The need to create an academic public, to instruct their students, and to give them the necessary tools to cope with Pound's poetry were impelling them towards work that would create Pound studies in the university from scratch. Both scholars were responding not only to what they perceived as student ignorance, but also to the poet's scorn of academic knowledge. Kenner continued:

> Emasculation of curricula // whew! I shall look up the Cairns/ Blackstone article. But Ez doesn't know the 'arf of it. "No history/

> NO classics/ now diminish modern langs/" Gad, I get the flower of the California school system here every semester, and mod. langs almost totally gone. Not a soul in a 3rd year class who cd translate phrase "idee recue" 'tother day. And as I discovered re interp. of a Marvell poem, NOT ONE student in a sophomore class knew what the north pole was. Just that it was cold there. I had to explain the concept of "axis" by getting 'em to imagine an orange with a knitting needle stuck thru it, poles being places where the needle pokes thru the skin. Which they had NEVER been told.[7]

Pound may have been impressed by this, since what Kenner and Edwards offered was the prospect of an academic public, and young minds he could instruct through the mechanisms of the university. Yet in the long run, the poet was unmoved, and preferred to channel his energies into little magazines, which he felt represented his agenda much better. This was observed by Montgomery Belgion, whose criticism of the *Newsletter*'s rapport with what really mattered to the poet must have shocked the editors who published it in the last number. Belgion pointed out that the newsletter did not give any indication of how projects that Pound wanted, such as the reprinting of Alexander Del Mar or a popular edition of William Blackstone's *Commentaries of the Laws of England* might be achieved. The poet may have hoped that students would do something more constructive than pore over his sources—they could have pursued studies he regarded as vital, whether individually or in groups. In a letter to Pound of August 10, 1956, Vasse admitted:

> Yes, Belgion is perfectly right: the Newsletter failed to get people to think. And no one is more aware of that than Edwards and I—because we had to sit here in Berkeley trying to make people work for us. And nothing much happened. At least nothing much that wasn't on the academic side of the fence. Of course, the fact that the University was putting up the money for the publication (and it was like pulling teeth to get as much as we did) set some limitations on what we could publish—not so much as to opinions but rather as to the sort of material that could go in. Still, I think that we could have at least made some start toward getting people together in the way that Belgion wanted, and this was one of the things that we wanted the Newsletter to do, too. Well, we arranged the party—but nobody came. And I am not yet sure just why, because we begged all sorts of people to do just this sort of thing and to contribute material toward it. As it was, we published almost all the material that did come in—even wrote ourselves when it didn't. And you know the final result. No, I am not trying to construct a defence; there are a lot of ways in which the Newsletter failed, and this is perhaps the most obvious failure of them all. (YCAL 43 53/2436)

Still, the *Pound Newsletter* had been a first effort to gather information, set up professional communication, create the foundations of research through bibliographies, annotate *The Cantos*, and even create a repository of new secondary literature on Pound at Berkeley. It did not demand a subscription fee from its readers, as Edwards had gotten modest funding from the university. But it is a shock to the contemporary scholar interested in academic archaeology to see what it really was—a set of mimeographed sheets that were occasionally kept together with a pin, or in the best of cases, stapled together. The newsletter may have been a periodical, but it was not a publication. Neither was *The Analyst*.

Retrospectively, the reasons it "failed" were quite different from Vasse's apology. From our 2018 perch, we realize that Carroll F. Terrell must have known them very well too. A newsletter was definitely not what academics wanted or what they were prepared to work for, especially so if it was not professionally printed, with an unfriendly, crowded, clumsy design, and a limited period of running. Participating in the work of a newsletter did not advance anyone's career; quoting from or citing it would not have been safe or reputable in any academic's publications list. An editor who wanted to establish an academically legitimate Pound periodical would have to strive for higher standards in all these aspects. The journal would absolutely have to be printed, include good quality essays, have a well-designed layout, and enact a certain convergence of standards between itself and the book format to ensure staying power: standard book dimensions (6 x 9 in.), bulk around 200 to 400 pages, glossy, professionally designed soft covers, good quality paper. The editor would have to be able to go the distance, not break after ten issues. The glossing of *The Cantos* would have to be complete, not stopping at position 11, or even 84. Edwards's and Vasse's partial projects had to be taken up and radically improved.

When considering the task ahead around 1971, Carroll F. Terrell must have known he was the one.

The Reaction against Eliot: Ezra Pound in *Agenda*, 1959–1972

When William Cookson's monthly, *Agenda*, started in London in January 1959, it looked more like a clandestine publication than a *bona fide* magazine. Looking at it with a curious eye, one could even say it was a revision of "little": as a putative revival of Dallam Simpson's American periodical *Four Pages*, it had, in a bow to its predecessor, only four pages.[8] It definitely looked like a one-man effort—someone who in the fire of a prophetic mission had just grabbed whatever publishing instrument was available and cheap because he had to deliver his message quickly and urgently. This personal, prophetic voice was not guided by Pound's poetry, but by his economics, which judging by Cookson's age at the end of the 1950s (he was twenty), was alive and well as an Ezuversity discipline. Throughout his later career, Cookson would say that Pound founded the magazine, or alternatively, that Pound's encouragement and mentorship caused *Agenda* to be born and exist.

Cookson's youthful enthusiasm and sense of mission overlapped entirely with Pound's own and reminds the informed reader of other young men whom Pound had mentored earlier in his career and assisted as editors and/or publishers: Ronald Duncan, James Laughlin, Dallam Simpson, John Kasper, David Horton, William McNaughton, and Noel Stock. All of them had benefited from the Ezuversity: they too had been sent out into the world or gently pushed to spread the word and work for Pound's sociopolitical ideas. Laughlin, who did his apprenticeship at Gorham Munson's Social Credit journal *New Democracy* in 1935–1936, was lucky to have found in Munson a second mentor who tempered the excesses of the first. Cookson was Pound's last disciple, and after Laughlin, the most successful. He was also fortunate to have met the poet, editor, and translator Peter Russell as a teenager, at the same time he was discovering Pound, around 1956. He was not quick to acknowledge Russell's value as a potential model. But it was Russell, not Pound, who encouraged Cookson to start *Agenda* independently. Russell, who gave Cookson the translation of a poem by Osip Mandelstam to print, was the magazine's first signed contributor. Russell introduced Cookson to important poets like Hugh MacDiarmid and Tom Scott, as well as to his future printers. And Russell's previous work, especially his periodical *Nine,* provided a possible model for *Agenda* and saved Cookson from the editorial impasse to which his exclusive discipleship to Pound had brought him.[9] Russell himself combined an admiration for Pound as poet and translator with an interest in his economics. He published six of Pound's pamphlets on money—four of them had been printed in Italian during the war (Alexander and McGonigal 46).

When *Agenda* reached adulthood with its twentieth anniversary issue in 1979/80, Cookson shaped it as a homage to Pound: at 299 pages, this was the longest number he had ever published. In it, he included a selection of his initial correspondence with the poet and recounted in an introductory note how he first contacted him and how *Agenda* was born: the miracle of his regular correspondence with Pound began in 1956, after he had sent the poet first some bad verses and then his plans for reviving verse drama. Pound responded on May 2, gently drawing the young man's attention to the Square Dollar series and the canon in economics he was trying to set up, mostly Alexander Del Mar and Thomas Hart Benton.[10]

> the styge and "drammer" [stage and drama] will remain cat shit as long as dummytists [dramatists] AVOID the MAIN vital fields of contest. without curiosity no life in writing. Nobody can write a live play NOW while ignoring matter such as in Sq $ series 4. 5. 6.[11]

Their correspondence took off when Cookson sent Pound a copy of the Westminster School literary magazine *The Trifler*, which he had been editing and where he had published a review of *Rock-Drill.* Pound liked the review, began to educate the young man and integrate him into his network of contacts. After Pound's release from St. Elizabeths, Cookson and his mother visited Pound at Brunnenburg in October 1958: the idea of *Agenda* grew from this visit. Initially, the intention was to organize a four-page section in an existing publication, possibly *Time and Tide*, but that did not pan out.[12] Pound would have preferred the title to be *Four Pages* to establish continuity with the past and correlate with other little magazines that he had supervised such as William McNaughton's *Strike* and Noel Stock's *Edge*. It seems that Cookson's first rebellion consisted in choosing the title. He felt, as he was later to declare, that he would soon go beyond the four pages (Alexander and McGonigal 53).

Pound's policy during his time at St. Elizabeths was to use young people's little magazines to plant short paragraphs on economic and political issues anonymously while pouring recommendations and guidelines to the editors via correspondence—this backseat driving had been successful, but short-lived in his previous attempts with *Four Pages, Strike,* and *Edge.* Cookson assumed it was his friendship with Edmund Gray, Laurence Binyon's grandson, that Pound particularly valued, but in retrospect, it is more likely that his editorship of the *Trifler* and his youth must have been decisive in Pound's willingness to mentor him. The samizdat quality of *Agenda* was not accidental, but expressed Pound's view of its mission—that of spreading his political agenda in the underground.

The first number of Cookson's four-page brochure was a résumé of Pound's economic and political opinions at the time when *Thrones* (i.e., Cantos XCVI–CIX) was in the works or just finished: taxes, Alexander Del Mar, coinage, Social Credit, and even the praise of Mussolini. No wonder: as Cookson was to reveal many years later (Alexander and McGonigal 53), the first issue was in part ghost-written by Pound himself.[13] It looked like a series of small-scale personal rants organized in the manner of a diary or scrapbook. The one-man tone was critical, missionary, and consistent. On the first page, the reader could find something like a justification for the periodical, though no heading would have indicated that this text was actually an editorial. Pound anonymously restated the idea of the necessity of communication between "isolated outposts"; he also reminded readers that London had no reporting on European thought and culture. Readers are free to draw their conclusions. *Agenda* was bridging the cultural gaps between England and the continent and was supposed to coordinate intellectual efforts at the European level. A bold mission for a serial in four pages.

Agenda's first number, January 1959, carried Pound's other unsigned contributions under the heading "Items" (3–4). For the rest, a small poem by Osip Mandelstam was wedged between two thick black lines between pages one and two. The poem had no title and looked seriously squeezed.

The first *bona fide* articles appeared in the second issue and were short pieces called, somewhat predictably, "Financial Reform" and "Planning Today." They had author bylines too and Cookson had received his first letter to the editor.[14] The only poem, by Peter Whigham this time, was better presented: it did have a title and was not divided by a page break; the text was centered, allowing for more space for the eye and showing more respect and care for the poem. The thick lines had mercifully disappeared, being replaced by thin centered ones. All in all, the second issue had improved design and readability.

The third issue stuck firmly with the economic agenda, but tilted it towards Pound's concerns of the late 1930s: the economic mainsprings of civilization, which he advocated in his Social Credit writings and *Jefferson and/or Mussolini*; and the definition of organic categories and the concern for education that is visible in the *Guide to Kulchur*.

The editor announced the introduction of one poem per issue. The roll of events superseded this announcement: *Agenda* no. 4 had only poems in it. It started with one by Noel Stock, a translation of Osip Mandelstam, a poem by Peter Russell, and yet another by Alan Neame. Cookson had found contributors! But no. 4 was just a breather: by *Agenda* 5, in May 1959, Cookson had returned to the vital question of education compounded with the monetization of debt and the conspiracy of finance. A strong anti-American wind blew through those pages, driven by the perceived necessity that British education should resist American modernization initiatives and protect the requirement of Latin in English schools as a basis and bulwark of culture.[15]

Finally, by *Agenda* 6, Cookson was ready for another editorial. Readers did not and would not know for another twenty years that this was his effort to modulate Pound's editorial policies, even as his own statement seems to reaffirm them. Here are the aims of his magazine:

> We are intended as a means of communication and to keep certain basic ideas in circulation.
> There will be a Poetry Issue every few months. By implied criticism, we hope to show that better poetry is being written than would be supposed from current literary periodicals.

> We have not yet become sufficiently a forum for intelligent discussion among those who are thinking actively at the present time. [. . .].
> The *use* of a publication of this size is to circulate ideas which are unlikely to get printed elsewhere, to form a group, to collect news and to indicate where active thinking is taking place. [. . .]
> We hope in "Agenda" to indicate lines along which vital study can be pursued.
> Underlying all this we are trying to keep curiosity alive, without which there can be no art or literature. (*Agenda* 1, no.6 [July-August 1959]: 1).

We recognize this agenda—it is not so much Cookson's as Pound's, expressed clearly in *Guide to Kulchur* as early as 1938 and reiterated in his letter to Cookson of June 17, 1959.[16] Ideas, usually "basic" ones, are "active," they are the sediment of consciousness and attuned to what people are ready to believe. The active ideas are those that infiltrate the status quo and change the profile of a culture. The "forum for intelligent discussion" is a resurfacing of another cherished idea of Pound's and a constant in his correspondence with Cookson, whom he constantly admonishes to form a group and not alienate his contacts. But into this agenda Cookson inserted the second paragraph, about poetry, which showed his groping toward a goal for his magazine he could really identify with and be his own. The correspondence reveals that he wanted to stop after the fourth number, and Pound agreed because he felt that Cookson was not pulling his weight and needed more time to mature and gather information.

But Cookson did not give up—he continued in the Poundian vein until he could see his own way forward. He took the *paideuma* principle to heart and attuned his budding periodical to the vital ideas of 1959: the changes that were occurring in education and the question of WWII. The short articles on education reform he undertook himself. On the war question, he published a piece by Stock, whom Pound admired at the time and recommended for his scholarly acumen.[17] Like Cookson, Stock followed Pound's political agenda closely, with hair-raising results. In a mockery of scholarship, Stock presented the "revisionist" point of view in a two-part article called "Where We Have Got To": the war had been started by Chamberlain's offering guarantees to Poland and by Roosevelt's desire to deflect from the economic crisis at home by engaging in the European war. Hitler was not the instigator; Mussolini "made sane efforts to prevent war and later to stop it." This argument is by now familiar from the right-wing propagandistic literature. Stock did not provide precise references for his various allegations, but added a bibliography, which, like revisionist bibliographies often are, was limited to several works by the same author. In the second installment of the article in *Agenda* 1.8 (November 1959) Stock went on to analyze the financial causes of the war. The result is predictable: these consisted in the influence of Jewish financiers on the heads of state in Great Britain and the United States. This time, Stock quoted liberally, but never contextualized or referred with precision to a source. His bibliography consisted of Pound's favorite authors: Alexander Del Mar, Thomas Hart Benton, Brooks Adams, Arthur Kitson, Eustace Mullins, and Pound himself.

It was a relief that the next issue (no. 9) included just new poetry (by Ronald Duncan, Noel Stock, and Alan Neame) and translations (from Catullus by Peter Whigham). It prefigured what was about to come: In its tenth number, April 1960, a year after it started, *Agenda* doubled its size to eight pages. It was Cookson's most ambitious issue to date. "Creative work is the most valid form of criticism," he declared in his editorial. The issue contained a poem by W. C. Williams and a long selection from Ronald Duncan's long poem, *Judas*. An article by David Gordon compared Homeric Greek with Mencius: Chinese ideograms ran on both sides of the text, from top to bottom, a unique feature for such a small-scale magazine.[18] Cookson felt secure enough to announce material that would be presented in the next issues: more translations, reviews (for the first time), announcements of recent books, and most importantly, poetry of value that was not published in the mainstream journals. He had shifted his emphasis from politics to Pound's works of literary theory, *How to Read* and *The ABC of Reading*. He declared that English poetry had forgotten its responsibility to language and ideas—it had made no progress since the 1890s, leaving progressive avant-garde poetry in the language to Scots, Irish, and Americans. Echoing Pound and also Hugh Kenner, with whom he shared this point of view and whom he had contacted at Pound's request,[19] Cookson asserted that:

> The poet is the most responsible member of the community; poetry is concerned with facts, details, emotions, every side of human activity: history, theology, science, the mysteries, economics, politics: the poet handles the sum of human knowledge as a scientist handles significant data and by defining his perceptions of these things with ever greater precision, the field of human understanding is widened: language becomes a subtler instrument of communication, intelligence is made active, but if poetry ceases to be concerned with things of vital importance, or, as has happened in England becomes the domain of amateurs and of no possible significance to anything, everything declines, and disintegrates. (*Agenda* 1, no.11 [June 1960]: inside of front cover)

Agenda had finally found its mission: to discuss, support, and promote British poetic talent and to correlate it with past traditions, as well as with poetry written in other countries. Pound continued to inform Cookson's personal education and criteria of literary value; however, it was another side of his mentorship that now became important: the disciple turned from affirming Pound's political and cultural opinions to affirming his beliefs about poetry; the ideas about culture and politics in general made way for a literary focus. The little magazine itself had changed in a direction its editor had not foreseen in the beginning: it became a periodical dedicated to new poetry, and its greatest successes relate to a consistent profile in its chosen domain as well as active research and presentation. Translations from modern poets and classics were included, as Pound had stipulated in *How to Read*. Indeed, the translation program of Cookson's magazine was every bit as impressive as the new poetry side of his periodical: among the poets included were Cocteau, Mandelstam, Catullus, and Nerval: the little mag did indeed connect English poetry with the continent, as Cookson, echoing Pound, had asserted in the first issue.

Starting with the eleventh number (June 1960), Cookson began publishing reviews on the inside of the back cover. Understandably, they were very short summaries, but the volumes of poetry he signaled were proof of the seriousness with which he scrutinized the field: Pound's *Thrones*, Duncan's *The Solitudes*, Williams's *Paterson* (Book V). Cookson's special reason for pride was that with his little—now eight-page—magazine, he could publish a special double issue dedicated to an English translation of a piece by Jean Cocteau, *Leoun*, translated by Alan Neame (another of Pound's recommendations), with a cover designed by the author himself—he often advertised this poem in various issues of *Agenda*.[20] Barely a full year had passed since the publication of the first issue. From his post on the inside front cover, Cookson, under the influence of his readings of new volumes (Pound's *Impact*, Duncan's *Judas*, and Tomlinson's *Seeing Is Believing*), again felt the need to redefine the meaning of his little magazine, which he did by relying on Pound's important letter of June 17, 1959:

> There are too many little magazines. Few justify their existence. The *use* of a publication of this size is: first, to print creative work; secondly, to form a group or nucleus with the object of establishing criteria and thirdly, to serve as a means of communication between those actively interested in the furtherance of civilisation in general and the writing of poetry in particular. (*Agenda* 2, no.2–3 [December-January 1960–61]: inside front cover).

Printing new creative work, poetry, translations, and essays became Cookson's prime goal. Within a year, he had certainly established a group of regulars around his magazine: Neame, Whigham, Stock, Duncan. It was a small group—but again, Cookson was only twenty-one. *Agenda* was not a looker—but it did publish Cocteau, Williams, and Mandelstam in its first year.

As an editor, Cookson still had to learn consistency: no sooner had he declared his interest in poetry that he decided to let Stock espouse Pound's economics in a longer article that took all but three pages of the issue, even counting both sides of the back cover.[21] It was clear that whenever he decided to print an essay, he would get into space difficulties. Almost surreptitiously, *Agenda's* number of pages was creeping up. By June 1962 (volume 2, issues 7–8) the magazine had grown to twenty-four pages and the space taken up by reviews was vying with that devoted to poetry. Cookson himself dispensed with editorials but often wrote reviews: Lowell's *Imitations*, Pound's *Treatise on Harmony*, Schafer's volume *Ezra Pound and Music* received long reviews from him. In March-April 1963, *Agenda* included "*from* Canto CXI"—which looked both like an homage of son to father and a blessing of father to son. The little magazine format was stable, the group of contributors growing, the reviews were becoming more substantial and even publisher advertising was coming Cookson's way.

Apart from the inclusion and discussion of questions of literary importance, Cookson was growing up and maturing as an editor and thinker through the agency of his magazine. In just four years, from 1959 to 1963, his voice became well defined, his style secure, logical, focused. If Cookson followed a *paideuma*, it was the idea of poetry as intellectual pursuit and key to unlock every domain of knowledge and feeling, an application of Pound's maxim: "Man gittin' Kulchur better try poetry first" (*GK* 121). Cookson had started his little magazine as a forum of ideas that were political and economic. After some circling around, after thinking of giving up and choosing to separate himself from Pound's agendas of the late fifties, he found that his magazine by a stroke of good fortune had unerringly taken him where he wanted to go. Poetry was key; poetry can and should express everything—it is the best, most efficient formulation, our religion and our music: its care, its cultivation was the mission of a lifetime.

Starting with its third volume, *Agenda* became a bi-monthly. The number of pages for the next four years continued to grow; the issues became more substantial and even showed a concern for design: David Jones created the lettering of the title and table of contents (*Agenda* 2, no.5 [September-October 1961]). Cookson was trying to shed the brochure image and had all but disappeared from the list of contributors. As ever, he was fighting a losing battle with the clock. In four years, from 1963 to 1967, he only published two volumes (twelve issues). But the discernment remained unchanged and the quality of contributions, poems, reviews, and essays was enhanced: Cookson published Williams's "Asphodel, that Greeny Flower" in a special issue dedicated to the American poet (3, no.2 [October-November 1963]); selections from what would become Pound's *Draft and Fragments* (3, no.3 [December-January

1963/64]); poetry by Roethke (*The Geranium* [3, no.3], *The Rose* (3, no.4 [April 1964], *Last poems* (3, no.5 [September 1964]); a special issue on Zukofsky (3, no.6 [December 1964]), and new English poetry by Geoffrey Hill, Ted Hughes, and Charles Tomlinson (4, no.1 [April-May 1965]).

For all this difficult progress, the second number of the fourth volume (October-November 1965) delivered something of a shock: *Agenda's* special issue on Pound's eightieth birthday had glossy cover and a photograph! This was unprecedented, a feat that Cookson would not be able to repeat for another two years. One cannot help feeling that this was a personal gift, a proof of love. The number started with the publication of Canto 115, continued with an essay on *The Cantos* by Alexander, and then turned to poets' testimonials: Robert Creeley introduced selections of his correspondence with Pound and delineated the older poet's influence on his generation; Marianne Moore quoted Pound's phrases that had taught her most; Robert Duncan had a long semi-biographical essay on Pound's "lasting contribution"; John Berryman a consideration on Pound and the Nobel; Robert Lowell wrote a tribute; Basil Bunting included his poem "On the Flyleaf of Pound's Cantos" comparing the poem to the Alps. Kenner had two essays, "Pound and Chinese" and "Pound and Money," Sullivan wrote about Propertius, Duncan on religion, and Whigham on Pound in the schoolroom. The issue ended on a biographical note, with a report on Pound at the Spoleto festival. It would be well to remember Russell's model of 1950 and Cookson's age at the time: he was twenty-five.

The Pound special issue was placed strategically between the number on English poetry that preceded it and one on American poetry that followed it. *Agenda* went back to its simple format, but by the end of 1965 it became consistently around eighty pages long. It kept to its blend of poems, essays, and reviews. The essays, especially, though longer, were not conceived as scholarly texts—they had the occasional footnote and reference, but addressed the educated reader, not the specialized academic. We may note the special issue on Pound's disciple, Basil Bunting, placing him in the context of the poets of his generation: Creeley, Zukofsky, Gunn, Tomlinson, and Hill, all of them in Pound's orbit of influence (vol. 4, nos. 5 & 6, autumn 1966).

The next turn came only two years after the birthday issue in Pound's honor. In spring-summer 1967, financial support from the Arts Council enabled *Agenda* to advance by a quantum leap. As a special issue dedicated to David Jones, this number was three issues in one: it had 176 pages and contained 19 black-and-white reproductions of Jones's artwork. The glossy cover showed an eerie landscape with animals and fairies and Jones's own typography in the title. The volume is a multifaceted exploration of Jones's work in poetry and graphic design: in his editorial note, Cookson briefly stated what fascinated him about Jones's poetry and naturally connected it to Pound's, which he had adopted as his standard of value. The David Jones issue shows how a dedicated editor enhanced and filtered Pound's influence in the British literary world: Cookson was investing all his energies into becoming an arbiter of true poetry, and his criteria of evaluation were derived from Pound's mature aesthetics. Until that time, Eliot's "technical" judgment of Pound as "a better craftsman" had been the reigning criterion of evaluating his oeuvre in the UK. Eliot had been Pound's editor and publisher at Faber since 1928. In his introduction to the *Selected Poems*, which he curated in that year, called "Isolated Superiority," Eliot had affirmed his belief that Pound's poetic merit lies in his technical prowess, which was unequalled in the poets of his generation, himself included. Eliot went on to say that he did not care much for *what* Pound says in his poetry, but *how* he says it, declaring that his ideas are "antiquated," following a Romantic tradition of the 1890s (Erkilla 168–69). This point of view helped Eliot and Faber navigate the dangerous political waters of Pound's reception after WWII—it was the position allowing both to continue publishing *The Cantos* despite Pound's anti-Semitic broadcasts, indictment for treason, subsequent incarceration in a mental institution, and final diagnostic of incurable insanity. As Coyle argued (1995), by publishing Pound's *Literary Essays* at Faber in 1954, a selection of articles Pound published in periodicals before 1935, Eliot continued to promote a de-politicized perspective, in a general strategy that emphasized the innocent literary texts and kept silent about the disreputable economic and political ones.

Cookson took issue with this point of view—he wanted to shape the way Pound was received in the UK and not leave that to Faber alone. His first move was to associate him with newer British poetry, like that of David Jones. In his editorial, he commented:

> His [Jones's] poetry and his painting are both filled with a numinous material detail: they contain a particular beauty which, while gathering strength from many various sources, holds its own haecceity that has a certain kinship to *Sir Gawain and the Greene Knight*. He has drawn from "the dark backward and abysm of time" radiant layers of past experience into a living cosmos—as Ezra Pound has written:
>
> There *is* subtler music, the clear light
> Where time burns back about th' eternal embers.[22]

The number was enthusiastically received in the *Guardian*, and Cookson took the liberty of quoting the laudatory reviews he had garnered in the press in the following issue: "that excellent magazine *Agenda*" had been devoting "sumptuous special issues" to the "older and less decorated captains of the modern movement." The David Jones issue was "an important collector's item" (5.4–6.1 [1967–68], inside front cover). If in 1966 *Agenda* was a bi-monthly of roughly eighty pages per issue, in 1967 it became a quarterly, hovering around 100 pages. Its minimalistic design was still the heir of the modest cover and size the magazine had in its beginnings, but the elegant white glossy surface with Jones's lettering made all the difference. The magazine now looked decidedly posh—it had indeed become collectable. Its list of contributors was prestigious, as it had been since its younger days. Cookson kept up his interest in Poundiana, acquiring the best emerging critical work for first inclusion in his magazine. He thus published a chapter from Kenner's *The Pound Era* as early as 1968. The chapter, called "The Muse in Tatters" was more academic than usual, since it also contained explanatory notes about Pound's use of names and references.

In the next number, Cookson printed a two-page review of the *Selected Cantos*, edited by Pound himself, which had been published by Faber in December 1967. The volume had a total of 121 pages, foregrounding the historical and economic side of the poem, at the expense of its other, erotic, paradisal, mythical, even Chinese aspects (Ten Eyck 33). Pound stated: "I have made these selections to indicate main elements in the Cantos. To the specialist the task of explaining them." The title of Cookson's review was "Main Elements in *The Cantos*": it was his most developed personal affirmation on Pound's poetry to date, intimating the course his own work was going to take (*Agenda* 6.3–4 [1968]: 143–44).

In taking up the "main elements" idea, Cookson's finally aired his subterranean gripe against Faber and against Eliot's way of presenting Pound to the world as a technician of prosody, a craftsman of verse. The Faber program was focused on the exclusively literary aspects of Pound's oeuvre and insisted on formalism to deflect attention from the ugly nitty-gritty of Pound's economic and political ideas. As a response to that, Cookson's "main elements" concerned content, not technique. The focus on economics and politics with which he had started his magazine had not disappeared, but sedimented in his mind, giving him a personal view of Pound as a poet. He affirmed it as a literary editor who had built up his own professional reputation and prestige:

> It is time that Pound's writings on money and history (some of them are collected in *Impact*, Regnery, 1960) were issued by an English publisher. Faber have done the poet a disservice by printing only his literary essays as this has helped to perpetuate the illusion of a fundamental split in his writing. (*Agenda* 6.3–4 [1968]: 143)

Perhaps more than anything else he ever published, this criticism of Eliot's selection in *Literary Essays* (1954) demonstrates Cookson's convictions: the exclusively literary point of view was mutilating Pound's vitality as a thinker. Both Eliot ("Isolated Superiority," 1928) and New Critics like Blackmur, Tate, and Winters had dismissed Pound's cultural ideas in their writings of the 1930s and 1940s, reducing him to what they thought Pound knew best—literature. Cookson's generation was ready to accept Pound integratively, taking account of both his whole poetic oeuvre and his later, post-1935 journalism.

From 1959 to 1968, Pound's lesson that economics is of vital importance to culture and contemporary life had remained central to the work of *Agenda,* even if it was not at the surface; indeed, Cookson applied this lesson to the MacDonald government then in power in the UK. Cookson realized very clearly that isolating the literary from the economic was doing great damage to a just evaluation of Pound's work. He continued:

> It would seem an opportune moment for a disinterested assessment of Ezra Pound's writings on "coin, credit and circulation." But, even if his monetary theories were proved to be mistaken, what ultimately counts for the poetry is his concern for justice in these matters; it is the economics and the history which give *The Cantos* order and profundity—without them the unsurpassed lyrical beauty would lack meaning beyond aestheticism—it would have no roots in reality. When all the errors have been forgotten, the humanity and inclusiveness of the concerns of Pound's poetry are the things which will be remembered. (144)

This short review and position-taking was followed up in the next number by Tom Scott's strong statement in the article "The Poet as Scapegoat." By publishing it, Cookson was showing the world where he stood in the controversy around Pound's fascism. Scott's ten-page article was a review of three books documenting Pound's life at St. Elizabeths and his release: Julien Cornell's *The Trial of Ezra Pound*, Michael Reck's *Ezra Pound: A Close-Up*, and Harry M. Meacham's *The Caged Panther: Ezra Pound at St. Elizabeths,* which documented Pound's American ordeal between 1945 and 1957. Scott cleared Pound of the insanity diagnosis, affirmed the poet's democratic right to speak his mind on politics, and absolved him of the charges of fascism and anti-Semitism. Pound was not a fascist, he averred, and the fact that he had criticized certain Jews did not make him an anti-Semite. Scott saw Pound as a profoundly innocent poet who had been made a scapegoat of the war and been mistreated by his country—the error should be recognized, amends should be made. (*Agenda* 7, no.2 [1969]: 49–58). By the time Scott's article appeared, *Agenda* was no longer a samizdat publication, but had earned its way into the mainstream of British literary life through its consistency as a quality poetry magazine, its design by Jones, its Arts Council funding, and its favorable reviews in the press. Its affirmations counted and pulled their weight against Faber's safe position in the Pound case. By publishing

Scott's review, Cookson partook of his dangerous and unpopular opinion, daring to stand behind a complete defense that in 1969 was restricted to the enthusiasts visiting Pound at St. Elizabeths.

At the turn of the 1970s, Cookson's magazine took another leap—the special issue dedicated to Wyndham Lewis had 224 pages and *color* illustrations. Tucked among articles documenting various aspects of Lewis's oeuvre, there was a biographical essay comparing Lewis and Pound along the years of their association and friendship, W. K. Rose's "Pound and Lewis: the Crucial Years." Cookson's policy was never to let Pound out of his view—in every issue, the reader would find documentation, extensive essays, and comparisons with other poets. Before Pound had a dedicated journal, Cookson published a forty-three-page essay by John Peck, made space for Kenner and Pearlman, published reviews, and included long articles on the later cantos, constantly placing Pound's work among that of other poets. If this was criticism, it was criticism by anthology, one of Pound's own methods.

Finally, by 1972, Cookson was ready: he published his edition of Pound's cultural criticism, *Selected Prose 1909–1965,* taking care to include writings on economics and culture that most illuminated the poetry. This volume was Cookson's major synthesis and the natural result of *Agenda*'s beginnings and development: it was meant to assist a reader's evaluation of *The Cantos* as a repository of ideas, not necessarily as a storehouse of poetic techniques. The first announcement appeared on the inside front cover of Cookson's magazine, advertised together with Kenner's *The Pound Era.* Hugh MacDiarmid published his review of the volume in *Agenda*, praising it for performing "a formidable task in a simple straightforward way." MacDiarmid deplored the mass of contemporary critical commentary that had no respect for the poet, particularly the error-hunting and the disparagement for lack of scholarship characteristic of the 1950s and 1960s. He remarked that Cookson had shown a true sense of measure and tact, with no excess of editorial apparatus. In his introduction, he had gone to the heart of the matter: this was to select the prose pieces by degree of relevance to *The Cantos*, so that they form a useful commentary. To prove the indivisibility of Pound's work, MacDiarmid especially prized the economic writings, which he defended against the accusation of eccentricity, recognizing their family resemblance to writings by Corbett, Ruskin, Carlyle, and the American populists. The main merit of the *Selected Prose* was to show how the middle and late cantos were articulated to a parallel prose discourse elucidating it (10.4–11.1 [autumn-winter 1972–73]: 139–45).

When in the summer of 1972 Terrell started *Paideuma,* the first academic journal exclusively dedicated to Pound's work (as the serial of the National Poetry Foundation, an organization he had just created at the University of Maine), he decided to include contributors that had been previously published in *Agenda*: Peck, Davie, Pearlman, Kenner, Stock, and Gordon. During the 1970s, Cookson seemed to diversify—he left the study of Pound to *Paideuma* but championed the work of Oppen, Zukofsky, and Bunting, poets that Terrell would also take a major interest in. Cookson was a step ahead in publishing Agenda Editions—volumes of original poetry and translations for which he started advertising in spring 1973. Terrell proceeded to extend the National Poetry Foundation with a book-publishing venture in 1974. The two journals would advertise and review each other, collaborate across the Atlantic, and nurture their sets of readers: Cookson's public was the British cultivated reader, whereas *Paideuma*'s was decidedly academic. Cookson's and Terrell's careers as agents of change, explicators, and arbiters of taste would henceforth run together.

Paideuma: Building up the Discipline

When the first number of *Paideuma* appeared on the stage of literary scholarship in the summer of 1972, one could well be reminded of the birth of Pallas Athene emerging in full armor out of the head of Zeus, her father: indeed, the title page of volume I issue 1 looks almost military: at the top of the page, the senior editors—the most prestigious names in the Pound scholarship of the day: Hugh Kenner and Eva Hesse, hovering like house deities above the editors, Davie, Gallup, and Leary; the managing editor—inconspicuous but in the very center of the page both on the vertical and horizontal axis—Carroll F. Terrell; under him, the associates, Cookson in London, Iwasaki in Tokyo, Singh in Belfast, de Roux in Paris, Meacham in New York, Tierney in Quebec and Patnaik in India! Under the associates, the editorial assistants, four of them. The journal also had an art director, a secretary, and a press director. Indeed, in retrospect, a word of homage is due to the art director, Arline Thomson, whose name appeared in small letters at the bottom of the title page: the design of the journal, the masthead, logo, type, and the artwork on the front and back covers have been the most resilient components of the *Paideuma* identity.

The organization of the journal reflected the concept of "paideuma" (defined as active ideas informing a culture) which Pound had adapted from the German anthropologist Leo Frobenius, and that of "ching ming" (the "right word"), which Pound took over from Confucius. The first concept was adopted as the journal's title, whereas the second was quoted as a constant reminder on the inside front cover of every issue. The "ching ming" was not an empty formula, but governed the approach that Terrell was to adopt for his creation, the most important of a lifetime: the Mandate of the Emperor is to use correct terminology to delegate responsibility to the best person to hold it. The edifice of *Paideuma*'s title page reflects this. Terrell's goal and ambition was to coordinate a whole discipline by the strength of his journal, harness the energies of all the scholars working in Pound studies in a forum where the best were to contribute, if possible regularly.

Force, architecture, perfection—these were the watchwords governing the founding of the journal. Unlike Cookson at the time of starting *Agenda*, Terrell was a mature scholar when he began his Pound project: there was no fumbling, no insecurity, no identity crisis, no growing up and maturing. On the back of the title page, Terrell already announced material that would be published in the next issues. The way forward was mapped out, the structure established, the contributors known. The categories which were to organize the scholarly material were also remarkably resilient and answered the immediate needs of studying Pound at the start of the 1970s: a generic rubric called "Periplum" held the articles that interpreted aspects of Pound's oeuvre; "The Explicator" clarified obscure allusions; "The Biographer" was to contain memoirs by people who knew Pound, thumbnail sketches that could be used for a long biography later. The first such testimony appeared in the second number—Richard Stern's account of visits to Calle Querini in the 1960s. The "Biographer" was also to contain information on people mentioned in *The Cantos*. Images had their place in a "Gallery." "The Documentary" was to highlight primary texts and bibliographic work on them. Finally, "Departments" would contain reviews and editorial correspondence. The first review, printed in the second issue, was Donald Davie's appraisal of Kenner's *The Pound Era*.

By the start of volume 2 in spring 1973, Cookson had dropped from the list of associates. The two journals, *Agenda* and *Paideuma*, worked together nevertheless, they advertised each other and reviewed each other's work. But professional association did not mean mercy: in 1974, Forrest Read published a damning review of Cookson's edition of Pound's *Selected Prose 1909–1965*, which had been published the previous year. The first complaint was that Cookson had simply reprinted and rearranged according to his own design a great number of prose pieces from an earlier collection edited by Stock in 1960: *Impact: Essays on Ignorance and the Decline of American Civilization*. Read's further objection was that important materials had been left out, the *ABC of Reading* and *The Chinese Written Character as a Medium for Poetry* among the most important. The *New Age* articles and items that had been published in fascist periodicals in the 1930s were woefully underrepresented. Of 464 pages, only 174 were reprints that were not readily available—that made the book "misleading and more or less redundant for the beginner": "Selection, editing, organization, and introduction make it a sketchy pastiche useless for serious reliance" (*Paideuma* 3, no.1 [1972]: 126). Read was particularly scornful of Cookson's effort to glide over Pound's fascism:

he quoted from favorable, even enthusiastic statements about Hitler that Pound made in 1939, 1941, and 1945. Read's review shows the extent of probity that Terrell was willing to practice and the merciless way in which professional standards were going to be applied.

In time, the journal sections became more clearly outlined and the senior editors were responding to scholarly queries. Reviews had their own section, separate from "Departments," which was subdivided into "Notes and Queries," "Letters to the Editor," "Bulletin Board," and "Notes on Staff and Contributors." Starting with the second volume, bibliographies also received their separate section. In retrospect, Terrell's foresight is impressive. He not only mapped out the needs of the present by concentrating the efforts of a scholarly community, developing and structuring a growing body of knowledge on Pound and his work, but also set the foundations for what would of necessity be written in the future: the extended monograph, the large biography, the editions of primary texts and of course, his own *Companion*, which would be the due heir of the "Explicator" and "Documentary" sections, but really would coordinate information derived from all the other journal categories. All these areas of study needed a foundation of research which the journal could amass over the years.

A careful look at *Paideuma's* first number gives us the answer to the question "How does one create a discipline from ground up?" The publication of the *Pound Era* and the eruption on the literary scene of *Paideuma*, the dedicated journal of Pound studies, blew away the possible fears and timidities of Pound's scholar-readers. They were encouraged to be bold, rally around their journal, and rely on the most brilliant book of criticism ever written on a modernist author. Between them, Kenner and Terrell sparked a classical era in Pound studies, ushering in the books and authors that we still read today. The 1970s were prolific, enthusiastic, hopeful, constructive. There was so much to find out, understand, and explore.

On to the Digital Age: *Make It New*

Not even the master wizard Carroll F. Terrell could have predicted the success of his Pound journal: *Paideuma* was the backbone of the discipline for much longer than he anticipated; not for ten but for thirty-three years it continued as an academic journal devoted to the poet. Looking at *Paideuma*'s website, we notice that the last number focused exclusively on Pound was volume 30 (2001) and it was in that year, at the turn of the new millennium, that the journal policy changed. The Board of the National Poetry Foundation announced the opening up of *Paideuma* to the poetry of English-language modernism broadly conceived. The Board might have realized that a journal dedicated to a single author was not in step with the times. As indeed it was not: in the era of the New Modernist Studies, an author-centered journal was undesirable. The new perspectives on modernism sought to escape the single focus on individual authors and survey the field in all its thematic variety (Harris 115). Moreover, Pound was in so many respects the wrong author: in the aftermath of deconstructive critique, his political image at the dawn of the millennium was even more tarnished than at the start of the 1970s; his canonical status was deflecting academic attention from modernist writers who had been marginalized unfairly on the grounds of gender, ethnicity and race; as a dead white male, the most elitist and difficult of modernists, and a fascist to boot, Pound enjoyed too much academic attention to the detriment of under-researched zones of modernism. In the new configuration, Pound had a place, but he was a poet among others, not the favorite. With this turn, Kenner's definition of modernism as a Pound era was officially closed. *Paideuma* no longer provided, and could no longer provide, the community glue that had been so strong in Terrell's days.

In many respects, *Paideuma* was Terrell's journal, and a lifetime project, as *Agenda* was Cookson's. When Terrell died in 2003, the focus was changed to adjust it to the professional ideologies of the present—the same thing that happened to *Agenda* at Cookson's own death in the same year. In both cases, a founding editor had invested his whole life in his periodical—those who took over from him shifted the focus and interest into another direction. Arguably, this led to a reorientation: Pound scholars spread out and published in other journals, like *Twentieth Century Literature, American Literature, Textual Studies*, and *Modernism/modernity.*

The frequency of *Paideuma* had played a role in its identity. The journal was strongly connected to Terrell's project of annotation that culminated in the *Companion to The Cantos of Ezra Pound.* As long as the *Companion* was in project phase, from 1972 to 1985, Terrell needed all the input on the poem he could get and produced two or three issues a year. The journal was very diverse, but the documentation, research, and interpretation of the poem played a prominent role in its pages. By 1984, when the *Companion* was finally ready and published, Terrell had been retired for three years. Even though he continued to work part-time and was involved in the journal until 1998, he managed only two issues per year; by 2002, when his successors had to do the work alone, *Paideuma* became an annual. Not only was the journal slowing down, its periodicity was compromised by great delays in publication, especially in the new millennium. The commemorative issue celebrating Terrell and Kenner, who had died five days from each other in November 2003, appeared two years later, and the next number after that, volume 36, appeared only in 2010. Pound continued to have great weight and importance in *Paideuma*: volume 37 was dedicated to Mary de Rachewiltz and volume 40 was a Festschrift issue for Burt Hatlen. They were conceived in the old format, and geared towards a readership of Pound scholars. But as an annual, *Paideuma* was an unlikely vessel to keep abreast of new events, conferences and publications, as it used to do.

As *Paideuma* slowed down, the world around it was changing dramatically. Academic journals were impacted by the digital revolution; their articles were digitized and integrated in specialized databases that made them searchable and their contents available at a touch of a key. This availability in turn was changing the behavior of students and researchers. Academic work began in the database and privileged electronic texts over printed ones. A journal had to have a digital edition to ensure that its contents were being accessed and used in research under this new framework. Yet *Paideuma* stuck to its print-only format, which made it rare and difficult to access. Its treasure—around thirty years of exclusive research on Pound—became all but hidden away in a few libraries. Then the price of producing the volume went up—for an annual, *Paideuma* became expensive—in 2018, it was $40 per issue. Certainly, libraries could buy it—but how many individual scholars, especially graduate students, could and did?

By 2013, five years after Hatlen's passing away, the channels of communication were disappearing—the only way Pound scholars could stay in contact with each other's current work, or keep informed about new research and publication was by attending the biennial Ezra Pound International Conferences. The needs of the day were to recreate a sense of community, bring scholars together, offer an outlet to young people to experiment with new digital methods and tools, put one's finger on the pulse of what was going on in the world of Pound studies—and beyond them, in the wide pastures of other media, art, and fandom he inspired. These needs would only be addressed in the new digital quarterly *Make It New*, which Preda started in 2014.

The rationale was that while *Paideuma* could continue to publish academic essays as an annual devoted to modernist literature, a sense of community liveliness derived from information on publications and events was missing. A society serial could be a cultural gazette, a review, and a workshop. Thus, *Make It New* did not aim to replace *Paideuma*, but to retrieve a sense of what made Pound interesting and valuable for life; it aimed to be a document that a scholar in the field might read with ease and pleasure. Preda designed the magazine as a forum for experiment which would bend the usual format of an academic journal. Hence, it relied on *Paideuma*'s earliest practices of regular information, as well as on the openness and flexibility of *Agenda* as possible models of editing.

Preda launched *Make It New* simultaneously with the Pound Society website in May 2014. The aim of the new serial was to inform members of society events (conferences and awards) as well as to announce and review new publications on or related to Pound. Hence the frequency of publication was much higher, aiming to respond quickly to the mass and quality of new publications, conferences, and events. If *Paideuma* in 2014 had been an annual publication for almost a decade, *Make It New* was a digital quarterly. What Preda did not foresee at the time was the speed with which the periodical would grow; also that the quality of submitted contributions would prove to be much higher than the framework of a society magazine led both editor and readers to expect. The first number had thirty-five pages, suitable for a "little magazine." The second almost doubled that, reaching sixty-two pages. The third and the fourth reached eighty-five and ninety pages respectively. The parameters were flexible—from the start, the quarterly included materials that straddled categories: review essays, like "Imagism Status Rerum and a Note on Haiku" by David Ewick (*MIN* 2.1) and "WHY Joe/ izza hiz/ Torian" by Richard Sieburth (*MIN* 3.2); reports on methodology research, like Jim Cocola's "Notes Toward a Draft of 'A Gazetteer to *The Cantos of Ezra Pound*'" (*MIN* 1.4); extended documentary and biographical reports, like Heriberto Cruz Cornejo's "From Arcadia to Hell: The Fate of Gerhart and Vera Münch, 1937–1947" (*MIN* 3.3); and multimedia experiments like Margaret Fisher's "Music Column" (*MIN* 1.1–2.4), which included audio examples alongside small-scale musical analyses.

Preda found herself doing bibliographic work, like Edwards before her (and doing it serially as well). She collaborated with Archie Henderson, whose bibliographic activities had started in a previous collaboration with Donald Gallup. This work, started in March 2015, found that the previous year had witnessed four books and forty-eight articles on Pound published in English alone. This came as a surprise to many, since the coverage of the *MLA Bibliography* had not been as extensive, and its very incompleteness gave a skewed idea of contemporary research on Pound. The digital medium was beneficial to this bibliographic work as well, since it permitted easy supplementation and correction. Moreover, since more and more secondary literature was available online, the bibliography could form a convenient starting point for new work, since it provided not only a complete tableau of publications, but also links to full-text resources.

Like Edwards and Terrell before her, Preda was correlating a bibliography, a project on Pound's *Cantos,* and a periodical, responding to the situation of Pound studies in her time. The transition to the digital medium she effected in Pound studies was done in parallel with overall efforts made by various forms of academic associations in all branches of the humanities, at a time that saw the rise of digital humanities as an academic discipline, the creation of gigantic databases for storing scholarly articles, and the scanning of books by Google and Internet Archive. Like monks in monasteries bent over their copying of old parchment scrolls into codices, or like the first printers using Gutenberg's press to make knowledge universal and accessible, contemporary scholars like Preda felt the need to ensure that Pound's work, as well as scholarship on it, are copied and developed into the new media, to allow access, preservation, development, and transmission of specialized knowledge to a younger generation of students and researchers.

Notes

[1] J. H. Edwards to Ezra Pound, June 15, 1953. YCAL 43 14/658.

[2] "The checklist went off to the publisher this morning. It is not as good as I wished it to be, of course, but it is as good as I could make it, working at this distance from major libraries and having to depend on various others sending in information. The full bibliography has yet to be done: this is meant to provide information in the meantime. It ought to function in that role." (J. H. Edwards to Ezra Pound, August 8, 1951. YCAL 43 14/658).

[3] While reporting his activities to Pound in 1953, trying to get his blessing and draw him in, Edwards remarked: "I have little doubts of your intense uninterest in said index. It is the sad fact that I have to live with" (November 2, 1953, YCAL 43 14/658).

[4] Vasse had his own correspondence with the poet: his letter of August 10, 1956 is a summing up and conclusion of his collaboration with Edwards for the *Pound Newsletter* and the *Index* (YCAL 43 53/2436).

[5] Alexander Del Mar was the author of *History of Monetary Systems*, a book that Pound was enthusiastic about and which he used as material for his canto XCVII.

[6] Hugh Kenner to Ezra Pound, November 28, 1952 (YCAL 43 27/1140: 2).

[7] Ibid., 3.

[8] Dallam Simpson edited *Four Pages* in 1948 in Galveston, Texas. The magazine ran for nine numbers and received from Pound an avalanche of recommendations, snippets, and advice re policy and contributors (Moody, *Ezra Pound: Poet* III: 291–92). Pound wanted Cookson's magazine to be a revival of Simpson's, telling him: "Dear C/n yes, I prefer title Four Pages to establish/ continuity, ultimately a reprint of useful parts of 4P/ Strike and Edg in some larger mag/ possibly Europ" (Pound to Cookson, [Oct/Nov 1958], published in *Agenda* 17, no.3–4–18.1 (1979/80). In this issue, Cookson published his early correspondence with Pound in facsimile, under the title: "Some Letters to William Cookson 1956–1970," 5–47. The pages are not numbered. All quotations and references from Pound's letters are taken from this source and will be referred to by date.

[9] Peter Russell published the eleven issues of his magazine *Nine* (after the nine muses) from 1948 to 1956. Cookson acknowledged his debt to both in his retrospective article "E. P. and *Agenda*: Autobiographical Fragments" (Alexander and McGonigal 46).

[10] The Square Dollar was a series of booklets priced at one dollar in which one of Pound's disciples at St. Elizabeths, John Kasper, republished authors that Pound considered important: Confucius, Ernest Fenollosa, Alexander Del Mar, Louis Agassiz, and Thomas Hart Benton. The series was published between 1951 and 1954 (Moody, *Ezra Pound Poet* III: 307).

[11] This letter (Pound to Cookson, May 2, 1956) is reproduced both in Cookson's *Agenda* 1979/1980 and in Alexander and McGonigal 45–46.

[12] Introductory note to "Some Letters to William Cookson 1956–1970" *Agenda* 17 1979/1980: 5.

[13] An undated letter of Oct./Nov. 1958 from Pound contains the text that Cookson used as his first editorial (*Agenda* 1979/1980). He added by hand: "the above is strictly ghost writ as from editors. not from EP." On February 3, 1959 Pound wrote: "Nope, please do not stick my name on anything unless specially requested."

[14] The letter to the editor was from J. F. C. Fuller (3). The articles were "Financial Reform," signed C.M.: 2–3; and "Planning Today," by Edmund Gray, 3–4, both in *Agenda* 1.2 (February 1959).

[15] The editorial was signed by David Gordon (*Agenda* 1, no.5 [May 1959]: 1–2. The issue also reprinted a comment about the creation of money from the *U.S. News & World Report* (2).

[16] "You have missed the point in letter of a couple of months ago. (1) The USE of a 4 page leaflet is to get over ideas unprintable elsewhere. They do NOT stay the same. No use in Agenda saying to 70 people what American Mercury, Candor, and even Action are NOW saying to MORE people. (2) to form a group. You went into reverse and lost BINbinides [Binyon's grandson] instead of finding a third man. Gordon might support you, BUT he really wants a place for his Mencius and what he was supposed to be doing needs more than a couple of pages. IF he can swing it. 3/ a group that collects news and/or indicates where lively articles are being printed, Agenda hasn't shown the seeing eye" (Pound to Cookson, June 17, 1959, in *Agenda* 1979/1980).

[17] Pound was highly impressed with Stock and recommended him to Cookson very early, in a letter of January 19, 1959: "Stock is a marvel for collecting and digesting information. I am too exhausted to keep up with him. He now probably knows as much as I do and is competent to carry on" (*Agenda* 1979/1980). By June, he was telling Cookson to put himself under Stock's orders so that he could learn both how to correlate important facts and manage contributors.

[18] David Gordon's article, "The Cyclops Ideogram," had also been mediated by Pound.

[19] "I don't know if you cd/ encourage the better side of him/ but always useful to review him/ commending his virtues/ mezzo-Possumik. He has been steadily constructive./ not protruding the nekk beyond the possible. [. . .] at any rate Correlate/" (Pound to Cookson, February 25, 1958, in *Agenda* 1979/80).

[20] Alan Neame's translation of *Leoun* was first published in Noel Stock's *Edge* 6 (Moody, *Ezra Pound: Poet* III: 672).

[21] Noel Stock "Ezra Pound and an American Tradition," *Agenda* 2, no.4 (June 1961): 4–10.

[22] William Cookson. [Editorial.] *Agenda* 5, no.1–3 (spring-summer 1967): 4.

Conclusion

He is very likely, in ways controversy still hides, the contemporary of our grandchildren.

—Hugh Kenner (1971)

I shall survive as a curiosity. The art of letters will come to an end before A.D. 2000.

—Ezra Pound (1910)

In *Orality and Literacy: The Technologizing of the Word* (1982), Walter Ong developed his theory of "secondary orality," a condition whereby the written word ceases to be the primary means by which a culture exchanges ideas and information. Ong couldn't, in 1982, have foreseen our twenty-first-century world where readers spend more time in front of screens than they do in the pages of books; a world where literature survives, but—almost reverting to its condition in the medieval or ancient worlds—increasingly does so as an art valued principally by elite culture. Ong couldn't have foreseen it, but in a curious way Pound did. The epigraph above comes from a letter he sent to his mother, at a time when his aspirations still absolutely eclipsed his accomplishments. The letter caught the attention of Mary Ellis Gibson, who quotes it at length:

> I shall survive as a curiosity. The art of letters will come to an end before A.D. 2000 and there will be a sort of artistic dark ages till about A.D. 2700.
>
> The last monument will be a bombastic, rhetorical epic wherethrough will move Marconi, Pierpont Morgan, Bleriot, Levavasour [*sic*] Latham, Peary [*sic*], Dr. Cook, etc. clothed in the heroic manner of Greek imitation. . . . I shall write it myself if threatened with actual starvation.[1]

In 1910, a twenty-five-year-old Pound was already imagining himself as a kind of Mauberley, born too late, a kind of relic living in a society that no longer values the art to which he has dedicated his life ("He strove to resuscitate the dead art / of Poetry"). He was also imagining that an epic poem for his time would necessarily include politics, economics, and history. He was anticipating, in other words, the kinds of trouble that awaited him, and awaited us. The story of Pound's reception is very much the story of our arguments with ourselves. We continue to debate the power of his work in large part because we remain uncertain about what it is we want from a great poet.

The scholars of Kenner and Terrell's generation assumed that Pound's poetry should be separated from the messiness of his political allegiances and regarded in strictly literary terms. Broadly, they knew a good part of what we know today, yet they chose to keep silent about the politics so as to concentrate on studying the work, in the honest belief that the two should and could be regarded independently. The poetry and the politics were kept apart even in the recognition that Pound was a poet who had been the most actively engaged of his time, a writer as committed to the politics of his age as Dante, Milton, and Shelley had been to theirs. These scholars created the foundation and organizational framework of Pound studies as a discipline and of all that we know about his work today, particularly *The Cantos*. It was they who first submitted Pound to the strictures and structures of professional attention. Kenner, especially, draped the study of modernism around Pound, placing him at its very heart. In launching Pound studies as a legitimized field of academic endeavor, Kenner's generation inadvertently laid the foundation for the next stage of development of English as a discipline.

This foundation, relying on the distinction between literature and politics, was radically undermined by forms of poststructuralist ideology critique that developed in the 1980s. In retrospect, this development, a kind of methodological backlash, was a well-deserved protest at the one-sided way in which Pound had been studied. Pound's anti-Semitism and his involvement in Italian Fascism were thoroughly explored and prosecuted: scholars argued fiercely that Pound's political convictions could not be separated from his poetry and that his fascist, anti-Semitic ideology vitiated his literary work and turned it into a veiled political apology. Casillo's study *The Genealogy of Demons* (1988) had far-reaching influence in turning scholarship away from the strictly literary towards a politically inflected inquiry into poetic rhetoric. Casillo aimed to demonstrate that Pound's whole work was fundamentally anti-Semitic and that there were no untainted periods or paradisal parts of his poetry where scholars could take refuge. Other critics, writing within the poststructuralist paradigm current at the time, went even further to argue that Pound's mature work, *The Cantos,* was tainted by what he detested most, usury and Jewishness.

Towards the end of the millennium, scholars began to see the limitations of the poststructuralist approach, whose ideology critique was as inward-looking and text-oriented as the previous literary-historical paradigm had been. A redefinition of modernist studies swept the whole discipline with sociologically oriented assumptions: professional Pound criticism was submerged in the wave, despite isolated efforts to resist it.

The new critical paradigm, called New Modernist Studies both by the founders of the Modernist Studies Association and also by the *Chronicle of Higher Education*,[2] internalized the political critique of the 1980s and aimed to loosen the grip of author societies on the study of modernism. The MSA founders sensed that the best way to move on from rhetorically framed moral outrage was to submit modernism, largely for the first time, to properly historical and historicizing study, as well as to the techniques of cultural semiotics. In many areas of modernist scholarship, this move was unproblematic. But no approach to Pound has yet proven problem-free. Every source of light casts a shadow. In retrospect, it is remarkable that all five members of the MSA's founding board of directors were scholars who had worked or were working on Pound: Michael Coyle, Gail McDonald, Cassandra Laity, Sanford Schwartz, and Mark Morrison. Indeed, one of the association's first two keynote speakers was a Pound scholar, Peter Nicholls.

Rooting Pound studies in cultural critique should not have been problematic. Kenner's work had demonstrated that engaging Pound required following at least some of his heterogeneous interests: Pound studies have always branched out naturally in perspectives on other modernist poets and artists. However, the New Modernist Studies worked against the politics of exclusion that Pound's centrality presupposed; they broadened the field of modernism to include those neglected and marginalized, they flattened the implicit hierarchies of Kenner's short list of relevant writers. Pound lost his central position and became a poet among others. His compromised politics continued to inform the way his poetry was read even as it was sometimes deployed in attempts to read him out of the canon. Scholars acknowledged the central role of fascism in Pound's poetics as a preamble to any topic under discussion. Starting with Redman's seminal study of Pound in the context of Italian Fascism (1991), the palette of approaches to Pound's political involvement was considerably broadened, to include historical analyses of Pound's propaganda; critiques of fascist aesthetic ideology and Pound's relationship with it; studies on Pound's economics; detailed analyses of the "Italian cantos" written in the desperate stages of the war; and extended explorations into Pound and the American and European Right.

The cultural studies turn has, to be sure, produced work of enduring significance. Let Rainey's *Ezra Pound and the Monument of Culture* stand as the pre-eminent example. But work of this kind sometimes functions to explain away greatness rather than lead new readers into it. That this is so follows in part from scholars who have followed Franco Moretti's lead in turning away from the tactics of "close reading" that served both the post-war and poststructuralist eras to the concept of "distant reading."[3] Such reorientations tend to divert attention from Pound's poetry, allowing for the resurfacing of the "new" argument that he was not an important artist in his own right, but rather a cultural figure, a mediator, promoter, and helper of other more deserving writers. Although often neglecting Pound the poet in favor of Pound the facilitator, the recent, sociologically inflected approach has been unable to dismiss his centrality; instead it has found itself confronted with it at every turn. Paradoxically, it could not avoid reaffirming it: scholars of modernism found Pound everywhere, in every topic they wanted to study, whether it was the involvement of modernism with mythologies, gender, race, history, museums, magazines, technology, new media, the arts, exile, the law. Some aspect of Pound's work had to be included in every handbook on modernism, every textbook for students. Books delineating his influence on poets, both British and American, established new genealogical lines. More significantly, since Pound's poetic practices had questioned and challenged the nature of the linguistic sign, the idea of the book, and the print medium, he seemed to anticipate the newest of the new, postmodernism and the digital revolution.

As we move into the third decade of the twenty-first century, it is clear that these various attempts at dislocation have been ineffective. Despite the political arguments against him, Pound continues to be read in and out of the professional community, a fact confirmed by Pound's strong presence on the internet, by the informal meetings of the Cantos Reading Group in London (2006 to the present), and by the number of lay attendees of the Ezra Pound International Conference events every two years. Dissertations continue to be written, translations continue to be made. The *Bibliography of English Language Scholarship on Ezra Pound*, assembled by Henderson and Preda for the Pound Society, demonstrates that scholarship dedicated to the poet has continued to thrive into the new millennium. Every scholar in the field has denounced or at least distanced him- or herself from Pound's fascism and anti-Semitism, yet this has not prevented the writing of an average of forty-five articles on Pound per year, nor the publication of new editions of his work, like Sieburth's edition for the prestigious Library of America series, nor the glossing of his work online, nor the most complex and detailed biography of him ever written, Moody's monumental three-volume *Ezra Pound: Poet* (Oxford University Press, 2007–2015).

This contradictory reality suggests that we do not need to kill Pound again, whether by merely denouncing, watering down, or silence. We do not need to be afraid that his fascism and anti-Semitism will magically rub off on us or compromise our good standing among fellow human beings. A better way seems to be to admit Pound's flaws, be aware of them at all times, but acknowledge that his place at the heart of modernism cannot be contested in good faith. His politics and his racism were his own—they are not and will not be ours. We now know who and what he was—his life has now been traced almost week by week. His texts have been kept, not destroyed—access to them has always been open. We know how others punished him for his actions and how he chose to punish himself.

He is not going to disappear.

A century ago, Pound was embraced by the best poets of the age, but we have not always remembered why, nor admitted his merits as an artist. Professional attention means responsible attention. As they conduct their work, scholars shoulder many, sometimes conflicting responsibilities: we serve the promotion of writing—now more than ever as we move into a post-literary culture; we serve historical truth; sometimes we serve political or ethical causes. For all of this, we need to remember some part of what Pound's peers always knew. W. B. Yeats, T. S. Eliot, James Joyce, Mina Loy, H.D. and Wyndham Lewis, among others, all recognized that the challenges Pound posed as an artist are worth meeting. In the twenty-first century, we are still learning to study Pound as we study them. It is time we engage with his work not by flickers of awareness and partial, timid projects but, in recognition of his status as a classic of modernism, finally make good on the scholars' dream. Possibilities include a critical edition of Pound's poetry on the model of the Eliot or Yeats editions;[4] a digital research environment dedicated to *The Cantos* as has now been started at the University of Edinburgh; a complete critical edition of his criticism in digital format along the lines of *The Complete Prose of T. S. Eliot*, currently being prepared at Johns Hopkins;[5] the complete correspondence in chronological order, on the model of the editions of Henry James's and T. S. Eliot's letters;[6] a digital *Variorum*; genetic editions; complete primary and secondary bibliographies in English as well as other languages; a dedicated journal and book series.

A new century is already bringing us a new Pound: a Pound that Ezra himself might not always have recognized but—in no small way owing to the development of new forms of professional attention—a Pound still very much alive, continuously modified in the guts of the living, as Auden would have it. "Transformation, translation, their systematic deformations," become themselves, to borrow one of Kenner's most Poundian phrases (170), "foci of attention." We explore Pound best when we misread him in new ways and adapt his work to understand our world. "Great bulk, huge mass, thesaurus" (V/17): we might remember that "thesaurus" means "treasure house" or "temple." *The Cantos* continues to serve as that kind of place—a locus for original thought and exploration, his and ours.

Notes

[1] Mary Ellis Gibson, *Epic Reinvented: Ezra Pound and the Victorians* (Ithaca: Cornell University Press, 1995), 83.

[2] Scott Heller, "New Life for Modernism," in the *Chronicle of Higher Education*, Nov. 5, 1999: https://www.chronicle.com/article/New-Life-for-Modernism/16279.

[3] Franco Moretti, *Distant Reading* (Brooklyn: Verso, 2013).

[4] *The Poems of T. S. Eliot*, edited by Christopher Ricks and Jim McCue, 2 vols. (London: Faber & Faber, 2015). *The Collected Works of W. B. Yeats* is published by Scribner: volume XIV came out in May 2015.

[5] *The Complete Prose of T. S. Eliot: A Critical Edition*, 8 vols. (Baltimore: Johns Hopkins University Press, 2014–). Six volumes are already published.

[6] *The Letters of T. S. Eliot* are being published by Faber. Volume 7 (1934–1935) came out in 2017. *The Complete Letters of Henry James* is being published by the University of Nebraska Press. The eleventh volume appeared in November 2017.

Chronology of the Bollingen Controversy

1935

January 11	Pound makes his first broadcast, for Minculpop—the Italian Ministry of Popular Culture.

1941

January 21	Pound begins regular broadcasting for the Italian Broadcasting Service.
Summer	Pound decides to return to the US for the duration of the war, but instead of renewing his passport, the US Chargé d'Affairs—in view of Pound's radio broadcasts—confiscates it on the spot. In mid-July the Government offers Pound a conditional passport allowing his return on condition that he remain in the United States for the duration of the war. Although he had himself planned to do just that, Pound refuses to be dictated to, and declines the conditions.
December	Pound is refused a seat on the last clipper out of Rome; told he must return to the US, but must do so by slow boat, risking mines and submarine attack. He decides to stay in Italy.

1942

January 6	Paul and Mary Mellon incorporate the Bollingen Foundation under the laws of the state of New York.
January 29	Pound resumes broadcasting.
June 23	Under pressure from the FBI, which was suspicious of its Swiss contacts, the Bollingen Foundation is liquidated entirely.
December	The FBI begins formal investigation of Pound.

1943

May — Allen Tate is appointed Consultant in Poetry to the Library of Congress.

July 26 — Pound is indicted *in absentia* for treason.

1944

May — Acting upon a suggestion of Allen Tate's, the Library of Congress appoints a body of fellows in American letters. The first fellows are: Conrad Aiken, W. H. Auden, Louise Bogan, Katherine Garrison Chapin, T. S. Eliot, Paul Green, Robert Lowell, Katherine Anne Porter, Karl Shapiro, Theodore Spencer, Allen Tate, Willard Thorp, and Robert Penn Warren.

1945

May 3 — Pound is taken prisoner by Italian partisans, who release him later in the day. He immediately surrenders to American troops, who require several days to decide what to do with him.

June — President Truman appoints Luther Evans Librarian of Congress, replacing Archibald MacLeish. Evans had already been serving as acting librarian since December of 1944, and had served in the same capacity before that from 1942-1943.

June 14–15 — After three weeks in "the gorilla cage," a cage hastily constructed for Pound of jagged air-strip metal (six by six-and-a-half feet), exposed to the elements and under intense floodlights at night, Pound suffers inflammation of the eyes, claustrophobia, and mental confusion.

November 18 — Pound is returned to the US on military transport and taken to the District of Columbia jail; the next day he is arraigned for treason.

December — Bennett Cerf, editor at Random House, decides to exclude Pound's work from a new "Modern Library Giant" anthology of twentieth-century American poetry.

1946

January 1 The Bollingen Foundation is revived under the laws of the Commonwealth of Virginia.

February 13 Declared of "unsound mind" and so unfit for trial, Pound is committed to St. Elizabeths Hospital, District of Columbia.

December Huntington Cairns, as trustee of the Bollingen Foundation, responding to *Poetry* editor Hayden Carruth's request, sponsors the first of several contributions to enable the Modern Poetry Association of Chicago to continue publishing *Poetry*. Over the next fifteen years the Bollingen Foundation grants the Association $82,500. This award is the first ever from a philanthropic foundation to a literary journal.

1947

January 31 The motion for bail filed on Pound's behalf by his lawyer, Julien Cornell, is dismissed. Pound is allowed only to move to a more comfortable ward within St. Elizabeths.

1948

January Tate proposes that the Fellows create an award in poetry. Librarian Luther Evans agrees. Tate successfully approaches Huntington Cairns, a trustee of the Bollingen Foundation; Cairns then proposes the donation to the foundation's finance committee, which votes an allocation of $10,000 for ten years of awards.

March 4 Luther Evans, having accepted the grant, announces the establishment of the Bollingen Prize in Poetry, a $1,000 annual prize for "the highest achievement of American Poetry" published in the previous year.

July 30 Publication of *Pisan Cantos.*

November At the annual meeting of the Fellows in American Letters, final nominations are reduced to four candidates. That night, at a dinner he gives for the Fellows, Cairns expresses hope that the prize will attract a little attention; Tate responds, "*Will* it attract attention."

1949

January — Informed of the Fellows' vote, Luther Evans warns that "the reaction would be, for the most part, emotional rather than intellectual; public conscience would be outraged; the progress of poetry would be arrested for a generation; international relations, particularly with Italy, would be embarrassed; confidence in the Library of Congress would be seriously impaired; their faculties would be suspected, their motives rejected, their principles deplored; Congress, inevitably, would intervene." The fellows persist in their choice.

Feb. 17 — The first Bollingen Prize is announced.

May — The *Partisan Review* publishes a forum on "The Question of the Pound Award," including comments from Auden, Shapiro, and Tate.

June 11 — The *Saturday Review of Literature* publishes Robert Hillyer's "Treason's Strange Fruit," the first of two attacks on Pound, the Bollingen Prize, and the Bollingen Foundation. The second article, "Poetry's New Priesthood," appears on June 18. Norman Cousins and Harrison Smith, in an editorial in the June 11 issue, predict, "if we read the signs of the time correctly, the Bollingen Prize given to Ezra Pound will eventually set off a revolution of no mean dimensions."

June 30 — Luther Evans, in his annual Report of the Librarian of Congress, first answers Hillyer's attacks.

August 19 — Joint Committee of Congress on the library unanimously agrees that the library should abstain from the giving of prizes or the making of awards.

August 27 — Peter Viereck's "My Kind of Poetry" is published in the *Saturday Review of Literature.*

October — Hayden Carruth, editor of *Poetry*, publishes the special issue *The Case Against the Saturday Review: The Attack of the Saturday Review on Modern Poets and Critics: Answered by the Fellows in American Letters of the Library of Congress, Together with Articles, Editorials, and Letters from Other Writers* as a seventy-five-page booklet distributed to subscribers and sold for $1.

1950

Early in year the Yale University Library, one of several applicants, is granted funds by the Bollingen Foundation to continue the Poetry Award. The winner of the award for 1949, announced shortly thereafter, is Wallace Stevens. Although the Bollingen Foundation ends its programs in 1968, the Andrew W. Mellon Foundation continues making the requisite donations to Yale, and in 1973 endows the Yale University Library with $100,000 to enable it to continue making the award *in perpetuo*. The prize continues to be called the Bollingen Prize. According to bollingen.yale.edu/about: "The Bollingen Prize is awarded every two years; winners are selected by the judges without any application on the part of the poet or publisher. The Bollingen Prize judges and the Beinecke Library do not accept nominations or submissions for the Bollingen Prize." Since 1963 the prize has been awarded every two years and includes a grant of $5,000.

1951

July 13 — Hugh Kenner's *The Poetry of Ezra Pound* is published. Kenner's book defines the terms by which "Pound Studies" will develop as a field, as it marks the point where controversy over the award moves from the public sphere into academe. Debate does not end at this point, but the manner in which it is conducted changes, and so, too, the stakes involved in further argument.

Works Cited

Archival Resources

Beinecke Library, New Haven. Ezra Pound Papers (YCAL 43). Cited by box no./folder no. Materials relating to Pound and particular scholars are listed below in "Works by Other Authors" under the scholar's name.

Works by Ezra Pound

Canti Postumi. Edited and translated into Italian by Massimo Bacigalupo. Milano: Mondadori, 2002.

Canto I. Genius.com. https://genius.com/Ezra-pound-canto-i-annotated.

The Cantos. New York: New Directions, 1998.

Complete Violin Works of Ezra Pound. Edited by Robert Hughes. Introduction by Margaret Fisher. Emeryville: Second Evening Art, 2004.

"Date Line." In *Literary Essays of Ezra Pound*. Edited by T. S. Eliot. London: Faber & Faber, 1954.

Drafts & Fragments: Facsimile Notebooks 1958–1959. Edited by Glen Horrowitz and Marcella Spann Booth. New York: Glen Horrowitz Bookseller, 2010.

EP to LU: Nine Letters Written to Louis Untermeyer. Edited by J. A. Robbins, Bloomington, IN: Indiana University Press, 1963.

Ezra Pound's Economic Correspondence, 1933–1940. Edited by Roxana Preda. Gainesville: University Press of Florida, 2007.

Ezra Pound's Opera "Le Testament." Text by François Villon. Edited by George Antheil. Conducted by Robert Hughes. Audio CD. Emeryville, CA: Second Evening Art, 2012.

Ezra Pound's Poetry and Prose: Contributions to Periodicals. 11 vols. Edited by Lea Baechler, James Longenbach, and Walton Litz. New York: Garland, 1991.

"A Few Don'ts by an Imagiste." *Poetry*, 1, no.6 (March 1913): 200–206.

Guide to Kulchur. 1938. London: Peter Owen, 1952.

"I Cease Not to Yowl": Ezra Pound's Letters to Olivia Rossetti Agresti. Edited by Demetres Tryphonopoulos and Leon Surette. Urbana and Chicago: University of Illinois Press, 1998.

"I Cease Not to Yowl": Reannotated. Edited by Archie Henderson. Houston, privately printed, 2009.

Impact: Essays on Ignorance and the Decline of American Civilization. Edited by Noel Stock. Chicago: Regnery, 1960.

Indiscretions; or, Une revue de deux mondes. Paris: Three Mountains Press, 1923.

Le Testament, an Opera by Ezra Pound. 1923 Facsimile edition. Edited by Robert Hughes and Margaret Fisher. Essays by Stephen J. Adams, Margaret Fisher, and Robert Hughes, annotations by Robert Hughes. Emeryville, CA: Second Evening Publishing, 2011.

Le Testament, Paroles de Villon. 1926 and 1933 Performance Editions. Emeryville, CA: Second Evening Publishing, 2008.

The Letters of Ezra Pound, 1907–1941. Edited by D. D. Paige. London: Faber, 1951.

Literary Essays of Ezra Pound. Edited by T. S. Eliot. London: Faber and Faber, 1954.

Personae. Edited by Lea Baechler and Walton Litz. New York: New Directions, 1990.

The Pisan Cantos. Edited by Richard Sieburth. New York: New Directions, 2003.

Poems and Translations. Edited by Richard Sieburth. New York: Library of America, 2003.

Posthumous Cantos. Edited by Massimo Bacigalupo. Manchester: Carcanet, 2015.

Selected Cantos. Ed. Ezra Pound. London: Faber, 1967.

The Selected Letters of Ezra Pound, 1907–1941. 1950. Edited by D. D. Paige. New York: New Directions, 1971.

Selected Poems. Edited with an introduction by T. S. Eliot. London: Faber & Faber, 1928.

Selected Prose 1909–1965. Edited by William Cookson. New York: New Directions, 1973.

Shih-Ching: The Classic Anthology Defined by Confucius. 1954. Cambridge Mass.: Harvard University Press, 1976.

XXX Cantos. Translated into Italian by Massimo Bacigalupo. Parma: Ugo Guanda, 2012.

Variorum Edition of Three Cantos by Ezra Pound. Edited by Richard Dean Taylor. Bayreuth: Boomerang Press-Norbert Aas, 1991.

"What I Feel about Walt Whitman." In *Selected Prose 1909–1965*, edited by William Cookson, 145–46. New York: New Directions, 1973.

Works by Pound with Others

Fenollosa, Ernest, and Ezra Pound. *The Chinese Character as a Medium for Poetry: A Critical Edition.* Edited by Haun Saussy, Jonathan Stalling, and Lucas Klein. New York: Fordham University Press, 2008.

Pound, Ezra, and Margaret Fisher. *The Recovery of Ezra Pound's Third Opera "Collis O Heliconii." Settings of Poems by Catullus and Sappho.* Emeryville, CA: Second Evening Art, 2005.

Pound, Ezra, and Robert Hughes. *Cavalcanti: A Perspective on the Music of Ezra Pound.* Emeryville, CA: Second Evening Art Publishing, 2003. Part II is a performance edition of Pound's "Cavalcanti."

Pound, Ezra, and Dorothy Shakespear. *Shakespear's Pound: Illuminated Cantos.* Edited by David A. Lewis and Omar Pound. Nacogdoches, TX: LaNana Creek Press, 1999.

Works by Other Authors

Abrams, M. H. "The Deconstructive Angel." *Critical Inquiry* 3, no.3 (Spring 1977): 425–38.

Ackroyd, Peter. *Ezra Pound and His World.* London: Thames & Hudson, 1980.

Adams, Robert M. "A Hawk and a Handsaw for Ezra Pound." *Accent* 8 (Summer 1948): 205–214.

Alexander, Michael. *The Poetic Achievement of Ezra Pound.* 1979. Edinburgh: Edinburgh University Press, 1998.

———. Review of *Studies in Ezra Pound*, by Donald Davie. *Agenda* 21, no.3 (1991): 64–66.

Alexander, Michael, and James McGonigal, eds. *Sons of Ezra: British Poets and Ezra Pound.* Amsterdam and Leiden: Rodopi/Brill, 1995.

Alvarez, A. "The Wretched Poet Who Lived in the House of Bedlam." Review of *The Life of Ezra Pound*, by Noel Stock. *Saturday Review*, July 18, 1970, 27–29.

"An American Poet Discovered in England." *Literary Digest* 39 (November 27, 1909): 958.

Antliff, Mark, and Scott W. Klein, eds. *Vorticism: New Perspectives.* Oxford: Oxford University Press, 2013.

Arrowsmith, Rupert Richard. *Modernism and the Museum: Asian, African, and Pacific Art and the London Avant-garde.* Oxford: Oxford University Press, 2011.

Auden, W. H. *Collected Poems.* Edited by Edward Mendelson. New York: Vintage, 1991.

Auden, W. H., W. Barrett, R. G. Davis, C. Greenberg, I. Howe, G. Orwell, K. Shapiro, and A. Tate. "The Question of the Pound Award." *Partisan Review*, 16 (May 1949): 512–522. Reprinted in O'Connor and Stone 54–56.

Babbitt, Irving. *Rousseau and Romanticism.* New York: Houghton Mifflin, 1919.

Bacigalupo, Massimo. "*The Cantos: Cantos LXXII–LXXIII.*" In *The Ezra Pound Encyclopedia*, edited by Demetres Tryphonopoulos and Stephen J. Adams, 39–41. Westport, CT: Greenwood Press, 2005.

———. *The Forméd Trace: The Later Poetry of Ezra Pound.* New York: Columbia University Press, 1980.

———. "The Poet at War: Ezra Pound's Suppressed Italian Cantos." *South Atlantic Quarterly* 83, no.1 (1984): 69–79.

Barbour, Douglas. Review of *Reading the Cantos: A Study of Meaning in Ezra Pound*, by Noel Stock. *Queen's Quarterly* 75 (1968): 550–51.

Barnes, David. "Fascist Aesthetics: Ezra Pound's Cultural Negotiations in 1930s Italy." *Journal of Modern Literature* 34, no.1 (2010): 19–35.

Barnes, David. *The Venice Myth: Culture, Literature, Politics, 1880 to the Present.* London: Pickering & Chatto, 2014.

Barnhisel, Greg. *James Laughlin, New Directions and the Remaking of Ezra Pound.* Amherst: University of Massachusetts Press, 2005.

Baro, Gene. Review of *Ezra Pound*, by Charles Norman. *The American Scholar* 30, no. 2 (Spring 1961): 284, 286.

Barrett, William. "A Prize for Ezra Pound." *Partisan Review* 16 (April 1949): 345.

Barry, Iris. "The Ezra Pound Period." *Bookman* 74 (October 1931): 159–71.

Baumann, Walter. *The Rose in the Steel Dust: An Examination of the Cantos of Ezra Pound.* Bern: Francke, 1967; Coral Gables, FL: University of Miami Press, 1970.

———. *Roses from the Steel Dust: Collected Essays on Ezra Pound*. Orono, ME: National Poetry Foundation, 2000.

Beach, Christopher. *ABC of Influence: Ezra Pound and the Remaking of the American Poetic Tradition*. Berkeley: University of California Press, 1992.

Beasley, Rebecca. *Ezra Pound and the Visual Culture of Modernism*. Cambridge: Cambridge University Press, 2007.

———. "Pound's New Criticism." *Textual Practice* 24, no.4 (2010): 649–68.

———. *Theorists of Modernist Poetry: T. S. Eliot, T. E. Hulme, Ezra Pound*. London: Routledge, 2007.

Bell, Michael. *F. R. Leavis*. London: Routledge, 1988.

Benét, William Rose. "The Phoenix Nest." *Saturday Review of Literature*, July 23, 1949, 28–29.

Benning, Sheri. "Critical Reception: 1980–2000." In *The Ezra Pound Encyclopedia*, edited by D. Tryphonopoulos and Stephen J. Adams, 72–74. Westport, CT: Greenwood Press, 2005.

Bernstein, Charles. "Pounding Fascism. Appropriating Ideologies—Mystification, Aestheticization, and Authority in Pound's Poetic Practice." Chap. 5 in *A Poetics*. Cambridge Mass.: Harvard, University Press, 1992. 121–27.

Bernstein, Michael André. *The Tale of the Tribe: Ezra Pound and the Modern Verse Epic*. Princeton, NJ: Princeton University Press, 1980.

Berryman, John. "The Poetry of Ezra Pound." *Partisan Review* 16 (April 1949): 377–94. Reprinted in Homberger, ed. *Ezra Pound: The Critical Heritage*, 388–404.

Bischoff, Volker. *Ezra Pound Criticism, 1905–1985: A Chronological Listing of Publications in English*. Marburg: Universitätsbibliothek Marburg, 1991.

Blackmur, R. P. *Language as Gesture: Essays in Poetry*. New York: Harcourt Brace, 1952.

———. "The Masks of Ezra Pound." *Hound and Horn* 7 (January 1934): 177–212.

Blish, James. "The Pound Scandal." *Sewanee Review* 67 (October 1959): 703–706.

Bloom, Harold, ed. *Modern Critical Views: Ezra Pound*. New York: Chelsea, 1987.

Bodenheim, Maxwell. "Isolation of Carved Metal." *The Dial* 72 (Jan. 1922): 87–91.

Bogan, Louise. "Pound." *New Yorker*, November 9, 1940, 76–78.

———. Review of *Eminent Domain: Yeats among Wilde, Joyce, Pound, Eliot and Auden*, by Richard Ellmann. *New Yorker*, March 30, 1968, 133–34.

———. Review of *Reading the Cantos: A Study of Meaning in Ezra Pound*, by Noel Stock. *New Yorker*, March 30, 1968, 134–35.

Bornstein, George. Review of *"To Write Paradise": Style and Error in Pound's "Cantos,"* by Christine Froula. *Journal of English and German Philology* 85, no.2 (1986): 301–3.

Bottrall, Ronald. "The Achievement of Ezra Pound." *Adelphi* 28 (May 1952): 618–23.

Breslin, James. *From Modern to Contemporary: American Poetry 1945–65*. Chicago: University of Chicago Press, 1986.

Brooke, Rupert. "*Personae* of Ezra Pound." *Cambridge Review* 31 (December 2, 1909): 166–67.

Brooker, Peter, and Andrew Thacker, eds. *The Oxford Critical and Cultural History of Modernist Magazines.* Volume 2: *North America 1894–1960.* Oxford: Oxford University Press, 2012.

Brooke-Rose, Christine. *A ZBC of Ezra Pound.* Berkeley and Los Angeles: University of California Press, 1971.

Brooks, Cleanth. *The Well-Wrought Urn: Studies in the Structure of Poetry.* New York: Harcourt Brace, 1947.

Brooks, Cleanth, and Robert Penn Warren. *Understanding Poetry.* New York: Holt, Rinehart & Winston, 1976.

Brown, John L. Review of *Discretions: A Memoir by Ezra Pound's Daughter*, by Mary de Rachewiltz. *Books Abroad* 47, no.1 (Winter 1973): 155.

Brown, Merle. Review of *The Poetry of Ezra Pound: Forms and Renewals, 1908–1920*, by Hugh Witemeyer. *Journal of Aesthetics and Art Criticism* 29 (1971): 412–14.

Bruns, Gerald. "The Newton of Modernism." *Modernism/modernity* 12, no.3 (2005): 477–81.

Bush, Ronald. *The Genesis of Ezra Pound's Cantos.* Princeton, NJ: Princeton University Press, 1976.

———. "'Unstill, Ever Turning': The Composition of Ezra Pound's Drafts & Fragments. In *Ezra Pound and Europe*, ed. Richard Taylor and Claus Melchior. Amsterdam: Rodopi, 1993.

———. "Walton Litz: Eminent Poundian (1929–2014)." *Make It New* 1, no.3 (September 2014): 52–54.

Butterfield, R. W. (Herbie). Review of *"I Cease Not to Yowl": Ezra Pound's Letters to Olivia Rossetti Agresti*, edited by Leon Surette and Demetres Tryphonopoulos. *Journal of American Studies* 36, no. 1 (Apr. 2002): 186–88.

———. Review of *Reading the Cantos: A Study of Meaning in Ezra Pound*, by Noel Stock. *Journal of American Studies* 2 (1968): 284–86.

Byron, Mark. *Ezra Pound's Eriugena.* London: Bloomsbury, 2014.

Carpenter, Humphrey. *A Serious Character: The Life of Ezra Pound.* New York: Delta, 1988.

Carr, Christopher. Review of *Variorum Edition of "Three Cantos" by Ezra Pound: A Prototype*, edited by Richard Taylor. *Text* 8 (1995): 477–88.

Carr, Helen. *The Verse Revolutionaries: Ezra Pound, H.D. and the Imagists.* London: Cape, 2009.

Carruth, Hayden. "The Anti-Poet All Told." In *The Case Against the Saturday Review of Literature.* Special issue, *Poetry* (October 1949): 46–58.

———. *The Case Against the Saturday Review of Literature: The Attack of the Saturday Review on Modern Poets and Critics: Answered by the Fellows in American Letters of the Library of Congress, Together with Articles, Editorials, and Letters from Other Writers.* Special issue, *Poetry* (October 1949).

Casillo, Robert. *The Genealogy of Demons: Anti-Semitism, Fascism, and the Myths of Ezra Pound.* Evanston, IL: Northwestern University Press, 1988.

———. Review of *Ezra Pound and Italian Fascism*, by Timothy Redman. *Modern Language Review* 88, no.1 (January 1993): 186–88.

Casper, Leonard. Review of *The Barb of Time: On the Unity of Ezra Pound's Cantos*, by Daniel Pearlman. *Thought* 45, no.4 (Winter 1970): 614–15.

———. Review of *Ezra Pound: The Image and the Real*, by Herbert Schneidau. *Thought* 45, no.2 (1970): 301–2.

Chace, William M. *The Political Identities of Ezra Pound and T. S. Eliot*. Stanford, CA: Stanford University Press, 1973.

Chase, Richard. "Pound of Flesh." Review of *An Examination of Ezra Pound: A Collection of Essays*, edited by Peter Russell. *Partisan Review*, September 1951, 586–90.

Cleophas, Sister Mary. Review of *Ezra Pound: Poet as Sculptor*, by Donald Davie. *Thought* 40 (Autumn 1965): 455–57.

Cockram, Patricia. "Collapse and Recall: Ezra Pound's Italian Cantos." *Journal of Modern Literature* 23, no.3–4 (2000): 535–44.

———. "Hypertextuality and Pound's Fascist Aesthetic." *Paideuma* 26, no.2–3 (1997): 151–63.

Cocola, Jim. "Notes Toward a Draft of 'A Gazetteer of Ezra Pound.'" *Make It New* 1, no. 4 (March 2015): 50–54.

Coffman, Stanley K., Jr. Review of *Ezra Pound's Mauberley: A Study in Composition*, by John Espey. *Books Abroad* 30 (Spring 1956): 222.

Cole, William. "Pound's Web: Hypertext in the Rock-Drill Cantos." *Paideuma* 26, no.2–3 (1997): 137–50.

Colum, Padraic. "Studies in the Sophisticated." *New Republic*, December 8, 1920, 52–54.

Cook, Reginald L. Review of *Motive and Method in The Cantos of Ezra Pound*, edited by Lewis Leary. *American Oxonian* 42 (April 1955): 103–4.

Cookson, William. "E.P. and *Agenda*: Autobiographical Fragments." In *Sons of Ezra*, edited by Michael Alexander and James McGonigal, 43–59. Amsterdam: Rodopi: 1995.

———, ed. "Ezra Pound. Some Letters to William Cookson 1956–1970." *Agenda* anniversary issue: 17, no. 3–4–18, no. 1 (1979/80): 5–47.

———. *A Guide to the Cantos of Ezra Pound*. London: Anvil, 1985, 2001.

———, ed. Introduction. *Selected Prose, 1909–1965*. New York: New Directions, 1973.

———. "Main Elements in *The Cantos*." Review of *Selected Cantos*, by Ezra Pound. *Agenda* 6, no. 3–4 (1968): 143–44.

———, ed. *Special Issue in Honour of Ezra Pound's Eighty-Fifth Birthday. Agenda* 8, no.3–4 (Autumn-Winter 1970).

Cornell, Julien. *The Trial of Ezra Pound: A Documented Account of the Treason Trial by the Defendant's Lawyer*. New York: The John Day Co., 1966.

Cournos, John. "Native Poet Stirs London." *Philadelphia Record*, January 5, 1913, 7.

Cousins, Norman, and Harrison Smith. "Ezra Pound and the Bollingen Award." *Saturday Review of Literature*, June 11, 1949, 20–21.

———. "More on Pound." *Saturday Review of Literature*, July 30, 1949, 22.

Cowie, Alexander. Review of *Motive and Method in The Cantos of Ezra Pound*, edited by Lewis Leary. *American Literature* 27 (1955): 443–44.

Cowley, Malcolm. "The Battle Over Ezra Pound." In *The Case Against the Saturday Review of Literature*. Special issue, *Poetry* (October 1949): 31–38.

Coyle, Michael. *Ezra Pound, Popular Genres, and the Discourse of Culture.* University Park: Penn State University Press, 1995.

———. "With a Plural Vengeance: Modernism as (Flaming) Brand." *Modernist Cultures* 1, no.1 (2005): 15–21.

Cruz Cornejo, Heriberto. "From Arcadia to Hell. The Fate of Gerhart and Vera Münch." *Make It New* 3, no. 3 (December 2016): 36–60.

Culver, Michael. *The Art of Henry Strater: An Examination of the Illustrations for Pound's A Draft of XVI Cantos.* Orono: National Poetry Foundation, 1983.

Daniel, Gabriel. *Hart Crane and the Modernist Epic: Canon and Genre Formation in Crane, Pound, Eliot, and Williams.* New York: Palgrave Macmillan, 2007.

Dasenbrock, Reed Way. *The Literary Vorticism of Ezra Pound and Wyndham Lewis.* Baltimore: Johns Hopkins University Press, 1985.

———. Review of *The Genealogy of Demons*, by Robert Casillo. *American Literary History* 1, no.1 (1989): 231–39.

———. "Saladin, Confucius and the Status of the Other in Dante and Pound." In *Dante e Pound*, edited by Maria Ardizzone, 63–76. Ravenna: Longo Editore, 1998.

Davenport, Guy. *Cities on Hills: Study of 1–30 of Ezra Pound's Cantos.* Epping: Bowker, 1983.

———. "Ezra Pound, the Poet?" Review of *The Life of Ezra Pound*, by Noel Stock. *Hudson Review* 23, no.4 (Winter 1970): 754–57.

Davie, Donald. *Ezra Pound.* London: Fontana-Collins, 1975.

———. *Ezra Pound: Poet as Sculptor.* New York: Oxford University Press, 1964; London: Routledge & Kegan Paul, 1965.

Davis, Earle. *Vision Fugitive: Ezra Pound and Economics.* Lawrence: University Press of Kansas, 1968.

Davis, Robert Gorham. "The New Criticism and the Democratic Tradition." *American Scholar* 19 (Winter 1949/50): 9–19.

———. "The Poem and the Poet." *New Leader*, December 11, 1950, 18.

De Nagy, N. Christoph. *Ezra Pound's Poetics and Literary Tradition: The Critical Decade.* Bern: Francke, 1966.

———. *The Poetry of Ezra Pound: The Pre-Imagist Stage.* Bern: Francke, 1960.

De Rachewiltz, Mary. *Ezra Pound, Father and Teacher: Discretions.* New York: New Directions, 1971.

Dekker, George. *Sailing after Knowledge: The Cantos of Ezra Pound.* London: Routledge & Kegan Paul, 1963.

Dembo, L. S. *The Confucian Odes of Ezra Pound: A Critical Appraisal.* Berkeley and Los Angeles: University of California Press, 1963.

———. Review of *Ezra Pound: Poet as Sculptor*, by Donald Davie. *Modern Philology* 63 (1965): 88–90.

———. Review of *New Approaches to Ezra Pound: A Co-ordinated Investigation of Pound's Poetry and Ideas*, edited by Eva Hesse, *Ezra Pound's Cathay*, by Wai-lim Yip, and *The Poetry of Ezra Pound: Forms and Renewals, 1908–1920*, by Hugh Witemeyer. *American Literature* 42, no.1 (March 1970): 111–13.

———. Review of *The Rose in the Steel Dust: An Examination of the Cantos of Ezra Pound*, by Walter Baumann. *American Literature* 39 (1968): 576–77.

———. Review of *Sailing after Knowledge: The Cantos of Ezra Pound*, by George Dekker. *American Literature* 36 (November 1964): 386–87.

Dempsey, David. "L'Affaire Pound." *New York Times Book Review*, January 1, 1950, 8.

D'Epiro, Peter. *Touch of Rhetoric: Ezra Pound's Malatesta Cantos.* Ann Arbor: UMI Research Press, 1983.

Derrida, Jacques. "Force de loi: Le Fondement mystique de l'autorité/Force of Law: The Mystical Foundation of Authority." Translated by Mary Quaintance. *Cardozo Law Review* 11 (1990): 919–1045.

———. *Memoirs of the Blind: The Self-Portrait and Other Ruins.* Translated by Pascale-Anne Brault and Michael Naas. Chicago: University of Chicago Press, 1993.

———. *Of Grammatology.* Translated by Gayatri Chakravorty Spivak. Baltimore: Johns Hopkins University Press, 1976.

———. "The Pit and the Pyramid." In *Margins of Philosophy*, translated and edited by Alan Bass, 69–108. Chicago: University of Chicago Press, 1982.

———. "Structure, Sign, and Play in the Discourse of the Human Sciences." In *The Structuralist Controversy. The Languages of Criticism and the Sciences of Man*, edited by Richard Macksey and Eugenio Donato, 247–264. Baltimore: Johns Hopkins University Press, 1970.

Desai, Meghnad. *The Route of All Evil: The Political Economy of Ezra Pound.* London: Faber & Faber, 2006.

Deutsch, Albert. Editorial. *New York Post*, February 28, 1949.

Dinsman, Melissa. *Modernism at the Microphone: Radio, Propaganda and Literary Aesthetics During World War II.* London, New York: Bloomsbury Academic, 2015.

Donoghue, Denis. "Poetry and Sanity." Review of *A Serious Character: The Life of Ezra Pound*, by Humphrey Carpenter and *The American Ezra Pound*, by Wendy Stallard Flory. *The New Republic*, March 6, 1989, 39–40.

Doob, Leonard, ed. *"Ezra Pound Speaking": Radio Speeches of World War II.* Westport CT: Greenwood Press, 1978.

Dougherty, J. P. Review of *The Political Identities of Ezra Pound and T. S. Eliot*, by William Chace. *The Review of Politics* 36, no.4 (1974): 621–23.

Drew-Bear, Thomas. Review of *Ezra Pound and Sextus Propertius: A Study in Creative Translation*, by J. P. Sullivan. *American Literature* 37 (January 1966): 503–4.

Driscoll, John. *The "China Cantos" of Ezra Pound.* Stockholm: Almqvist and Wicksell, 1983.

Droysen, J. G. 1868. *Outline of the Principles of History.* Boston: Ginn and Co, 1897.

Duffy, Bernard. Review of *Ezra Pound's Mauberley: A Study in Composition*, by John Espey. *American Literature* 27 (January 1956): 601–2.

———. Review of *New Approaches to Ezra Pound: A Co-ordinated Investigation of Pound's Poetry and Ideas*, edited by Eva Hesse and *The Poetry of Ezra Pound: Forms and Renewals, 1908–1920*, by Hugh Witemeyer. *South Atlantic Quarterly* 69 (1970): 297–99.

Durant, Alan. *Ezra Pound, Identity in Crisis: A Fundamental Reassessment of the Poet and His Work.* Brighton: The Harvester Press, 1981.

Eastman, Barbara C. *Ezra Pound's Cantos: The Story of the Text 1948–1975.* Orono, ME: National Poetry Foundation, 1979.

Eberhart, Richard. "Pound's New Cantos." *Quarterly Review of Literature* 5, no.2 (December 1949): 174–91.

Edwards, John Hamilton. Correspondence with Ezra Pound. Beinecke YCAL 43 Box 14 Folder 158.

———. "A Critical Biography of Ezra Pound: 1885–1922." Unpublished dissertation.

———, ed. *The Pound Newsletter.* January 1954–May 1956.

———, ed. *A Preliminary Checklist of the Writings of Ezra Pound.* New Haven: Kirgo Books, 1953.

Edwards, John Hamilton, and William W. Vasse, eds. *Annotated Index to the Cantos of Ezra Pound: Cantos I-LXXXIV.* Berkeley and Los Angeles: University of California Press, 1957.

Eliot, T. S. *Ezra Pound: His Metric and Poetry.* New York: Knopf, 1917.

———, ed. and introd. *Ezra Pound Selected Poems.* London: Faber & Gwyer, 1928.

———, ed. Introduction to *Literary Essays of Ezra Pound.* London: Faber; Norfolk, CT: New Directions, 1954: ix–xv.

———. "Isolated Superiority." *The Dial* 84 (January 1928): 4–7.

———. "The Method of Mr. Pound." *Athenaeum*, October 24, 1919, 1065–1066.

———. "The Noh and the Image." *Egoist* 4, no. 7 (August 1917): 102–3.

———. "A Note on Ezra Pound." *To-Day* 4 (September 1918): 3–10.

———. "On a Recent Piece of Criticism." *Purpose* 10 (April–June 1938): 90–94.

———. *The Poems of T. S. Eliot.* Vol. I: *Collected and Uncollected Poems*, edited by Christopher Ricks and Jim McCue. London: Faber & Faber, 2015.

———. "Tradition and Individual Talent." In *Selected Essays 1917*–1932, 3–11. New York: Harcourt Brace, 1932.

Ellmann, Maud. "Ezra Pound: the Erasure of History." In *Poststructuralism and the Question of History*, edited by D. Attridge, Geoff Bennington and Robert Young, 244–63. Cambridge: Cambridge University Press, 1987.

Ellmann, Richard. *Eminent Domain: Yeats among Wilde, Joyce, Pound, Eliot, and Auden.* New York: Oxford University Press, 1967.

Emery, Clark M. *Ideas into Action: A Study of Pound's Cantos.* Coral Gables, FL: U of Miami Press, 1958.

Erkilla, Betsy, ed. *Ezra Pound: The Contemporary Reviews.* Cambridge: Cambridge University Press, 2011.

Espey, John. "Ezra Pound." In *Sixteen Modern American Authors.* Volume 2: A Survey of Research and Criticism since 1972, edited by Jackson R. Bryer, 519–57. Durham and London: Duke UP, 1990.

———. *Ezra Pound's Mauberley: A Study in Composition.* 1955. Reprinted London: Faber; Berkeley: University of California Press, 1974.

———. Review of *Ezra Pound's Poetics and Literary Tradition: The Critical Decade*, by Christoph de Nagy. *American Literature* 39 (1968): 577–78.

———. Review of *The Poetry of Ezra Pound: Forms and Renewals, 1908–1920*, by Hugh Witemeyer. *Modern Philology* 68 (1971): 403–5.

Evans, David W. "Ezra Pound as Prison Poet." In *Ezra Pound: A Collection of Critical Essays,* edited by Walter E. Sutton, 80–86. Englewood Cliffs, NJ: Prentice, 1963.

Evans, Luther H. "The Bollingen Prize in Poetry." *Annual Report, Library of Congress,* June 30, 1949: 88–94.

Ewick, David. "Imagism Status Rerum and a Note on Haiku." (Review essay). *Make It New* 2, no. 1 (June 2015): 42–58.

Feldman, Matthew. *Ezra Pound's Fascist Propaganda, 1935–1945.* London: Palgrave Pivot, 2013.

———. "Ezra Pound's Political Faith from First to Second Generation; or, 'It is 1956 Fascism.'" In *Modernism, Christianity and Apocalypse,* edited by E. Tonning, M. Feldman, and D. Addyman, 279–300. Leiden: Brill, 2014.

Feldman, Matthew, and A. Rinaldi. "'Penny-wise . . .': Ezra Pound's Posthumous Legacy to Fascism." *The Post-War Anglo-American Far Right,* edited by P. Jackson and A. Shekhovtsov. London: Palgrave Pivot, 2014.

Feldman, Matthew, Erik Tönning, and Henry Mead, eds. *Broadcasting in the Modernist Era.* London: Bloomsbury, 2014.

Ferlinghetti, Lawrence. Review of *Ezra Pound and the Cantos,* by Harold H. Watts. *San Francisco Chronicle,* May 25, 1952, 31.

Fisher, Margaret. *Ezra Pound's Radio Operas: The BBC Experiments, 1931–1933.* Cambridge, MA: MIT Press, 2003.

Fitts, Dudley, "Music Fit for the Odes," *Hound and Horn* 4, no. 2 (Jan.–Mar. 1931): 278–89.

Flack, Leah Culligan. *Modernism and Homer: The Odysseys of H.D., James Joyce, Osip Mandelstam, and Ezra Pound.* Cambridge: Cambridge University Press, 2015.

Flint, F. S. Review of *Canzoni,* by Ezra Pound. *Poetry Review* 1 (January 1912): 28–29.

Flory, Wendy Stallard. *The American Ezra Pound.* New Haven: Yale University Press, 1989.

———. *Ezra Pound and "The Cantos": A Record of Struggle.* New Haven: Yale University Press, 1980.

Foerster, Norman. *American Criticism: A Study in Literary Theory from Poe to the Present.* New York: Houghton Mifflin, 1928.

———. *Towards Standards: A Study of the Present Critical Movement in American Letters.* New York: Farrar & Rinehart, 1930.

Foucault, Michel. *The History of Sexuality: An Introduction, Volume 1.* Translated by Robert Hurley. New York: Vintage, 1978.

Fox, Margalit. "C. David Heymann, Biographer of the Rich and Famous, Dies at 67." *New York Times,* May 10, 2012. http://www.nytimes.com/2012/05/11/books/c-david-heymann-biographer-of-rich-and-famous-dies-at-67.html?_r=0.

Frankenberg, Lloyd. "Ezra Pound—and His Magnum Opus." *New York Times Book Review,* August 1, 1948, 14.

Fraser, George S. *Ezra Pound.* London: Oliver & Boyd, 1960.

Fraser, John. Review of *The Early Poetry of Ezra Pound,* by Thomas H. Jackson. *Dalhousie Review* 48 (1968): 563–64.

Frohock, W. M. "The Revolt of Ezra Pound." In *Ezra Pound: A Collection of Critical Essays,* edited by Walter E. Sutton, 87–97. Englewood Cliffs, NJ: Prentice, 1963.

Froula, Christine. "Hugh Kenner's Modernism and Ours." *Modernism/modernity* 12, no.3 (2005): 471–75.

———. *"To Write Paradise": Style and Error in Pound's* Cantos. New Haven: Yale University Press, 1984.

Fuller, Torrey E. *The Roots of Treason: Ezra Pound and the Secret of St. Elizabeths.* New York: McGraw Hill, 1983.

Gabriel, Daniel. *Hart Crane and the Modernist Epic: Canon and Genre Formation in Crane, Pound, Eliot, and Williams.* New York: Palgrave Macmillan, 2007.

Gall, Sally, M. Review of *A Companion to The Cantos of Ezra Pound: Volume II (Cantos 74–117)*, by Carroll Terrell and *A Guide to the Cantos of Ezra Pound*, by William Cookson. *The Journal of English and Germanic Philology* 85, no.4 (1986): 593–95.

Gallup, Donald. *Ezra Pound. A Bibliography.* Charlottesville: The University Press of Virginia, 1983.

Gelpi, Albert. Review of *The Pound Era*, by Hugh Kenner. *American Literature.* 44, no.3 (1972): 502–4.

Genauer, Emily. "Still Life with Red Herring." *Harper's Magazine*, September 1949, 88–91.

Gibson, Andrew, ed. *Pound in Multiple Perspective.* London: Macmillan, 1993.

Gibson, Mary Ellis. *Epic Reinvented: Ezra Pound and the Victorians.* Ithaca, NY: Cornell University Press, 1995.

Glenn, E. M., et al., eds. *The Analyst.* March 1953–April 1969.

Goodwin, K. L. *The Influence of Ezra Pound.* London: Oxford University Press, 1966.

Gordon, David. "The Cyclops Ideogram." *Agenda* 1, no. 10 (April 1960): 2–6.

Granville, Charles. "Modern Poetry." *Eye-Witness*, August 10, 1911, 247–248.

Grattan, Harvey. *The Critique of Humanism.* New York: Brewer & Warren, 1930.

Graves, Robert. *The Crowning Privilege.* New York: Doubleday, 1956.

Grigsby, Gordon K. Review of *Ezra Pound: Poet as Sculptor*, by Donald Davie. *South Atlantic Quarterly* 64 (Summer 1965): 423–424.

Grimes, Peter. "Charles Norman, 92, Poet and Biographer." *New York Times*, September 14, 1996. http://www.nytimes.com/1996/09/14/arts/charles-norman-92-poet-and-biographer.html (accessed June 6, 2016).

Gross, Andrew. *The Pound Reaction: Liberalism and Lyricism in Midcentury American Literature.* Heidelberg: Universitätsverlag Winter, 2015.

Hale, William G. "Pegasus Impounded." *Poetry* 14, no.1 (April 1919): 52–55.

Hallberg, Robert von, ed. *Canons.* Chicago: Chicago University Press, 1984.

[Hamburger, Michael.] "Complete Poet's Poet." [Review of ten titles on Ezra Pound.] *Times Literary Supplement*, August 21, 1970, 925–26.

Harmon, William. "Beat, Beat, Whirr, Pound." Review of *A Companion to The Cantos of Ezra Pound*, by Carroll F. Terrell. *The Sewanee Review* 94, no. 4 (1986): 630–39.

———. "Yes, We Have No Psychiatrists." Review of *"Ezra Pound Speaking": Radio Speeches of World War II*, edited by Leonard W. Doob and *Instigations: Ezra Pound and Remy de Gourmont*, by Richard Sieburth. *Sewanee Review* 87, no.2 (1979): xxxiv–xxxviii.

Harris, Kaplan. "Editing after Pound." *Paideuma* 40 (2013): 107–25.

Hassan, Ihab. *The Dismemberment of Orpheus*. Oxford: Oxford University Press 1971; Madison: University of Wisconsin Press, 1982.

Hatlen, Burt. "Carroll Terrell and the Great American Poetry Wars." *Paideuma* 26, no.2–3 (1997): 33–62.

Healy, J. V. "Pound and Tate." *Western Review* 13 (Winter 1949): 115–18.

Heller, Scott. "New Life for Modernism." *Chronicle of Higher Education*, Nov. 5, 1999: https://www.chronicle.com/article/New-Life-for-Modernism/16279.

Henderson, Archie, and Roxana Preda. *Bibliography of English Language Scholarship on Ezra Pound 2000–2018. ezrapoundsociety.org*. Ezra Pound Society, 2015-. http://ezrapoundsociety.org/index.php/2015 (accessed June 10, 2018).

Henriksen, Line. *Ambition and Anxiety: Ezra Pound's "Cantos" and Derek Walcott's "Omeros" as Twentieth-Century Epics*. Amsterdam: Rodopi, 2007.

Heringman, Bernard. Review of *Ezra Pound*, by Charles Norman. *Wisconsin Studies in Contemporary Literature* 2, no.2 (Spring-Summer, 1961): 62–66.

Hesse, Eva, ed. *New Approaches to Ezra Pound: A Co-ordinated Investigation of Pound's Poetry and Ideas*. Berkeley and Los Angeles: University of California Press; London: Faber, 1969.

Heymann, David C. *Ezra Pound: The Last Rower: A Political Profile*. New York: Viking, 1976.

Heywood, C. Review of *Sailing after Knowledge: The Cantos of Ezra Pound*, by George Dekker and *The Poetry of Ezra Pound: The Pre-Imagist Stage*, by Christoph de Nagy. *English Studies* 47 (1966): 457–59.

Hickman, Miranda B. *The Geometry of Modernism: The Vorticist Idiom in Lewis, Pound, H. D., and Yeats*. Austin: University of Texas Press, 2006.

———. "Pamphlets and Blue China (Or, 'Cheap Books of Good Work'): Pound's Preference for Plainness in the 1950s." *Paideuma* 26, no.2–3 (1997): 165–79.

———. "'to Facilitate the Traffic' (Or, 'Damn Deluxe Edtns'): Ezra Pound's Turn from the Deluxe." *Paideuma* 28, no.2–3 (1999): 173–92.

———. "Vorticism." In *Ezra Pound in Context*, edited by Ira Nadel, 285–97. Cambridge: Cambridge University Press, 2010.

Hillyer, Robert. "Poetry's New Priesthood." *Saturday Review of Literature,* June 18, 1949, 7–9, 38.

——— "Treason's Strange Fruit: The Case of Ezra Pound and the Bollingen Award." *Saturday Review of Literature*, June 11, 1949, 9–11, 28.

Hobsbaum, Philip. Review of *Ezra Pound and Sextus Propertius: A Study in Creative Translation,* by J. P. Sullivan. *Listener* 74 (1965): 279.

Homberger, Eric. "A Close Look at the *Cantos*." Review of *A ZBC of Ezra Pound*, by Christine Brooke-Rose. *Times Literary Supplement*, June 2, 1972, 624.

———, ed. *Ezra Pound: The Critical Heritage*. London: Routledge, 1972.

Howard, Alex, ed. *Astern in the Dinghy: Commentaries on Ezra Pound's "Thrones de los Cantores 96–109." Glossator* 10 (2018).

Hutchins, Patricia. *Ezra Pound's Kensington: An Exploration, 1885–1913*. London: Faber, 1965.

Huyssen, Andreas. *After the Great Divide*. Bloomington: Indiana University Press, 1986.

Hynes, Samuel. "The Case of Ezra Pound." *Commonweal* 63, December 9, 1955, 251–54.

Jackson, Thomas H. *The Early Poetry of Ezra Pound.* Cambridge: Harvard University Press, 1968.

Janssens, G. A. M. Review of *Reading the Cantos: A Study of Meaning in Ezra Pound*, by Noel Stock. *Levende Talen* 250 (August/September 1968): 584.

Jarman, Mark. "Your Anonymous Correspondent: Ezra Pound and the 'Hudson Review.'" *The Hudson Review* 59, no.3 (2006): 359–75.

Jauss, Hans Robert. "Literary History as a Challenge to Literary Theory." Translated by Elizabeth Benzinger. *New Literary History* 2, no.1 (Autumn 1970): 7–37.

Jin, Songping. *The Poetics of the Ideogram: Ezra Pound's Poetry and Hermeneutic Interpretation.* Frankfurt am Main: Peter Lang, 2002.

Joost, Nicholas. "Poets, Critics and Myth." *Renascence* 9 (Spring 1957): 140–49.

Kaplan, Harold. *Poetry, Politics, and Culture: Argument in the Work of Eliot, Pound, Stevens, and Williams.* New Brunswick, NJ: Transaction, 2006.

Katz, Daniel. *American Modernism's Expatriate Scene: The Labour of Translation.* Edinburgh: Edinburgh University Press, 2007.

Kenner, Hugh. "The Broken Mirrors and the Mirror of Memory." In *Motive and Method in The Cantos of Ezra Pound*, edited by Lewis Leary, 3–32. New York: Columbia University Press, 1954.

———. Correspondence with Ezra Pound. Beinecke YCAL 43 Box 27/Folder 1140.

———. "Gold in the Gloom." Review of *Ezra Pound and the Cantos* by Harold H. Watts. *Poetry* 81 (November 1952): 127–32.

———. *Historical Fictions.* Athens: University of Georgia Press, 1995.

———. *A Homemade World.* New York: Knopf, 1975.

———. "Incurious Biographer." Review of *The Life of Ezra Pound*, by Noel Stock. *New Republic*, October 17, 1970, 30–32.

———. "Introduction." In *Ezra Pound's Cantos: The Story of the Text 1948–1975.* Edited by Barbara Eastman, xi–xix. Orono: National Poetry Foundation, 1979.

———. "The Making of the Modernist Canon." In *Canons,* edited by Robert von Hallberg, 363–76. Chicago: University of Chicago Press, 1984.

———. "*Mauberley.*" In *Ezra Pound: A Collection of Critical Essays,* edited by Walter E. Sutton, 41–56. Englewood Cliffs, NJ: Prentice, 1963.

———. *The Mechanic Muse.* Oxford: Oxford University Press, 1988.

———. "The Muse in Tatters." *Agenda* 6, no.2 (Spring 1968): 43–61.

———. "New Subtlety of Eyes." In *An Examination of Ezra Pound: A Collection of Essays*, edited by Peter Russell, 84–99. Norfolk, CT: New Directions, 1950.

———. "Notes on Amateur Emendations." In *A Poem Containing History: Textual Studies in "The Cantos,"* edited by Lawrence Rainey, 21–29. Ann Arbor: University of Michigan Press, 1997.

———. *Paradox in Chesterton.* New York: Sheed & Ward, 1947.

———. *The Poetry of Ezra Pound.* New York: New Directions; London: Faber, 1951.

———. *The Pound Era.* London: Faber, 1971.

———. Review of *Ezra Pound: Poet as Sculptor*, by Donald Davie. *American Literature* 37 (January 1966): 502–3.

Kindellan, Michael. *The Late Cantos of Ezra Pound.* London: Bloomsbury, 2017.

Kronick, Joseph. Review of *Ezra Pound and the Monument of Culture. Text History and the Malatesta Cantos*, by Lawrence Rainey. *The Journal of English and Germanic Philology*, 92, no.4 (Oct. 1993): 586–88.

LaCapra, Dominick. *Madame Bovary on Trial.* Ithaca, NY: Cornell University Press. 1986.

Lan, Feng. *Ezra Pound and Confucianism: Remaking Humanism In the Face of Modernity.* Toronto: University of Toronto Press, 2005.

Landini, Richard G. "A Fairer Appraisal." Review of *Ideas into Action: A Study of Pound's Cantos*, by Clark Emery. *Renascence* 13 (Autumn 1960): 49–51.

Latham, Sean, and Gayle Rogers. *Modernism: Evolution of an Idea.* London: Bloomsbury, 2015.

Lauber, John. "Pound's 'Cantos': A Fascist Epic." *Journal of American Studies* 12, no.1 (1978): 3–21.

Laughlin, James. *Pound as Wuz: Essays and Lectures on Ezra Pound.* Minneapolis: Graywolf Press, 1987.

Le Brun, P. Review of *The Influence of Ezra Pound*, by K. L. Goodwin. *Review of English Studies* 19 (1968): 235–38.

Leary, Lewis, ed. *Motive and Method in The Cantos of Ezra Pound.* New York: Columbia University Press, 1954.

———. Review of *The Poetry of Ezra Pound: The Pre-Imagist Stage*, by Christoph de Nagy. *American Literature* 33 (March 1961): 98–99.

Leavis, F. R. "Ezra Pound." In *Ezra Pound: A Collection of Critical Essays*, edited by Walter E. Sutton, 26–40. Englewood Cliffs, NJ: Prentice, 1963.

———. *New Bearings in English Poetry.* 1932; rpt. London: Routledge, 1988.

Lee, Robert. Review of *Discretions*, by Mary de Rachewiltz. *Studies: An Irish Quarterly Review* 62, no.246 (Summer 1973): 182–86.

Leick, Karen. "Ezra Pound vs. *The Saturday Review of Literature.*" *Journal of Modern Literature* 25, no.2 (Winter 2001–2002): 19–37.

Lentricchia, Frank. *After the New Criticism.* London: Athlone Press, 1980.

Lewis, Wyndham. "Ezra Pound." In *An Examination of Ezra Pound: A Collection of Essays*, edited by Peter Russell, 257–66. Norfolk, CT: New Directions, 1950.

———. *Time and Western Man.* 1927. Edited by Paul Edwards. Santa Rosa, CA: Black Sparrow Press, 1993.

Liebregts, Peter. *Ezra Pound and Neoplatonism.* Madison, NJ: Fairleigh Dickinson University Press, 2004.

Lindberg, Kathryne V. *Reading Pound Reading: Modernism after Nietzsche.* New York: Oxford UP, 1987.

Litz, A. Walton, and Lawrence Rainey. "Ezra Pound." In *The Cambridge History of Literary Criticism.* Volume VII: *Modernism and the New Criticism*, edited by A. Walton Litz, Louis Menand, and Lawrence Rainey, 57–92. London: Cambridge University Press, 2008.

Longenbach, James. *Stone Cottage: Pound, Yeats & Modernism.* Oxford: Oxford University Press, 1988.

Louchheim, Aline B. "The State and Art." *New York Times*, September 4, 1949, 8. Reprinted in *The Case Against the Saturday Review of Literature*. Special issue, *Poetry* (October 1949): 39–42.

Lucas, John. Review of *The Poetry of Ezra Pound,* by Hugh Kenner. *Furioso,* Winter 1952, 63–66.

Lucie-Smith, Edward. Review of *Ezra Pound: Poet as Sculptor*, by Donald Davie. *Listener* 73 (1965): 569–70.

Lyotard, Jean François. 1979. *The Postmodern Condition*. Manchester: Manchester University Press, 1984.

M., W. P. Review of *The Poetry of Ezra Pound,* by Hugh Kenner. *Dublin Magazine,* October 1951.

MacDiarmid, Hugh. Review of *Ezra Pound. Selected Prose 1909–1965*, ed. William Cookson. *Agenda* 10, no. 4–11, no. 1 [Autumn–Winter 1972–73]: 139–45.

MacDonald, Dwight. "Homage to Twelve Judges: An Editorial." *Politics* 6 (Winter 1949): 1–2. Reprinted in *Memoirs of a Revolutionist: Essays in Political Criticism*. New York: Farrar, 1957.

Macksey, Richard, and Eugenio Donato, eds. *The Structuralist Controversy. The Languages of Criticism and the Sciences of Man*. Baltimore: Johns Hopkins University Press, 1970.

MacLeish, Archibald. *Poetry and Opinion: The Pisan Cantos of Ezra Pound: A Dialog on the Role of Poetry.* Urbana: University of Illinois Press, 1950.

Makin, Peter. Review of *A Companion to The Cantos of Ezra Pound. Volume II: Cantos 74–117*, by Carroll F. Terrell; *Digging for the Treasure: Translation after Pound*, by Ronnie Apter. *The Modern Language Review* 83, no. 2 (1988): 435–37.

———. Review of "*To Write Paradise*": *Style and Error in Pound's "Cantos,"* by Christine Froula. *The Modern Language Review* 82, no.3 (1987): 720–22.

Malm, Mike W. *Editing Economic History: Ezra Pound's "The Fifth Decad of Cantos."* Frankfurt am Main: Peter Lang, 2005.

Mangiafico, Luciano. "Attainted: The Life and Afterlife of Ezra Pound in Italy." *Open Letters Monthly* (September 2012), http://www.openlettersmonthly.com/attainted-the-life-and-afterlife-of-ezra-pound-in-italy/ (accessed August 7, 2016).

Marcus, Jane, ed. *The Young Rebecca*. New York: Viking, 1982.

Marsh, Alec. *Ezra Pound*. London: Reaktion, 2011.

———. *John Kasper and Ezra Pound: Saving the Republic*. London: Bloomsbury, 2015.

———. *Money and Modernity: Pound, Williams, and the Spirit of Jefferson*. Tuscaloosa: University of Alabama Press, 1998.

———. "Pound and Eliot." *American Literary Scholarship*, 2000–. [A standard feature/section of each volume.]

Marshall, Margaret. "The *Saturday Review* Unfair to Literature." *The Nation*, December 17, 1949, 598.

Martin, Wallace. Review of *Ezra Pound's Poetics and Literary Tradition: The Critical Decade*, by Christoph de Nagy. *English Studies* 52 (1971): 85–87.

———. Review of *The Early Poetry of Ezra Pound*, by Thomas H. Jackson. *English Studies* 53 (1972): 171–73.

Matterson, Stephen. "The New Criticism." In *Literary Theory and Criticism: An Oxford Guide*, edited by Patricia Waugh, 166–76. Oxford: Oxford University Press, 2006.

Maxwell, J. C. Review of *Ezra* Pound, by G. S. Fraser. *Durham University Journal* 24 (December 1962): 76–77.

Maxwell-Mahon, W. D. Review of *Sailing after Knowledge: The Cantos of Ezra Pound*, by George Dekker. *Unisa English Studies* 15.2 (September 1977): 66–67.

Mayo, Robert. Review of *Motive and Method in The Cantos of Ezra Pound*, edited by Lewis Leary. *Modern Language Notes* 71 (April 1956): 311–13.

McDonald, Gail. *Learning to Be Modern: Pound Eliot, and the American University*. Oxford: Clarendon Press, 1993.

McDowell, Colin. "Meeting Terry." *Paideuma* 26, 2–3 (1997): 71–74.

McGann, Jerome. "The Text, the Poem and the Problem of the Historical Method." In *The Beauty of Inflections*, 111–32. Oxford: Oxford University Press, 1985.

———. *The Textual Condition*. Princeton NJ: Princeton University Press, 1991.

McGann, Jerome J., ed. *Lord Byron: The Complete Poetical Works*. 7 vols. Oxford: Clarendon Press, 1983–1992.

McGuire, William. *Bollingen: An Adventure in Collecting the Past*. Princeton, NJ: Princeton University Press, 1982.

McLuhan, Herbert Marshall. "Pound's Critical Prose." In *An Examination of Ezra Pound: A Collection of Essays*, edited by Peter Russell. Norfolk, CT: New Directions, 1950.

———. Review of *The Letters of Ezra Pound*, edited by D. D. Paige, *An Examination of Ezra Pound*, edited by Peter Russell, and *Poetry and Opinion*, by Archibald MacLeish. *Renascence* 3, no. 2 (Spring 1951): 200.

McNaughton, William. Review of *Ezra Pound: The Last Rower: A Political Profile*, by David Heymann. *Paideuma* 5, no.3 (1976): 473–84.

Meacham, Harry M. *The Caged Panther: Ezra Pound at St. Elizabeths*. New York: Twayne, 1967.

Menand, Louis. "The Pound Error: The Elusive Master of Allusion." *The New Yorker*, June 9, 2008, 123–27.

Merritt, Robert. Review of "*I Cease Not to Yowl*": *Ezra Pound's Letters to Olivia Rossetti Agresti*, edited by Leon Surette and Demetres Tryphonopoulos. *ANQ: A Quarterly Journal of Short Articles, Notes and Reviews*, 13, no.4 (Fall 2000): 46–48.

Meyers, Jeffrey. *The Enemy—A Biography of Wyndham Lewis*. London: Routledge, 1980.

Miller, Hillis J. "Stevens' *Rock* and Criticism as Cure. II." *Georgia Review* 30, no.2 (1976): 330–48.

Millett, Fred B. Review of *The Poetry of Ezra Pound: The Pre-Imagist Stage*, by Christoph de Nagy. *Modern Philology* 61 (1964): 322–23.

Miyake, Akiko. *Ezra Pound and the Mysteries of Love: A Plan for The Cantos*. Durham, NC: Duke University Press, 1991.

Modernist Studies Association. "About." [Ca. 1998] *msa.press.jhu.edu*. Johns Hopkins University, https://msa.press.jhu.edu/about/index.html (accessed November 24, 2017).

Montgomery, Marion. Review of *Vision Fugitive: Ezra Pound and Economics*, by Earle Davis. *Georgia Review* 24 (1970): 508–11.

Moody, A. David. *Ezra Pound: Poet.* 3 vols. Vol. 1: *The Young Genius, 1885–1920* (2007); vol. 2: *The Epic Years, 1921–1939* (2014); vol. 3: *The Tragic Years, 1939–1972* (2015). Oxford: Oxford University Press.

———. "Interview with A. David Moody," by Roxana Preda. Part I. *Make It New* 3, no.1 (June 2016): 35–47. Part II. *Make It New* 3, no.2 (September 2016).

Moore, Marianne. "The Cantos." *Poetry* 39 (October 1931): 37–50. Reprinted in *Ezra Pound: The Contemporary Reviews*, edited by Betsy Erkilla, 185–91. Cambridge: Cambridge University Press, 2011.

———. Review of *A Draft of XXX Cantos*, by Ezra Pound. *Criterion* 13 (1934): 482–85.

Moran, Margaret. Review of *The American Roots of Ezra Pound* [and three other titles], by J. J. Wilhelm. *American Literature* 58, no.1 (March 1986): 114–17.

More, Paul Elmer. *Shelburne Essays.* 7 vols. London: G. P. Putnam, 1904–1910.

Moretti, Franco. *Distant Reading.* Brooklyn: Verso, 2013.

Morse, Jonathan. Review of *"I Cease Not to Yowl": Ezra Pound's Letters to Olivia Rossetti Agresti*, edited by Leon Surette and Demetres Tryphonopoulos. *University of Toronto Quarterly* 69, no.1 (Winter 1999/2000): 280–81.

Mullins, Eustace. *This Difficult Individual: Ezra Pound.* New York: Fleet Publishing Corp., 1961.

Nadel, Ira, ed. *The Cambridge Companion to Ezra Pound.* Cambridge: Cambridge University Press, 1999.

———. *Cathay: Ezra Pound's Orient.* London: Penguin, 2015.

———. *Ezra Pound: A Literary Life.* London: Palgrave, 2004.

———, ed. *Ezra Pound in Context.* Cambridge: Cambridge University Press, 2010.

Nicholls, Peter. "Bravado or Bravura? Reading Ezra Pound's *Cantos.*" In *Modernism and Masculinity: Literary and Cultural Transformations,* edited by Natalya Lusty and Julien Murphet, 233–54. Cambridge: Cambridge University Press, 2014.

———. *Ezra Pound: Politics, Economics and Writing; A Study of "The Cantos."* London: Macmillan, 1984.

———. "Late Pound: The Case of Canto CVII." *Journal of Philosophy: A Cross-Disciplinary Inquiry* 8, no.20 (Fall 2015): 1–16.

———. "'2 doits to a boodle': Reckoning with Thrones." *Textual Practice* 18, no.2 (2004): 233–49.

Nolde, John J., *Blossoms from the East: The China Cantos of Ezra Pound.* Orono, ME: National Poetry Foundation, 1983.

Norman, Charles. *The Case of Ezra Pound.* New York: The Bodley Press, 1948.

———. *Ezra Pound.* New York: Macmillan, 1960.

North, Michael. *The Final Sculpture: Public Monuments and Modern Poets.* Ithaca, NY: Cornell University Press, 1985.

———. Interview with Michael North, Author of "Novelty." *Critical Margins*, Feb. 12, 2014, http://criticalmargins.com/2014/02/12/interview-michael-north/ (accessed October 18, 2015).

———. *The Political Aesthetic of Yeats, Eliot, and Pound.* Cambridge: Cambridge University Press, 1991.

———. *Reading 1922: A Return to the Scene of the Modern.* New York: Oxford University Press, 2000.

O'Connor, William Van. *Ezra Pound.* Minneapolis: University of Minnesota Press, 1963.

O'Connor, William Van, and Edward Stone, eds. *A Casebook on Ezra Pound.* New York: Crowell, 1959.

Olson, Paul A. "The Bollingen Controversy Ten Years After: Criticism and Content." *Prairie Schooner* 33 (Fall 1959): 225–29.

Ong, Walter. *Orality and Literacy: The Technologizing of the Word.* New York: Routledge, 1982.

Orage, Alfred R. "Readers and Writers." *New Age*, July 25, 1918, 201.

Paige, D. D., ed. Pound special issue. *Quarterly Review of Literature* 5, no.2 (December 1949).

Parker, Andrew. "Ezra Pound and the 'Economy' of Anti-Semitism." *boundary 2* 11, no.1–2 (1983): 103–28.

Parker, Richard. *News From Afar: Ezra Pound and Some Contemporary British Poetries.* Bristol: Shearsman, 2014.

———, ed. *Readings in "The Cantos."* Clemson, SC: Clemson University Press, 2017.

Parkinson, Thomas, ed. *Hart Crane and Yvor Winters: Their Literary Correspondence.* Berkeley: University of California Press, 1978.

———. "Method in *Motive and Method.*" *Pound Newsletter* 4 (October 1954): 7–8.

Paul, Catherine. "Ezra Pound, Alfredo Casella, and the Fascist Cultural Nationalism of the Vivaldi Revival." In *Ezra Pound, Language and Persona*, edited by Massimo Bacigalupo, 91–112. Genova: Quaderni del Palazzo Serra, 2008.

———. "Italian Fascist Exhibitions and Ezra Pound's Turn to the Imperial." *Twentieth-Century Literature* 51, no.1 (Spring 2005): 64–97.

———. *Poetry in the Museums of Modernism: Yeats, Pound, Moore, Stein.* Ann Arbor: The University of Michigan Press, 2002.

Pearlman, Daniel. "The Anti-Semitism of Ezra Pound." Review of *"Ezra Pound Speaking": Radio Speeches of World War II*, by Leonard W. Doob and Ezra Pound. *Comparative Literature* 22, no.1 (1981): 104–15.

———. *The Barb of Time: On the Unity of Ezra Pound's Cantos.* New York: Oxford University Press, 1969.

———. "The Blue-Eyed Eel. Dame Fortune in Pound's Later Cantos." *Agenda* 9, no.4–10, no.1 (Autumn–Winter 1971–72): 60–77.

Peck, John. "Landscape as Ceremony in the Later Cantos" *Agenda* 9, no. 2–3 (1971): 26–69.

Peel, Robert. "The Poet as Artist and Citizen." *Christian Science Monitor*, December 9, 1950, mag. sec.: 7.

Perloff, Marjorie. "Hugh Kenner and the Invention of Modernism." *Modernism/modernity* 12, no.3 (2005): 465–69.

———. Review of *Ezra Pound Poet III: The Tragic Years 1945–1972*, by A. David Moody. *Times Literary Supplement,* November 4, 2015, 5, 7.

"*The Pisan Cantos* Wins for Ezra Pound First Award of Bollingen Prize in Poetry." Library of Congress Press Release no. 542, February 20, 1949. Reprinted in *A Casebook on Ezra Pound*, ed. William Van Connor and Edward Stone. New York: Cornwall Press, 1959.

"A Poet's Prize." *New York Herald Tribune*, February 21, 1949, 20.

Porteus, Hugh Gordon. "Pound Saved Again—." Review of *Ezra Pound and Sextus Propertius: A Study in Creative Translation*, by J. P. Sullivan. *Spectator* 215, October 1, 1965, 423.

"Pound, In Mental Clinic, Wins Prize for Poetry Penned in Treason Cell." *New York Times*, February 20, 1949, 1, 14.

Powell, Jim. "A Conspiracy of Scholars, a Tribe of Poets." Review of *The Tale of the Tribe: Ezra Pound and the Modern Verse Epic*, by Michael André Bernstein; *A Companion to The Cantos of Ezra Pound: Volume I (Cantos 1–71)*, by Carroll F. Terrell. *The Threepenny Review* 10 (Summer 1982): 11–13.

Preda, Roxana. The Cantos Project. http://thecantosproject.ed.ac.uk.

———, ed. The Ezra Pound Society. http://ezrapoundsociety.org.

———, ed. *Ezra Pound's Economic Correspondence, 1933–1940*. Gainesville, FL: University of Florida Press, 2007.

———. *Ezra Pound's (Post)modern Poetics and Politics: Logocentrism, Language, and Truth*. New York: Peter Lang, 2001.

———, ed. *Make It New: The Ezra Pound Society Magazine*. http://makeitnew.ezrapoundsociety.org.

Pressman, Jessica. *Digital Modernism*. Oxford: Oxford University Press, 2014.

Qian, Zhaoming, ed. *Ezra Pound and China*. Ann Arbor: University of Michigan Press, 2003.

———, ed. and introd. *Ezra Pound's Cathay. The Centennial Edition*. New York: New Directions, 2015.

———, ed. *Ezra Pound's Chinese Friends*. Oxford: Oxford University Press, 2008.

———. *The Modernist Response to Chinese Art: Pound, Moore, Stevens*. Charlottesville: University of Virginia Press, 2003.

———. *Orientalism and Modernism: The Legacy of China in Pound and Williams*. Durham, NC: Duke, 1995.

"The Question of the Pound Award." *Partisan Review* 16 (May 1949): 512–22. Contributors: W. H. Auden, William Barrett, Robert Gorham Davis, Clement Greenberg, Irving Howe, George Orwell, Karl Shapiro, Allen Tate. Reprinted in *A Casebook on Ezra Pound*, ed. William Van O'Connor and Edward Stone. New York: Crowell, 1959.

Quinn, Sister M. Bernetta. "Ezra Pound and the Metamorphic Tradition." *Western Review* 15 (Spring 1951): 169–81.

———. *The Metamorphic Tradition in Modern Poetry: Essays on the Work of Ezra Pound, Wallace Stevens, William Carlos Williams, T.S. Eliot, Hart Crane, Randall Jarrell and William Butler Yeats*. New Brunswick, NJ: Rutgers University Press, 1955.

———. "The Metamorphoses of Ezra Pound." In *Motive and Method in The Cantos of Ezra Pound*, edited by Lewis Leary, 60–100. New York: Columbia University Press, 1954.

———. "A Poem Too Interesting for Burial." Review of *Ezra Pound's Mauberley: A Study in Composition*, by John Espey. *Pound Newsletter* 7 (July 1955): 1–3.

Rabaté, Jean-Michel. *Language, Sexuality and Ideology in Ezra Pound's Cantos.* Albany: SUNY Press, 1986.

Rainey, Lawrence. *Ezra Pound and the Monument of Culture: Text, History, and the Malatesta Cantos.* Chicago: University of Chicago Press, 1991.

———, ed. "Introduction." In *Modernism. An Anthology.* Oxford: Blackwell, 2005, xix–xxix.

———. *Institutions of Modernism.* New Haven, CT: Yale University Press, 1998.

———, ed. *A Poem Containing History: Textual Studies in "The Cantos."* New Haven: Yale University Press, 1997.

———. Review of *The Genealogy of Demons*, by Robert Casillo. *The Journal of English and German Philology* 88, no.4 (1989): 559–63.

———. Review of "*To Write Paradise*": *Style and Error in Pound's "Cantos,"* by Christine Froula. *Modern Philology* 83, no.4 (1986): 441–45.

Ransom, John Crowe. *The World's Body.* New York: Scribners, 1938.

Read, Forrest. "A Man of No Fortune." In *Ezra Pound: A Collection of Critical Essays,* edited by Walter E. Sutton, 64–79. Englewood Cliffs, NJ: Prentice, 1963.

———. Review of *Ezra Pound Selected Prose 1909–1965*, edited by W. Cookson. *Paideuma* 3, no.1 (1974): 126–28.

Reck, Michael. *Ezra Pound: A Close-Up.* London: Hart-Davis, 1968.

Redman, Tim. "An Epic is a Hypertext Containing Poetry." In *A Poem Containing History: Textual Studies in "The Cantos,"* edited by L. Rainey, 117–50. New Haven, CT: Yale University Press, 1997.

———. *Ezra Pound and Italian Fascism.* Cambridge: Cambridge University Press, 1991.

Review of *Ezra Pound's Mauberley: A Study in Composition*, by John Espey. *Times Literary Supplement,* March 18, 1955, 162.

Review of *Reading the Cantos: A Study of Meaning in Ezra Pound*, by Noel Stock. *New York Times Book Review*, September 17, 1967, 38.

Richards, I. A. *Practical Criticism: A Study of Literary Judgment.* New York: Harcourt Brace, 1929.

Ricks, Christopher. "Davie's Pound." *New Statesman*, April 16, 1965, 610.

Robinson, Lillian, and Lise Vogel. "Modernism and History." *New Literary History* 3, no.1 (1971): 177–99.

Robson, W. W. Review of *The Pound Era,* by Hugh Kenner. *Partisan Review* 40, no.1 (1973): 136–41.

Rorty, Richard. *Consequences of Pragmatism.* Minneapolis: University of Minnesota Press, 1982.

———. "Deconstruction." In *The Cambridge History of Literary Criticism.* Vol. 8. *From Formalism to Poststructuralism,* edited by Raman Selden, 166–96. Cambridge: Cambridge University Press, 1995.

Rose, William K. "Pound and Lewis: The Crucial Years." *Agenda* 7, no. 3–8, no. 1 (1969–70): 117–33.

———. Review of *Eminent Domain: Yeats among Wilde, Joyce, Pound, Eliot and Auden*, by Richard Ellmann. *American Literature* 40 (November 1968): 415–16.

Rosenthal, M. L. "The *Cantos.*" In *Ezra Pound: A Collection of Critical Essays,* edited by Walter E. Sutton, 57–63. Englewood Cliffs, NJ: Prentice, 1963.

———. *A Primer of Ezra Pound*. New York: Macmillan, 1960.

Russell, Peter, ed. *An Examination of Ezra Pound: A Collection of Essays*. Norfolk, CT: New Directions, 1950.

———, ed. *Ezra Pound: A Collection of Essays to be Presented to Ezra Pound on His Sixty-Fifth Birthday*. London: Nevill, 1950.

———. "Vingt-Cinque Ans Apres: An Editor's Personal Retrospect." In *An Examination of Ezra Pound: A Collection of Essays*, edited by Peter Russell, 267–304. New York: Gordian Press, 1973.

Russo, John Paul. "The Tranquilized Poem: The Crisis of New Criticism in the 1950s," *Texas Studies in Literature and Language* 30, no.2 (1988).

Ruthven, K. K. *A Guide to Ezra Pound's "Personae" (1926)*. Berkeley and Los Angeles: University of California Press, 1969.

San Juan, Epifanio, ed. *Critics on Ezra Pound*. Coral Gables, FL: University of Miami Press, 1972.

Sandburg, Carl. *Home Front Memo*. New York: Harcourt Brace. 1943.

Sanders, Frederick K. "The View Beyond the Dinghey." *Sewanee Review* 79 (Summer 1971): 433–60.

Sansone, Claudio, and Massimo Bacigalupo, eds. *The Online Bibliography of Italian Pound Studies (OBIPS)*. *ezrapoundsociety.org*. Ezra Pound Society, 2014-. http://ezrapoundsociety.org/index.php/obips.

Schneidau, Herbert. "Accelerating Grimace." Review of *The Life of Ezra Pound*, by Noel Stock. *The Nation*, August 17, 1970, 122–23.

Schneidau, Herbert N. *Ezra Pound: The Image and the Real*. Baton Rouge: Louisiana State University Press, 1969.

———. Review of *The Barb of Time: On the Unity of Ezra Pound's Cantos*, by Daniel Pearlman. *American Literature* 42 (January 1971): 597–98.

Schneider, Isidor. "Traitor or Holy Idiot: The Case of Ezra Pound." *New Masses*, December 11, 1945, 13.

Scholes, Robert, and Clifford Wulfman. *Modernism in the Magazines: An Introduction*. New Haven: Yale University Press, 2010.

Schulman, G. *Ezra Pound: A Collection of Criticism*. New York: McGraw Hill, 1974.

Schwartz, Delmore. "A Literary Provincial." *Partisan Review* 12 (Winter 1945): 142.

———. *Selected Essays of Delmore Schwartz*. Ed. Donald A. Dike and David H. Zucker. Chicago: University of Chicago Press, 1970.

Schwartz, Joseph. Review of *Vision Fugitive: Ezra Pound and Economics*, by Earle Davis and *The Early Poetry of Ezra Pound*, by Thomas H. Jackson. *Spirit* 37.2 (Summer 1970): 42–46.

Scott, Tom. "The Poet as Scapegoat." *Agenda* 7, no.2 (1969): 49–58.

Seferis, George. "The Cantos: A Note Appended to His Translation of Three Cantos." In *An Examination of Ezra Pound: A Collection of Essays*, edited by Peter Russell, 77–83. New York: Gordian Press, 1973.

Sergeant, Howard. Review of *Ezra Pound's Mauberley: A Study in Composition*, by John Espey. *English* 10 (Summer 1955): 192–93.

Shapiro, Karl. "Ezra Pound: The Scapegoat of Modern Poetry." In *In Defense of Ignorance,* 61–85. New York: Random House, 1960.

———. Letter to the editor. *Baltimore Sun,* February 25, 1949.

———. *Reports of My Death*. Chapel Hill, NC: Algonquin, 1990.

Sheerin, J. B. "The Pound Affair." *Catholic World* 169 (August 1949): 322–23.

Sherman, Stuart. *On Contemporary Literature*. New York: Henry Holt, 1917.

Shioji, Ursula. *Ezra Pound's Pisan Cantos and the Noh*. Frankfurt: Peter Lang, 1997.

Sicari, Stephen. *Pound's Epic Ambition: Dante and the Modern World*. New York: State University of New York Press, 1991.

Sieber, H. A. "Notes on the Ezra Pound Matter." *Carolina Quarterly* 12, no.1 (Winter 1959): 14.

Sieburth, Richard. "He Do the Enemy in Different Voices." Review of "*Ezra Pound Speaking*": *Radio Speeches of World War II*, by Leonard W. Doob and Ezra Pound. *Poetry* 134, no. 5 (1979): 292–302.

———. "In Pound We Trust: The Economy of Poetry/The Poetry of Economics." *Critical Inquiry* 14, no. 1 (1987): 142–72.

———. "WHY Joe/ izza hiz/ Torian." Review essay of *Joe Gould's Teeth*, by Jill Lepore. *Make It New* 3, no. 2 (September 2016): 43–58.

Simpson, Louis. *Three on the Tower: The Lives and Works of Ezra Pound, T. S. Eliot and W. C. Williams*. New York: William Morrow, 1975.

Sisson, C. H. "Ego Scriptor: The *Pisan Cantos* of Ezra Pound." *New English Weekly*, July 28, 1949. Reprinted in *The C. H. Sisson Reader*, edited by Charlie Louth and Patrick McGuiness, 194–97. Manchester: Carcanet, 2014.

Sitwell, Edith. "Ezra Pound." In *An Examination of Ezra Pound: A Collection of Essays*, edited by Peter Russell, 37–65. Norfolk, CT: New Directions, 1950.

Smith, Harrison. "End of Controversy." *Saturday Review of Literature*, September 3, 1949, 23.

Southworth, James G. "Ezra Pound." *More Modern American Poets*. New York: Macmillan, 1954. Reprint, Freeport, NY: Books for Libraries Press, 1964, 18–34.

Spector, Robert D. Review of *A Primer of Ezra Pound*, by M. L. Rosenthal. *New York Herald Tribune Book Review*, September 4, 1960, 6.

Spoo, Robert. "Ezra Pound's Copyright Statute: Perpetual Rights and Unfair Competition with the Dead." In *Without Copyrights: Piracy, Publishing, and the Public Domain*. Oxford: Oxford University Press, 2013.

Stein, Sol. Review of *An Examination of Ezra Pound: A Collection of Essays*, ed. Peter Russell. *Arizona Quarterly* 7 (Summer 1951): 184.

Stern, Richard. "A Memory or Two of Mr. Pound." *Paideuma* 1.2 (1972): 215–19.

Stilwell, Robert L. Review of *This Difficult Individual: Ezra Pound*, by Eustace Mullins. *Books Abroad*, 36, no.1 (winter 1962): 76.

Stock, Noel. "Ezra Pound and an American Tradition." *Agenda* 2, no.4 (June 1961): 4–10.

———, ed. *Ezra Pound Perspectives: Essays in Honor of His Eightieth Birthday*. Chicago: Henry Regnery, 1965.

———. *The Life of Ezra Pound*. London: Routledge, 1970.

———. *Poet in Exile: Ezra Pound*. Manchester: Manchester University Press; New York: Barnes, 1964.

———. *Reading the Cantos: A Study of Meaning in Ezra Pound*. New York: Pantheon, 1966; London: Routledge & Kegan Paul, 1967.

———. "Where We Have Got To." [Part I] *Agenda* 1, no.7 (September-October 1959): 1–4; [Part II] *Agenda* 1, no.8 (November 1959): 1–3.

Stoicheff, Peter. *The Hall of Mirrors: Drafts & Fragments and the End of Ezra Pound's Cantos.* Ann Arbor: University of Michigan Press, 1995.

Strachey, Lytton. "Doctor, Heal Thyself!" *This Quarter* 4 (1931–2): 555.

Sullivan, J. P., ed. *Ezra Pound: A Critical Anthology.* Harmondsworth: Penguin, 1970.

———. *Ezra Pound and Sextus Propertius: A Study in Creative Translation.* Austin: University of Texas Press, 1964; London: Faber, 1965.

Surette, Leon. *The Birth of Modernism: Ezra Pound, T. S. Eliot, W. B. Yeats, and the Occult.* Kingston and Montreal: McGill-Queen's University Press, 1993.

———. *Dreams of a Totalitarian Utopia: Literary Modernism and Politics.* Montreal and Kingston: McGill-Queen's University Press, 2011.

———. *Ezra Pound in Purgatory: From Economic Radicalism to Anti-Semitism.* Evanston: University of Illinois Press, 1999.

———. *A Light from Eleusis.* Oxford: Clarendon Press, 1979; XLibris, 2000.

Sutton, W. Review of *The Political Identities of Ezra Pound and T. S. Eliot*, by William Chace. *American Literature* 47, no.2 (1975): 284–85.

Sutton, Walter E., ed. *Ezra Pound: A Collection of Critical Essays.* Englewood Cliffs, NJ: Prentice, 1963.

Swabey, Henry. "Towards and A.B.C. of History." In *An Examination of Ezra Pound: A Collection of* Essays, edited by Peter Russell, 186–202. Norfolk, CT: New Directions, 1950.

Tate, Allen. "Ezra Pound's Golden Ass." *The Nation*, June 10, 1931, 632–34.

———. "Further Remarks on the Pound Award." *Partisan Review* 16 (June 1949): 666–68.

———. *Reactionary Essays on Poetry and Ideas.* London: Scribner's, 1936.

Taylor, Richard Dean. "Editing the Variorum Cantos: Process and Policy." *Paideuma* 31, no.1-2-3 (2002): 311–34.

Taylor, Richard Dean. "The Tragi-Comical History of the Variorum Project and Its Betrayal by Cambridge University Press." *richard-dean-taylor.de*, [2013]. http://richard-dean-taylor.de/index.php?id=14 (accessed January 29, 2016).

Ten Eyck, David. "Evaluating the Status of Ezra Pound's *Selected Cantos.*" In *Selected Poems: From Modernism to Now*, edited by Hélène Aji and Jennifer Kilgore-Caradec, 23–40. Newcastle upon Tyne: Cambridge Scholars, 2012.

Ten Eyck, David. *Ezra Pound's Adams Cantos.* London: Bloomsbury, 2012.

Terrell, Carroll F. *A Companion to The Cantos of Ezra Pound.* 2 vols. Berkeley: University of California Press, 1980–1984.

———. "Wanted: A Phalanx of Particulars." *Paideuma* 1, no.1 (Spring 1972): 103.

Terry, Arthur. Review of *Ezra Pound*, by William Van O'Connor. *Modern Language Review* 61 (1966): 701.

———. Review of *The Poetry of Ezra Pound: The Pre-Imagist Stage,* by Christoph de Nagy. *Modern Language Review* 56 (1961): 305.

"That's All, Fellows." *Time*, August 29, 1949, 11.

Thomas, Edward. "Exotic Verse." *New Weekly*, May 9, 1914, 249.

———. *Letters from Edward Thomas to Gordon Bottomley*. Edited by R. George Thomas. London: Oxford University Press, 1968.

———. "The Newest Poet." *Daily Chronicle*, November 23, 1909, 30.

———. "Two Poets." Review of *Personae* by Ezra Pound. *English Review* 2 (June 1909): 627–30.

Tietjens, Eunice. "The End of Ezra Pound." *Poetry* (April 1942): 38–40.

Tomlinson, Charles. "Lives and Works." Review of *A Serious Character: The Life of Ezra Pound*, by Humphrey Carpenter. *The Hudson Review* 42, no. 2 (Summer 1989): 191–200.

———. "The Tone of Pound's Critics." *Agenda* 4, no.2 (October-November 1965): 46–49.

Torrey, E. Fuller. *The Roots of Treason: Ezra Pound and the Secret of St. Elizabeths*. New York: McGraw-Hill, 1984.

Tryphonopoulos, Demetres P. *The Celestial Tradition: A Study of Ezra Pound's "The Cantos."* Waterloo, ON: Wilfrid Laurier University Press, 1992.

Tryphonopoulos, Demetres P., and Stephen J. Adams, eds. *The Ezra Pound Encyclopaedia*. Westport, CT, London: Greenwood Publishing Group, 2005.

Tytell, John. *Ezra Pound: The Solitary Volcano*. New York: Anchor Press, 1987.

Van Doren, Mark. "Letter to Harrison Smith" (May 26, 1949). In *The Case Against the Saturday Review of Literature*. Special issue, *Poetry* (October 1949): 62.

van Wick, Brooks. *The Pilgrimage of Henry James*. New York: E. P. Dutton & Co., 1925.

Vasse, William. Correspondence with Ezra Pound. Beinecke Library. YCAL 43 Box 53/Folder 2436.

Végsö, Roland. *The Naked Communist: Cold War Modernism and the Politics of Popular Culture*. New York: Fordham University Press, 2013.

Viereck, Peter. "My Kind of Poetry." *Saturday Review of Literature*, August 27, 1949, 7–8, 35–36.

———. "Parnassus Divided." *Atlantic Monthly* 184 (October 1949): 67–70.

———. "Pure Poetry, Impure Politics, and Ezra Pound: The Bollingen Prize Controversy Revisited." *Commentary*, April 1, 1951. https://www.commentarymagazine.com/articles/pure-poetry-impure-politics-and-ezra-pound-the-bollingen-prize-controversy-revisited/ (accessed August 28, 2016).

Walkiewicz, E. P. Review of *"I Cease Not to Yowl": Ezra Pound's Letters to Olivia Rossetti Agresti*, edited by Leon Surette and Demetres Tryphonopoulos. *English Literature in Transition, 1880–1920* 43, no.1 (January 1, 2000): 120–24.

Walton, Eda Lou. "Obscurity in Modern Poetry." *New York Times Book Review*, April 2, 1933, 2.

Wang, Guiming. *A Study of Ezra Pound's Translation: An Interpretation of* Cathay. Beijing: Foreign Language Press, 2013.

Watts, Harold H. "Art in Fiction: The Intellectual and Artistic Development of Lord Lytton." PhD diss., University of Illinois, 1932.

———. "The Devices of Pound's Cantos." Special issue of *Quarterly Review of Literature* 5, no.2 (December 1949): 147–73.

———. *Ezra Pound and The Cantos*. London: Routledge & Kegan Paul, 1951; Chicago: Henry Regnery, 1952.

———. *Modern Readers' Guide to the Bible*. New York: Harper & Brothers, 1949.

———. "Philosopher At Bay." *Cronos* 2 (March 1948): 1–17.

———. "Points on the Circle." Review of Ezra Pound, *Pisan Cantos*. *Sewanee Review* 57 (Spring 1949): 303–6.

———. "Pound's Cantos: Means to an End." In *Ezra Pound Issue*. Special issue of *Yale Poetry Review* 6 (1947): 9–20.

———. "Reckoning." In *Ezra Pound: A Collection of Critical Essays,* edited by Walter E. Sutton, 98–114. Englewood Cliffs, NJ: Prentice, 1963.

Weatherhead, A. Kingsley. Review of *Ezra Pound: The Image and the Real*, by Herbert Schneidau and *The Barb of Time: On the Unity of Ezra Pound's Cantos,* by Daniel Pearlman. *Criticism* 12 (1970): 358–60.

Weyl, Nathan. *The Bollingen Award*. New York: Crowell, 1959.

Whitaker, Thomas R. Review of *The Barb of Time: On the Unity of Ezra Pound's Cantos*, by Daniel Pearlman. *Modern Philology* 69 (1971): 91–94.

Wilcox, Ella Wheeler. "A New Singer of Songs: The Greeting of a Poetess of Established Fame to a Newcomer Among the Bards." In *Ezra Pound: The Contemporary Reviews*, edited by Betsy Erkilla. Cambridge: Cambridge University Press, 2011. Originally published in *American Journal Examiner*, December 14, 1908.

Wilhelm, James J. *The American Roots of Ezra Pound*. New York: Garland, 1985.

———. *Dante and Pound: The Epic of Judgement*. Orono, ME: National Poetry Foundation, 1974.

———. *Ezra Pound in London and Paris*. University Park and London: Pennsylvania State University Press, 1990.

———. *Ezra Pound: The Tragic Years, 1925–1972*. University Park and London: Pennsylvania State University Press, 1994.

———. *The Later Cantos of Ezra Pound*. New York: Walker, 1977.

Williams, William Carlos. "Excerpts from a Critical Sketch." In *William Carlos Williams: Selected Essays*. New York: New Directions, 1969, 105–12.

Williamson, George. *A Reader's Guide to T. S. Eliot*. New York: Noonday Press/ Farrar Straus, 1953.

Wilson, Edmund. *Axel's Castle: A Study in the Imaginative Literature of 1870–1930*. New York: Scribner, 1931.

Wilson, M. T. Review of *The Poetry of Ezra Pound*, by Hugh Kenner. *University of Toronto Quarterly* (January 1953): 210–11.

Wimsatt, W. K. "The Intentional Fallacy." In W. K. Wimsatt and M. Beardsley. *The Verbal Icon*, 3–20. Louisville: University Press of Kentucky, 1954.

Winters, Yvor. "The Critiad," in *Uncollected Poems of Yvor Winters, 1929–1977*, ed. R. L. Barth. Edgewood, KY: R. L. Barth, 1997.

"The Objectivists." *Hound and Horn* 6 (October 1932): 158–60.

———. "Primitivism and Decadence. A Study of American Experimental Poetry." In *In Defense of Reason*, 90–103. Chicago: Swallow Press, 1947.

Witemeyer, Hugh H. *The Poetry of Ezra Pound: Forms and Renewals, 1908–1920*. Berkeley and Los Angeles: University of California Press, 1969.

Wood, Frederick T. Review of *Ideas into Action: A Study of Pound's Cantos*, by Clark Emery. *English Studies* 41 (1960): 407.

Woodward, Anthony. Review of *A Companion to The Cantos of Ezra Pound:* Volume II: *Cantos 74–120*, by Carroll Terrell. *The Review of English Studies*, n.s. 38, no.149 (1987): 127.

———. Review of "*To Write Paradise": Style and Error in Pound's "Cantos,"* by Christine Froula. *Review of English Studies* 37, no.148 (1986): 594–95.

Woolf, Virginia. "The New Biography." 1927. In *Granite and Rainbow: Essays by Virginia Woolf*, edited by Leonard Woolf, 149–55. New York: Harcourt Brace and Company, 1958.

Wright, Elizabeth. Review of *Ezra Pound: The Image and the Real*, by Herbert Schneidau. *American Quarterly* 22, no. 2 Part 2 (Summer 1970): 314.

Xie, Ming. *Ezra Pound and the Appropriation of Chinese Poetry: Cathay, Translation, and Imagism*. New York/London: Garland Publishing, 1999.

Yeats, William Butler. *The Collected Poems of W. B. Yeats*. Edited by Richard J. Finneran. 2nd revised edition. New York: Scribner, 1996.

———. *Essays and Introductions*. Edited by Georgie Hyde-Lees Yeats. New York: Collier, 1961.

———. Introduction to *The Oxford Book of Modern Verse, 1892–1935*. Oxford: Clarendon, 1936: v–xlii.

———. *The Letters of W. B. Yeats*, edited by Alan Wade. London: Hart Davis, 1954.

———. "A Packet for Ezra Pound." In *The Collected Works of W. B. Yeats*. Volume XIV. *A Vision*. The Revised 1937 Edition, edited by Margaret Mills Harper and Catherine E. Paul, 3–22. New York: Scribner, 2015.

Yip, Wai-Lim. *Ezra Pound's Cathay*. Princeton, NJ: Princeton University Press, 1969.

Zukofsky, Louis. "A Draft of XXX Cantos by Ezra Pound." *Front* 4 (June 1931): 364–69.

———, Louis. "Ezra Pound: His Cantos." *Memphis Observer* 2 (January-February 1934): 3–4, 8.

Index

Lightning Source UK Ltd.
Milton Keynes UK
UKHW041406161118
332458UK00001B/87/P

9 781571 131928